A PREFACE TO URBAN ECONOMICS

A PREFACE TO
URBAN
ECONOMICS

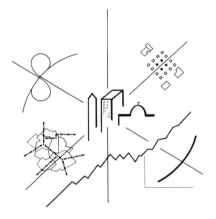

WILBUR R. THOMPSON

published for
RESOURCES FOR THE FUTURE, INC.
by
THE JOHNS HOPKINS PRESS, BALTIMORE

Resources for the Future is a nonprofit corporation for research and education in the development, conservation, and use of natural resources. It was established in 1952 with the co-operation of The Ford Foundation and its activities since then have been financed by grants from that Foundation. Part of the work of Resources for the Future is carried out by its resident staff, part supported by grants to universities and other nonprofit organizations. Unless otherwise stated, interpretations and conclusions in RFF publications are those of the authors; the organization takes responsibility for the selection of significant subjects for study, the competence of the researchers, and their freedom of inquiry.

This book is one of RFF's regional and urban studies, which are directed by Harvey S. Perloff. Wilbur R. Thompson, professor of economics at Wayne State University, began the present study in 1961 as an RFF research associate, while on leave from his university. Through an RFF grant to Wayne State he began another assignment with RFF in 1964 as staff director of the Committee on Urban Economics.

Director of RFF publications, Henry Jarrett; *editor,* Vera W. Dodds; *associate editor,* Nora E. Roots.

PREFACE

Three years ago the author undertook to describe and evaluate a subject matter which gave promise of becoming a new field of thought: the economics of urban growth and development. Very early in this effort it became clear that the inexorable trend toward very large, extremely complex, urban places would make the understanding and management of the process of urbanization one of the two or three most challenging and critical domestic issues of the latter half of the twentieth century. And it seemed inconceivable that the skills of the economist would not be needed.

A corollary judgment was also reached that since the city is much less a pure economic organism than the firm or industry with which economists have traditionally been concerned, the conventional wisdom of economics would not translate easily nor even be enough. A long study was in prospect. Further, the distinguishing characteristic of economics is the rigor that is achieved through formal methods of analysis—mathematical and statistical techniques. But the promise of economic analysis is realized only when the simplifications that permit the construction of formal analytical models do not entail too great a cost in realism and social significance. The research strategy chosen, therefore, was to break the surface of this new and strange world by first composing a preface to urban economics, skipping lightly across nearly the full reaches of the city. Only then, with some feeling for the half-dozen or so critical variables that determine in large part the form and functioning of the city, might significant progress be made toward formulating theories and setting forth rigorous principles. A decade would surely be needed to prepare a true "principles of urban economics." The work of testing and reformulating hypotheses has, of course, no end.

This preface to urban economics is, then, a first step or at best an intermediate product. But a new field can languish for lack of easily accessible educational materials. University faculty members, for example, are most reluctant to teach courses in new fields, prior to the existence of textbooks or reasonable facsimiles thereof; it is very difficult and inefficient to base courses on fugitive, specialized pamphlets and journal articles existing only in single library copies. State and local finance, a subject closely related to urban economics, is still an infrequently scheduled course, reflecting decades of bare existence without good teaching materials. Today specialists in this field are very rare and much sought after. While the appearance of this work may in some respects seem premature, it is offered in the belief that an introductory work in urban economics, however tentative, will encourage faculties to offer courses in the subject sooner and more often than they otherwise would have done.

The book is a substantial revision of a preliminary multilith version that was used experimentally in about twenty classrooms across the country in the fall of 1963. The reader is presumed to have completed a one-year "principles" course in economics (or be willing to remedy such deficiency by reading the national income and price theory parts of any standard text) and to have attained the general level of intellectual maturity ordinarily associated with senior undergraduate standing. Thus the book can also be used as collateral reading in upper-division or graduate school courses in business administration, political science, sociology, urban planning, or urban-regional geography.

A second objective is to share these early thoughts with fellow students of the city, especially those with whom the author is unacquainted. The market in ideas is quite as imperfect as most of the others with which economists must deal. These two objectives are, moreover, interrelated because most of the new urban economists will have to come from the uncommitted generation of economists-to-be now in classrooms. The surest, if not the shortest, road to good research is roundabout through the classroom.

The history of economic thought teaches us that the pace of intellectual development is slow; a gestation period of a generation for a new field is not unusual. The generation that lights the torches is not likely to balance the scales.

This book is, therefore, directed to the student who is willing to trade the neat catechism of the textbook in a mature field for the mildly chaotic excitement of the tract in a new one.

The author is greatly indebted to the Committee on Urban Economics of Resources for the Future, Inc., for the financial support which made possible the year of uninterrupted thought and writing which culminated in the first draft of this work. CUE also financed a limited distribution of multilith copies of the second draft for experimental use in classrooms in the fall of 1963. The author thanks those who participated in the classroom experiment for their comments and suggestions.

The author is especially indebted to Harvey Perloff for promoting the sequence of events that produced the most personally rewarding (and, he hopes, socially valuable) epoch in the author's academic life. He acknowledges the stimulating conversations, over coffee and under the elms of Dupont Circle, with Harvey, Lowdon Wingo, and Jack Lessinger during that most productive first year at RFF and since then. Where their ideas left off and his began, the author will never know. To Harold Barnett belongs the credit for seeing the pressing need for classroom materials in this field at the earliest possible time.

Wayne State University contributed significantly to this work by granting released time from other duties and by extending financial aid at many critical junctures. But even more important, the University freed the author to experiment with a series of courses in this new field—perhaps a little prematurely at times—ahead of the imminent respectability of "urban economics." Much of what follows took shape on the blackboard, unexpectedly if not accidentally; the author's students contributed patience as well as constructive criticism.

The author's greatest debt is to his colleague John Mattila, with whom these ideas have been discussed at various stages over too many years to remember. Many others have contributed to this very eclectic work, but the author will limit his specific acknowledgments to just three more: Edgar M. Hoover, for ideas first transferred via the printed page years ago, changing to more personal exchanges in recent years; Henry Jarrett for editing in the spirit of the writing; and David Felix, for just being a kindred spirit.

As is customary, the subtle and unobtrusive contributions of the author's wife are acknowledged last. But the last shall be first. Finally, the author acknowledges, with this evolving work, personal responsibility for the inescapable fact that Philip, Martha, and Andrew and their generation will have to live in the cities that he and his generation create.

WILBUR R. THOMPSON
Washington, D.C.

January, 1965

CONTENTS

PART II

PRESCRIPTION: PROBLEMS AND POLICY IN THE URBAN ECONOMY

A PREFACE TO URBAN ECONOMICS

INTRODUCTION

Already for more than two out of every three Americans, community life is city life and local government is city government; with each passing year the proportion increases. Moreover, it is the great metropolitan centers of a million or more population that seem to be the most viable and that steadily gain in share. As the United States tends more and more to be a country of very large cities, the critical national problems of growth and development, stability, greater and more equal opportunity and, ultimately, the pursuit of the "good life" become urban problems.

In this study the subject matter of urban economics has been organized in two parts. Throughout most of Part I the urban area is seen as a single local labor market—as the primary unit of employment and income generation. The performance of this "little economy" is measured and evaluated by the same three basic indexes of economic welfare that are used at the national level. Thus, we begin by focusing on the local economic goals of:

1. Affluence: expressed as a high and rising level of income, measured in money terms first but translated into real terms by taking full account not only of local differences in the cost of living but, perhaps more important, local differences in the range of goods and services available;

2. Equity: expressed as a "fair" distribution of income, considering both the distribution of earned income under a free market price system and the redistribution of income effected by local government taxes, services, and transfer payments;

3. Stability: expressed as seasonal, cyclical, and growth stability, seen as a problem both of maintaining employment and income and of achieving efficiency in the use of resources—avoiding peak congestion and off-peak idle capacity.

A full chapter is devoted to each of these three goals—or performance criteria, if a less normative term is desired—emphasizing basic determinants and processes much more heavily than policy.

But policy does enter Part I implicitly in the lengthy discussion of urban growth in Chapter 1. Few would question the identification of affluence, equity, and stability as goals of community economic welfare, but aggregate growth is more a process than a goal. In a normative

1

context, economists can hardly be accused, at least since Malthus wrote one hundred and fifty years ago, of unquestioningly accepting an increase in total population as economic progress. And so, while much urban-regional development literature is unabashedly and indiscriminately expansionist, we view urban growth here, especially to the degree that it is controllable, as more a strategy than a goal—more a means than an end.

The fundamental normative assumption here is that the local growth rate is a lever through which desirable changes in the level, distribution, and stability of income may be achieved. Much of what we label urban problems are, in fact, undesirable rates of local growth. To grow too slowly is to invite chronic unemployment and poverty, the *symptoms* of which are slums, blight, and crime. To grow too fast is to invite the capital shortages that lead to the irritating delays and expensive congestion that can be just as damaging to the quality of urban life in the short run, as exemplified in traffic jams, and in the long run, in crowded schools on half-day sessions. Thus the opening chapter on urban growth is more than an introduction to urban growth analysis; it has the more ambitious objective of contributing to an understanding of the nature of the principal instrument—the key "controllable variable"—in the hands of local government. For only by understanding the local growth process can local government hope to be even partially master of its own destiny.

The level, distribution, and stability of local income are analyzed in the spatial context of the local labor market and in the analytical framework of the "export base theory," which relates the income characteristics of the local economy to the income characteristics of those local industries that sell outside the local labor market. Simply said, high-wage export industries produce a high-income town and stable exports create a stable local economy. Some evidence is offered, moreover, that specialization in manufacturing lessens the degree of income inequality, due in part to a relatively narrow range of skills in mass production work and in part to the egalitarian influence of trade unions. In sum, the local economy is seen as the lengthened shadow of its export industries. The power of the exogenous forces with which the local economy must contend is stressed.

Although the demand for local exports is also emphasized in the growth chapter—the *current* rate of growth of an urban area is explained more by the growth rate of its export sector than any other single factor—even greater emphasis is placed on the supply side of growth, the local economy's comparative advantage in land, labor, capital, and entrepreneurship. Thus, despite the fact that the export base theory was developed as an explanation of the long-run aggregate growth of small-area economies, its explanatory power is greatest over short periods during which the export base remains relatively unchanged, such as over the business cycle, and it loses power over time as the local industrial specialization undergoes the inevitable metamorphosis of all living and growing phenomena. The very essence of long-run growth is, in fact, the transition—sometimes orderly, sometimes chaotic—of the local economy from one export base to another as the area matures in what it can do, and as rising per capita income and technological progress change what the national economy wants done. Thus the emphasis in our growth analysis is on the process by which each round of economic development leaves an industrial legacy of skills, wage rates, business services, social overhead, entrepreneurial talent, and so forth, which shapes the developmental path and constrains the policy choices of the next round. The power of endogenous forces in urban growth are heavily stressed, and there is less precedent here.

Finally, the influence of city size runs throughout Part I. Not only is city size a large question in its own right (is the higher money income associated with big cities dissipated in higher prices or enhanced even more through greater range of choice in goods and occupations?) but the tight mathematical bond between the rate of growth and total size forces us to make consistent choices extending over both variables. Clearly, an urban area cannot choose to grow but not become bigger. The complementaries and trade-offs forced on a community by virtue of this iron bond between growth and size are played through all three goals of economic development. Finally, what are the implications to the nation of a continuation of current urban growth trends, and what is the federal role in achieving a desirable system of cities?

To the extent that an urban economy is a bundle of industries in space—and it is that in part, but much more too—the national system of cities follows from the national system of industries. Huge plants built on great "internal economies of scale" assemble large labor forces and create middle size cities almost singlehandedly. High transportation costs of intermediate products, as in steel making and chemical processes, pull successive stages of production together in space, and form "industrial complexes" that create large cities. And "external economies" in the form of a well-developed set of business and professional services (finance, law, engineering, marketing, advertising, and so forth) and of social overhead (good schools, leading universities, research centers) draw the newer industries and the smaller firms to create great cities. Industry trends shape urban trends; industry analysis underlies urban analysis; national industrial planning must be coordinated with national urban planning. We cannot, therefore, design our preferred systems of industries and cities independently. Accordingly, in Part I, we move back and forth between industries and cities freely; in our export-base constructs, we regard an urban economy as a bundle of industries in space and in our "stages of growth" analyses we see it as an organic entity with a life of its own. There are elements of both at work.

Part I does not stress public policy partly because the author has not progressed in his own thinking to the point of clear prescription. Still, the analysis is oriented toward public policy. It is unrealistic to assume that the lack of an explicit comprehensive national urban policy means that the federal government has not had a powerful impact on the relative growth rates, the size distribution and the locational pattern of our system of cities. The Area Redevelopment Administration struggles to lure plants to depressed areas; the Department of Defense opens and closes military installations and shifts procurement with heavy employment impacts; the Bureau of Public Roads connects or bypasses towns, thereby inducing either booms or stagnation; the Urban Renewal Administration pursues policies that directly influence the attractiveness and efficiency of central cities and indirectly shape their expectations; the National Aeronautics and Space Administration creates great research and development capabilities here and there, leading to whole new local development sequences. On balance, are we subsidizing the big or the small cities? Are we forcing a clustering or dispersion of our cities? What trade-offs among affluence, equity, and stability follow from various patterns of urban growth rates, population sizes, and locational constellations? If we are not well aware of the consequences of different courses of action and ready for strong prescriptions, surely serious study of the national interest and federal role in the system of cities is long overdue.

An *inter*urban income and employment analysis which stresses structure and process in Part I gives way in Part II to an *intra*urban analysis more heavily oriented to problems and policy. The standard problems approach is reflected in the subdivisions of this latter part: unemployment, poverty, and welfare; urban public services under political fragmentation and multilevel government; renewal, race, and sprawl; transportation and traffic. Nominally, the taxonomy is the traditional one of the "awful mess." But throughout, three basic themes are played—three deep roots of urban problems are examined: (1) The causes and consequences of poverty, (2) the neglect of the role of price, and (3) the social, economic, and political implications of great size.

Many so-called urban problems are, in one guise or another, simply symptoms of poverty. Slums are the home of the poor; the affluent flee from the poor to insulate their culture from contamination; central city budgets become unbalanced as they are left with the heavy public service needs of the poor and without the tax base of the rich; historical discrimination in education and current discrimination in the job market transform racial segregation into income inequality; a "white noose" of suburbs tightens around the central city; a growing nonwhite population crowds core-area housing, raises rents, and further impoverishes workers with the most menial jobs; inexorable growth does push back the housing line but the addition of contiguous neighborhoods to the core housing supply does not break the pattern of segregation but only enlarges the reach of the ghetto; the ghetto grows in size until its radius is great enough to shut off the slum child from any and all nonslum contacts however nominal. And downtown dies a slow death too as it becomes an island in the most dilapidated area of the city. Not just the downtown of the department store, as retailing quite logically follows its market to the suburbs, but the downtown of the theaters, museums and restaurants also languishes. The ramifications of urban poverty are far-reaching. Quite understandably, the economist exhibits a prejudice for opening a discussion of urban problems with a policy-oriented analysis of unemployment, unemployability, and welfare.

In one way or another, any comprehensive analysis of the city must resolve the role and relevance of the price system. Again, many so-called urban problems arise out of the fact that behavior is not subject to any disciplinary force such as price. This is especially true of that class of urban phenomena which are most demanding of what is usually the scarce factor—urban space. If, for example, we place too low a price on the extension of local public services and/or utility services to the sparsely populated urban fringe areas, we encourage a profligate use of space—"urban sprawl." Or if we do not charge extra for moving large private vehicles through narrow city streets at peak periods, we do not ration urban space efficiently. Thus sprawl and congestion are less "problems" in themselves than symptoms of a more basic malady—the lack of any disciplinary force, such as price, which forces individuals to bear the financial responsibility for their actions.

This is not to say that the extension of the price system to the realm of private public goods is ever easy or even often possible; the difficulties of administration are exceeded only by those of cost accounting. Still, we should always be aware that the price mechanism is a powerful control, and one not only compatible with but also indigenous to our culture (although not necessarily familiar and easily acceptable to the citizen-voter in this new context). As such the rule of price, although it may be *explicitly* rejected where inappropriate, must not be ignored.

The third major theme is far less central to economics: urban land use patterns. While urban economics is concerned with the locational patterns of all major land uses, this study emphasizes the residential land use pattern, even if this had to be at the considerable cost of slighting the treatment of industrial and commercial locational patterns. Residential patterns are emphasized because they are so critical to human resource development (antipoverty) programs and to judging the appropriate size of local government in the politically fragmented metropolitan area. As our urban areas grow to giant size, the long standing practice of residential segregation by income threatens to sever all contact between the slum dwellers and the middle- and upper-income classes. Removed from good schools and good examples, out of the main stream of American culture in a time of rapid technological change and of a need for a high level of personal achievement and adaptability, the disadvantaged fall farther and farther behind.

Further, to the extent that income-homogeneous neighborhood communities (ghettos) grow large relative to the political subdivisions of the large metropolitan areas, the latter framed in fixed boundaries, income segregation becomes institutionalized, greatly complicating fiscal transfers at the local level. To the extent that we complicate the redistribution of income by disorganizing those local public services that extend economic opportunity to the poor, we make a mockery of equal opportunity and/or invite the centralization of social welfare programs at the federal level. Certainly, the trade-off between (1) a fine-grain income mixing in our residential patterns, which would strengthen "grass roots" political democracy by matching tax base and public service needs so that small local government might also be socially responsible government, and (2) the current pattern of segregation to preserve various neighborhood amenities of communities homogeneous in income (and thereby in culture) is subtle and complex, but the issue needs to be laid out boldly and clearly. The broad social implications of the residential-income pattern are traced through: (a) core renewal strategy, (b) the design of "new towns" in the suburbs, (c) school districting, (d) the building of better youth and casual labor markets, and (e) the journey to work, both the personal burden imposed and the social investment required.

The lack of integration between the two halves of the book reflects the belated entry of the economist into this field and the fact that urban planners and administrators have been forced to rely on their own economic analyses. Economists on the whole, and especially those in the main stream of thought, have only recently discovered the city. With some notable exceptions, it is very difficult to identify an "economist" (in the tradition of Marshall and Keynes) who has reflected on the nature and problems of cities for as long as a decade, although one can identify a number of "urbanists" from other origins who have, out of sheer necessity, developed into very presentable economists by avocation. And a real and sure feeling for a phenomenon as complex and subtle as the city does not come quickly and easily, as those of us hurrying to catch up have found. All in all, as this first attempt is made to throw a net over the whole field of urban economics, no apology need be offered for the inevitable fact that the mesh of the net is very large and many of the strands are stretched dangerously thin.

PART I

PRINCIPLES:
Goals and Processes
in the Urban Economy

CHAPTER I

Economic Growth and Development: Processes, Stages, and Determinants

AN ABRIDGED OVERVIEW OF
THE URBAN GROWTH PROCESS

The principal cause of the dramatic urban growth experienced by the United States since the turn of the century is the great rural to urban migration. By now, however, the significance of the continuing shift from farm to city is well appreciated; we need pause only briefly to recall its main characteristics as background for the principal concern of this chapter.

In brief, a steady advance in agricultural technology has greatly enlarged farm output per man-hour. The rate of annual increase has risen from a little over 1 per cent in the twenties to more than 5 per cent in the years since the Second World War. Our rapidly growing per capita income—the reflection of a generally advancing technology —has not, however, increased the demand for foods and fibers at anywhere near the same rate; food consumption is increasing only about half as fast as over-all productivity and per capita income, and not much more than half as fast as the productivity growth rate in agriculture itself. Thus, national economic development has required that the agricultural sector decline sharply in relative share. The percentage of the labor force engaged in agriculture plummeted from

An earlier draft of this chapter, together with a heavy abridgment of those scattered parts of Chapters 2–5 which also deal with growth, appears as "Urban Economic Growth and Development in a National System of Cities," in Philip M. Hauser and Leo F. Schnore (editors), The Study of Urbanization, The Committee on Urbanization of the Social Science Research Council (New York: John Wiley & Sons, Inc., 1965).

11

12 to 6 per cent between 1950 and 1960—while manufacturing and services absorbed expanding shares.

Farm to city migration was, then, dictated by national demand and supply forces and would have occurred even if demographic patterns had been neutral. But a farm birth rate considerably above the urban one resulted in more than proportionate manpower additions in agriculture, during a period when few additions were needed. In sum, the great shift from farm to factory and office is the most basic explanation of urban growth up to now.

But the nation's rural areas are rapidly emptying out; the great farm to city migration has about run its course and will soon belong to economic history. Today, the most challenging urban growth theory and the most compelling urban growth problems arise out of interurban competition for growth and the development of the national system of cities. It is in the size distribution and the spatial pattern of cities that the new vitality of urban economics lies. This chapter emphasizes, then, not the rural to urban migration of the past but the interurban interactions of the present and near future.

The Many Lines of Linkage

Some appreciation of the fine web of urban growth forces can be gained by working through a much oversimplified presentation of the lines of linkage between a hypothetical urban area and the outside world, as outlined in Figure 1. We arbitrarily break into the pattern of urban economic development by beginning with three local meat-packing plants (1) which sell outside the locality. These have been drawn together by the mutual advantages they enjoy in tapping a large local pool of specialized and skilled labor (2), created by their own *combined* demand. Because they have clustered together, these three plants have attracted a common supplier, a plant manufacturing meat cutting tools (3), and this integration of sequential operations has added to local exports, indirectly, by increasing the proportion of the meat products sales dollar that remains within the area. In other words, as vertical integration in the local export industries progresses, local value-added and income generated become a higher proportion of sales.

Local slaughtering produces hides as a by-product and this encourages shoe firms (4) to locate nearby to save transportation costs on their chief raw material. The horizontal agglomeration of shoe

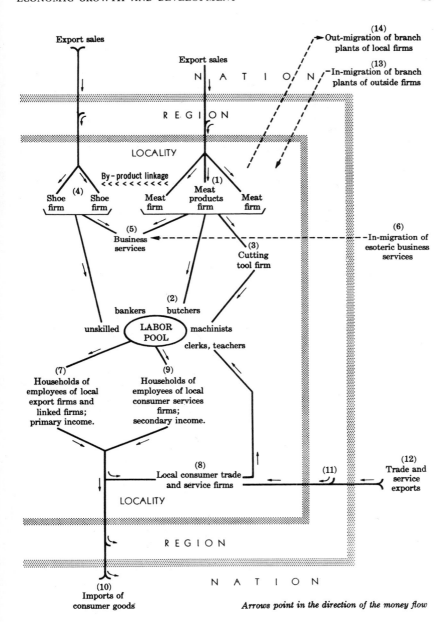

Figure 1. The urban growth complex.

plants may be reinforced by the fact that shoes are subject to comparative shopping by wholesalers and retailers and an out-of-the-way shoe plant is at a severe disadvantage. All of this greatly increases the demand for local business services (5), such as transportation, financial, and marketing services, and thereby improves their quality and variety and lowers their cost.

As local business services become more varied and improve in quality, they steadily replace similar services (6) previously imported from larger, more highly developed neighboring cities. While the net effect is for the local economy to become ever more self-sufficient in business services, the growing complexity of the local economy will bring a need to import at least a modest amount of new, more esoteric business services (e.g., specialized financial and commercial services related to importing foreign steels for the meat cutting tool firm). Simultaneously, the addition of successive firms augments local payrolls and personal income of local households (7) which, in turn, enriches the consumer service sector (8). As successive consumer spending mounts, the variety store gives way to the department store, and then the "custom shop" and the "salon" are added.

Consumer expenditures rise faster than export industry payrolls as the "multiplier effect" takes hold and employees of the local service facilities (9) take incomes earned by servicing the households of employees of the export industries and the linked business service and cutting tool firms, and spend them for more locally produced goods and services. Parallel to the pattern developing in the local business service sector, as the local consumer service sector matures imports of consumer goods and services (10) will decrease, in relative terms, although the absolute amount of consumer imports will probably increase as the local economy grows in size and complexity.

Our hypothetical urban area is now moving up in rank in the hierarchy of cities. As it becomes first a provincial and then a regional capital, its rising status is explicitly recognized by an industrial structure which changes to reflect its new role: an exporter of services. A true metropolis as a "mother city" reaches out and renders the more specialized and skill-demanding administrative, financial, legal, educational, recreational, medical, and governmental services to its satellites. The first step, usually, is to export a growing range of services to nearby cities of the next smaller size (11), which in turn merchandise a somewhat abridged line of services to the next lower level of cities. With growth, however, the metropolis may extend its reach to embrace the whole nation or a very large portion of it (12) for a much narrower group of services: New York with finance, corporate administration, entertainment, and others; Chicago with nearly as broad a group; Miami, recreation and amusement; Washington, government and tourist services; Boston, education and research.

Even local manufacturing tends to become more diversified and self-sufficient, as the growing local market attracts the branch plants of outside firms (13), while the branch plants of the growing local firms are spun off in complementary fashion to the large and growing metropolitan areas elsewhere (14). Piece by piece, additional business and consumer services and manufacturing operations are added to the local economy, as the growing local market affords ever more economies of scale and cuts the cost of local production to the point at which the remaining cost disadvantage vis-à-vis the bigger and/or most efficient operations elsewhere is less than the transportation costs from each of them.

Finally, the metropolis, with its universities, museums, libraries, and research laboratories, becomes one big, spatially integrated "coffee house," where bright minds out of diverse cultures clash and strike sparks that ignite the fires of new products and processes—new export industries. We have now come full circle to where we began, or better, we have entered upon an endless and self-regenerative growth cycle.[1]

The Stages of Urban Growth

Can the many aspects of urban-regional growth be grouped and arranged in a time sequence of distinct stages?

We might identify, first, the *Stage of Export Specialization* in which the local economy is the lengthened shadow of a single dominant industry or even a single firm. This initial stage gives way with growth and size to the *Stage of the Export Complex* in which local production broadens to other products and/or deepens by extending forward or backward in the stages of production, by adding local suppliers and/or consumers of intermediate products. Next, the *Stage of Economic*

---

[1] This summary and loose synthesis of the complex of forces underlying urban-regional economic growth and development draws liberally, of course, from innumerable sources, and only an unabridged history of doctrine in this field of thought would suffice to assign credits of authorship. The most comprehensive review of this literature and the most exhaustive bibliography published to date (or likely to be published for some time to come) is in Walter Isard, *et al., Methods of Regional Analysis: an Introduction to Regional Science* (New York: John Wiley and Sons, Inc., 1960).

Maturation (Local Service Sector Puberty) follows, in which the principal expansion of local activity is in the direction of replacing imports
with new "own use" production; the local economy fills out in range
and quality of both business and consumer services. Fourth, the *Stage
of Regional Metropolis* is reached, when the local economy becomes
a node connecting and controlling neighboring cities, once rivals and
now satellites, and the export of services becomes a major economic
function.

One more common phase is the *Stage of Technical-Professional
Virtuosity;* national eminence in some specialized skill or economic
function is achieved. This stage may succeed or precede the status of
regional metropolis: Detroit was a national center of automotive
design and engineering long before it became a regional metropolis,
if indeed it is one now. Boston's acknowledged eminence in education
and, more recently, research and development, followed its role as the
capital of New England. San Francisco is a national cultural center,
perhaps second only to New York, quite apart from its co-captaincy
with Los Angeles of the West Coast region.

These purported stages of urban growth are, of course, highly impressionistic generalizations and deserve a hearing only as the most
tentative hypotheses from which careful empirical work might be
begun. Moreover, these growth sketches leave much too strong a feeling
of the inevitability of growth and development—onward and upward
forever. And yet we see many examples of local economic stagnation
and decay and even demise. What are some of the dampening and
restraining forces that surely must exist?

Failure of Momentum between Stages in Growth

Suppose the original growth stimulus—the economic environment
at genesis—did not generate a sufficiently strong impulse to lift the
economy to a level at which derivative growth forces could take over.
For example: the local harbor and connecting waterways may not
have been so superior or the local ore deposit so rich, given the current
ore prices and the remoteness of the mine and so forth, to create a
town large enough or a technology advanced enough to build an
attractive labor force. Without this latter attraction, the local economy
never drew the manufacturing plants which would have moved the
local economy into the second stage of export diversification and into
a state of general industrial enrichment, before the preferred mode of

transportation changed or the vein of ore gave out. Or, if the small port or mining economy did manage to add a few manufacturing firms and limp through the second stage of growth, not enough of an industrial complex was created to develop the local market to a point where a strong surge of local service industry formation developed, replacing imports with local production. Thus the growth of a local economy may hesitate and stagnate between any of these stages if the momentum at the end of a phase is not strong enough to carry the economy to the point at which the mechanism of the next stage is activated.

An insufficiency of momentum may be relative rather than absolute, especially with reference to the fourth stage, metropolis formation. Typically, one city will rise from a group of rivals to become the "mother city" of the group. Whichever city gets the jump on the others and achieves early economic dominance usually finds that success breeds success as external economies of service industry agglomeration pave the way for progressive, cumulative coups.[2] The wholesale trade center for the group may stand in good way to become the financial center and the latter gain may commonly lead to administrative dominance and subsequent legal eminence and so forth. The sequence as sketched is purely illustrative because historical and/or statistical-empirical work on this facet of urban growth dynamics is scarce.[3]

[2] For example, in the historic rivalry between Chicago and St. Louis for supremacy in the Middle West and as a gateway to the West, natural factors, such as the Mississippi River, as a north-south transportation facility and as an east-west barrier, and social factors, such as a a river-minded leadership group in St. Louis and the disruptive effect of the Civil War on the border-state hinterland of St. Louis, all combined to edge Chicago past St. Louis. Cumulative forces in growth then widened the gap. See Lewis F. Thomas, "Decline of St. Louis as Midwest Metropolis," *Economic Geography* (April 1949), pp. 118–27, for a brief account, or Wyatt Winton Belcher, *The Economic Rivalry between St. Louis and Chicago, 1850–1880* (New York: Columbia University Press, 1947), for a more extended treatment.

[3] A number of static, cross-section studies have been made which classify cities according to their principal economic function—manufacturing, wholesale trade center, transportation center, seat of government and so forth. But dynamic analyses which take a city through a sequence of functions with sufficient analytical rigor to permit generalization are still to be done or lie hidden in fugitive materials. On the classification of U.S. cities according to economic function see Chauncy D. Harris, "A Functional Classification of Cities in the United States," *Geographical Review* (January 1943), pp. 86–99, and Howard J. Nelson, "A Service Classification of American Cities," *Economic Geography* (July 1955), pp. 189–210, both reprinted in Harold Mayer and Clyde F. Kohn (editor), *Readings in Urban Geography* (Chicago: University of Chicago Press, 1959), Gunnar Alexandersson, *The Industrial Structure*

Promotion up through the hierarchy of cities is, then, partly a matter of the right timing, usually an early lead amply fortified with local leadership. And we count, of course, more losers than winners in this interurban competition; too little and too late, relative to neighboring cities, is a powerful constraint on urban growth and development.

To be sure, a lagging city can forge ahead to dominance through some exceptionally fortunate circumstance, such as being the chance host to a firm which is destined to become the individual "success story" of *the* growth industry of the era (e.g., Ford Motor Company and Detroit) or through the discovery of great natural wealth (e.g., Houston). Ordinarily, however, success breeds success and the rich get richer, at least in the urban growth process.

"Challenge and Response": A Tale of Three Cities

If the rich always did get richer (and the poor poorer) in inter-regional competition, long-range urban forecasting would be much easier than it actually is. But victories can bring complacency and defeats can be challenges. We might postulate a crisis theory of human behavior in regional economic development: a community rises to the occasion in a variation on the Toynbee theme of "challenge and response."

When urban growth slackens or stalls—when the rate of growth of new jobs falls below the rate of natural increase in the local labor force—heavy, chronic unemployment creates local crises: personal, social and governmental. Out-migration, the economist's solution, is often sluggish, especially in a time of ever more pervasive home ownership, tighter job seniority, and broadening unemployment compensation. (Millions for unemployment compensation, but not one cent for relocation expenses!) In depressed areas, sagging tax collections and soaring welfare costs upset municipal budgets and force politicians and public administrators to strain for more imaginative and incisive programs of area industrial development.

Agonizing reappraisals are made of local business taxes relative to competing urban areas, and the efficacy of tax concessions, subsidies

---

of American Cities (Stockholm: Almquist and Wiksell, 1956), and Otis Dudley Duncan, W. Richard Scott, Stanley Lieberson, Beverly Duncan, and Hal H. Winsborough, *Metropolis and Region* (Baltimore: The Johns Hopkins Press for Resources for the Future, 1960).

in the form of rent-free use of vacant buildings, and other industrial lures are reviewed. One can almost predict the likelihood of "another" state-local tax study from the current rate of local unemployment relative to the current national rate. Comparative transportation facilities, wage rates, utility rates, and other leading plant location factors will also come in for close scrutiny during these trying times. If necessity is the mother of social, as well as technical, invention, the probability of imaginative and effective local action, both public and private, designed to improve the local business climate and nurture new industrial growth will be significantly increased in time of local stagnation.[4]

Perhaps, on close inspection, the recent economic histories of Boston, Pittsburgh, and Detroit would exhibit evidence of a challenge-and-response developmental syndrome. Boston was the first of the three to experience economic stagnation and was a declining economy prior to the outbreak of the Second World War. But shortly after its end, building on a base of superior higher educational facilities that area spawned a complex of research and development work and manufacturing activity in R & D-oriented industries (e.g., electronics, instruments) almost overnight, greatly softening the blow of losing the textile and shoe industries to the South. How much of this new work was generated by increased organized efforts at industrial development and how much was due to the presence of Harvard University and Massachusetts Institute of Technology in the area is impossible to tell. But there is at least evidence of local awareness of a need to rebuild a faltering economy on a new industrial base in the mass of economic studies and reports on the area that poured forth in the prewar and early postwar period.[5]

Contrast the case of Boston with that of Pittsburgh, an economy which boomed during the war and briefly in its aftermath as it worked

[4] Perloff and associates found a low *negative* correlation between the location of growth industries and the local growth rate. Harvey S. Perloff, Edgar S. Dunn, Eric E. Lampard, and Richard F. Muth, *Regions, Resources, and Economic Growth* (Baltimore: The Johns Hopkins Press for Resources for the Future, 1960), p. 68. Perhaps this is due to the tendency of invention, innovation, and promotion to come more than proportionately out of the industrially mature regions, a point they themselves make later in their work. This more than proportionate incubation of new industries in the older industrial areas may originate in their greater technological sophistication, and then again it may originate in purposeful desperation as local entrepreneurs rise to the challenge of heavy local unemployment and business losses.

[5] Culminating in *The New England Economy*, A Report to the President by the Committee on New England Economy of the Council of Economic Advisers (Washington: U.S. Government Printing Office, 1951).

to supply the backlog demand for steel. Hard hit by the first postwar recession in 1949, for the next half-dozen years Pittsburgh stagnated as local leadership went through a period of intellectual and emotional readjustment, apparently culminating in a clear understanding that this urban area could either stagnate as a steel city or hunt for some broader industrial base for a resurgence. The striking rebirth of Pittsburgh—through smoke abatement programs; physical renewal in the Golden Triangle; the sponsorship of a highly sophisticated economic development study in co-operation with the local universities;[6] and, most recently, the $250 million research center sponsored by the universities of the area—gives every evidence of being just as spectacular as the Boston rebirth, at least if it is conceded that in an age of education and affluence the image and long-run prospects of a steel city are decidedly inferior to those of a center of culture.

Consider now the third city, Detroit, an area which rode through the first two postwar recessions (1949, 1954) relatively unscathed on a huge backlog demand for automobiles. Not until 1955, much later than the other two cities, did automobile manufacturing employment in Detroit reach its peak. For almost five years thereafter, as manufacturing employment sagged lower and lower, the local industrial pundits misread warning signs of structural transformation in the local economy as signaling only a temporary cycle trough. About 1960, the chronic nature of the crushing unemployment left in the wake of an automobile industry which had matured, decentralized, automated and demilitarized—all in an indigestibly short period of time—began to percolate through to the opinion molders in the local economy. True, the first serious stirrings had begun about two years before, with an epic state tax study[7] and a few small-budget industrial development

[6] The Economic Study of the Pittsburgh Region was jointly financed by the Commonwealth of Pennsylvania and The Ford Foundation as a successor to the New York Metropolitan Area Regional Study and was sponsored by The Pittsburgh Regional Planning Association and directed by Edgar M. Hoover. The last of the four volumes was published by the University of Pittsburgh Press in late 1964; this study will probably be judged the best piece of empirical work on urban economics to date.

[7] *Michigan Tax Study, Staff Papers,* Legislative Committee, House of Representatives, Lansing, Michigan, 1958. This is one of the two best analyses of state and local finance extant, including academic efforts, the other is the earlier *Report of the Governor's Minnesota Tax Study, 1956.* The latter, which goes beyond the usual coverage of such studies to include an excellent analysis of regional economic growth factors was also initiated in response to a local "crisis" of slower-than-average economic growth.

analyses,[8] but serious efforts at organizing industrial development investment funds, industrial parks and the like were five or six years behind the turning point of a trend in local manufacturing employment. The concept of a research park tied in with two large universities of the area was independently "discovered" in 1961 about six years after the first signs of crisis and perhaps a dozen years after Boston's successful venture in hothouse research and development.

An interesting and supporting sidelight here is that Detroit could have carried on its World War II work in aircraft, at least in aircraft engines, granting Southern California's advantage in climate for final assembly and testing. But impatience to get back to the more lucrative automobile business was so great that airplane production was not even accorded a secondary place on Detroit's postwar industrial agenda. Conversely, Los Angeles, with nothing as profitable as making automobiles to reconvert to, fought for and won the postwar airplane business. Accordingly, Michigan's share of total military procurement fell from 10.5 per cent in 1940–45 to 2.7 per cent in 1962, while California's was rising from 9.1 to 23.9 per cent.

On careful quantification, we might find that the challenge of an employment crisis elicits its response in a resurgence of local economic leadership with various lags of roughly predictable length, under various sets of circumstances. For example, in these three industrially mature cities, about a half-dozen years elapsed between the beginning of steady deterioration and widespread appreciation of the structural character of the local malady. Public and private counteraction, in magnitude commensurate with the gravity of the challenge, lagged by another half-dozen years. And industrial reconversion may take a decade or so. Thus, over all, as much as two decades may elapse between shifts from one economic base to a substantially new one. Of course, this is the very kind of knowledge which, once revealed, might effect changes in the developmental pattern and might even shorten the period of response.

The Urban Size Ratchet

If the challenge of economic adversity does indeed beget the response of renewed community leadership and individual creativity, how can

[8] For example, William Haber, Eugene C. McKean and Harold C. Taylor, *The Michigan Economy: Its Potentials and Its Problems* (Kalamazoo, Mich.: The W. E. Upjohn Institute for Employment Research, 1959) and Paul W. McCracken (editor), *Taxes and Economic Growth in Michigan* (Kalamazoo: Upjohn, 1960).

we explain abandoned towns and depressed areas?[9] The coal towns of Pennsylvania, West Virginia, and Kentucky have been challenged by chronic unemployment for decades now with little evidence or prospect of significant response; the smaller urban places in Nebraska, the Dakotas and Montana—the wheat belt—have been declining for decades and give every indication of continuing to do so.

But these illustrations are all of the smaller urban areas. Clearly a scale factor is at work: witness the difficulty of finding a similar illustration of an urban area of over half a million population, one which has suffered an absolute decline in population. How far down in population size must we go to name an urban area that has lost population? Perhaps some critical size exists, short of which growth is not inevitable and even the very existence of the place is not assured, but beyond which absolute contraction is highly unlikely, even though the growth rate may slacken, at times even to zero. In sum, at a certain range of urban scale, set by the degree of isolation of the urban place, the nature of its hinterland, the level of industrial development in the country, and various cultural factors, some growth mechanism, similar to a ratchet, comes into being, locking in past growth and preventing contraction.

A number of possible rationalizations of a hypothetical urban-size ratchet could be adduced. One argument would be that with growth and size comes industrial diversification, and even a random blending of young, mature, and decadent industries tends to produce local growth rates which deviate only slightly from the national average rate, or the rate applicable to the surrounding region. Freedom from rapid rates of decline, moreover, provides the large urban area a grace period in which to react to adversity. Finally, the rich industrial diversification of the large urban area is fashioned in part out of many small firms with extensive and complex linkages to other local businesses. Clearly, it is much harder for these firms to relocate than it is for the large self-sufficient plant characteristic of a small urban area.

A second possible basis for irreversible urban growth after achievement of some threshold size is simply power politics. With a larger population comes greater electoral strength at both the state and

---

[9] See *Distressed Areas in a Growing Economy*, A Statement of National Policy by the Research and Policy Committee of the Committee for Economic Development (New York, June 1961), and current unpublished memoranda on area redevelopment circulated by the Manpower and Social Affairs Committee of the Organisation for Economic Cooperation and Development (Paris). The former is directed to U.S. depressed area problems and the latter to the European counterparts.

national levels and with reference to both executive and legislative bodies. True, political power may increase less than proportionately with population increase, as in malapportioned state legislatures and in the United States Senate; nevertheless, it does increase significantly. Thus, to the extent that federal and state financial aids and public works projects can revive faltering urban economies, the bigger urban areas are the gainers, for they can press harder for government support.

Third, and somewhat related, is the fact that tremendous amounts of fixed capital have been sunk in social and private overhead in the very large urban area—streets, sewers, schools, water mains, electric power lines, stores and housing—so that even if the area's productive facilities for export are worn out or technically obsolete, public service and utility costs are low enough to make it uneconomic to abandon so much immobile capital. No nation is so affluent that it can afford to throw away a major city.

Fourth, a greater and greater proportion of industrial activity is oriented to customers rather than to sources of supply, and the larger urban areas amass potential customers. A large local economy becomes almost self-justifying as a rich product market. New industries, born elsewhere, eventually reach a stage of development at which they are likely to establish branch plants in this large local market, sustaining local growth. Also, the current shift from manufacturing to service activity favors local market-oriented production. With growing size comes a steady improvement in an area's transportation position; every large urban area becomes a transportation hub regardless of its geographical position. In a day when the giant corporation engaged in nationwide operations is growing ever more dominant, the frequency of jet air service may be the critical factor in choosing an area for a headquarters or even a branch operation.

Finally, a large urban area is more likely to give birth to new industries at critical points in its life cycle than is a small urban area—an industrial birth which rescues it from the brink of stagnation or decline. While a large place may not produce more new ideas per thousand population per year than a small place—and some evidence will be cited below to suggest greater industrial creativity in larger places—a surer and steadier supply of invention, innovation, and promotion is to be expected in larger places. To illustrate, suppose that an entrepreneurial genius occurs only once in every 10,000 births, then a 50,000-population urban area with, say, 1,000 births per year will produce this key person only once every ten years, on the average. This area may not have a new industrial savior ready at the time of critical need, whereas the 500,000-population urban area, spawning a genius a year, almost certainly will. Gifted persons, moreover, born in smaller places tend to migrate to bigger cities. Sheer size may stabilize the supply of the key human resources necessary to economic growth and development.

In sum, if the growth of an urban area persists long enough to raise the area to some critical size (a quarter of a million population?),[10] structural characteristics, such as industrial diversification, political power, huge fixed investments, a rich local market, and a steady supply of industrial leadership may almost ensure its continued growth and fully ensure against absolute decline—may, in fact, effect irreversible aggregate growth.

Management as the Scarce Factor in Urban Growth

Absolute size may also be a brake on rate of growth as cities experience, after a certain critical level, increasing cost of public services due to density, congestion, bureaucracy, and so forth. Few statistical studies of public service production functions are available and even with a full portfolio of them one would have to exercise great care in generalizing across diverse urban areas. The principal diseconomy of scale may well turn out to be managerial efficiency, with a high variability between areas. The impression that management may be the limiting factor in urban scale is partly inferential by analogy from orthodox economic thought and partly intuitive.

In search of a theoretical constraint on size of firms, without which neither competition nor the self-regulating price system itself could be preserved, economists long ago found that they were forced to rely primarily on the limited expansibility of the managerial factor. The supply of land, labor, and capital does not seem to pose serious constraints on firm size. Apart from the managerial limitation, economists could rationalize firm-size limits only by turning to imperfect competi-

[10] Of the 212 Census-defined standard metropolitan areas, only seven experienced population losses between 1950 and 1960: Texarkana (92,000 population), Altoona (137,000), Wheeling (190,000), Scranton (235,000), Johnstown (280,000), Wilkes-Barre-Hazleton (347,000) and Jersey City (611,000). If Jersey City, N.J., is regarded as one of the central cities of the consolidated New York-Northeastern New Jersey metropolitan area, and it is alternatively classified that way by the Census, then we find no absolute declines in the one-half-million-and-over class and only two cases in the one-quarter to one-half million population class. U.S. Bureau of the Census, *Statistical Abstract of the United States: 1961*, Washington, 1961, Table 10.

tion or the inability of a firm to sell an endless amount of a given product at a constant price (i.e., a "downward sloping demand curve").[11] If price cuts are necessary to sell additional product, the firm realizes steadily diminishing net additions to revenue and profit with each additional sale, even if its unit costs do not begin to rise. While the firm might continue to grow even here by adding new product lines, multiproduct operations pose even greater managerial demands. Sooner or later, management would come to be the principal limitation or scarce factor, albeit it later with multiproduct expansion.

The managerial factor may also be the critical limitation on city size. As the city grows in total population, density of population, and physical extent, a point may be reached at which the unit cost of public services begins to rise or the quality of the service begins to fall appreciably. If so, a force which tends to dampen urban growth will have come into being. Local export firms, with their costs of production rising, find themselves disadvantaged in interregional competition for shares of the national market; manufacturing firms must move their trucks through congested streets to cramped loading docks, while paying higher property taxes for the less efficient urban public services. The city size at which increasing public service costs first turn sharply upward is probably, in large measure, a matter of the current level of urban technology. While the state of the arts in such diverse fields as urban transportation, communication, governmental decision making, and personnel administration is common to all urban areas—for knowledge is freely available—the competency and creativeness of various sets of local public officials are not nearly so uniform. And it is the local public officials, elective and appointive, who are the principal instruments of urban efficiency, together with the private managers of a few key local service industries, such as the utilities, banks, and local transportation and communication systems.

The parallel to the multiproduct firm is the highly interrelated set of local public services that must be integrated or co-ordinated to preserve the efficiency of the city, seen now as a huge factory with its streets, power lines, and pipes as the assembly lines, and its complex of legal, financial, and technical services as a magnified version of the "front office." If we believe that success in business is closely tied

---

[11] See the chapter on "monopolistic competition" in any standard Principles of Economics textbook. This idea dates back to the brilliant article by Piero Sraffa, "The Laws of Returns under Competitive Conditions," *The Economic Journal*, Vol. 36 (1926), reprinted in George J. Stigler and Kenneth E. Boulding (editors), *Readings in Price Theory* (Chicago: Richard D. Irwin, 1952), especially pp. 189 ff.

to the efficiency and creativity of the firm's management, is it not
equally likely that the efficiency of the local public economy will vary
widely from place to place according to the quality of urban management? Just as efficient management of the General Motors Corporation
can push back the point at which net diseconomies of scale take effect,
so public service inefficiency and rising unit costs can be postponed
considerably, even if not indefinitely, by able and experienced local
public legislators and administrators.

But recruiting able public administrators at the local level is no
easy matter. The Municipal Manpower Commission found:

> *Low prestige of government employment adversely affects the qual-
> ity of local government personnel.* . . . Nearly half of the responses
> to a survey of local officials conducted by the Public Personnel
> Association said that low prestige was a major obstacle to recruiting
> persons to fill key positions in local governments. A still more strik-
> ing manifestation of the effect of this low prestige of employment
> in local governments is found in the attitudes of municipal execu-
> tives themselves. The Commission's study of 1,700 local executives
> revealed that only 17 per cent would recommend a career in local
> government.[12]

It is not enough to recruit talented people to serve as public officials,
develop a science of local public administration, and professionalize
urban management. The organizational and institutional framework
within which all this functions is paramount. Even the most able
urban managers may not be able to provide efficient government in a
politically fragmented, unco-ordinated urban area. The problems of
recruitment and political fragmentation, moreover, interact, worsening
the situation. The Municipal Manpower Commission also reported
that:

> A lack of clear-cut community-wide objectives and of permanent
> machinery for area-wide planning and policy formulation. . . .
> The fragmentation of the geographical area among numerous local
> governments and many leadership groups is a serious barrier to the
> solution of metropolitan problems which are beyond the capacity
> of any single jurisdiction or civic organization; it is a cause of frus-

---

[12] *Government Manpower for Tomorrow's Cities*, A Report of the Municipal
Manpower Commission (New York: McGraw-Hill Book Co., Inc., 1962), pp. 44–46.

tration for municipal manpower. . . . Furthermore, the small-scale problems faced by such units do not offer much attraction to experienced and able personnel.[13]

Ultimately, then, diseconomies of scale in public services and quasi-public services, such as water supply, sewage disposal, electricity, gas and transportation, may constrain the size of the city; but only if technological progress, political innovation, and administrative ingenuity do not keep pace. Despite the built-in frailties that have been mentioned, they have up to now.

URBAN GROWTH ANALYSIS: THE DEMAND SIDE

One of the simplest and most useful analytical frameworks within which to view the urban economy is the highly popular "export-base" construct, an analytical rationalization of the urban economy first set forth explicitly in 1928 in Robert M. Haig's classic study of the New York region and more recently integrated into the mainstream of economic theory in the work of Charles Tiebout.[14] The urban area is depicted as a wide-open economy, heavily dependent on external trade, quite like the small, industrially advanced nation in the world market, only more so. Both Switzerland and Denver must export or die. A small metropolitan area (50,000–100,000 population) may devote as much as one-half of its economic activity to producing goods for sale outside of its borders, greatly surpassing even the most trade-oriented

[13] *Ibid.*, pp. 30–32.

[14] Robert M. Haig, *Major Economic Factors in Metropolitan Growth and Arrangement*, Vol. I, *Regional Survey of New York and Environs* (New York, 1928). The economic base or export-base logic of urban-regional growth has a long history of conceptual development traced through most thoroughly in the first of a series of articles by Richard B. Andrews, "Mechanics of the Urban Economic Base: Historical Development of the Base Concept," *Land Economics* (May 1953), pp. 161–67. The full series of ten articles together with eleven others are reprinted in Ralph W. Pfouts (editor), *The Techniques of Urban Economic Analysis* (West Trenton, N.J.: Chandler-Davis Publishing Co., 1960). Economic base theory was developed more rigorously in two articles by Charles M. Tiebout, "The Urban Economic Base Reconsidered," *idem*, pp. 279–89, and "The Community Income Multiplier: A Case Study," pp. 341–58, and reaches its height of elegance in Tiebout's *The Community Economic Base Study*, Supplementary Paper No. 16, Committee for Economic Development (New York: December, 1962).

small nation in this regard.[15] With the proceeds of its "export" sales, complementary goods are purchased from outside ("imported"), roughly equivalent in dollar amount to the value of the area exports.

The Role of the Export Sector

Those who have tried to fathom the processes and patterns of small-area economic development—largely planners trying to anticipate the future and business groups promoting local industrial development, and only rarely economists—have gained valuable insights into the process of city formation and growth through these domestic, inter-national-trade-type models. Because the city planners and area development people were most often concerned with long-range growth trends, the customary use of the export-base model was to project the future size and shape of the total local economy from the projected size and shape of the area's export sector. Since the export base of most urban economies is dominated by a relatively small number of manufacturing activities, the usual procedure was simply to estimate the number of manufacturing workers that would be employed locally at the target date and then add on the number of local service employees needed to accommodate the export industry workers and their families, and, of course, to serve each others' families.[16] Further, if the projected export and service industry workers were summed and this number multiplied by the average number of dependents per worker, the future total population of the area fell neatly into place. (It is a fact, however, that the ratio of labor force to population does vary

[15] Exports may account for a full one-half of local economic activity in urban areas with as many as a quarter of a million people, in cases of heavy industrial specialization. For example, the Flint, Michigan, "urbanized area," with a total population of 278,000 and an employed labor force of 100,000, had over 51,000 workers in manufacturing of which close to 50,000 were producing motor vehicles or related intermediate products. Almost all of the automobile output, one-half of total local activity, is sold outside of the Flint area. Derived from the U.S. Bureau of the Census, *U.S. Census of Population: 1960, General Social and Economic Characteristics, Michigan* (Washington: U.S. Government Printing Office, 1962), Tables 32 and 75.

[16] With repeated handling, and the occasional intervention of economists, the export-to-service ratio became more sophisticated. An appreciation of the way in which it changes (decreases) with larger city size is most clearly conveyed in Irving Morrissett, "The Economic Structure of American Cities," *Papers and Proceedings of the Regional Science Association,* Vol. 4, 1958, pp. 239–56.

appreciably between urban areas, due to the availability of jobs for women, family income levels, and other factors. This is brought out in Chapters 2 and 3.)

Applicability of the Export-Base Logic

Thus the export sector is cast in the key role as the active instrument of change, the point of contact between the national and the local economies; and national forces are presumed to be more powerful and more autonomous than local forces. "As the export industry goes, so goes the total local economy" might be the watchword. A typical characterization of the urban growth process, at least as it has evolved in the literature of regional geography and city planning, is that a given number of export workers "supports" a given number of local service workers. This has given rise to a long and sometimes bitter dispute over who "supports" whom. The export-base advocate argues that if the export jobs were to disappear, the local service jobs would also be lost—the very town would vanish—but if, instead, some part of the local service work were lost, say, through business failures, re-placement service business would spring up automatically.

But this is not wholly convincing because one might also argue that replacement export firms could also be reborn on the base of a viable local service sector, if the reason of being for that industry in that place still exists; even new, unrelated export complexes might be generated if the town as a whole still has a *raison d'être*. Going behind local services, *per se*, an urban economy based on natural or persistent economic advantages (e.g., a good port and railhead, a pleasant climate and topography, the homes of skilled workers who resist migration) may give birth to wholly new export industries to replace lost ones with only modest labor pains. The champions of the local service sector, led by Blumenfeld,[17] rising to the challenge, have even argued that it is really the local service sector which is basic and enduring, and that this latter sector supports the chameleon-like export sector which, taking a very long view, is founded on transitory manufacturing firms. In short, a severed export appendage of the urban corporate

---

[17] See especially, Hans Blumenfeld, "The Economic Base of the Metropolis," *Journal of the American Institute of Planners* (Fall, 1955), pp. 114–32, reprinted in Pfouts, *op. cit.*, pp. 230–77.

body can, in time, be regenerated by a viable and efficient local service sector.

The phrase "in time" is critical. In the analysis of local business cycles the export-base logic is employed, quite legitimately, under the reasonable assumption that the industrial composition of the export sector of an urban economy is highly unlikely to experience any substantial amount of structural alteration in the short space of time within which business cycles take place. Not only the same industries but even the precise firms will probably remain intact. The local service industries, moreover, are probably not going to alter the competitive position of the local economy in any major way through increases or decreases in the cost or quality or availability of services rendered. Therefore, in analyses which extend over periods of time so short that the industrial structure—both export and local service— is largely fixed in kind and quality, the primacy of the demand for export products in effecting change seems clear and incontestable.

When the time dimension is extended, however, circularity sets in. The demand for local services is derived indirectly from the external demands for the export products of the area and directly from the local spending of payrolls and profits generated by that export production. In that sense the export sector is primary. On the other hand, local services are important inputs in export production and the efficiency of the local service sector is critical to export firms. An abiding electric utility and commercial bank that successively serve the firms and employees of, first, a wagon maker, and then an unsuccessful automobile firm, and then a railroad car firm, and so on, have strong claims to be counted "basic" in the local economy. But in order to avoid flagrant bias in the argument, we should note that the area exporter could well have been the same steel plant, year after year.

We observe the opening of an iron mine in Minnesota (export industry) stimulating the growth of a whole town (with its complex of derivative local service industries); alternatively, we observe the existence of a farm service center in Iowa with an efficient and pleasing local service sector (e.g., schools, utilities, shopping centers) attracting a manufacturing plant (exporter) which, of course, generates more local services. In a growth context, this is a chicken-and-egg problem which, if treated at the level of gross generality, can become a fool's game. When treated in a specific context, such as the emphasis on external demand and the export base in local business cycle analysis, selective emphasis can be both proper and incisive.

Urban Economic Projection as Demand Analysis

Still, the complexity of urban-regional growth does not completely vitiate the value of the simplistic export-base logic. One important element in any long-range growth prognosis is a projection of the demand for the area's current mix of export products—the lengthened shadow of the sales charts of a handful of key industries. While the export-base lines of causation in the growth process become adulterated with larger city size, demand projections for the current export mix still provide as good a place as any at which to begin.

One can begin an analysis of the trends in demand for an area's leading exports with a standard economic concept: income elasticity of demand, the ratio of the per cent change in spending on a good to the per cent change in disposable income. A 10 per cent increase in income might increase cigarette sales by only a couple per cent—an income-inelastic good—while sales of fashion dresses might increase by 20 per cent—an income-elastic good. We are interested here in identifying which are the "inferior" goods from which the consumer turns as his living standard rises secularly (e.g., grits and rice, bus and rail transportation), and which are the "superior" goods to which he turns in response to a steadily rising income (e.g., beef and wine, automobile and air transportation). The critical concept in our growth context is the *long-run* income elasticity of demand, a consumption-to-income trend line that abstracts from cycle swings.[18] Time is clearly on the side of those urban areas which are producing goods for which the long-run income elasticity of demand is greater than unity, the "luxury" goods, and the reverse. And this is obviously an operational concept, although precise measurement is difficult.

---

[18] One must take care to distinguish between the deliberative reaction of buyers to the slow, steady increases in per capita income which come with economic development and the quick, first response of buyers to sudden (cyclical) fluctuations in their income. The distinction is a major one. In cycle analysis the durability of the good—the ease of postponing the replacement of an aging automobile or refrigerator—is the single most critical factor in determining income elasticity of demand, but in growth analysis the durability-postponability characteristic is of little interest. The time period spanned by a growth study is much too long to reflect the transitory postponements and accelerated purchases of durable goods that are part of the buyers' business cycle strategy. Compare the treatment of income elasticity of demand in any standard text on business cycles or national income with its treatment in any standard text on price theory. For example, Robert M. Biggs, *National-Income Analysis and Forecasting* (New York: W. W. Norton and Co., Inc., 1956), pp. 319–20, and Richard H. Leftwich, *The Price System and Resource Allocation* (New York: Holt, Rinehart, and Winston, 1961), pp. 83–86.

A second set of factors which bears on the growth prospects of an urban area, via the demand for its exports, is changes in the relative prices and availabilities of the principal substitutes for the local exports. Rising costs of production in rival urban areas, due perhaps to a growing scarcity of raw materials in their hinterlands relative to local environs, would tend to raise the prices or lower the quality of these competing goods, thereby shifting demand toward the local product. Of course it cuts both ways: improvements in the resource position of competing areas act to lower their prices or improve their quality relative to that of the local economy, and shift demand adversely.[19]

The adverse effect of the depletion of the natural resource base on which a town is built is a clear and obvious case. But mining towns may face more subtle threats too. A coal town stagnates when households in the areas it serves shift to oil or gas heat as supplies of these fuels increase or become more accessible. In the near future, electricity, an even cleaner and more flexible form of heat, may become competitive in price for space heating as it already has for cooking. At that time, the gas and oil areas may slump a little and, in certain circumstances, the coal towns could revive. New coal mining techniques—such, for example, as pumping coal slurry through pipes to electricity generating plants—might underlie the falling electricity costs, or long-distance transmission might be accomplished with much less fall in voltage. And in the more distant future, as the huge public investment in atomic power technology pays off, plants using fission fuel may replace those using fossil fuel, in which case the outlook for coal towns darkens again.

Next, changes in tastes—autonomous changes now, not changes in consumption patterns in response to higher income or altered relative prices through diverse income elasticities of demand—have always been an important source of change, perhaps now more than ever before. Despite isolated instances of extreme and self-conscious individualism (e.g., "beatniks"), the prevailing opinion seems to be that we are moving toward a mass culture, with our society pursuing security and finding it in increasingly close conformity. The image here is

[19] For a succinct treatment of the natural resource impact, see Harvey S. Perloff and Lowdon Wingo, Jr., "Natural Resource Endowment and Regional Economic Growth," *Natural Resources and Economic Growth*, Papers presented at a conference held at Ann Arbor, Michigan, April 7–9, 1960, under joint sponsorship of Resources for the Future, Inc., and Committee on Economic Growth of the Social Science Research Council (Washington: Resources for the Future, Inc., 1961).

nationwide television networks and Madison Avenue. And by coupling uniform consumption patterns to a high and rising per capita income, an ever greater share of which is "discretionary income," the danger is that capricious shifts in consumption spending may come to dominate the pattern of economic activity.

"Discretionary spending" could come to ebb and flow in massive tides as fads and fashions dictate: from big cars and small boats to small cars and big boats. Manufacturing plants selling in national markets may increasingly find themselves alternately awash with demand, then left stranded on the beach. Even whole industries may rise and fall over very short time periods. The remote small urban economy exporting a single product, probably even a single brand, would run the greatest risks, especially if it is a "luxury" good. Small one-industry towns, long subject to the risk of great cyclical instability, may no longer be a viable long-run form of socioeconomic organization in the Age of Affluence.[20]

Economic Viability of the Remote Small Urban Area

Other disadvantages of the remote small urban area in today's fierce competition for industry can be cited. Highly automated factory and office operations will assemble labor forces too small to support a community,[21] especially in the light of the growing range of goods and services that are considered necessary. Not only "bright lights and action" but also good museums, technical libraries and community colleges are urban "necessities" today and they cross the threshold of economical operation at relatively large population sizes. Only the clustering of many automated operations will provide the necessary supporting population. Further, more and more industries are clustering into mutually supporting complexes, based on input-output linkages, complementary labor demands, technological interactions and

---

[20] John Kenneth Galbraith in *The Affluent Society* (Boston: Houghton Mifflin, 1958), introduced the first systematic analysis of the economics of affluence; however, he laid siege to orthodox economic theory, and questioned the central concept of *unlimited* human wants as an *inexhaustible* spur to greater production. Here, however, we are concerned less with the rationality or morality of artificially stimulating wants (e.g., advertising, promoting materialistic social values) and more with the destabilizing effect of affluence—a large and growing proportion of income spent for goods which satisfy weakly-felt wants.

[21] See Aaron Fleisher, "The Influence of Technology on Urban Forms," *Daedalus*, Winter, 1961, p. 55, for bare mention of this provocative point.

so forth. Linked, individual firms cannot enter or leave their present location easily or unilaterally; therefore, an urban area finds it more difficult to attract interdependent firms. In sum, bigger, tighter-knit industrial complexes imply larger and fewer manufacturing centers.

The economic uncertainty and instability of the small urban area will tend to be reflected in higher labor costs—either compensatory higher wage rates for high-grade labor or the need to depend on lower-grade labor—and other competitive disadvantages, such as the alternating periods of capital shortages (congestion) and idle capital (heavy overhead costs) which accompanies heavy fluctuations in economic activity. All in all, when we add together (a) the precariousness of specialization in discretionary goods in the affluent society to (b) the difficulty of supporting a community on the base of a "worker-less" plant to (c) the trend toward more integrated industrial complexes, it is difficult to be sanguine about the economic prospects of small towns or even small cities.

While the remote small one-industry town would seem to be highly vulnerable, even obsolete, in a country which has achieved an advanced stage of economic development, an interesting and perhaps highly significant exception may exist. A number of small and medium size urban areas, connected by good highways and/or other transportation facilities may form a loose network of interrelated labor markets. With widespread ownership of automobiles or a well-developed bus system, and with expressways permitting average speeds up to fifty miles an hour between home and work place, such a network could extend radially for twenty-five to thirty miles around one of the larger urban places or embrace a square fifty miles on a side and still be tied into a single, integrated local labor market. A half-dozen towns of, say, 25,000 population with two or three main industries each plus a dozen small one- or two-industry towns of half that size add up to a 300,000 population, extended local labor market, built on the moderately broad base of a couple of dozen separate industries. This federated local economy may achieve the minimum size necessary to activate the urban size ratchet effect mentioned above, preserving the *collective* existence of these smaller urban places.

The case for the federated local labor market can be made more programmatically. A number of small nearby towns could join with a few medium size places to develop a co-ordinated employment service. The local labor market could then achieve the scale necessary to acquire the counseling and teaching talent and facilities to become viable in our rapidly changing economy. At a bare minimum a very good vocational education institution is required.[22] In addition, area industrial development efforts designed to attract new firms could be co-ordinated, even to the point of developing common research and industrial parks at central points. Some evidence of this pattern can be seen in North Carolina, a state filled with small and medium size urban areas, where a research and development triangle is being created in the Chapel Hill-Durham-Raleigh triangle, fifteen to thirty miles on a side, and enclosing about a quarter of a million people.[23]

A less noted example of urban confederation to achieve economies of scale and greater range of choice is occurring in upstate Michigan. Three cities, Saginaw, Bay City, and Midland, ranging in population from 30,000 to 100,000, are forming the first loose bonds to effect a working coalition spanning an area of some 350,000 population. This latter figure is, incidentally, precisely the one we have suggested above as the critical size at which no absolute declines in population have been observed.[24]

[22] Vocational education institutions will probably be placed only in large or centrally located places. The President's Committee on Youth Employment recommended that "area skill centers, or technical or vocational schools should be established in many new central locations. . . . These schools should draw their pupils from a large enough area to permit full staffing and equipment, and should offer a wide variety of courses . . . there may be a number of centers in a large city, or a single center for several counties." *The Challenge of Jobless Youth*, President's Committee on Youth Employment (Washington: U.S. Government Printing Office, April 1963), p. 11.

[23] Malcolm Ross, "North Carolina, Dixie Dynamo," *The National Geographic*, February 1963, especially pp. 141–49. Ross writes, "visit the State capital, Raleigh, and the first thing you hear about is the Research Triangle." The Triangle connects the State College of Agriculture and Engineering at Raleigh, Duke University at Durham, and the University of North Carolina at Chapel Hill, and encloses the Textile Research Center and other industrial laboratories.

[24] Linkages between the three cities originated in many individual private actions, such as the fact that almost one-half of the 10,000 employees of the chemical firm that is the chief employer in Midland commute from Bay City and Saginaw. Subsequently, more official co-operation has solidified these linkages in the form of the Tri-City Airport, centrally located, and a new community college, appropriately named Delta, to be followed with a senior college, Saginaw Valley College. More subtle evidence can be found in the fact that area directories contain some fifty firms with the words Tri-City or Delta in their names. Finally, the critical cultural considerations in achieving viability are reflected in interest in a regional orchestra and the exchange of newspaper articles by entertainment critics among the three cities to effect an informally consolidated regional theater. The principal problem will probably be to co-ordinate local government; few serious efforts have been made and interest is even lagging. And with eight cities, five villages and fifty-seven townships encompassed in the three counties, management of the public sector could be the limiting factor in efficiency and growth. Abridged from William W. Lutz, "New Metropolitan Area for Michigan," *The Detroit News*, February 6, 1964, p. 14-D.

The long-range viability of the smaller urban areas can be assured, however, only if one other ingredient is added to the recipe. The current generation of young adults will probably not be satisfied with rural or small town life; they are an urban generation. The pictured loose federation of towns could, however, support a rather wide range of consumer services and urban amenities if they joined forces. Differentiation of urban function could be accentuated far beyond that which has naturally evolved. The smaller urban places could become analogous to the dormitory suburbs of the large metropolitan area, with their central business districts becoming regional shopping centers. The largest or most centrally located town could become the central business district—downtown—for the whole network of urban places, with travel times not significantly greater than those which now exist in the typical million population metropolitan areas.

The fate of whole regions, the West North Central wheat belt and the Appalachian Mountain area for example, may rest on the ability of conurbations of smaller urban places to emulate the spatial-functional form of the large metropolitan areas. While local jealousies and capital gains and losses in real property are not to be taken lightly, the depth of the local crises which attend inaction may prompt bold measures. Both public and private investments could be planned strategically. Instead of a half-dozen small, bare community halls sprinkled across the area, one generous size, acoustically pleasing auditorium could be built where good music could be heard. In place of a couple of two-year community colleges staffed as extensions of the local high schools, a full-fledged, four-year college of high standards could be supported. Low-tuition colleges where the student can live at home cheaply while attending—and keep his part-time job—may be critical in holding the talented young from middle- and low-income homes, and in attracting those families in the first place.

Again, museums, professional athletic teams, complete medical facilities, and other accoutrements of modern urban life could be supported collectively. As these federated places grew and prospered the interstices would, of course, begin to fill in, moving the area closer to the large metropolitan area form. But alert action in land planning and zoning could preserve open spaces in a pattern superior to those found in most large urban areas.[25]

[25] The concept of a city-region can, of course, be traced back to Christaller and Lösch and, in a more limited sense, further back to Von Thünen. And geographers have been doing empirical work on city-regions for years. See, for example, Robert E. Dickinson, *City, Region and Regionalism* (London: Kegan Paul and New York:

The political difficulties of achieving the federated urban area are substantial and should not be waved aside, but the constituent political entities are the creations of and subject to the state. Without predicting that it will move into this vacuum, the state could, at will, implement the spatial-functional form suggested here, and the alternatives seem bleak.

URBAN GROWTH ANALYSIS: THE SUPPLY SIDE

While a demand orientation has been the more fashionable for the past decade, the existence of a supply side to urban-regional economic development has long been recognized, even antedating the demand (export-base) model. A supply orientation is implicit in the typical "inventory" of local resources with which many area development studies begin—and too often end. A supply approach need not be naïve, for it holds considerably greater potential for unraveling the pattern and determinants of urban growth than does the relatively static export-base logic.

We might generalize to the effect that the longer the time period under consideration, the greater the relative importance of supply— local resource endowment and industrial culture. The recent New York study, for example, highlighted the fact that the New York metropolitan area grew by incubating new functions, nurturing them

---

Oxford University Press, 1947). Again, Karl Fox has been developing a nationwide system of "functional economic areas," which integrate the Census standard metropolitian areas and Bogue's "state economic areas" into a single comprehensive system of city-regions which exhaust the land area. See Karl A. Fox, *Economic Models for Area Development Research,* Workshop on Area Development, Stillwater, Oklahoma, May 8–9, 1963 (mimeo.) for a recent formulation or "The Study of Interactions between Agriculture and the Non-farm Economy; Local, Regional and National," *Journal of Farm Economics* (February 1962), pp. 1–34 for an earlier published account.

But the community of interest between city and hinterland in these works is based on their economic complementarity and the resulting trade. What is offered in this study is quite different: namely, that a cluster of small cities with more or less parallel industrial structures may find their community of interest in combining to achieve economies (and qualities) of scale in public investment and other kinds of social overhead. Small, vulnerable one-industry towns, facing stagnation or even extinction, form a "region" for developmental purposes. For a likely new source of additional material on these matters which came to the author's attention too late for substantive comment here, see F. Stuart Chapin, Jr., and Shirley F. Weiss (editors), *Urban Growth Dynamics: In a Regional Cluster of Cities* (New York: John Wiley & Sons, Inc., 1962), a treatment of the Piedmont Industrial Crescent of North and South Carolina.

and finally spinning them off to other sections of the country, all the while regenerating this cycle. The flour mills, foundries, meat packing plants, textile mills and tanneries of the post-Civil War period drifted away from New York, their place taken by less transport-sensitive products, such as garments, cigars, and office work. Currently, New York is losing the manufacturing end of many of its most traditional specialties, as garment sewing slips away to low-wage Eastern Pennsylvania leaving only the selling function behind, and as printing splits away from immobile publishing. But New York's growth never seems to falter as the new growth industries are much more than proportionately regenerated in its rich industrial culture.[26]

Further testimony to the fact that the relative proportion of growth industries in the local economic base is a most undependable guide to aggregate area growth can be drawn out of the work of Perloff and associates. They found "no positive correlation between the proportion of workers in 'growth industries' and the relative rates of increases in total economic activity among the many states."[27] A number of possible explanations come to mind: growth industries are (a) quantitatively dwarfed by other activity, or (b) they are based on new products which are most likely to be invented and/or innovated in mature (slow-growing) industrial areas either out of superior know-how, or (c) out of desperation, as suggested above in the challenge-and-response argument. In any event, the industry-mix approach—a demand-side technique which ignores new industry—can only provide a partial basis for a long-run growth theory.[28] We turn, therefore, to a brief survey

[26] Raymond Vernon, *Metropolis 1985* (New York: Doubleday and Co., Inc., 1960), pp. 35ff. This historical evidence of New York's vitality as an industrial innovator-promoter is later supplemented with a more analytical exposition attributing New York's growth over the past three decades to its absolute and comparative advantage in the "external-economy industries" (pp. 61–62). Large metropolitan areas, in general, must and can depend on relatively tight-knit industrial complexes for their growth, and on the related group of industries which draw broadly on a well-developed social overhead, ranging from private consultants to public libraries.

[27] See footnote 4, above.

[28] Raymond Vernon's New York study moves from historical description to a statistical analysis of industrial change over the past thirty years. The area is characterized as having had an industry mix relatively rich in the fast-growing industries but whose "promise was not realized" as these industries grew locally at rates slower than their national counterparts. While this is a statistically valid explanation of the Region's slower than average total growth, a more revealing formulation might be to see the area as one which grows, despite the fact that it steadily loses share (spins off) in almost every activity it undertakes, by constantly creating some new *raison d'être*. If, indeed, New York is the birthplace of new ideas and new industries, much more than proportionately, and it did not experience a declining market

of the supply side of urban growth, conventionally enough with the economist's classic four factors of production: land, labor, capital, and entrepreneurship.

Labor

The historical pattern of industrial development in an urban area may greatly influence its future pattern of growth, and inherited traits may be especially noteworthy with reference to the local labor force. A farm market town on the verge of its industrial baptism can look to only the most routine kinds of manufacturing operations—a work-shoe factory, a textile mill, a food processing plant. After a decade or so of apprenticeship in low-skilled work, the area may be in a position to offer a large supply of semiskilled workers and perhaps a few highly skilled workers, and ultimately the area will have passed from apprenticeship to journeyman status as a local labor market. Moreover, as skill levels rise, so do wage rates, and the higher local standard of living may automatically evoke a middle-class morality that further spurs growth. Personal achievement—"success"—is not only reasonably attainable now, it is highly emphasized and the financial means are at hand with which the principal instrument toward that end—education—can be applied. Further, personal saving and capital formation become a basic cultural trait, opening the way to entrepreneurship in the form of new small business formation.

Seldom, however, is an appreciation of this process accompanied by a sense of the time dimension of the industrial acculturation process. Do the steps upward in labor skill span a decade? A generation? What is the principal channel for transmitting skills: through the industrial base and personal contact (from father to son) or through earnings and improved public services (from productivity to income to tax base to good schools)? Clearly, a rapidly advancing technology favors the latter.

But "what is past is prologue" may cut both ways. If a strong and aggressive local union presses for wage rate increases in excess of the

---

share of these industries as they matured, the New York area would come to embrace most of the nation's economic activity and population. The great value of the New York study is precisely that it demonstrates that giant metropolises grow by serving an entrepreneurial not a caretaker function. This message does come through but only obliquely, probably partly because the historical work showing the long-run industrial sequences and the short-run, industry-mix analyses were performed by different persons. Raymond Vernon, *op. cit.,* Chapter 3.

rate of increase in local labor productivity, and if the local employer
is confident that he can easily pass along the increase in labor costs
(plus his markup), because his competitors are few and collusive
(oligopoly), and similarly circumstanced (nationwide union), the union
is likely to find the employer quite accommodating, with only token
resistance for the sake of appearance. But a day of retribution arrives
when the local economy, affluent beyond its expectation or merit, must
face the task of gaining additional employments.

Even if the local export oligopolist survives forever, it is highly
unlikely that this firm will add continually to *local* operations, as the
typical pattern is for a growing firm to move to multiplant operations
and to disperse its plants to minimize transportation costs. But, the
natural increase in local population and labor force alone demands
expanding employment, and because technological advances ("automation") will probably *reduce* employment in the local plant appreciably,
new firms must be acquired and they will probably have to be recruited almost entirely from industries new to the area. But high local
wage rates would tend to put most of the low-wage, nondurable goods
industries out of reach, as long as large pools of cheap labor exist
elsewhere, and high wage rates *relative to local skills* dim the prospects
of getting even new durable goods industries. Probably a significant
part of the current stagnation and structural unemployment of the
Pittsburgh area is traceable to wage rate increases that outran skill
and productivity gains during the long, lush periods of the Second
World War and its early aftermath. Painful wage rate adjustments
under the pressure of protracted unemployment may be an integral
part of the industrial redevelopment of heavy-industry towns.[29]

But the local industrial legacy influences the local labor market in
ways other than through labor skills and wage rates; in labor mobility,
for example. A growing preference among new entrants to the labor
force—the younger generation—for the broad welfare fringe benefits
and the prestige of employment in a large corporation is becoming
evident. Personnel placement and job recruiting studies have demonstrated that "name" corporations do, in fact, find recruiting easier,[30]

[29] Absolute reductions in the local wage rate are rare, especially under trade
unionism, but the reluctant acceptance of wage increases of less than average
amount is quite common; indeed wage freezes at the current level for a year or two
are accepted even under unionism in emergency cases. Thus local wage deflation
ordinarily takes the form of a *relative* decrease, as local wages stand still or lag
behind national increases.

[30] Henry C. Thole, *Shortages of Skilled Manpower: Implications for Kalamazoo
Businessmen* (Kalamazoo: The W. E. Upjohn Institute for Community Research,
1958), especially pp. 26–39.

as retirement and stock purchase plans attract the young men and glamorous buildings in exciting central locations attract the young women.[31] The security-glamour effects must be separated from the fact that the big corporation also has the added advantage of recruiting with a full-time, professional personnel staff.

Not only does firm size help to augment the local labor force, thereby widening and deepening the selection of human resources available at that location, but the large corporation may also facilitate a more orderly contraction of the local economy under adverse business conditions. Big firms are usually multiproduct operations and are spatially dispersed; therefore when demand or supply conditions change the requisite adjustments in their labor force can often be swiftly and smoothly accomplished within the protective shell of the corporate family. A worker may be shifted from a failing to an expanding line of production within the same plant, assuming the skill level is about the same, or he may be transferred without job change to a distant plant serving a region growing more rapidly than the nearby region, although often not without strong "persuasion." That the new jobs of a firm will be offered first to their own displaced workers seems ever more certain as the courts continually expand their interpretation of property rights to cover jobs,[32] and as the unions win fringe benefits covering this same contingency. In sum, big multiproduct firms probably increase the mobility of labor both in and out of their local labor markets, and thereby both enrich the local supply of labor, and also reduce frictional and structural unemployment in the area. This would seem to be a testable hypothesis.

[31] In a slightly different context, Hoover and Vernon observe that "The young women's preference for a job in the central business district today . . . is based . . . on the increased opportunities for after-hours recreation, lunch-hour shopping (or window-shopping), and the greater opportunities for husband-hunting." Edgar M. Hoover and Raymond Vernon, *Anatomy of a Metropolis* (Cambridge, Mass.: Harvard University Press, 1959), p. 102.

[32] On the Fall 1961 docket of the United States Supreme Court were two cases turning on the question of whether employees of a firm that has relocated its operations have seniority rights to jobs at the new site. One case was filed by Teamster Union Local 852 against the Glidden Company (paints and chemicals) for damages to workers at the old Elmhurst, N.Y., plant who were not offered jobs at the new Bethlehem, Pa., site. In the second case, five employees of the Gemmer Manufacturing Co. (steering gears) of Detroit, Mich., were suing the company for agreeing to hire only local workers at the new Lebanon, Tenn., site, in return for a $2.4 million plant construction loan extended by the community. In both cases, the lower court had ruled in favor of the employees. Reported in *The Evening Star*, Washington, D.C., August 30, 1961, p. B-9.

Finally, *unbalanced* local labor demands have very long-run supply repercussions which may stimulate local growth. If the local industries hire only males, this creates a shortage of jobs for women and, while temporarily depressing to average family income, the surplus pool of female labor tends to attract industries with complementary labor demands. Hoover cites the classic examples of silk mills being drawn to the Pennsylvania coal towns, and shoe and textile industries to the New England port towns.[33] Clearly, this argument carries more force in a full employment economy than in one with widespread unemployment; moreover, the long experience of Cincinnati, Pittsburgh, and other places with unbalanced labor demands has shown that righting the balance may be greatly delayed—commercial and financial secretarial work does not flow readily into isolated places or gray factory towns. More often the young women leave for the centers of commerce. Still, Boston's industrial resurgence is due in part to a good supply of experienced female workers, highly valued in electronics manufacturing, a legacy of textile-mill days.

Another very long-run dynamic of the local labor market operates through work standards and work rules. Strong, imaginative entrepreneurs combined with anxious, pliable labor produce an immediate industrial environment especially hospitable to local innovation and economic growth. This is especially true with reference to major changes in production processes which disrupt established work standards and may be darkly seen as a "speed-up" by the workers. Warner has noted the developmental advantages of flexible work rules as far back as Philadelphia in the early nineteenth century.

> The contrast between the vitality and rapid progress of Philadelphia's machine and foundry trades and its resistance to innovation in textiles can perhaps be explained by two factors: differences in business leadership and differences in the organization of the city's labor force. Philadelphia had the unaccountable good fortune to be the place of work of a few great innovator-businessmen in the machine and foundry trades. . . . Before the Civil War Philadelphia had no such outstanding textile-innovator-businessmen. . . .
>
> The condition of the city's work force also contributed to the slow modernization of its textile manufactures. In the machine trades

---

[33] Edgar M. Hoover, *Location of Economic Activity* (New York: McGraw-Hill Book Co., Inc., 1948), pp. 118–19.

no established crafts were threatened by the innovations. . . . Fully integrated and mechanized textile mills presented quite the opposite case. . . . The late arrival of cotton mills to the city proper, despite the cheap coal and steam power of Philadelphia, suggests that labor opposition kept the mills out of the city until after the Civil War. In Lowell, hand weavers of rugs were replaced immediately upon the invention of a power loom which could be tended by women . . . [indicating] the Lowell mill owners had strong control over the local labor force. In Philadelphia, however, the weavers were numerous and well organized . . . [leading to] a series of strikes, riots . . . to defend their trade.[34]

Thus a powerful "long wave" may be at work in the process of urban growth. An established center of an industry has a strong comparative advantage in the early period of the industry's development due to all the external economies that are so familiar—the presence of "skills in the air," local financial, marketing, engineering, and repair services that support the industry are better developed, and so forth. But a radical change in industrial technology not only undercuts some of the older center's comparative advantage but may even reverse it if the veteran labor force resists work standard changes dictated by the new technology. And if, as frequently happens at the blue-collar level, the new production techniques are less demanding of skill than the old, the "labor-harassed" firm is likely to relocate. The relocation will probably be gradual, however, taking the form of adding new facilities elsewhere over a period of time while slowly closing down the old ones. The steady migration of textiles from New England to the South Atlantic region probably had more than a little of this force underlying it: labor's collective resistance to increasing the number of spindles tended in the textile mills is very much in line with this kind of development. The influence of work standards on industrial location is, moreover, not likely to lessen in the near future, with even more changes in industrial technology in the offing (e.g., computers).

Urban growth analysis has much to glean from historical studies-in-depth of local labor markets.

[34] Sam B. Warner, Jr., "Innovation and the Industrialization of Philadelphia 1800-1850," *The Historian and the City*, Oscar Handlin and John Burchard (editors), (Cambridge: The M.I.T. Press and Harvard University Press, 1963), pp. 66–69.

Entrepreneurship

Students of regional economic development are inclined to admit defeat too quickly when faced with the task of quantifying the presumably more qualitative aspects of growth. No one denies that entrepreneurship—inventiveness, promotional artistry, organizational genius, venturesomeness, and so forth—lies at the very heart of industrial development, yet we hurriedly pay our formal respects to this critical factor and then move on in embarrassed haste to surer, more easily charted grounds, such as the rate of capital formation, capital-to-labor ratios and the like. But this is a mistake; we cannot act so cavalierly toward the entrepreneur, least of all in long-term growth analysis.

A number of naïve but intriguing hypotheses on the role of entrepreneurship in urban-regional growth literally cry out for even the loosest testing, so that we may then strike more sophisticated reformulation. For example, Chinitz offers one that emphasizes risk-taking:

> My feeling is that you do not breed as many entrepreneurs per capita in families allied with steel as you do in families allied with apparel, using these two industries for illustrative purposes only. The son of a salaried executive is less likely to be sensitive to opportunities wholly unrelated to his father's field than the son of an independent entrepreneur. True, the entrepreneur's son is more likely to think of taking over his father's business. My guess is, however, that the tradition of risk-bearing is, on the whole, a more potent influence in broadening one's perspective.[35]

Perhaps one might argue in rebuttal that the relative security of a managerial position in one of the entrenched oligopolies characteristic of heavy industry is somewhat counterbalanced by the cyclical instability also characteristic of much of this sector (e.g., steel, metal, fabricating, machinery, automobiles). But violent fluctuations in production and blue-collar employment probably do not pose much personal risk to an entrenched management of these financially secure behemoths, much as they may unsettle corporate earnings and dividends. The steel executive is ordinarily not held accountable for the national business cycle.

A complementary hypothesis offered here is that there are local recurring "cycles" of entrepreneurial vigor. (Perhaps "long waves" of

[35] Benjamin Chinitz, "Contrasts in Agglomeration: New York and Pittsburgh," *American Economic Review* (May 1961), pp. 284–85.

entrepreneurship, more analogous to the Kondratieff long cycles than to the traditional business cycle, would be a more appropriate analogy.) We might argue, again, the dynamics of "challenge and response" at the local level on a more individualized basis. A dynamic entrepreneurial group—even a single outstanding figure—arises in a particular area, perhaps due to mere chance, and this group generates rapid industrial development in that locality. Commercial success and the resultant rise of large local firms produces an environment characterized by complex managerial routines, and administrative talents become both the critical local need and the *sine qua non* of local industrial leadership. The rough and unorthodox inventor-innovator-promoter type is pushed into the background as "scientific management" takes over. The new gods are efficiency and stability and industrial statesmanship.

As the new industry matures, the local giants begin the almost inevitable regional decentralization, as branch plants are spun off into major product markets to minimize transportation costs. This leads inevitably to a slowing rate of *local* employment growth in this industry, and a concomitant growth in local unemployment, as population and labor force grow faster than job opportunities. With local stagnation the dominant concern, necessity becomes the mother of invention, literally, as a frantic search is conducted for unexploited old opportunities and renewed emphasis is placed on concocting new products and processes. Efficiency pales alongside creativity or promotional artistry; the inventor is king again and the unorthodox is welcomed, almost uncritically.

As a corollary to this set of propositions, we might also hypothesize that inventor-innovators tend to bunch in time and space; dynamic persons create an atmosphere that attracts more of the same, to share the fraternity of protest against the old and excitement in the new. The bar-room of the old Pontchatrain Hotel in Detroit is reputed to have been a hot-house of early automotive technology in the early years of this century. Later the burgeoning automobile industry attracted financial wizards (e.g., William Durant who put General Motors together) and finally that host of apt managers who see any rapidly expanding, and therefore mildly chaotic, industry as an escalator to rapid promotion.[36]

---

[36] See Lawrence Seltzer, *A Financial History of the American Automobile Industry* (Boston: Houghton Mifflin Company, 1928), especially Chapter IV, "The General Motors Corporation." Seltzer writes: "William C. Durant was a vigorous promoter

To argue that Henry Ford and some associates and imitators turned Detroit from a middle size regional center into a huge industrial center is not to advance a "great man theory of *economic* history." Certainly, the commercially successful private automobile would have been introduced in the United States by someone else within a few years if Ford had not acted first—but probably not in Detroit. Nor would any other new industry of comparable potential have been developed. Henry Ford, as an individual, was highly substitutable for the nation and probably did not materially alter what would have happened had he never been born, but Detroit today would probably have about one-half its present population.[37]

The parallel between the challenge-and-response and long-wave hypotheses at the community level, outlined earlier in this chapter, and at the firm level, at issue here, may even be extended to suggest the possibility of some direct linkages between them. For example, the stellar local firm(s) may well catch the brightest young men of the community in its web of glamour, power, and financial security; local public service may have to make do with lesser talent. Both for this

---

and salesman rather than an operating executive; and the career of the General Motors Combination, until very recent years, has largely reflected his personality. His temperament and his unbound confidence in the automobile industry led him to seek rapid growth. . . . He was ready to expand by acquisition . . ." pp. 223–24.

[37] At the turn of the century, Detroit was about three-quarters the size of Cleveland and the supporting hinterlands of these two regional metropolises were of roughly equal size. (True, the population of Ohio was about two-thirds again as large as Michigan, but this rich base of support was shared with Cincinnati, a city closely pressing Cleveland in population.) Now let us imagine that Henry Ford and R. E. Olds and others had been born in Massachusetts or Illinois and that the automobile industry had never developed in Michigan, except for the occasional assembly plant that has been the lot of nearly every concentration of population the country over. But, instead, suppose that Detroit had garnered a Cleveland-like share of manufacturing—a very handsome industrial fortune, even if not the Arabian wealth of the automobile legacy. With a manufacturing base comparable to that of Cleveland and a hinterland to service of similar size, the population of the Detroit metropolitan area in 1950 would probably have been near Cleveland's 1.3 million instead of the actual count of 2.4 million.

Consider, in parallel fashion, Milwaukee, a neighboring lake city somewhat north of the main east-west stream of commerce (like Detroit), a comparable center of heavy industry and endowed with a work force at least as highly skilled as that of Detroit. Even adjusting for the fact that Milwaukee's Wisconsin hinterland is only two-thirds as heavily populated as Michigan, the base of Detroit—raising the expected Detroit population to about one and one-half times that of the Wisconsin regional metropolis—we again arrive at an expected population of one and one-half million persons at most for the Detroit (*sans* auto industry) metropolitan area in 1950. The conclusion is offered that this area is nearly twice as large as the most sophisticated forecaster could have foreseen a half-century ago. Wilbur R. Thompson, "Detroit's Economic Future," *The Michigan Economic Record*, June 1960, p. 7.

reason and because of sheer corporate power, the local legislative and public administrative bodies may be dominated by local big business. In such an event, one would expect the business values to prevail in the community and be reflected in a relatively *efficient* local public economy. But an imaginative and, consequently, unorthodox, local political leadership would hardly be expected, and might not even be tolerated. Thus as the local corporate giant decentralizes and precipitates a local employment crisis, a political revolution may well be a prerequisite to effective community response. That is, political innovators may be—must be—spawned to complement the economic ones generated in the private sector.

We have hypothesized that the presence of the giant manufacturing firm turns a local economy into an "organization man" town, temporarily breaking the tradition of individual enterprise, at least in manufacturing, and dampening creative effort. This is offered as a research hypothesis, not a value judgment. The hypothesis might have been formulated otherwise. For example, giant firms, with their market power and administered prices, are much more likely to have the funds necessary to support a large research and development program. Oligopolists, moreover, have the feeling of permanence to give them the extended time horizons which justify more roundabout research and which permit more deferred payoffs—basic research can lead to radical breakthroughs. And the long view that favors basic research may be even more characteristic of the public utility; the Bell Telephone laboratories are probably unexcelled in their field.

True, some students of research and development have expressed strong reservations about the capability of large corporations to perform significant creative work, or at least the likelihood of their doing so.[38] They have argued that truly creative work almost invariably disturbs production schedules until the "bugs" are worked out, imposes large redesign and retooling costs, and challenges the conventional wisdom laid down by the senior members of management—an attack on older ideas may be construed as an attack on older and wiser heads. Moreover, with their current line of products highly competitive with newer products, by sheer force of market control if nothing else (e.g., saturation advertising, exclusive dealerships, and omnipresent service organizations), oligopolists can often suppress or soften the necessity that mothers invention.

[38] See John Jewkes, David Sawers, and Richard Stillerman, *The Sources of Invention* (New York: St. Martin's Press, 1958), for example.

But even granting all this—and this would be too generous—if it is local leadership in the formation of new industries that is at issue, and not contributions to scientific progress per se, the advantage may lie with that local economy which serves the oligopolist who, however much he may bide his time in *invention*, retains a fine sense of timing in market *innovation*. In short, the glistening, well-equipped laboratories of the giant firm may be quite conventional in research and development but still spawn greater aggregate local growth than an equivalent amount of small business, simply because it is better able to commercialize its own research.[39] The giant corporation is also in a better position to exploit the diamond-in-the-rough creations of the alley workshop inventor and therefore can offer him a more certain, smaller payoff, which he probably prefers to the heavy risk of the grand reward—especially under high income tax rates. Still, an intuitive presumption in favor of the giant firm does not necessarily favor the host local economy because their innovations may be launched elsewhere in branch plants, whereas the smaller firm is more likely to innovate at home. Clearly, we need empirical work here to strike a net balance.

To sound the call for research on the role of entrepreneurship in urban-regional economic growth and development without admitting that the measurement and data problems are most difficult would be pure exhortation. But the data supply is growing with each passing year; reports of research and development expenditures and related research are issued regularly and frequently by the National Science Foundation. One problem, however, is that almost all of the data available to date are by national aggregates, stymieing regional comparative analysis. At the conceptual level, the papers of a recent joint Universities-National Bureau of Economic Research-Social Science Research Council Conference on "The Rate and Direction of Inventive Activity" should provide a number of highly relevant, testable hypotheses.[40]

How does one go about measuring entrepreneurship, especially interregional differentials in that elusive quality? Attempts have been made

[39] One can do little better than refer the reader to the imperishable work of Joseph A. Schumpeter. See especially Chapter VII, "The Process of Creative Destruction," in *Capitalism, Socialism and Democracy* (New York: Harper Brothers, 1942).

[40] *The Rate and Direction of Inventive Activity: Economic and Social Factors*, a Conference of the Universities-National Bureau Committee for Economic Research and the Committee on Economic Growth of the Social Science Research Council (Princeton: Princeton University Press, 1962).

to express the propensity to invent in both input and output terms through surrogates that may only reflect inventive activity but are in themselves more quantifiable. The most notable stand-ins are (the input of) expenditures of money, and/or manpower by business on research and development, and (the output of) patents issued. No comparative regional analyses, or even isolated case studies, of inventiveness using expenditure data can be cited, probably largely due to the absence of regional breakdowns on the national aggregate expenditure data; and only one such analysis uses manpower data.[41] Except for one early incidental use of patent data at the state level by Ullman,[42] the only regional analyses with this latter index that can be reported are two experimental efforts made by the author. First, an attempt was made to introduce patent-grants-to-local-residents-in-selected-patent-classes (e.g., "metal working") as an independent variable into employment growth estimating equations for associated Census industry groups (e.g., "fabricated metal products"), as part of a broad-gauge, cross-sectional, multiple regression analysis of 1947–54 state growth. This effort had limited success.[43] Second, the same patent data were later disaggregated and reclassified by the metropolitan area of residence of the patentee in a paper published as part of the proceedings of the Inventive Activity Conference referred to above. This latter effort succeeded in identifying patentees (and presumably inventors) as city-dwellers, rather than rural tinkerers:

> The best estimate is now this: the approximately 57 per cent of the population who resided in standard metropolitan areas (in 1945) or within 25 miles of the central city of such an area received (in 1947–

[41] George Perazich, *Growth of Scientific Research in Selected Industries, 1945–60*, Report to the National Science Foundation by Galaxy Incorporated (Washington, October 14, 1957, mimeo.).

[42] Edward L. Ullman, "Regional Development and the Geography of Concentration," *Papers and Proceedings of the Regional Science Association*, Vol. IV (Philadelphia: Regional Science Research Institute, 1958), pp. 189–91.

[43] Patents granted in an aggregate of five chemistry classes did join with plant and equipment expenditures as the two independent variables in the best employment estimating equation for "chemicals and allied products," fitted to the 1947–54 data, a period of very rapid growth. While the chemical industry equation exhibited one of the lowest multiple correlation coefficients—was one of the poorer fits—the patent variable was sufficiently promising in each of the seven industries in which it was tried to warrant further work with this index. Patent grants were, for example, much more promising than many of the old perennials in area industrial development analysis, such as the relative level of state and local taxes. Wilbur R. Thompson and John M. Mattila, *An Econometric Model of Postwar State Industrial Development* (Detroit: Wayne State University Press, 1959), pp. 6, 11–12, 18, 23–25, 43, 63–64.

48) approximately 90 per cent of the patents granted in sixteen selected patent classes covering chemistry, metal, machinery and engine products and processes.[44]

This study did not succeed in identifying any significant relationship between either city size or industry mix and the rate of inventiveness of the local population, or the lack of any such relationship. This appeared to be due mainly to various statistical difficulties. But progress was made toward preparing the patent variable for subsequent inclusion in some broader analytical framework of urban-regional growth analysis.

A second facet of entrepreneurship, the ease of entry of new blood into the top echelon of management, might be estimated by working with the length of time spent in grade at the various intermediate levels by those who eventually rose to the top, in a given firm. Intellectual nepotism might be assessed by the degree of concentration of background and training among the top management—a preponderance of lawyers, for example. The willingness to accept new managerial technology might be related to such measurable indexes as investment in electronic data processing facilities (adjusted to allow for ostentatious display and other extraneously motivated purchases) and to the proportion of the junior executive group exposed to postgraduate university work in management science (e.g., game theory, operations research, and other quantitative innovations in business school curriculums that have occurred since the present management graduated). Whether or not this advanced training was pursued on company time or with the company paying tuition fees might also be quite relevant.

Certainly, these concepts are difficult to quantify. Moreover, the underlying functional relationships are almost certainly multivariate rather than single variate, and curvilinear rather than linear (e.g., top level management turnover should not be too high or too low). But if promotion within the firm has any substantial quantitative foundation, interfirm (interregional) comparative analysis is feasible. Besides, if one rules out of bounds every facet of growth that is difficult to count or weigh with precision—inventiveness, managerial skill, the productivity of the labor force, the supply of risk capital and so on— nothing but second-rate determinants will be left. Growth analysis

[44] Wilbur R. Thompson, "Locational Differences in Inventive Effort and Their Determinants," *The Rate and Direction of Inventive Activity, Economic and Social Factors, op. cit.,* p. 259.

will remain purely deductive and at roughly the same stage that business cycle analysis was at in the twenties, when, too often, a distinguished professor was distinguished by having his very own business cycle theory.

Capital

Before becoming deeply enmeshed in the role of local capital supplies in urban-regional growth, one would do well to be sure that a regional context is relevant. Capital more than any other of the four co-ordinate factors of production is highly mobile. The capital market may be almost wholly a national market to which all firms have equal access no matter where located.[45]

The fact of a national capital market would probably make for greater regional growth differentials than would be probable in a set of semiautonomous local capital markets because there would be little or no spatial friction to prevent unlimited amounts of the full national supply of savings from flowing to any given region. In sharp contrast, labor and entrepreneurship move much more sluggishly and the friction of migration dampens the growth of the most buoyant areas and retards contraction and collapse of disadvantaged areas. We have assumed above that a unique local labor market does exist and is highly relevant to much of urban economics, and more hesitantly that a unique local entrepreneurial "market" probably also exists, especially relevant to growth questions. Is there a local capital market of any consequence? Or are interest rates everywhere the same and risk capital everywhere equally available?

The very large, nationally known corporation does operate largely in a national capital market. Its financial needs are such that the urban areas in which it is located could hardly be the dominant sources of funds without precariously concentrating the investment portfolios

---

[45] Edgar M. Hoover observed some time ago that "capital funds for new investment, however, are highly mobile and show relatively small geographic differentials in price. Interest rates exhibit a tendency to vary with distance from major financial centers but are rarely a significant factor of location within any one country." *The Location of Economic Activity, op. cit.,* p. 70. Hoover cites the empirical work of August Lösch, *The Economics of Location* (New Haven: Yale University Press, 1954), pp. 461, 505. Interestingly, later works have ignored regional aspects of the capital market. Neither the most comprehensive general reference work on location theory, Isard, *op. cit.,* nor that on regional growth, Harvey S. Perloff, *et al., op. cit.,* include "interest" in their very detailed subject indexes.

of local individuals and financial institutions. Besides, commercial banks are prohibited by law from lending to a single borrower sums greater than a specified proportion of their net worth, generally about 10 per cent.[46] Moreover, the larger well-known corporation probably finds that its credit does not suffer appreciably with distance from its physical operations. In short, we may be able to disregard the very large borrowers for our present purposes.

The very small firms, especially the prospective new entrants into business, are usually known only locally (and personally) and can secure outside capital only on the most adverse terms. To them the capital market is predominantly a local market. And we would be surprised if careful study of the medium size firms did not place them firmly in the middle of this spectrum. Less obvious, however, is whether distance makes much difference after the boundaries of the home area have been passed. Can a medium size business in Akron borrow on as good terms in St. Louis as in nearby Cleveland? In general, if we could quantify the degree of a firm's attachment to the local capital market by firm size, size of home area, type of industry or whatever proves to be relevant, subsequent urban-regional growth analyses could move more quickly and surely to those parts of the local capital market that justify studies-in-depth.

When we turn from the users of funds to the sources of funds, we find that it is not so easy to dismiss some sectors to concentrate on others. We must run the gamut from individuals to the largest commercial banks. The widely publicized, purported shortage of risk capital suggests the importance of individual investors, specifically those willing and able to make equity investments. We may care, then, whether a given local economy has more or less than its share of wealthy residents. While the total amount that this group is willing to invest in any given firm may be trivial compared to the needs of a very large corporate business, resident wealth might easily marshal enough capital to build a veritable hot-house for the growth of small firms. Through general and limited partnerships and subscriptions to small local stock offerings, the wealthy residents of an area may serve as financiers and patrons to local inventors and innovators.

The interesting questions concerning local wealth and growth become ones of relative magnitudes. How common is the occurrence of

---

[46] Harry G. Guthmann and Herbert E. Dougall, *Corporate Financial Policy*, Third Edition (Englewood Cliffs, N.J.: Prentice-Hall, Inc., 1955), Chapter 20, especially p. 423.

an urban area wherein a small wealthy group could appreciably affect the local supply of risk capital? Are these wealthy groups more inclined toward area industrial development or toward retarding local industrialization and urbanization to keep the area pleasantly rural for residential amenities? These two questions may well be closely interrelated: the smaller urban areas are probably both the places where resident wealth is a more significant component of the local capital supply and where the residential amenity factor is more critical. Which way it goes depends on whether the locality will be deemed by the local rich to be a more pleasant place to live if it remains small and bucolic or grows large and exciting.

Finally, are the local rich venturesome, as those of Houston have often been characterized, or are they inclined toward graceful living, as is often reputed to be the case for most of the Deep South and some of the more idyllic places, such as Denver?[47] At issue here is the kind of capital which is most critical to growth and the source which is most distinctively local. The question is basically one of quantitative significance and therefore demands an empirically based answer.

While the importance of equity capital is universally recognized, the critical role of commercial banks and other suppliers of working capital loans is not so thoroughly appreciated, especially in the case of new and growing businesses. In the early stages of its life cycle, a firm economizes on fixed capital by leasing its plant (an old vacant store or loft spaces in a run-down section of the city)[48] and subcontracts much of its fabricating and sub-assembling to economize on machinery. Often the young firm is most sorely pressed for working capital to pay wages and buy supplies and to extend credit to customers, and short-term borrowing of working capital can be very expensive for small, unknown firms.[49] The point is that the speed and ease with which new and small firms can gain access to the larger and lower-cost sources of short-term credit (commercial banks, for the most part) is

---

[47] J. Schaefer, "Denver: The Mountain Metropolis," *Holiday* (September 1961), pp. 56–69.

[48] Edgar M. Hoover and Raymond Vernon, *op. cit.*, pp. 49–55.

[49] A small business that is forced to sell or borrow on its accounts receivable at a discount of face value, to get cash sooner than the normal business sequence would provide, will have to pay interest rates of 12 per cent and over, in most places and at most times. Passing up trade discounts allowed for prompt payment of its own bills is usually even more expensive, for example, one of the more common trade terms ("2/10, net 30") is convertible into an annual interest rate equivalent to about 36 per cent. See Guthmann and Dougall, *op. cit.*, p. 441.

perhaps just as important to local growth as the more dramatic supply of risk capital.[50]

To be quite clear, we do not suggest here that local commercial banks seriously consider increasing their loans to small local firms, with other loans and investments remaining the same. Local banks would lose reserves, on net, if they expanded total loans and investments faster than banks in other areas. We suggest only that local commercial banks might consider lending more to small local firms and less to larger ones. The larger ones are better able to borrow outside anyway. And this could redound to the benefit of local bankers, in the aggregate, if it accelerated local economic development, that is, lending more to riskier small business could be in the *long-run* self-interest of local bankers.

What determines the receptivity of commercial bankers to the needs of smaller, riskier business—how quickly they will pick up the account of a new business? One factor comes easily to mind: alternative opportunities. If local bankers can keep fully loaned-up on prime commercial paper—the business of the bigger and safer local firms—they can minimize administrative costs and maximize safety by ignoring the needs of small business. This may be most likely to occur during periods of rapid local growth, when the local market is a lenders' market. Conversely, when local growth has slowed, excess reserves (unused lending power) pile up and the local commercial banks may begin to take an interest in the more marginal borrowers in the area. At this point, one is tempted to infer that commercial banks, as suppliers of local working capital, act as governors in local economic development by slowing rapid growth and stimulating slow growth. But this sounds much too good to be true and it is much too early in the conceptual stage of so complex a subject to take any purely deductive proposition very seriously.

While no attempt is being made to construct a full-blown model of the local capital market, one further point needs at least a formal acknowledgment. A recurrent theme throughout this section has been that the historical evolution of a local industrial complex leaves a legacy to the present that greatly influences future economic development in that area. We argued above that aging oligopolies might

[50] For a most dramatic case of the critical character of working capital in the early years of a new small business, see J. Keith Butters and John Lintner, *Effects of Federal Taxes on Growing Enterprises* (Division of Research, Graduate School of Business Administration, Harvard University, Boston, 1945), Chapter XII, "Lithomat Corporation."

dampen venturesomeness and even prevent potential entrepreneurs from being "born," as the giant corporations recruit the most talented local graduates. We hypothesize here that aging oligopolies might also, indirectly, lay a heavy hand on local financial practices. Chinitz, reflecting on the state of the stagnant Pittsburgh economy, has guessed that:

> When banks cater to competitively organized industry, they are more likely to accept the insurance principle of making money, not on each customer, but on the average customer. If you have U.S. Steel and Westinghouse on your rolls, you do not have to learn to make money on the insurance principle.[51]

The willingness of Detroit bankers to back the fledgling automobile industry has been cited as an important factor in the rise of that industry in that area.[52] Eastern bankers were reportedly much more reluctant to support the struggling young eastern automobile firms. Has this characteristic of Detroit bankers endured, or did they also become conservative with success and affluence? Perhaps there are "long waves" of local venturesomeness and conservativeness in financing. Are Detroit bankers becoming more inclined toward risk taking now that the automobile industry has matured and growth must be sought elsewhere—among small firms with radical new products and processes?

The Detroit area capital market is, moreover, further complicated by the fact that the now giant automobile firms raise their capital in a national capital market and local bankers are now left with surplus loanable funds which they have had to dispose of in other urban areas. In short, the development of big firms and local maturity would seem to leave the area with the funds for an industrial rebirth, awaiting only entrepreneurial talent and a venturesome spirit among local bankers.

One final caveat lest the unwary be misled by irrelevant relative magnitudes. Since big business accounts for a very large part of total activity and since big business raises new capital largely out of retained

---

[51] Chinitz, *op. cit.*, p. 286.

[52] Lawrence H. Seltzer, *op. cit.*, pp. 29–30. The author quotes Roy D. Chapin, a man identified with the automobile industry in its early years, as telling him, in a personal interview, that "the banks here played an important part. There was a great deal of prejudice in other parts of the country on the part of bankers, particularly in the east. They lacked the business sense that was needed. The Detroit bankers had it and were not afraid of our sight drafts."

earnings and from security sales in a national capital market, one might too quickly conclude that local capital supplies to small business are dust in the balance. But a handful of these small businesses of today are destined to become the industrial giants of tomorrow. Thus the availability of local capital to small business today may be a major determinant of the rate of the area growth a decade hence. The tail does come to wag the dog.

The more one pursues the question of the impact of local capital supplies on regional growth, and, conversely, of growth on regional capital supplies, the more one feels that there is highly useful knowledge to be gained in this direction.

Land

The economist's "land"—natural resources in the broadest sense—would seem to be the least likely of the four classical factors of production to be important in *urban* economic development. But this is not the case. Let us begin by considering the relevance of the rural hinterland of a city to the economic development of that city. The quality of the soils, mineral deposits, and forest resources determine the productivity and income of the surrounding farms, mines, and lumbering operations, and the owners and employees of these facilities are the customers of the trade and service establishments of the central city of the area. Thus the quality and quantity of nearby rural natural resources are important economic factors in urban growth to the degree that the urban economy is a service exporter. While rural area market towns are typically the smaller urban places, even very large cities may depend *indirectly* on rural prosperity by functioning as service centers to middle size cities which serve as service centers to the smaller ones which serve the rural areas directly. The Chicago economy is undoubtedly quite sensitive to changes in the prosperity of the corn-and-hog economy of the Middle West, albeit indirectly.

Further, rural areas are not only important immediate customers of urban areas, they are also suppliers to the cities. A given city may be disadvantaged in interurban competition for industry and share of the national market if the sites of accessible extractive activity are experiencing depleting supplies and/or rising costs relative to the raw material producing areas closer to its manufacturing rivals.

Raw material processing is ordinarily carried on quite close to the source of the material and is therefore ordinarily located in the more remote, small towns. Still, a number of very large urban areas have a very important stake in raw material processing, at an intermediate if not primary stage. For example, the Twin Cities metropolitan area, thirteenth largest in the nation, has more employment in food products manufacturing than any other of the twenty major industry groups in manufacturing, reflecting its rich agricultural hinterland.

Family costs of living also are involved. New York and Buffalo lose ground relative to Chicago and Milwaukee as preferred residential areas when dairying, poultry raising, and truck gardening costs in New York State rise relative to similar costs in Wisconsin. Blending the two concepts together, natural resources developments which favor the Middle West over the East also favor Chicago over New York by enriching the customers of Chicago's service industries—a money income effect—and by lowering food prices in Chicago—a real income effect.

But if reaching into the rural hinterland of a city to relate "land" to urban economic development is regarded as straining a point, we could confine ourselves to the impact of urban land on urban growth. Flat land, for example, promotes urban efficiency by reducing street construction and maintenance costs and by smoothing and speeding traffic flow. Flat land also lowers housing costs by simplifying grading operations and by facilitating mass production building. But hills provide more pleasing housing sites.[53] The net balance of these opposing values of terrain is not so much blurred as variegated. A low-income family would probably choose to have a larger house and lower cost transportation, while the higher-income family might even pay to have the hill built. The half-serious hypothesis is offered that flat terrain raises lower incomes and lowers higher incomes, that is, effects greater income equality, and hilly terrain does the reverse. Further, if the upper-income groups make the basic industrial location decisions that apply at the interurban level, and if they are guided in these business decisions to some appreciable degree by the personal considerations of residential amenities, the hilly, scenic areas might be favored in aggregate growth, or at least suffer a lesser disadvantage than physical efficiency considerations alone would dictate.

[53] Homer Hoyt long ago called attention to the tendency for the upper income groups to choose the high ground for residential sites, "The Pattern of Movement of Residential Rental Neighborhoods," *The Structure and Growth of Residential Neighborhoods in American Cities* (Washington: Federal Housing Administration, 1939), reprinted in *Readings in Urban Geography, op. cit.,* p. 504.

Natural resource endowments other than topography and economic considerations other than construction costs bear heavily on urban growth prospects. What is the net effect on population growth of Los Angeles' sunshine and ocean frontage on the one hand and its smog and water shortage on the other? How does one weigh the rivers of the Washington, D.C., area, rivers which create both traffic congestion and recreational opportunities, with bridges easing the former and pollution burdening the latter?

Practically everyone writing today on industrial location and regional growth hastens to point out the growing role of the natural features that make for pleasant living, especially climate, on locational patterns and trends.[54] With rising productivity, every year more of us can afford the luxuries of living where climates are pleasant, scenery attractive and outdoor recreation facilities convenient—and if the most attractive sites are not also the most efficient ones we do pay a price in foregone production and money income to live there. In addition, that part of our increased productivity which we take in shorter hours of work also operates to move us toward the sites of greatest amenities, as greater leisure may become merely prolonged idleness and weigh heavily unless the environment is enhanced. Exaggerating to illustrate, it may be cheaper to move our cities than to build mountains and lakes. We shall probably do a little of both over the next decade.

To further ensure that the inclusion of "land" as a fourth factor and full partner in this supply approach to urban growth is not regarded as strictly academic, an impressionistic model of the location of economic activity in an Age of Research and Development is offered. Suppose automation reduces the weight of the labor factor in industrial location by reducing the amount of direct labor input and unionization continues to spread its influence equalizing wages everywhere, especially for key skilled labor. Suppose differentials in capital supply to be of only minor importance, as giant enterprise, omnipresent, creates a national capital market. Entrepreneurship could then become the critical locational factor, especially if inventors and innovators do bunch in time and space, as hypothesized above. But what is more footloose, in aggregate, than an entrepreneurial complex; there is no obvious reason why an exciting and fruitful inventive-innovative environment might not be developed in a pleasant place to live rather

---

[54] The best known work here is Edward L. Ullman, "Amenities as a Factor in Regional Growth," *The Geographical Review* (Vol. XLIV, 1954), pp. 119–32.

than a less pleasant one. What could be more logical than for these intellectual-industrial centers to be consciously implanted in two distinctive environments: places which offer natural beauty and good outdoor recreation, and places which offer the height of urban culture and indoor recreation? The case for Palo Alto and Santa Monica, California, as centers of research and development does not need extended argument; it is hard to argue with success. Similarly, the superb consumer capital (e.g., museums, libraries, theaters, and so forth) in New York and Boston have made it possible for those areas to hold their own in competition for research and development activity with the natural garden spots.

We take limited exception here, then, to the hypothesis above that small towns are not viable in today's economy. Small towns in very *scenic, accessible* locations may well be on the verge of a local boom, and become quite viable—as middle size cities, as they attract research, pilot plants, and even full-scale manufacturing operations.

––––––––––––––

Manchester, England: Case History in Urban Growth. Many case studies and much empirical work will have to be brought to bear on the subtle and complex process of urban growth to translate the fragile chain of hypotheses in this chapter into a system of soundly grounded principles. In closing, a single historical example of Manchester, England, in the nineteenth century drawn from a classic article by Eric Lampard is offered, less to support the arguments of this chapter than to illustrate the course of the urban growth process in one city and to suggest the potential value of the historical method.

The earliest factories in textile districts using water-wheels were commonly situated outside of the urban center, but "they had to be near a town . . . to be close to a market, both for buying and selling purposes. Labour was needed, not only for the actual work in the factory, but also for the subsidiary domestic industries [hand weavers]." . . . Manufacturing capitalists were then [in the 1820's] obliged to install the improved power loom and "to integrate the spinning, weaving, and finishing branches in single establishments employing from 300 to over 1,000 hands." . . .

More significant, from the standpoint of our general theory of urbanization, was the tendency for other concerns to congregate around the cotton manufacture . . . foundries were casting wheels and pipes for steam engines and shafts, while tin-platers, braziers and harness makers were putting out the parts for spinning frames . . . a whole array of activities developed in the service of the mills and their operatives: railways, building, brewing, chemicals, coal supply and numerous wholesale trades. . . . The Bank of England felt obliged to come to town in the late twenties and several joint stock companies got underway. . . .

From the mid-18th century cotton merchants and manufacturers . . . offered attractive rewards for practical inventions. The "Manchester Literary and Philosophical Society" debated the application of science to the industrial arts. . . . These same business leaders gave a new meaning to the word "freedom" . . . "whereby trade has been kept open to strangers of every description, who contribute to its improvement by their ingenuity." . . . Manchester society was open for achievement. The early industrialists had mostly risen from the ranks of skilled craftsmen. . . .[55]

Thus the story of Manchester takes us from a natural resource base (water power) linked to a labor pool, up through the internal economies of vertical integration in textiles and the external economies of the clustering of support industries and business services, to the height of industrial arts: invention and entrepreneurship. In short, one thing leads to another.

It may be that a rigorous synthesis of many such case studies is needed to unlock the secrets of the urban growth process; the economic historian may have fully as much to contribute to urban growth theory as either the economic theorist or the econometrician.

[55] Eric E. Lampard, "The History of Cities in Economically Advanced Areas," *Economic Development and Cultural Change* (January 1955), pp. 81–136.

CHAPTER 2

Money Income and Real Income: From Labor Markets to Urban Efficiency

While there are other individual and social objectives, at least as important as making money, money income provides the principal measure of performance of the urban economy.[1] When one views the city from this vantage point, the first strong impression is one of surprise at the relatively narrow variation in family incomes between urban areas, relative to interstate variations. Median family income in the richer states is almost three times that in the poorer ones, while the richer metropolitan areas have family incomes only about one and three-quarters times as high as the poorer ones. This reflects, of course, the great disparity between urban and rural incomes which shows up when larger land areas with very different urban-rural mixes are compared. Still, interurban income differentials are sufficiently great to invite analysis, and the search for an explanation leads into a thorough appreciation of the urban area as a local labor market and of interurban income differentials as primarily a wage phenomenon. More specifically, local income analysis leads quickly into a statistical manipulation of the local industry mix and a conceptual reexamination of the nature of labor mobility—industrial, occupational, and spatial.

But a labor mobility study is largely a study of the supply side of the labor market, and the demand side must also be considered. The demand for labor is largely determined by its productivity, but labor productivity is a complicated phenomenon, especially when both the output per worker and the price at which that product is sold are considered. Labor *value* productivity can be traced back to the amount

[1] See Kenneth E. Boulding, *Principles of Economic Policy* (Englewood Cliffs, N.J.: Prentice-Hall, Inc. 1958), pp. 21–27, for a clear, broad-gauge treatment of economic "progress." Boulding suggests both output per man-hour and its first cousin, income per capita, as proper measures of economic progress.

of capital per worker, political factors, and the structure of markets—
that is, to the degree of competition in the local labor market and in
those national product markets important to the locality. Finally, city
size is reviewed as a proxy variable—not without a liberal measure of
mystique—in local income determination.

Although money income levels are remarkably alike between cities,
a firm conclusion on comparative levels of living between cities is
thwarted by the utter lack of cost-of-living indexes with which to
deflate the money income figures. Nor will the construction of a really
useful index be achieved easily or soon, for a host of qualitative and
intangible factors must be resolved. To illustrate, the range of choice
in consumer goods varies greatly with city size, as does the range of
choice in occupations, with the latter factor figuring just as importantly
in the local level of living. Interurban variations in the efficiency of
the local public sector—the cost and quality of police protection and
the speed and comfort of movement about the city—are hard to
quantify, but they are the real meat of urban analysis. Further interactions occur as a high local money wage is not only a source of income but also a cost to be borne, as the local residents not only earn
but must also buy back those wages in purchasing local services from
each other—the people of a city do exist in part by "selling oranges
to each other."

All in all, while interurban money income differentials seem on first
blush to be relatively minor compared to interstate income differentials, we really are not prepared to render a final verdict until we can
make the more critical real income comparisons. Interurban income
analysis has not yet moved much beyond the near tautology that
urban areas with the higher paying industries have the higher per
capita incomes. Let us at least identify what we need to know.

LESSONS OF THE INTERSTATE INCOME
ANALYSIS: PROLOGUE AND LEGACY

The nature and cause of interregional income differentials have
received a decent amount of serious attention only at the state and
multistate levels of area subdivision. The emphasis on analysis at the
state level and above, to the neglect of interurban focus, is largely
attributable to a rich supply of state income data, reported annually
and by distributive shares and by industrial origin; the meager supply

of urban data are largely confined to the *Decennial Censuses of Population.*[2] So, while it might seem diversionary to pause here in brief pursuit of the findings of these state studies, we should search these testaments for whatever they may offer because they contain most of the legacy with which urban income analysis begins life. True, the interstate income analyses of Hanna[3] and Perloff-Muth[4] provide only indirect evidence on the matter now at hand, and then only by tenuously extending the patterns exhibited by a group of industrially heterogeneous states to a quite distinctive set of economically integrated urban economies. Still, their empirical findings do provide us with a feeling for our subject matter and with some useful methodology. What, then, is the magnitude and character of interstate income variation and what are the lessons to be learned about the operational usefulness of various analytical techniques from the experience at this next higher level of subnational income analysis?

Property versus Participation Income

The first and strongest single impression gained from the interstate income analyses is the almost unbelievable dispersion of per capita income, ranging widely in 1950 from Mississippi's $729 annual per capita income to Delaware's $2,153.[5] These numbers, standing alone, place a high priority on regional income analysis as an indispensable complement to national income analysis—a priority as high as that long accorded to the disaggregation of national income by distributive share (wages, interest, rents, and profits) or by industrial origin. A

[2] State personal income estimates are reported annually in the August issue of the U.S. Department of Commerce, Office of Business Economics, *Survey of Current Business* (Washington: U.S. Government Printing Office). Urban income data was first collected and reported in the 1950 *Census of Population* and again in the 1960 *Census.* A frequency distribution of the number of families by income classes, for a dozen classes, is reported for urban places of 10,000 or more population, urbanized areas and standard metropolitan statistical areas.

[3] Frank A. Hanna, *State Income Differentials* (Durham: Duke University Press, 1959).

[4] Harvey S. Perloff, Edgar S. Dunn, Jr., Eric E. Lampard, and Richard F. Muth, *Regions, Resources, and Economic Growth* (Baltimore: Johns Hopkins Press for Resources for the Future, 1960).

[5] *Ibid.,* p. 494. Since the purpose here is to review the interstate studies which precede us, these interregional comparisons draw on data which are now over a decade old. The corresponding figures for 1960 are $2,996 for Delaware and $1,169 for Mississippi, a somewhat reduced gap. U.S. Department of Commerce, *Survey of Current Business,* August 1962, Table 2, p. 11.

second clear impression is that interstate income differentials are not "merely" reflections of the regional distribution of wealth. That is, what we see here is not a simple reflection of high property incomes in a "monied East." True, of the many kinds of income, property income is the most variable between states, but earnings from wealth constitute only about one-eighth of total income and even that relatively small share is highly correlated with "participation income" (wages and net income of unincorporated business).[6] Thus interstate variation in the dominant share, "work" income, is roughly the same as in total income—a threefold spread in 1950. (By 1960 the variation from bottom to top had narrowed somewhat to a factor of two and a half.) The tentative moral that we derive from this is that the local labor market is likely to be the place to which our search for the major source of interarea variation in living standards will lead us.

Demographic Characteristics and Labor Force Participation

Thus far the local living standard has been expressed as per capita income without any explicit mention of the precise head count that serves as the denominator of the ratio. By implication the "population" among whom the aggregate local income is divided is total population —all persons, regardless of age or sex or other demographic characteristics. But such a base tends to depress the income figures for areas with abnormally large proportions of nonproducers, namely, housewives, children, handicapped persons, elderly persons, and so forth. That total population may not faithfully reflect labor force participation may be quite unimportant if the objective is to measure levels of consumption, although even here the fact that children have lower consumption requirements than adults creates at least a minor bias. But if inferences about the relative level of local productivity is the objective, then such a gross count as total population is not an acceptable denominator. Because the proper deflation of income is such an easy statistical operation, the best practice would be to use some variant of population in welfare measurements and employment in productivity measurements.

To distinguish between the total population and the participants in production is not a trivial adjustment; the empirical work cited

[6] *Ibid.*, pp. 493–95.

suggests that interstate income differentials are reduced by perhaps 20 to 25 per cent by adjusting for nonproducers.[7] Demographic variation *between states* in average age at leaving school, age of mother at birth of first child, proportion of homes with a second income earner, average age at retirement and other relevant factors are, of course, considerably greater than their *interurban* counterparts because states mix factories and farms in widely different proportions, and it is urban-rural differentials in demographic composition that are most notable. We should, therefore, take care to discount somewhat the influence of the population mix when we translate these findings from the state to the urban context. Still, if even one-half of the observed interstate variation in labor force participation rates carries over into the interurban framework, we have more than ample cause to undertake careful demographic-labor force participation analyses. The growth of retirement communities such as St. Petersburg, Florida, for example, suggests that substantial differentials in labor force participation will cloud any interurban income analysis that ignores them.

Moreover, while interurban variations may be substantially less than urban-rural variations on the supply side (demographic composition), interarea variation in the demographic structure of the *demand* for labor is much more an urban phenomenon. (Female and child labor on the farm is impartially welcomed and left uncounted.) In a preliminary report issued by the Pittsburgh Economic Study, the labor-force-to-population ratio in that area is judged to be about 8 per cent below the all-metropolitan-area average, due mainly to the lack of employment opportunities for women in a steel making economy.[8] With allowance for the lower wage rate of women workers, the Pittsburgh area income is, then, about 5 per cent below what it would be and could be if a complementary demand for female labor could be generated by selective industrial development of the area. The Detroit area exhibits a similar pattern.

[7] Hanna, *op. cit.*, p. 203. By using the population 20–64 years old (roughly, the working age population) in place of total population, Hanna's interstate coefficient of variation in per capita income (1950) fell from 23.2 to 18.5, a 20.3 per cent reduction. By substituting the total labor force, the coefficient fell to 17.9, a 22.8 per cent reduction (Table 48).

[8] Melvin Bers, "Labor Force Participation in the Pittsburgh Standard Metropolitan Area," Working Paper No. 2, Economic Study of the Pittsburgh Region, Pittsburgh Regional Planning Association, April 12, 1960 (mimeo.), p. 1. See also, *Region in Transition*, Report of the Economic Study of the Pittsburgh Region (Pittsburgh: University of Pittsburgh Press, 1963), Chapter 3.

State Poverty as Farm Poverty

The interstate income studies strongly suggest that the degree of agricultural specialization, more than any other single factor, is the key to income differentials; the farm poverty problem is the heart of the state poverty problem. With farm median income generally running at about 60 per cent of urban median income, region by region, to identify a state as agricultural is tantamount to characterizing it as impoverished—with a few notable exceptions. To take a slightly different cut at this, if we were to confine our interstate comparison to the industrial heartland of the nation (Massachusetts west to Illinois and north of the Ohio River; ten states) the 1950 per capita income range is greatly narrowed, $1,522 (Indiana) to $1,903 (Connecticut). A range now of, not 3 to 1, but only 5 to 4. Almost the same amount of compression can be accomplished, while admitting the whole country to the sample, by explicitly eliminating the farm factor and one other, color, about which more will be said later. *Urban white* per capita income ranged in 1950 from $2,472 (Mississippi) to $3,380 (Michigan), a very similar 4 to 3 variation.[9]

In the course of identifying the leading role of farm poverty in interstate income differentials, our predecessors have not only pointed up the limited transferability of their conclusions to our urban focus but also the shortcomings of the state as a unit for comparative income analysis. Certainly, the proportion of the state labor force engaged in agriculture (or farm income as a per cent of total income) can be introduced into a state-level regional income analysis, but if a rural-poverty variable proves to be dominant, or even major, then one can get a clean shot at the other (urban) variables only by disentangling urban and rural-farm areas. Otherwise our strictly urban variables can be only dimly seen as a blurred residual of the hybrid state economy. The shortcomings of the industrially heterogeneous state as a unit of income analysis do not apply to the urban area, a much more integrated and functional region.

[9] Perloff, *et al., op. cit.*, p. 496. Again, we might update the figures to show the persistence of greater variation between states. Connecticut with a median family income of $6,887, exhibited an advantage of 2.4:1 over Mississippi ($2,884), while Washington, D.C., with the highest median family income of any metropolitan area of 250,000 or more population ($7,577), exhibited an advantage over the poorest of these large urban areas, Tampa-St. Petersburg ($4,490), of only 1.7:1. U.S. Bureau of the Census, *U.S. Census of Population, 1960, General Social and Economic Characteristics, United States Summary*, Table 148.

The use, in regional income analysis, of some extended urban area such as the Census standard metropolitan statistical area thus has compelling advantages, despite the gaps in data. The demand and the supply for labor operate in two quite distinct spatial frameworks. First, we may conceive of a local labor market as the area bounded by the commuting radius around a district of concentrated employment opportunities, such as the core of a city. This is a "short-run" labor market; a labor market that is especially revelant during a period of time so short that a worker is tied to his current residence. Second, we may conceive of a national labor market within which the citizen feels free to roam in the "long run," as he has time to make reasonably deliberate changes of residence and to prepare himself (and his family) for the modest social and cultural changes entailed. The conceptual superiority of the metropolitan area—the local labor market—as *the* subnational spatial unit for income analysis would not seem to require labored argument, although, admittedly, at this time state data are inestimably richer.

While the imaginative urban researcher should draw on the plentiful state data for perspectives and hypotheses, as we have done, the danger is that the income analyst may, like the proverbial drunk, continue looking too long in a place where he has not lost anything just because the light is better there. Thus, it is as a labor market and hence as a unit of income and welfare analysis that the economist usually catches his first strong feeling for the urban area as a significant unit of economic analysis—an analytical unit on a par with the time-honored "industry."

URBAN INCOME ANALYSIS AS
LOCAL LABOR MARKET ANALYSIS

If, then, the urban economy is above all else a labor market, the first step toward understanding the general level of economic well-being in an urban area would seem to be a serious analysis of the local wage structure. In this matter we may borrow advantageously in both concept and technique from the interstate income analyses that have preceded us. Local labor income differentials may be factored out into: (1) industry mix, (2) occupation mix, and (3) intra-area components. A numerical example is the shortest and clearest path to the understanding of these three simple ideas, and their not-so-simple interrelationships. Let us suppose that Area A has a higher over-all average wage rate than Area B, $2.25 compared to $1.75, and it is our purpose to explain this fact, or at least to describe it analytically.

Industry Mix and Earning Rates

Since even the most casual observation shows that some industries pay wage rates substantially higher than others, the customary first operation on the data is to "standardize" them for the local industry mix. The objective is to assess the contribution that the locality's distinctive industrial structure makes to its relative wage level. A hypothetical labor income is derived for the area by multiplying each *local* employment by the *national* average wage rate for that industry, industry by industry. The sum of all the hypothetical wage payments becomes the total local labor income that would be realized by that area if indeed the national average wage rates did apply locally. Divided by the number of employees, the standardized (hypothetical) total wage bill is converted into the "rate-constant" local wage rate. In our numerical example (see table below), we *impute* to Area A the

Industry	National average wage rate	Employment in:		Standardized earning in:	
		Area A	Area B	Area A	Area B
Chemicals (local export)	$2.50	4	0	$10.00	
Food (local export)	2.00	0	4		$ 8.00
Local services	1.75	4	4	7.00	7.00
All industries	2.00	8	8	$17.00	$15.00

$2.50 per hour national average wage rate in the chemical industry and the $1.75 per hour that is typical of the local services trades (retail clerks, bus drivers, and so forth), for an "expected" over-all average local wage rate of $2.12 (a total wage bill of $17.00 spread over 8 workers). By a parallel operation we derive an over-all average local wage rate of $1.88 for Area B out of the national average wage rates for food processing and local service employment.

Our analysis begins to take on substance when we compare these hypothetical local wage levels to the national average wage rate for all industries of, say, $2.00 per hour. From this comparison we infer that Area A has a "favorable" industry mix (chemicals) which lifts the local economy about 6 per cent ($2.12/$2.00) above the national average wage level, and that Area B has an "unfavorable" industry mix (food processing) which depresses the local economy to about 6 per cent ($1.88/$2.00) below the national average.

We may go even farther than this in sorting out the components of the relative local labor income in these two areas by comparing the hypothetical wage rates we have computed to the observed or actual local wage rates. With an observed wage rate of $2.25 per hour, Area A is twice-blessed, for its actual wage rate structure averages 6 per cent above its expected wage ($2.25/$2.12), and, as we have already seen, this latter figure is in turn 6 per cent above the national average wage. That is, the Area A firms pay wage rates above average for their industries and their industries pay above average. Conversely, Area B is twice-damned with low-wage industries and wage rates that are relatively low even for those industries, with an expected wage rate ($1.88) 6 per cent below the national average ($2.00) and an actual wage rate ($1.75) 6 per cent below expected. Area B does not even realize its dismal expectations.

Occupational Mix and the Capital-to-Labor Ratio

Conceptually and operationally this all seems quite simple and straightforward, but bisecting observed earnings into an industry-mix component and an earnings-rate component may not really come off cleanly. What is it that makes for a favorable or unfavorable industry mix? The mix may be favorable because it is compounded out of more of the higher- and less of the lower-skilled occupations. Turning now to a more detailed version of our numerical example (see table below), the chemical industry of Area A employs a favorable "occupational mix" of three skilled technicians to only one semiskilled material-handler, while the food processing industry in Area B employs a relatively unfavorable occupational mix of two skilled technicians and two material-handlers.

Occupation	National average wage rate	Local wage rate in:		Employment in:	
		Area A	Area B	Area A	Area B
Technician	$2.50	$2.60	$2.50	3	2
Material-handler	2.00	2.20	1.50	1	2
Retail clerk	1.75	2.00	1.50	4	4

But the example has been so constructed that other factors which make for a favorable or unfavorable industry mix are also at work. The chemical industry in Area A pays a much higher wage to its material-handlers, perhaps because they work with more capital (are mechanized) and presumably are more productive. If the chemicals material-handler works with a hydraulic lift truck while his counterpart in the food industry is struggling with a hand truck, this suggests that perhaps the former is really a different and more skilled occupation than the latter despite the similarity of end function because there is a machine to operate and maintain. Thus, in practice, it often becomes difficult to separate out interindustry earnings-rate differentials that are due to different capital-to-labor ratios from the skill (occupational) differences which complement them. The favorable industry mix is usually a subtle blend of a favorable occupational mix and a relatively high capital-to-labor ratio—skills and tools.

Note, however, that this simple numerical example has been further complicated by assigning a slightly higher wage to the "technician" in the chemicals industry than to his professional colleague in the food processing industry, who may be performing nearly identical work. The former job may pay more simply because the chemical industry is currently more profitable than the food industry, either because it is enjoying a boom or because it is less competitive and administers ("fixes") its product price to ensure high profits. Certainly, interindustry competition tends to eliminate such differentials, especially for the very skilled workers, but imperfect communication and sluggish migration stretch out the responses of semi-isolated local labor markets to ever changing labor demands.

Intra-Area Labor Mobility and the Export-Base Logic

Our example reveals one final co-ordinate force operating in our hypothetical labor markets: interindustry, intra-area labor substitution. Up to this point, we have been implicitly assuming that labor markets are organized along either industrial or occupational lines, not by area. That is, a material-handler employed in a Buffalo area chemical plant will, if laid off, seek work in a neighboring chemical plant but lacking that he will turn to another chemical plant in Charleston or Akron, or perhaps material-handling work of a roughly similar nature in a Buffalo area warehouse or railroad depot, but not to other kinds of work in the Buffalo area. Alternatively, we might posit that workers change industries and occupations more easily than places of residence. Labor market competition then occurs between neighboring firms selling different products and employing slightly different skills. We might assume that workers can move between various trades with a negligible amount of retraining, or at least with a lesser sacrifice in lost skills than the loss entailed by migrating to pursue the same work elsewhere. By emphasizing spatial immobility—the reluctance to migrate for whatever reason—the local labor market becomes partially autonomous and the local balance of demand and supply becomes critical in setting the local wage rate.

The numbers in our example will help fix this concept in our minds. When we compare the two tables above we note, from the first table, that the national average wage rate in the chemical industry is $2.50 per hour and, from the second table, that the local branch of that industry in Area A is also paying a $2.50 average rate (the weighted average of three wages at $2.60 and one at $2.20). How, then, can Area A enjoy an observed *over-all* average wage rate that is 6 per cent above that area's favorable industry mix, as was posited above? The answer, of course, is that one-half the jobs, the local service trades, pay wage rates that are over 12 per cent higher than the national average. (The figure is more than 12 per cent because the service sector accounts for less than one-half of the labor income.) Our example has been so constructed that the wage "roll-out" from the basic export industry, chemicals, to the local service trades has so raised the wage rate in that latter group that they are "responsible" for the whole positive residual of the observed over the expected (industry-mix standardized) rate. And, just as the retail trade clerks in Area A are paid $.25 per hour more than the national average, so those same workers in Area B are paid an equal amount below national standards, because theirs is a poor labor market built on an unfavorable industry mix—keyed to the lower-paying food industry.

Let us look more closely into the meaning of "intra-area wage roll-out." If the local export industries, those selling outside the local labor market, pay high wages, one would expect the contagion of a high wage rate to run throughout the whole labor market, if we assume some significant amount of labor substitution between industries and occupations and some significant resistance to migration. Specifically, the local department stores, banks, and bus companies have to at least partly meet the competition of the steel mills, automobile factories, and chemical plants, especially for the more versatile and venturesome workers. We have created a partially autonomous *local* labor market in which national labor market forces enter mainly through the export industries which in turn transmit these exogenous forces in modified form to the balance of the local economy through interindustry compe-

tition of local firms for the labor services of local residents. The very
concept of a "local labor market" implies the assumed resistance to
migration and some appreciable labor mobility between different kinds
of work, that is, an area-effect component of the local wage "relative"
(level relative to other areas).

Our numerical example demonstrates how interindustry, intra-area
labor competition could operate. Now let us turn to some empirical
findings which suggest that our example is not unrealistic.

In his monumental examination of interstate income differentials,
Hanna found.

> There is a marked tendency for states with unfavorable industrial
> compositions to have earning rates below the national average for
> their industries and, conversely, for states with favorable industrial
> compositions to have above-average earning rates. . . . There is also
> a tendency for states with extreme percentage departures in com-
> position to have extreme percentage departures in the same direc-
> tion for earning rates.[10]

Moreover, he offers as one possible explanation of this dichotomous
pattern of twice-blessed or twice-damned the hypothesis that, in subnational economies,

> . . . the demand for higher skills differs from their potential supply.
> In an area in which low-earning industries predominate, the lack
> of enough high-earning jobs to absorb all those qualified to hold
> them would have a depressing effect on earning rates. Conversely,
> in areas with high-earning industries, the search for a qualified labor
> force may lead to the inauguration of training programs, upgrading,
> pirating and other practices which inflate earnings. Moreover, in such
> an area, the low-earning industries might find it necessary to raise rates
> in order to attract and hold a labor force. Such an explanation does
> not depend upon a differential distribution of skills among regions.
> Migration from the lower- to the higher-earning areas presumably
> would operate in the direction of leveling out the earning differen-
> tial between areas, but the barriers to migration at any one time
> are probably enough to maintain regional differentials.[11]

If migration is sluggish, another force may operate to narrow interurban wage differentials: product competition. A steel making area
must take care not to pay its labor much above the going wage rates

---

[10] Hanna, *op. cit.*, p. 188.
[11] *Ibid.*, p. 190.

(unless higher productivity is induced). Thus the struggle for shares of a national product market tends to equalize wage rates within a given industry, wholly apart from migration. But consumer substitution between different products is much weaker than between only nominally distinctive brands of what is basically the same product; cost-price competition is a weak substitute for migration as we move across industries. Accordingly, steel making areas tend to have similar wage rates, as do plastic making areas, but the two groups may be quite unlike each other.

Thus, the wage rates in the export industry of an area may be quite distinctive (to that industry) and to the extent that the export industry wages roll out into the local service sector and produce atypical service industry wage rates—schoolteachers make more in a high-wage steel town than in a low-wage textile town—we have a variant on the export base doctrine. Just as we argued in Chapter 1 that a fast-growing export sector produces a fast-growing local service sector, and as we shall argue below in Chapter 4 that a cyclically unstable export sector transmits above average instability to the local service sector, we argue here that a high-wage export industry enriches an area not only directly through its own employees but also indirectly by raising local service sector wage rates through intra-area competition for labor. The hypothesis central to much of Part I is that the export industries of an area tend to characterize that area—at least in growth and income characteristics.

Labor Mobility and the Concept of a Local Labor Market

Let us see now where all this has led us. An analysis of the level of income in an urban area should probably begin with the dominant share, wage income, and identify first the influence of the local industry mix. This presumes a relatively small dispersion in wage rates between firms in an industry and a rather wide variation in wage rates between industries, so that a first approximation of area income level from industry mix is significant. This will be so to the extent that either labor mobility between firms in the same industry is greater than between industries, or that in the absence of easy intra-industry labor mobility (because of, say, spatially dispersed firms and a reluctance to migrate), cost competition between producers of highly similar products works to equalize wage rates within the industry. Or, third, because the organization of labor unions is likely to be along industry lines, industry-wide unions may simply impose identical wage patterns across the country. This is often the most powerful force of all acting to compress intra-industry wage rate variation.

The dominant importance of high- and low-paying industries and the power of unions to compress wage differentials between firms are intuitively impressive, but deductive vision may become clouded by the data unless proper care is taken in the empirical work. Industry wage schedules may apply broadly across the country but if the local branch of an industry is not truly representative, the result may be a distinctive occupational mix that nets out to be decidedly favorable or unfavorable to the locality. That is, the local automobile factory may be a low-skilled assembly or a high-skilled machining operation. This may be interpreted as "nothing more" than the failure to define "industry" narrowly enough. But to define an industry even conceptually, not to mention an *operational* definition, is a Herculean labor. Moreover, the distinctive local occupational mix may be complexly bound up with a higher or lower capital-to-labor ratio in the local plant, and this will raise or lower the local labor productivity and pay rates.

Only by the most careful adjustments for occupation mix can one even roughly isolate the influence of industry-mix earnings rates, and only by determining which local industries pay earnings rates above the national average for their industry can one clearly establish whether an "area effect" is operating. If the observed higher-than-national-rate wages are being paid mainly in the area export industries, we would probably lean toward some labor productivity theory of the favorable local differential, perhaps based on a high local capital-to-labor ratio or perhaps local union power, as discussed below. If, on the other hand, the higher than expected local wage rates are exhibited mainly by the local service industries, we might be more inclined toward an intra-area, export-industry-wage-roll-out rationale. Only if a significant "area effect" really does exist can we talk about a true *local* labor market, in contrast to just the fact of local employment of local residents. Does the local labor market have sufficient personality to endow it with a significantly distinctive *schedule* of wage rates for given industries and occupations?

Comparative Labor Mobility and Local Wage Rate Analysis

The issue reduces to this: do the wage rates of medical technologists and retail clerks in Detroit reflect more the national demand and supply for these skills or the pay scales in the nearby automobile factories? Posing the alternatives so starkly that one is forced to choose between industrial and area labor markets, as has been done in the examples and discussion above, can be defended only on pedagogical grounds. No such clear dichotomy is realistic; no such hard choice need be made. In fact, the two illustrative occupations highlight the relevance of labor skill. The highly skilled medical technologist will probably change residence, if need be, to preserve his or her vocation, with its educational investment and work satisfactions. The retail clerk will probably change occupations, if need be, to preserve his housing investment or social ties.

By working on the demand side, with some combination of labor substitution and employer competition and, on the supply side, with worker skills and demographic characteristics as they affect the propensity to migrate, we might be able to arrange some rough deductive and/or empirically based ordering of broad labor force classes, according to the dominance of an industry or occupation or area effect in their wage rate determination. For example, highly skilled employees of local export industries would tend to be both more likely to migrate and more subject to nationwide cost competition and, therefore, these workers would tend to receive wage rates determined in national intra-industry labor markets. At the other end of the spectrum, unskilled employees of local service industries would tend to resist migration and cast about locally for other kinds of work. These latter workers would tend to be well or poorly paid depending on the relative pay scales of the dominant local export industry; theirs is a largely local labor market.

The other two mixed cases do not merit detailing here because this classification is purely illustrative; a fully operational design would call for the integration of a number of other contributing factors. The social-economic characteristics of the labor force by industry and occupation may deserve explicit recognition in certain cases. The contrast in age, family size, and homeownership attributes between construction and custodial workers, especially as they affect the propensity to migrate, is suggestive of this point. Again, the national level of unemployment may be critical in shaping the process by which wage patterns are formed. Widespread unemployment may tend to reduce the area-effect in high/rising wage areas by spurring migration from the slack labor markets into this tight one, and it may increase the area-effect in low/falling wage areas as the redundant local labor is held captive with no place to flee. Conversely, national full employment would tend to cause labor shortages to persist in high/rising wage areas, raising wages perhaps most among the unskilled workers in the local service industries as the export industry employers are forced to lower standards and have to range farther afield to recruit workers; and weaken the area-effect in the low/falling wage rate areas by prompting the doubly low-paid service industry workers to seek better jobs elsewhere. All of which becomes even more complicated if migration is asymmetrical; in-migration may be faster and smoother than out-migration because in expansion a given area can draw the most mobile workers from all over but in contraction workers who are less and less mobile must be induced to leave the area.

The sum of this admittedly cavalier treatment of wage determination is that (a) an interurban income analysis reduces in large measure to labor market analysis, (b) the urban area is a local labor market par excellence, the elemental unit of income determination, and (c) the urban income analyst must ferret out the lines of interaction by which wage impulses are transmitted between and within industries, occupations, and areas and, of course, their relative magnitudes.

There seems to be room for both large-scale cross-section statistical analyses of the Census and Labor Department data for metropolitan areas, building on the work of Hanna and Perloff-Muth, and for a series on intensive studies of individual labor markets, wherein with local data, interviews and observation, the dynamic process of labor substitution and mobility can be traced.

Perhaps the most promising entry into local labor market income analysis is to follow the path blazed by Gladys Palmer in her survey of patterns and factors in labor mobility for the period 1940–50.[12] She compared the relative ease with which workers move between industries, occupations, and areas, the very essence of our analysis above. (The assumptions employed above to bring out the conceptual framework are, incidentally, generally consistent with her empirical findings.) Her work might well be updated and carried forward one more step by being tied into the local wage making process, again in a number of areas to permit comparison and generalizations. An integrated analytical framework that ties together the industrial-occupational structure of an urban area (the demand side) with the relative mobility of local labor as between industry, occupation, and area (the supply side) would almost certainly lead us very close to understanding

---

[12] Gladys L. Palmer, *Labor Mobility in Six Cities* (New York: Social Science Research Council, 1954).

and predicting the relative wage level of a given local labor market and would also be the longest single step that could be taken toward explaining the relative over-all per capita income of a given urban economy.

LOCAL PRODUCTIVITY AND THE
LEVEL OF MONEY INCOME

The standardization technique which allows us to separate out the relative roles of industry mix, occupational mix, and the area effect in setting the local wage structure is methodologically neat and substantively enlightening. But even the best standardization technique takes us only part way and is essentially more descriptive than truly analytical *per se,* however well it paves the way or poses the questions for further analysis. To say an area is affluent because it has the highest paying industries is, of course, close to a tautology and, in any event, does not explain how it came by this good fortune. And separating out the industry-mix component from the earnings-rate differential, however neatly, still leaves the earnings-rate differential to be explained. To suggest, moreover, that local labor markets become semiautonomous to the degree that intra-area, interindustry (interoccupational) mobility takes place only whets our interest in the enabling conditions underlying such an environment. While none of these questions can be examined in full, a quick review of some of the more readily deduced factors at work will at least provide a beginning. Let us start with an examination of some of the more obvious influences on labor productivity: the local capital-to-labor ratio, the nature of the price-making process in the area's main export markets, and the role of city size in local income determination.

Investment and Productivity

When comparative wage rates are mentioned, in almost any context, the first factor which comes to mind is differentials in the amount of capital per worker. We are, quite rightly, impressed with the tremendous lift given to labor power by the machine and we would expect that where labor works with more capital its productivity and wage rate will be higher. And very great differences in assets per worker are manifest between industries, ranging from well over $100,000 per worker in petroleum to less than $4,000 per worker in apparel manufacturing, with the average about $16,000 in assets per worker in manufacturing. But data on the capital stock (investment) per worker are not available on any systematic or comprehensive basis, least so for small areas such as our preferred metropolitan area. Still, it does seem that much more could be done even with existing data.

Capital per worker by industry and by area might be estimated by cumulating the annual plant and equipment expenditures data reported in the various *Censuses* and *Annual Surveys of Manufacturers*. The *Censuses* of 1947, 1954, and 1958 report expenditures on new plant and equipment by standard industrial classification at the "three-digit" level (e.g., industry #331, Blast furnaces and steel mills) for the larger standard metropolitan areas. In the intervening years, 1948–53, 1955–57, and 1959 to date, recourse would have to be had to the more aggregated two-digit major industry groups (e.g., industry #33, Primary metals), further aggregated to the state level, as reported in the *Annual Surveys*. These latter data might, however, be broken down into three-digit figures for metropolitan areas by applying the appropriate ratios drawn from the benchmark Census years. To illustrate, the proportion of 1950 plant and equipment expenditures in the transportation equipment industry group (#37) in Michigan that was invested in the Detroit metropolitan area in the subdivision of that broad industry group devoted to the manufacture of motor vehicles (#371) might be derived by interpolating (three-sevenths of the way) between the 1947 and 1954 benchmark *ratios* of Detroit area investment in industry #371 to Michigan investment in major industry group #37. Or some more sensitive method might be devised instead.

With an annual plant and equipment expenditure series covering fifteen years, we might attempt a capital stock estimate by simply cumulating the figures. We would lack, of course, two important quantities, the original stock at the beginning of the period and the appropriate rate of depreciation and obsolescence. We might assume that the capital stock in being at the beginning of the period, 1947, was of little value by the end of the period, 1962, and write it off, or that its value was approximately equal to the depreciation during the period so that the addition for beginning stock and subtraction for capital consumption during the period nearly offset each other, leaving us with the sum of new investment as the approximate current stock. Or we might assume a slower rate of depreciation and guess that the beginning stock stood in some systematic relation to the subsequent additions to stock. In this latter case, we might extrapolate the investment trend backward in time, imputing to urban areas whose shares of new additions to facilities have been declining since 1947 a greater share of the beginning stock, to reflect their earlier dominance. Or the rate of depreciation and obsolescence might be assumed to be faster than in the first case, so that the beginning stock could also be assumed to be zero and the annual post-1947 additions reduced proportionately between areas, year by year. (The totals would not be reduced proportionately for each urban area; those areas in which relatively more of their postwar investment was in the earlier years would sustain a greater than average reduction in total capital stock and those areas in which relatively more of their capital expansion occurred recently would sustain a lesser over-all depreciation rate.)

Whatever may turn out to be the most sensible set of depreciation assumptions, some first steps toward constructing an interregional capital-to-labor cross-sectional analysis seem to be quite manageable, from this Olympian vantage point. Surely, there will be many a slip twixt cup and the lip—data problems are almost always minimized from afar—but the possibility of getting even rough figures on fixed capital for the larger urban areas is most intriguing. What is especially significant is that both the capital and the associated employment figures apply to a mutually consistent areal unit—the plant and equipment figures and the related employment figures both apply precisely to an area circumscribed by the job commuting range.

For another facet of labor productivity, human capital, the measurement problem is easier in some ways and harder in others. Labor skill is an obvious factor to be considered in explaining labor productivity and relative wage rates. Here, surrogate indexes can be compiled more easily than for capital, but the indexes are of more tenuous linkage. The quality of the labor resources of an urban area—a matter of skill and experience—may be approximated by a host of educational indexes easily available in the *Decennial Censuses of Population.* "Median school years completed by persons 25 years old and over," and "per cent of persons with 4 or more years of college" are but two examples. The nature of the association between the level of general education and the level of industrial skill is, however, quite uncertain and a very liberal measure of empirical skill will be required to construct a sensitive index coupling the two, using only the available data. However, the resourceful investigator might find other less obvious data to serve his ends. For example, various college entrance examinations are administered nationwide (e.g., the graduate record examination) so that interarea differentials in scholastic performance might be analyzed. The military selective service tests are another possibility.[13] Whether a given examination measures intelligence, educational experiences, or cultural background is left for others to judge, but the intercorrelation of these performance measures with interarea differentials in labor productivity and rewards is clearly within the domain of the urban economist.

The complex of interacting forces that influence labor productivity is sufficiently intricate to caution the investigator against expecting easy answers to these hard questions. To cite just one possible source of ambiguity, a direct correlation between the amount of capital per worker and the wage rate might be rationalized quite conventionally, as the manifestation of greater productivity through the mechanization of work. But it is more than barely possible that another force is also at work. A large amount of capital per worker implies a heavy total investment in the relevant industry which in turn suggests the likelihood of both large outputs (to spread the heavy fixed cost) and also difficult entry into that industry. In sum, a high capital-to-labor ratio is probably associated with the concentration of activity among a few large firms—oligopoly. A few firms are much more able and much more likely to refrain from active price competition with each other, and the higher product prices which probably follow make it financially possible for oligopolies to pay higher wages than more competitive industries. Thus, while a high capital-to-labor ratio may raise the physical productivity of the workers, this may be only part of the explanation of their high wages because that same capital intensiveness may bring a diminution of competition which acts just as powerfully to raise wage rates above the level that these workers would earn elsewhere.[14]

---

[13] The proportion of selective service registrants examined and disqualified for failing the mental test is reported, annually, by states, by the Department of the Army, Office of the Surgeon General, and published in the *Statistical Abstract of the United States.* Selective service mental test data were used to help evaluate the comparative skill and potential of the Minnesota labor force in the *Report of the Governor's Minnesota Tax Study Committee, 1956,* p. 46 and Table 1.18, p. 48.

[14] Perloff estimated the amount of capital per person employed in an industry by subtracting total wage income per person from total income per person employed in the industry. His data show a modest tendency for wage income per worker to vary directly with the amount of capital per worker. But there are many exceptions: high wage rates in low capital intensity industries (e.g., construction, engineering services, radio and TV) and low wages in relatively capital-intensive operations

The relationship of "administered prices" and monopoly power to local income levels deserves further comment, to which we now turn.

Public Policy and Productivity

Productivity and pecuniary reward are not tied together in a simple bond. The *physical* productivity of an economic group may rise; but, if the prices at which their products are sold fall appreciably with the increase in supply, their gross income may rise but little and their net income may even fall. In fact, if the percentage fall in price is greater than the percentage increase in the volume of output sold (i.e., if the demand for their product is "inelastic"), even the gross income may decline. Farmers can testify to the seeming paradox of a larger harvest bringing a smaller gross income. Therefore, it is *value* productivity which commands our attention and this is a product of physical productivity and product price. The prosperity of a given industry and of the locality in which it is situated is as much a matter of the relevant price making process as of their physical efficiency.

Many product prices are greatly influenced by public policies, such as our agricultural price support programs. And agricultural price supports are relevant to urban economics, most directly to the urban areas that supply the farm market. A major determinant of value productivity (income level) of urban areas that specialize heavily in the manufacture of farm implements is the federal farm price support program which indirectly supports farm machinery prices by supporting the incomes of the machinery buyers. Waterloo, Iowa, and the tri-cities of Davenport, Rock Island, and Moline are good examples.[15]

Other dramatic examples of urban economic dependency on farm income can be found among the innumerable small urban economies

---

(e.g., medical services, tobacco manufacturing, legal services). And the capital intensity-ease of entry-monopoly power thread was not unravelled. Harvey S. Perloff, "Interrelations of State Income and Industrial Structure," *Papers and Proceedings of the Regional Science Association, 1956, Vol. II*, 81–83, also in *The Review of Economics and Statistics,* May 1957.

[15] "The key to Waterloo's fortunes has been its location in the heart of the Corn Belt. . . . Waterloo's 'export' economy is specialized in an even more dramatic way: the Rath Packing Company and the John Deere Tractor Works together produce 70 percent of the area's 'export' earnings and provide over two-thirds of the community's factory jobs." (Tractor manufacturing accounted for slightly over one-half of this joint product.) *Five Midwest Cities,* 1955 Annual Report of the Federal Reserve Bank of Chicago, pp. 22–25.

that serve as trade and service centers of both producers and consumers goods for the surrounding farm area—the farm market towns. When the farm state representatives rise on the floor of Congress to warn that the plague of falling farm prices and incomes will spread to the cities, they often overstate the national case for such contagion; but they might easily pinpoint a number of urban areas that are as dependent on these political prices as are the farmers.

"Political productivity" is not confined to farmers and a few urban manufacturers and merchandisers of farm products or caterers to farm families. The great wealth and high income of the oil cities[16] is at least as much a product of highly favorable depletion allowances on gas and oil in determining federal income tax liability as it is a product of the bountifulness of nature. Actually, the magnanimity of nature is often embarrassing to the oil industry, as heavy domestic supplies frequently depress prices, and protective tariffs and quotas are erected to choke off the influx of the ever increasing foreign supplies. The protective tariff is, indeed, a means of politically enhancing local earning power which is much more pervasive, industrially and geographically, than either of the political aids to the extractive industries discussed above. The very breadth and depth of tariff protection become most evident every couple of years when another unsuccessful attempt is made to enlarge the tariff reducing power of the President under the Reciprocal Trade Act.

Communities usually perceive clearly the advantages that accrue to them through political market intervention and they are usually quite adept at protecting and perpetuating their political "rents," even when clear conflict with a superior national interest is evident. Where the real challenge to the small-area economic analyst often lies is in identifying and quantifying the usually less direct and more diffused economic losses that are the reverse side of the coin of political price making. To continue with the foreign trade case, tariff reduction *would* increase our imports of bicycles and wine and cut into the sales of

---

[16] Beaumont-Port Arthur, with about three-quarters of its manufacturing employment in petroleum refining, had a median family income of $5,910 in 1960. Of the roughly two-dozen standard metropolitan areas in Texas and Oklahoma, only Houston's median family income of $6,040 exceeded it, and Houston is a city built on the ownership of oil wealth and has about a quarter of its manufacturing employment in petroleum refining. The average of the median incomes of the nonoil cities of this region is about $4,800, almost 20 per cent below the Beaumont-Port Arthur figure. Figures derived from *U.S. Census of Population,* 1960. The 1950 *Census of Population* figures show a similar pattern, with the oil cities at least 20 per cent above the regional average in median family income.

domestic producers of those goods, but increased imports imply increased exports because foreign countries now have more dollars to spend for American goods. A careful analysis of those local industries which could expect to share in a growing volume of American exports, either in direct foreign sales or indirectly as suppliers of raw materials or semifinished goods to other American businesses stimulated by growing foreign sales, would greatly aid the community in achieving a more balanced perspective on its stake in world trade. Further, the gains to the local consumer through the lower prices brought about by creating international competition should be quantified because this is the gain which usually tips the scales in favor of free trade and best reflects the national interest in promoting closer international economic relations.[17]

The purpose of evaluating the impact of national economic policies on the local economy is not only to prepare the urban area to perceive its own interests so that it may pursue them intelligently—lobby rationally—but also to smooth local adjustments to national policy changes not of the community's own making or liking. Specifically, a clear conception of the vulnerability of the local economy to foreign imports may not enable the community to halt a reduction in the protective tariff, but this knowledge may well alert the community to the coming change and suggest alternative avenues of adjustment. If, moreover, recurring proposals for federal aid to areas hard hit by expanded foreign trade ever materialize in legislation, those urban areas which are both able to diagnose their coming injury and prescribe their own remedy in a technically impressive manner would surely present a much stronger petition for financial aid. Perhaps only a minority, although probably a sizable one, of the urban areas are so intimately and significantly involved in foreign trade that a local-impact-of-foreign-trade study rates a high priority, but the value productivity and income level of almost every urban area is so deeply affected by one or another set of national economic policies that at least one serious analytical exercise in "political productivity" would seem to be highly relevant to almost every urban area study.

---

[17] The most sophisticated and comprehensive study in this area is the *Local Impact of Foreign Trade*. A Staff Report of the National Planning Association, prepared by Werner Hochwald, Herbert E. Striner and Sidney Sonenblum (Washington: NPA, July 1960). This study in local impact analysis attempts to trace both the direct and indirect effects of foreign trade through three communities: Gloversville, N.Y., Kalamazoo, Mich., and Mobile, Ala.

Monopoly Power and Productivity

The principal means of administering ("fixing") prices is not through politically inducing government market intervention, although this tack is of growing importance, but rather through the subtler, implicit collusion inherent in oligopoly. When a few big firms dominate an industry they become very conscious of their impact on each other and, given the pressure of the heavy fixed costs that arise out of their typically large capital investments in a typically complex technology, they become especially sensitive to the grave financial threat that they pose to each other. Accordingly, the game of competing for shares of the market is usually conducted under a kind of Marquis of Queensbury set of rules whereby only the relatively soft rivalry of product differentiation and supersalesmanship is permitted. Price competition might shift the market shares so drastically as to endanger the financial solvency of the loser. Nor will this soft nonprice competition produce the much feared cut-throat price war which, if the product demand is price-inelastic, dries up the total revenue stream for the whole industry and poses the gravest kind of threat to all the players in the game. The oligopolistic industry, then, tends to have product prices appreciably higher than those that would prevail under price competition, and income generated per participant in production tends to be higher too, ignoring for the moment how the aggregate earnings are distributed.

Still, specializing in an oligopolistic industry which administers its product price does not in itself ensure local prosperity—witness the tobacco manufacturing areas. If the local representative of an oligopolistic firm is a branch plant of a nationwide corporation with headquarters elsewhere, then not only will the control of the local industrial wealth rest elsewhere; but, of more immediate concern, the ownership of it will almost certainly be preponderantly external, shared by stockholders throughout the nation. Therefore, almost all of the nonwage (property) income will flow out of the local economy. In all probability, the local branch of the national corporate oligopoly will enrich the local economy only to the extent that it pays high wages.

But the fact that there are few firms in an important industry usually implies big plants, as does a complex technology with heavy fixed investment. The chances are, therefore, that employment in the local branch plant will pay well. The big plant will probably have a high capital-to-labor ratio and this will make for high labor productivity; capital-intensive production usually implies a high level of labor skill which also suggests the likelihood of high wage rates. Perhaps even more important, although much less studied, is the even greater probability that the big plants will raise local wage rates by creating a monopoly-monopsony complex in the local labor market. A single large plant may command a sizable fraction of the total local labor supply and may have a significant degree of control over the price of labor. But this often calls forth a vigorous response; "company towns" were among the first to spawn militant unions—the mining, textile, and steel towns for example.[18]

Thus, the urban area that houses the national oligopoly is also likely to be host to a "countervailing power"[19]—a "local" of a national, industrial-type labor union.

We need add only the final assumption that the demand for the product of "our" (local) oligopolist is price-inelastic (that consumption is reduced but little in response to a price increase) and we have all the conditions necessary for local affluence. And this latter is a reasonable assumption in that we have greatly weakened the opportunity of our external customers to turn to a cheap substitute for our export product if we should raise our prices, because the few other brands available are produced by firms in tacit price collusion with our oligopolist. Buyers can resist our price increases only by substituting entirely different products—a weak position.

Now it becomes quite clear how a high local wage rate and its reflection, a high per capita income, may be achieved by specializing in an export industry which brings together a secure and aggressive nationwide industrial union on one side of the bargaining table with an oligopoly selling a product with an inelastic demand on the other

---

[18] The sophisticated conservative position on labor unions is based on spatial monopsony—big firms in small local labor markets. Machlup put this succinctly: "Labor markets which are either geographically or occupationally isolated are certainly not the norm, but they are not too rare exceptions. We all know of company towns where workers have no chance of alternative employment and only an expensive chance of moving away . . . where skilled workers have only one possible employer in their trade. . . . This is probably the strongest case for the creation of labor monopolies to avoid monopsonistic wage determination [although] not yet a sufficient justification for the creation of labor monopolies all over the map." Fritz Machlup, "Monopolistic Wage Determination as a Part of the General Problem of Monopoly," in *Wage Determination and The Economics of Liberalism,* Chamber of Commerce of the United States, 1947, reprinted in Samuelson, Bishop and Coleman, *Readings in Economics* (New York: McGraw-Hill Book Co., Inc., 1952), p. 292.

[19] The classic statement on the tendency for economic power to beget "countervailing power," as well as the origin of the term, is John Kenneth Galbraith, *American Capitalism, The Concept of Countervailing Power* (Boston: Houghton Mifflin Co., 1952).

side. Together, the union and the firm—the whole local community
when wage roll-out is considered—can exploit the nation, or that
portion of it tributary to the local export plant, by raising industry
wage rates considerably above the national average for the associated
degree of skill and passing these higher-than-competitive costs on to
the consumers at large through administered prices—*firm and union*
administered.

If this union is nationwide or can prevent flight to nonunion areas,
that is if it can in general control the use of nonunion workers, the
monopoly wage power and its concomitant, an artificially high local
standard of living for the areas that specialize in the industry, may
persist and be exploited indefinitely. It would probably take the lure
of nonunion, low-wage areas to break the high wage scale, although
a downward shift in product demand or the "automation" of production would reduce employment and the leverage of these high-wage
jobs on the local service industries' wage scales. The community may
pay for its monopoly advantages at a much later date and in the form
of delayed industrial readjustment, as was discussed above (p. 40).

It is hard to argue with conviction that empirical work in this field
must await better data; there is little evidence that anyone has tried
very hard to test any of these propositions with the existing data. Any
number of studies of industrial concentration have estimated the
proportion of total industry activity controlled by the leading firm
or by some "Big Three." Admittedly, the identification of an "industry" is difficult, but sensible estimates and analyses are continually
made in antitrust and other research. Again, union strength and
aggressiveness may not be readily quantifiable concepts but helpful
surrogates may be found, for example, proportion of the industry
employment working under union shop contracts (or even just unionized) and other indirect evidence of union "security" may be brought
to bear.[20] Estimates of the elasticity of demand for the oligopolists'
product and the derived demand for the associated labor is difficult
but still familiar ground to the economist.

The great wealth of Census and other data holds out the promise
of some very fruitful inquiries, especially cross-sectional statistical

---

[20] For a start, the Bureau of Labor Statistics reports the "approximate per cent
of all office and plant workers employed in large- and medium-size establishments
in which a contract or contracts covered a majority of the workers" for 65 labor
markets, U.S. Department of Labor, Bureau of Labor Statistics, *Wages and Related
Benefits, 82 Labor Markets, 1960–61* (Washington: U.S. Government Printing Office,
December, 1961), Bulletin No. 1285–83, Table B-33b, p. 121.

analyses of some of the smaller, more specialized metropolitan areas. It is not unreasonable to feel that the effects of oligopoly and unionism may be roughly traced through some of the simpler urban economies, such as automobile-dominated Flint and textile-dominated New Bedford, to take extremes in the scale of industry competitiveness. In any event, the hypotheses strike at such obviously powerful themes that to ignore monopoly power is to risk a serious loss in any analysis of interurban income differentials.

City Size and Money Income

In what seems at times to be a trackless maze of interacting variables, the hope, perhaps borne of desperation, arises that some simple surrogate—like city size—might, by some mysterious process, rationalize and structure the whole host of underlying socioeconomic forces that influence the level of local income. The stick which complements this particular carrot is the urgent need of the city planner for some economic guidelines toward his holy grail—optimum city size.

Economists, with a few notable exceptions, have not shown any substantial or prolonged interest in the relationship between city size and the level of local income. Still, city size considerations are so central to city planning that the economist may well have a moral obligation here to render a cross-disciplinary service. Even just a handful of moderately firm numbers here would aid immeasurably in cleaning up a lot of loose generalization on central city "sprawl" versus "new town" colonization, and on suburbs versus satellite cities and so forth. While it is fashionable among planners to lament their lack of control over city size and spatial form, their work lacks convincing evidence of what should be done if such power were to be conferred.[21] Specifically, can metropolitan growth be checked with greenbelts and satel-

[21] A number of city planning axioms are much less inviolable than their dogmatic promulgation implies. The notion of "urban sprawl" as a "devastating" phenomenon of the "Auto Age" has been so widely popularized that documention is made to seem superfluous, but some appreciation of the implicit assumptions on which it is precariously balanced and of the case *for* sprawl can be gained from the highly challenging article by Jack Lessinger, "The Case for Scatteration," *Journal of the American Institute of Planners*, XXVIII, No. 3 (August 1962), pp. 159–69. Lessinger argues that the open spaces left scattered about as residential subdividers leapfrog across the urban-rural fringe ensure against having vast tracts of uniform age housing which would all wear out together, creating future slums. He also argues that open spaces ensure land-use flexibility for adjustment to change, e.g., easements for superhighways.

lite cities, without significant loss of productivity and income? Could we all move to small cities *à la* Mumford,[22] with economic impunity? At what cost? Quantification imposes a healthy intellectual discipline.

The principal empirical findings by economists on city size and income level are the well-guarded observations of Hanna and Mansfield[23] that "some tendency" exists for the urban income level to increase with city size. While the observed income differences between city size classes are small (roughly a $600 increase in 1949 median annual family income from $2,400 to $3,000 over eight classes, or about $75 per step upward in city size), they are statistically significant. The rank relationship is, moreover, quite regular and moderately impressive, especially when the number of city size classes is reduced to about five, with the lower limits of 2,500, 10,000, 50,000, 250,000, and 500,000. The disquieting element is that the variation within classes is almost as large as the variation between class medians from top to bottom. Precautions were taken to guard against the danger that a strong regional effect did not lay at the base of this finding, with the typically large cities of the high income North misleadingly compared to the typically small cities of the low income South. When the influence of location within the nation is removed, a direct relationship between city size and income level persists within each of the nine Census "divisions," varying from a greater city size effect in the three southern divisions to a lesser size effect in the two westernmost divisions.

The finding that income differentials between cities in any given size class tend to be greater than the income differentials between city size classes within any given region, prompts Hanna to argue that further classification is mandatory. He argues, however, that the available Census data are not sufficiently detailed by city size to test the really interesting and significant questions such as: Do higher-skill industries tend to locate in the larger cities? Do industries tend to

[22] Lewis Mumford, *The City in History* (New York: Harcourt, Brace and World, 1961). Mumford looks approvingly on England's New Towns—"relatively self-contained, balanced communities, with a sound industrial base—amply demonstrated" (p. 557)—but a later observer argues that "we shall have to revise our ideas about their [New Towns] most appropriate size; there is nothing to suggest that a population of 80,000 to 100,000 is necessarily ideal and experiments should begin with new communities two or three times that size." Gerald Manners, "The Crisis of Regional Planning," *Westminster Bank Review*, August 1962, p. 20.

[23] Edwin Mansfield, "City Size and Income, 1949," *Regional Income: Studies in Income and Wealth*, Volume Twenty-One (Princeton, N.J.: Princeton University Press, 1957) and Frank A. Hanna, *op. cit.*, pp. 204–14.

pay higher wage rates for a given skill in the larger cities? Do young workers migrate to the larger cities and after spending their most productive years therein leave when past their earnings peak? While Hanna's familiarity with Census data is such as to give his words on this subject great weight, his own tables indicate that a modest return on invested effort can still be realized by poring over the existing data. Using Census data, he characterizes the large metropolitan area as a place with a high labor participation rate, a high proportion of multiple-income consumer units, manufacturing specialization, a high ratio of males to females and a high population growth rate—a not inconsiderable description.

But even more indicative of what can be done with existing data, the weak relation he finds between city size and education (median school years completed by the adult population) might be considerably strengthened if the two city size groups which are out of rank (10,000 to 25,000 and 25,000 to 50,000 population) were "edited" to remove those cities which are dominated by large (state) universities. The college town links, spuriously, a high educational level to a low median income, largely due to part-time student workers (e.g., Ann Arbor, Bloomington, Iowa City, Ithaca, State College, Pa., and so on). The opportunities for imaginative detective work using just the existing Census data should excite the imagination of every urban researcher.

Again, one of his tables shows that the two largest city size classes (250,000 to 500,000 and 500,000 and over) rank very low (third and second lowest, respectively, out of seven) in proportion of population 65 years old and over, but very high (fourth and tie for seventh, respectively) in median age. The only way that a city with a relatively small elderly group could have a high average age is by having a very high proportion of middle-aged persons, and so we infer this to be true of the larger cities, especially the very largest cities. Since these two city size classes also have the highest median incomes, this is rather impressive support for his own hypothesis that many workers tend to spend the years of their greatest productivity in big cities and then return in old age to the places from which they came or ones of similar size. Are we not now moving toward the tentative conclusion that large cities have higher per capita incomes partly because they have a favorable age mix? Further thought joined with imaginative piecing together of the available data might well point the way to some set of demographic standardizations that would break out other components of the observed income advantages of urban scale.

REAL INCOME AND THE EFFICIENCY
OF THE LOCAL SERVICE SECTOR

From Money to Real Income:
Interregional Variations in the Cost of Living

As little as we know about interurban variation in money income, we know even less about the relative cost of living between cities. And surely we cannot rationally choose between big and small cities, either on grounds of personal preference or national policy, without some reasonably firm basis on which to translate urban money income differentials into real income differentials by adjusting for variation in local price levels. At this point the local service sector emerges from the shadow of the export sector. If the export sector is the breadwinner of the city, then the local service sector is the housekeeper, bearing primary responsibility for the efficiency of the city as a consuming unit. The housewife raises the real income of a given money income by purchasing and preparing food skillfully and by choosing shrewdly between competing brands of washing machines. Because from one-half to three-quarters of an urban area's expenditures are for locally produced goods and services, the resident's stake in the efficiency of the local service sector is as obvious as it is pervasive. A big pay check won from the local manufacturing plant can be at least partly offset by a decrepit, mismanaged bus system, an inefficiently small (high cost-high price) municipal water plant, or a collusive and rigidly conventional retail trade industry.

We could, quite logically, treat urban efficiency in full at this juncture, as the bridge between money income and real income. We shall not do so, however, because this work has been so divided that Part I tends to stress those industries through which the urban economy maintains contact with the nation—the breadwinner's work—while Part II will emphasize the housekeeping tasks of city life. Still, some limited pursuit of urban efficiency as the major determinant of the local "cost-of-living" is useful here.

Let us begin with a word about imports. Our export industry emphasis in the treatment of money income should remind us that imports are an important ingredient in the consumers' diet and that the *delivered* price of imports should enter our conceptual local-cost-of-living index. Clearly the more isolated urban economies must bear the higher transportation costs and the higher delivered prices for their imports. True, the more isolated urban area will tend to pro-

duce domestically some goods which comparable urban areas closer
to the main centers of population ordinarily import. But high-cost local
production is economical only relative to *very high* freight charges
on imports and the less isolated area still finds its cost of living lower
by paying the low transportation costs necessary to bring goods in
from regions which have a more than compensating comparative advantage in production—production cost savings which more than
offset *low* transportation costs. A careful comparison of living costs
between, say, isolated Spokane, Washington, and Indianapolis, Indiana,
nestled in our industrial heartland, would certainly be instructive.
But our current consumers' price indexes are confined to measuring
change over time in a given area and we do not have good measures
of the relative living costs between areas, a deplorable statistical gap.

The replacement of imports by local production can be seen in a
much broader and more significant frame of reference. Much more
dramatic than the shift to "own use" production forced by spatial
isolation is the growing variety of local production that normally and
naturally accompanies the growth of the local market. An appreciation
that the degree of specialization is determined by the extent of the
market dates back to Adam Smith. In a local market framework, as
an urban place grows to city status the variety store gives way to the
modern department store and, as the city becomes a true metropolis,
the department store is joined by a host of custom trades and specialty
shops selling a bewildering array of highly differentiated products and
the most esoteric collectors' items.

Increasing local self-sufficiency is, therefore, most often attained
gracefully and economically through growth and large size, as the
growing local market pulls one activity after another across the
threshold of economic local production.[24] And as the local market
continues to grow, these new local activities are likely to experience
economies of scale so that savings in production cost may be added on
to the savings in transportation costs.

The large urban economy raises the real income of its inhabitants
by extending the range of effective consumer choice for three interrelated reasons. First, goods which in smaller urban places would be

[24] The literature on the size of the local market and the range of available goods,
and on the "threshold" concept is relatively large and well developed. See P. S.
Florence, "Economic Efficiency in the Metropolis," *The Metropolis in Modern Life*
(Garden City, New York: Doubleday and Co., Inc., 1955) and Duncan, *op. cit.* (Ch. 1
footnote 4), Chapters 3 and 4.

imported can be produced efficiently in the large urban economy, with the saving in transportation cost accruing to the consumer. Second, many of the goods offered locally would not be available at all in a small city because of prohibitively high transportation costs—professional and personal services which must be performed on the spot and would entail the most expensive kind of transportation, the movement of people. Third, the wealthier persons tend to settle in the larger urban areas, partly to enjoy their money incomes to the fullest— it is difficult to spend, rationally, a high money income in a smaller urban place with only a severely limited range of goods and services. To the extent that the larger cities become enclaves of wealth, they become the prime markets for luxury goods and provide the cumulative force of attraction for other wealthy persons seeking that which their predecessors have already begun to provide—variety.

This third point has been introduced with some hesitancy because whether the agglomeration of the rich, through its impact on the trade and service structure of the area, raises or lowers the real income of the other residents or of the whole urban society is a moot point. An ostentatious display of wealth can breed invidious comparison and foster jealousy. Still, many external benefits accrue to the neighbors of the rich at little or no extra cost to them. The privately supported museums, even though they may have been endowed by wealthy patrons fully as much to enrich their own environment as to democratize culture, illustrate this spill-over effect. The existence of unusually attractive residential areas, such as Georgetown in Washington, probably produce a net favorable sensory-emotional gain to all but the most fervently egalitarian area residents.

Thus, the real obstacle in quantifying the change in consumer welfare lies not so much in measuring the cost of a given market basket of goods and services available in two different cities, as in assessing the value of having a greater selection from which to choose in the larger city, that is, in assessing the "cost" of not being able to buy a given good or service in a smaller place. (Can one impute the price of attending an opera in Scranton, Pennsylvania, by adding in the cost of transportation to New York, including lost time and possibly food and lodging while away from home?) Thus it is the esoteric services of the big city that provide the principal measurement problem, and this is not trivial because it is precisely these services which are the attraction of the metropolis, and which acquire increasing importance with high and rising levels of income.

Monopoly and Efficiency: Local Trades and Services

A fourth point may be derived from the discussion immediately above, one which also works against real income in the smaller urban place, namely, the degree of competition in the local trades and services. Monopoly in a local export industry, like piracy, raises the money income level of insiders by extracting tribute from outsiders. But a purely internal monopoly in the local service sector is more akin to mutiny with both the monopolist and his customers now all in the same boat. Not only does local monopoly capriciously redistribute income away from the competitive ("fair") pattern which better reflects ability and sacrifice, but the urban economy loses efficiency as well as equity because the pattern of production in local trades and services becomes disoriented from the optimum pattern of consumption. While the total local *money* income may well remain largely unchanged—the housewife's money loss is the monopolist's gain— aggregate *real* income will fall as local consumers are forced to distort their preferred consumption patterns by making forced substitutions. They buy "too little" of the overpriced monopolized goods and services and "too much" of the relatively underpriced, competitively sold products. Probably even more critical, in the long run, "local monopoly" may burden the local economy in a more dynamic context by stifling invention and innovation in merchandising, medical care, and so forth.

Monopoly power in the local service sector may assume many guises. Collusion among retail stores may be informal and covert (e.g., gentlemen's agreements and price leadership) or formal and overt (e.g., "fair trade" legislation). The legislation may be designed to protect existing businesses by restricting entry (e.g., licensing and zoning) or by suppressing innovation (e.g., discriminatory chain store taxation). Obviously, the burden of local monopoly is borne mainly by the small urban economy that can support only one or a few firms in a given local service activity. Even when the population of a small urban place passes the "threshold level" so that it can finally support its first small hospital or full-fledged department store, only the first step has been taken along the tortuous road to an efficient and variegated consumer complex. A second less appreciated step in the direction of extending consumer choice and lowering living costs is taken when the number of independent firms in the area grows to the point where active price competition and rivalry in product development occurs. And in this age of mass communication and mass tastes, the place of variety and innovation in raising real income should not be regarded lightly; neither should the role of vigorous competition as its instrument.

Monopoly and Efficiency: Local Public Services

Local monopoly, the bane of the small urban place as it reduces the efficiency of private enterprise in trade and services, becomes the small city's strength in terms of the efficiency of public services. The larger metropolis often suffers the disorganizing effects of *too little monopoly*. Public services play a much more fundamental role in living standards in urban areas than in rural, as many services that an individual can supply for himself in a rural setting must be collectivized and supplied by the local government to city dwellers: water supply, garbage and sewage disposal, transportation and outdoor recreation. The socialization of these activities does not occur suddenly, across the board, at the first signs of urban status; rather the scope of the public economy increases in breadth and depth as the city grows in size and density. Only in the larger cities do the latter two functions, transportation and outdoor recreation, become mandatory public responsibilities. Therefore, efficiency in the public economy becomes a more critical element in urban real income in proportion to city size. But the larger the population and spatial extent of the urban area, the greater the likelihood that this population will spill over the political boundaries of the central city—the original political entity—and form a myriad of suburbs and satellite cities. Political fragmentation of what was previously a single public service district brings with it economic fragmentation in the production of water supplies, sewage disposal, and transportation services, often at the expense of economies of scale.

Fragmented urban public services may labor under *"internal* dis-economies of scale" resulting from plants which are too small to exploit the optimum technology, or if of optimum size they are being operated at too low levels of output to take advantage of their low cost potentials. True, the service areas of the central cities' public plants in the fragmented large metropolitan areas may be fully as big or bigger than those of politically unified small urban areas, so that the internal economies of scale are comparable. But the larger area central city could achieve even lower costs for all of its political sub-divisions if its service area were extended into the suburbs, and a foregone gain is a true cost.

But unplanned subdivision of the natural service area is even more critical in the matter of *"external* economies of scale." External diseconomies of political fragmentation follow from the inability to engross in one accounting and decision-making unit the major benefits and costs of a public service. An action or activity which could render a net total social gain will be thwarted if one autonomous entity bears substantially more of the cost and another reaps more of the benefits. The central city, for example, is understandably loath to remove valuable property from its tax rolls to build expressways that will speed the high-income suburbanites into town and induce more of their number to migrate out of town, taking their tax payments with them and leaving their traffic costs behind. Similarly, storm water runoff in one political subdivision floods basements in another, causing a greater dollar amount of damage than the cost of correcting the situation, with no recourse open to the injured party except the traditional, slow, and cumbersome legal remedies.

External diseconomies of political fragmentation do not occur only in the beggar-thy-neighbor situations illustrated above where one subdivision's *large* loss is another's *small* gain. A case in which all subdivisions may well lose is in police protection, as economies of scale and/or qualities of scale (a better service for the same cost) are sacrificed to provincial pride; problems of communication and co-ordination between the subdivisions may lower the level of public protection below that of the small city police force. In sum, the production function in public services is such that lower unit costs depend not only on the absolute level of output (internal economies of scale) but also on the proportion of the optimum service area that is unified under a single decision-making authority (the degree to which the external economies are made internal).

From Individual Prices to an Urban Price Index

There are diseconomies of scale too. Land values and their reflection in housing rents may rise very rapidly with urban size—as much as one-third of the price of a home is land value in parts of the New York metropolitan area, whereas land may account for as little as one-tenth of the combined land and house value in a small town. Again, the cost of commuting to work in the very large urban area, including tension and fatigue, is clearly high, especially when compared to the advantages of walking to work in a small urban place.

Again, the cost of outdoor recreation may range with increasing urban size from practically nothing to virtual unavailability. Here again is the difficult task of comparing the price of a service to the "cost" of doing without it.

There is a subjective facet of cost-of-living comparisons which is at least as critical in quantification as specification of the objective price indexes. Even if we knew the price of each good and service both in some isolated small town and in one of the big cities of the Atlantic Coast "megalopolis"—even if we had all the "price relatives"—we could construct a composite price index which would synthesize and summarize this bewildering mass of information only if we knew what "weights" to use. That is, the weight we attach to the "fact" that opera is cheaper in the big city and to the fact that outdoor recreation is cheaper in the small urban place must reflect the frequency with which the consumer chooses the two activities—the relative quantities consumed.[25]

Clearly the same set of price relatives might show that a low-income family, with only a grade school education and only recently removed from rural surroundings, might find the cost of living lower in a small town, given their preference for picnicking and fishing and their relatively heavy expenditures on rent and transportation. Conversely, the upper-income, educated, confirmed urbanite would apply a wholly different set of weights to these same price relatives and would choose the big city at the same or even a lower money income to attain the highest real income—satisfaction. Fortunately, we do not need to quantify individual taste patterns. If we could but provide the major price relatives—the price of housing, transportation, food, recreation, and so forth—in various places, we might then trust the individual to do his own weighting, and multiplying, and summing, and to make his own locational decision.

But if we are, in fact, developing into a nation of very large city-states (not autonomous city-states in the Greek tradition, but united city-states in a giant "common market"), then the relationship between the size of an urban area and the local level of money and real income may come to be less significant than the internal variations within metropolitan areas, that is, between the large central city and the small suburbs located on the urban-rural fringe—the latter-day analogue

---

[25] See any standard economics statistics text on price index construction, especially the "weighted average of price relatives" or the "weighted aggregate" indexes, for example, Frederick C. Mills, *Statistical Methods*, Third Edition (New York: Henry Holt and Co., 1955), pp. 448–54.

of the isolated small town. This would be especially true if the effect of size on the level of income were largely confined to the range from small to medium, or even medium-large size cities, say, ten thousand to one-half million population, and the proportion of our national population residing in urban areas of over one-half million were to rise from the current 45 per cent[26] to 67 per cent within the next couple of decades.

The intrametropolitan area distribution of money income will be considered in the next chapter. Let us close here with passing notice of the effect of intrametropolitan variations in the cost of living. The line of reasoning employed here would be almost identical to that suggested above in handling cost-of-living differentials between small and large cities. Individuals and families face an array of possible residential sites from which to choose; the core area, the inner ring, suburbia, and exurbia (leaving aside for the moment the very real and critical social problem of racial discrimination in housing).[27] Conceptually, the householder begins from the objective base of a set of price relatives which apply to each of the various goods and services at each of the many residential sites (e.g., the relative cost of travel to downtown and back, land values and rents, the relative accessibility of open space and outdoor recreation and other living cost differentials at the various residential sites) and from the objective base of his given money income (largely unrelated to his place of residence because the metropolitan area is a single local labor market). The householder then proceeds to select, from those sites he can afford, that site at which he realizes the greatest satisfaction ("utility"), given his individual taste pattern—his preference for museums and restaurants or fishing and barbeque pits.

The modern, large metropolitan area offers its inhabitants variety ranging from "cliff-dwelling" at the edge of a vibrant downtown to garden patches under near-rural conditions at the urban fringe, virtually matching within one urban area the variety of many separate

[26] In 1960, approximately 81 million of the 180 million population of the United States (45 per cent) resided in Census-defined "standard metropolitan statistical areas" of over one-half million population.

[27] For example, the Negro population in the Detroit area was more residentially segregated in 1960 than in 1950, 1940, or 1930. See Albert J. Mayer and Thomas F. Hoult, *Race and Residence in Detroit* (Urban Research Laboratory, Institute for Urban Studies, Wayne State University, August 1962). Or, in a broader context, the Advisory Commission on Intergovernmental Relations also found that "population is tending to be increasingly distributed within metropolitan areas along economic and racial lines," *Government Structure, Organization, and Planning in Metropolitan Areas* (Washington: U.S. Government Printing Office, 1961), p. 7.

cities.[28] And when we recall that this very substantial range of residential choice is coupled with the opportunity to choose from a wide selection of jobs without having to change one's residence, then a strong case can be made that freedom of choice has been extended by the development of the very large metropolitan area. And extended choice can be associated with an increase in individual and social welfare more unequivocably—with fewer academic reservations—than almost any other alternative goal that we might pursue.

In sum, the argument here is that the trend toward population concentration in a relatively few, very large metropolitan areas will tend to narrow interurban differentials in money income very greatly, as each urban area assembles a random (and similar) mix of industries and occupations and age groups, but that the cost of living at various sites within the metropolitan area, broadly interpreted to include range of choice and amenities, will come to vary even more than at present, so that urban income analysis may come to concern itself at least as much with intrametropolitan area patterns as with interurban patterns, and with real income as much as with money income.

Technical Appendix

THE INTERRELATION OF
MONEY AND REAL INCOME

Finally, and perhaps most far reaching of all, money and real income levels may be intertwined, as wage rate differentials may be directly correlated with local cost of living differentials. An urban area not only earns its money wage rate but it must also buy it back, as the cost of the goods and services produced by the local service industries are largely determined by the local wage rate. If, for example, automobile or steel workers have higher wage rates than manufacturing in general and if the "area effect" (or "wage roll-out") is substantial, so that retail clerks, bus drivers, and domestic service workers in an auto or steel town make more than their national counterparts, then the cost of living will be higher in these towns, unless the productivity of these latter workers is commensurately higher.

A simple arithmetic example will help here. Suppose that the local manufacturing (export) workers average $4.00 per hour, compared to a national

[28] See Charles M. Tiebout, "A Pure Theory of Local Expenditures," *Journal of Political Economy*, October 1956, pp. 416-24, for a defense and rationalization of political fragmentation as a means of extending the range of choice in residential and community environmental arrangements, and Chapter 7 in this volume.

average in manufacturing of only $3.00, and that they account for 40 per cent of total local income. Suppose, further, that the local service workers in that town average $2.50 per hour, compared to a national average of $2.00, because of the competitive influence of the high wage rates earned in the export sector. With 40 per cent of total local economic activity in the export sector, we can assume that approximately 60 per cent of the purchases of the area's households are for locally produced goods and services, produced at wage rates 25 per cent above the national level ($2.50/$2.00). (Area exports are approximately equal to area imports at 40 per cent of total activity; we assume here that local business services supplied to area exporters are included in exports as intermediate product.) Thus, with 60 per cent of household purchases subject to a wage-and-price-index of 125 (the locally produced and consumed goods and services) and 40 per cent purchased in national markets at a price index of 100 (area imports), the local price index averages out to 115. The local manufacturing money wage of $4.00 deflates to only $3.50 ($4.00/115 × 100) when adjusted for the fact that the high export industry wage rate has created a high-wage town—the steel worker shares his good fortune with his neighbors and he pays for it.

The argument that a high money wage must be deflated for this roll-out effect becomes quite convincing when we recall that local service industries are protected from outside competition by the high cost of transportation of their "product." Personal and professional services usually require the movement of people, either the customer (e.g., retail trade) or the producer (e.g., domestic service) or both (e.g., hospitalization, where both patient and doctor travel), and personal transportation is the most costly of all. Therefore, a high wage rate in the local service industries would seem to be at least as protected from interregional competition as its progenitor, a high export wage rate. Conversely, low-wage export industries depress local service industry wage rates, so that a relatively low local cost of living somewhat softens the money income disadvantage. In sum, the wage roll-out effect, if in fact one does exist, tends to compress money wage rate and income differentials between urban regions into a smaller interarea variation of real income.

But, then, one can quickly fabricate any number of plausible *a priori* economic models purporting to describe the mechanics of local wage determination, even many variations on just the wage roll-out effect. This fact testifies, of course, to the need for some systematic empirical work to determine which of the various models occur most frequently. No attempt will be made here to trace through the almost endless possibilities. Still, a few of the more obvious internal labor market linkages can be quickly sketched in such a way as to suggest more rigorous work on the part of others.

We begin with a simplification to the effect that our local labor market has two interrelated sectors: the export labor market and the local service labor market. To further simplify, let us assume that our local economy has a single export industry, embracing a number of independent firms, and that labor is highly mobile between the various local service jobs so that we may

treat the service sector labor market as if it, too, were a single industry.
And we also assume just one grade of labor, more or less mobile between
all jobs in the locality—occupational mobility between factory and store.

How would an increase in demand for the area's exports be likely to affect
the local wage rate? An increase in demand for local exports will increase
the "derived demand" for export industry labor, as shown in Figure 2-A by
the arrow labeled (1). The export wage rate would tend to rise (2) and at
the higher wage rate more labor would be offered and employed (3). The

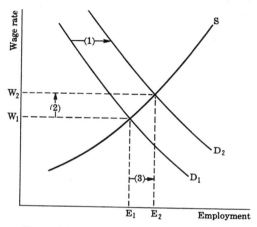

a. Export labor market

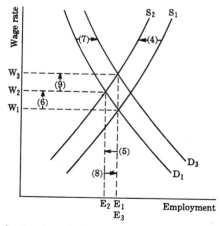

b. Local service labor market

Figure 2. Likely effects of increase in export demand on local wage rates.

new export industry workers would presumably be recruited, at least in part, from the local service sector (and part by in-migration), causing, as shown in Figure 2-B, a decrease in supply of labor (4) and employment (5) in the service labor market resulting in a higher wage rate for service work (6). Thus, the higher wage rate in the export sector has rolled out into the service sector, somewhat deflating the higher money income of the export workers, as suggested above, but permitting all laborers in the local economy to share the favorable effects of an increase in the demand for local exports.

A secondary effect or derived impulse follows, which may or may not be significant. The increased wage rates and employment in both sectors serve to expand local payrolls (income) and thereby increase the demand for local services and service workers (7), lessening the net shift of workers from the service to export sector (8). The combination of a reduced supply of and an increased demand for service workers may raise service wage rates about as high as export wage rates (9).

If we extend our time period sufficiently to allow for substantial in-migration, the relatively high local wage level will attract workers from elsewhere, increasing the supply of labor and (slowly) deflating the local wage level back to, say, its beginning position of parity with other nearby local labor markets. But in-migration may be so sluggish that labor supply increases more slowly, (8) in Figure 3-A, than a continually rising demand for local exports (9), as the local economy rides the boom in its industrial specialty onward and upward. Thus, in this more dynamic formulation the local wage rate may continue to rise slowly even in the "long run," even with significant in-migration. Alternatively, if we assume (Figure 3-B) easy and swift in-migration (10)—a rapidly increasing supply of local labor—and only moderately increasing demand for local exports (11), we set the stage for a slow deflation of the recently inflated local wage level back to about the original (parity) level.

Thus a high money wage rate in the export sector would tend to roll out into the service sector and raise wage rates and the price of local services (deflating local real income) only if entry into the local market (in-migration plus access to employment) is restricted or sluggish, or if the rate of increase in demand for local exports is extremely rapid. We would look for the real income deflating effect of wage roll-out especially in urban areas specializing in very rapidly growing industries (e.g., Detroit during the decades of the twenties and from 1941–53, and Los Angeles throughout the postwar period) or in areas with significant impediments to in-migration (e.g., various Alaskan urban areas).

Suppose instead, that we begin on the supply side of the export labor market by assuming that the export industry labor force is tightly organized both locally and nationwide. Let us further assume that the local export industry is an oligopoly which can and does administer prices and is able to pass on all wage increases as price increases with only token buyer re-

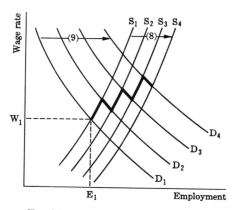

a. Sluggish in-migration

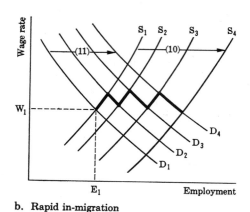

b. Rapid in-migration

Figure 3. Ease of in-migration and the wage rate pattern.

sistance (i.e., the demand for the product is highly inelastic). Next, assume the union demands and gets a sizable increase in the wage rate, (1) in Figure 4. This higher wage rate will not automatically roll out into the local service sector via increased competition for the limited local labor force, as in the preceding case. In fact, the higher export wage rate will tend to reduce employment (slightly) in that sector (2) and some of the released workers will compete for the available jobs in the local service industries, increasing supply there (3) tending to lower local service wage rates (4).

Just as before, however, we must consider a secondary effect through payrolls and income generation, which is an offsetting force this time. We have assumed that the demand for export workers to be inelastic, and if it were

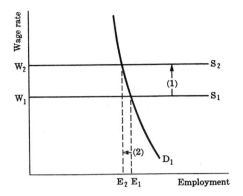

a. Export labor market

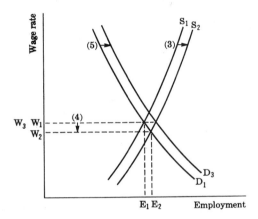

b. Local service labor market

Figure 4. Wage rate pattern in a tightly organized export labor market.

not true that an increase in the wage rate led to a less than proportionate reduction in employment so that the product of the wage rate times employment (total wage bill) were not greater, it is highly doubtful that the union would have pressed for the substantial wage increase which we assumed. Therefore, the higher wage rate will produce a higher export payroll ($W_2 E_2 > W_1 E_1$) and the increased income and spending for local services will increase the demand for service workers (5), tending to raise local service wage rates. The net effect of these two forces, an increased supply of and increased demand for local service workers may operate to raise or lower the local service wage rate, W_3, depending on their relative magnitudes. In general, the more inelastic the demand for export workers, the more likely it is that the local service industry wage rate will also rise. The greater the inelasticity of demand for export workers, the smaller the number of export workers released and thrown on the local service sector (the smaller the supply increase) and the greater the increase in export payrolls and spending for local services (the greater the demand increase). Thus, the greater the inelasticity of demand for export labor, the greater the wage roll-out effect in the local service labor market.

In addition, the propensity to migrate should be integrated into the model to convert reduced employment in the export industry into increased labor supply in the local service sector. The greater the propensity to migrate, the smaller the increase in local service following from a given cutback in export employment and, following the reasoning advanced earlier in this chapter, the greater the degree of skill, the greater the propensity to migrate in the event of discharge. Finally, the elasticity of demand for local service labor is also highly relevant, with an elastic demand for local service labor lessening the wage depressing effect of a given increase in local service labor supply. Thus, the roll-out effect of a given increase in export wage rates, achieved by labor bargaining power, may be either positive or negative, and will tend to increase local service wage rates to the extent that (a) the demand for export labor is inelastic, (b) out-migration is quick and easy, (c) the demand for local service workers is elastic, and (d) the marginal propensity to consume locally produced goods and services is high—the more that additions to the export wage bill are spent for local services.

Clearly, the purpose of these rather tortuous analyses is to serve as *caveats* against accepting the wage roll-out (real income deflating) hypothesis too quickly or unreservedly. What is most needed is some empirical work. While it would be most difficult, if not impossible, to quantify the various micro-economic functions at issue here (e.g., the various elasticities), some macro-economic slice that more modestly tries only to net-out the various forces at work is quite within the power of existing statistical and econometric techniques. Is the wage roll-out effect greater in urban areas with rapidly growing export industries than in areas dependent on mature but powerful, unionized oligopolies, as our deductions here would seem to suggest? Does spatial isolation enhance the roll-out effect by dampening in- and out-migration? How is the roll-out effect related to the size of the urban area—dissipated by lengthening lines of interaction? These questions would seem to be susceptible to operational formulation and empirical testing.

CHAPTER 3

Income Inequality: Personal and Governmental Poverty

The study of income distribution is perhaps the most under-developed area in the world of economics. The hesitancy of economists to tackle this subject is partly due to the inherent complexity of the material and partly due to the rapidity with which almost all analyses of income distribution "degenerate" into value judgments or ethics—leave the comfortable and dispassionate realm of pure theory so hospitable to the "scientific method." Firm conclusions on small questions seem to be more satisfying than rough, tentative judgments on big ones.

With very little literature to summarize and evaluate, with almost no empirical findings to report, our best course of action would seem to be to cast about for a conceptual framework within which subsequent empirical efforts might be organized. A three-part, integrated schema is suggested as a point of departure.

First, we begin by considering the metropolitan area as a whole in its capacity as a single local labor market, within which the basic degree of local interpersonal income inequality is determined. The likely influence of the local population size, industry mix, and racial composition on the degree of interpersonal income inequality will be considered.

Second, given this basic amount of area-wide, interpersonal income inequality, we move to the submetropolitan area level and examine the degree to which it is translated into intergovernmental differentials in per capita income. Because the political subdivisions of a metropolitan area are largely autonomous in matters of local public finance, differentials in per capita income create inequalities in both fiscal capacity and public service needs between municipalities. And because we entrust local government to effect substantial redistribution of real income through local public services, a serious problem follows from the divorcing of income from need.

105

Third, within each of these political subdivisions, residences may be clustered by income class (segregated), posing a quite different set of socioeconomic problems. If sophisticated human resource development programs require some reasonable close contact between the rich and the poor, income (and racial) segregation debilitates key programs that range from welfare to education, and span this generation and the next. Thus, the spatial pattern of residences by income class—the physical and social distance separating the rich and poor—influences acculturation and opportunity and, thereby, the basic degree of interpersonal income inequality within the whole metropolitan area—the point from which we began.

In sum, our basic frame of reference is a comparative analysis of income inequality within the area as a whole, between its parts and within each part, doubling back on the area as a whole.

METROPOLITAN AREA-WIDE INTERPERSONAL INCOME INEQUALITY

City Size, Opportunity, and Industry Mix

How might the size of the urban area affect interpersonal income inequality within the local economy as a whole? Since we have already identified the urban area as a local labor market, let us begin by examining deductively some of the forces which might create dispersion in wage rates and/or annual earnings from labor services.

On the supply side, we quickly recognize differentials in general education, vocational training, and in intensity of application of talent and skill among workers. We would expect the larger urban area to exhibit greater interpersonal variation on these scores for a number of reasons. Large cities tend to attract the most gifted and ambitious individuals and accentuate these great differences in natural ability by offering the most advanced technical and professional education. Large cities, moreover, tend to receive a sufficiently heavy influx of displaced farm laborers and other low-skilled rural workers to hold the lower end of the wage-skill spectrum in place. Thus, with their human resources ranging from the most talented and aggressive to the most marginally employable, not to mention sizable populations of students, social rebels, skid row derelicts, and other very low income groups, a compelling deductive argument that labor income inequality increases with city size can be built up solely from the supply side.

The demand side, moreover, is deductively complementary, but only in part. The large city is more likely to be the home office of the "name" corporation with its "executive suite" and research laboratory, and all the ancillary business services that call for the highest professional skills (e.g., corporation lawyers and financial counselors). In sharp contrast, the smaller city seems more often to be built on routine mass production activities, with the concomitant narrow range of skills and with wage rates further compressed by the egalitarian influence of the labor union. Further, while the more routine jobs on the assembly line may not call for any greater skill than the most menial jobs in service work, the manufacturing jobs typically pay much better, as workers displaced from factory to services trades are discovering to their dismay.

But the greater variety of jobs offered by the large city also implies greater opportunity to hold a second job ("moonlighting") or to have a second income earner in the family. Jobs for women are, moreover, much more plentiful in the large commercial, financial, or governmental center. The effect of more second jobs for the head of the household is probably to reduce income inequality, as this is probably practiced more among the lower-income groups. The big city's greater variety of jobs also makes multiple-earner families more common. To the extent that working wives come from the higher-income households with fewer children, where the wife pursues her "career" partly out of boredom with housekeeping, second earners in the family tend to increase income inequality. But the preliminary findings are that working wives are more a lower-income family phenomenon,[1] so big cities and occupational variety tend more to produce greater income equality via multiple earners as well as second jobs. While much more empirical work remains to be done, our tentative judgment is

[1] Mincer has shown that the participation of married white women is positively related to the wages offered to women and negatively related to husband's income, with the relation being stronger with transitional components of the husband's income than with the permanent components. Preliminary results from the work of Glen Cain at the University of Chicago suggest the same variables explain, in roughly the same manner, cross-sectional differences in the labor force participation rates of married non-white women, though Cain has not yet been able to settle on any one explanation of why the rates for non-white women are higher than for white after many kinds of standardization.
Comment by Albert Rees in *Human Resources in the Urban Economy*, Mark Perlman (editor), (Washington: Resources for the Future, Inc., 1963), p. 114.

that the effect of the greater occupational variety characteristic of big cities is ambivalent, so that we can not deduce the likely net relationship between city size and labor income inequality operating on the demand side. Taking the demand and supply sides of the labor market together, however, we sense some tendency toward increasing income inequality with greater city size.

We would also hypothesize a greater variability in the large city of profits in local trades and services—the net income of unincorporated business is probably about as close as we can get to an empirical measure. Almost by definition, the profits of proprietorships, partnerships, and closely held local corporations engaged in local trades and services can be very large only if the local market is very large. This suggests a parallel tendency for profit income inequality to increase with increased city size, but to make a really good case for this effect one should show that noncorporate profit income is as large a share of total income in the large city as it is in the small one. When we recall that the small urban place often is an important exporter of trade and personal services to its hinterland and that these activities are predominantly small businesses, it seems quite possible that the noncorporate profit share decreases with city size.[2]

Finally, if large cities are the home of the very rich to a more than proportionate degree—again, a very large income would be redundant in a small city with its limited offering of consumer goods—we would expect "property earnings," which are usually the foundation of the very highest incomes, to contribute to the greater income inequality hypothesized as typifying large cities. This completes the tour of income sources, but such a long train of deduction is much too fragile

[2] The smallest region for which data on the functional distribution of income are readily available is the state. Still we can get some feeling for the relationship between city size and profits as a share of total income by comparing 1960 "net nonfarm proprietors' income" as a per cent of total personal income for states with mostly small cities and states with large urban concentrations. For example, Maine, New Hampshire, and Vermont had nonfarm proprietorship profit shares of 9.40, 8.71, and 10.45 per cent, respectively, while Massachusetts, with Boston, and Rhode Island, dominated by Providence, had smaller proprietorship profit shares of 7.01 and 6.71 per cent, respectively. And highly urbanized New York and New Jersey, while not quite as low, also fell below the small-town northern New England level with 8.46 and 8.75 per cent, respectively. Again, the more densely populated East North Central region exhibits a nonfarm proprietor profit share of 8.23 per cent, well below the sparsely populated West North Central region's figure of 10.81 per cent. All in all, good reason exists to suspect that the proprietors' profit share decreases with city size, but it would be well to dismount and inspect the terrain more carefully. See, *Survey of Current Business,* Office of Business Economics, Department of Commerce, August 1961.

to do more than suggest hypotheses and point up the need for empirical work.

The empirical work will have to be subtle and sophisticated. For example, the smallest urban places are often largely engaged as service centers for their rural hinterlands; intermediate size cities are usually highly specialized in manufacturing for far-flung markets, with from 40 to 60 per cent of total employment in manufacturing quite common; and the very largest urban areas seldom have more than 35 per cent of their employment in manufacturing (only Detroit and Pittsburgh are exceptions) and often run as low as 20 per cent (e.g., San Francisco), with a median of about 30 per cent.[3] Further, manufacturing economies tend to be characterized by greater equality than service-oriented economies, because of some combination of a narrower range of skills in blue-collar work, less risk-taking (fewer small businesses), and the absence in the service sector of any counterpart to the egalitarian labor union.

All of this combines to suggest the hypothesis that the small city, with a large share of income originating in small business "profits," has a relatively high degree of income inequality, but as this (typically) regional service center acquires factories and grows in size it probably also becomes a more egalitarian society. With further growth and true metropolis standing, ever more esoteric services are acquired and exported over ever greater distances (e.g., administrative, legal, financial), probably turning the income distribution back again toward greater inequality by expanding both the opportunity to express personal talents and to manipulate private property.

Industry Mix, Race, and Inequality: Some Empirical Evidence

In addition to the opportunities for adding to the stock of knowledge about urban income distribution through deductive work, enough data exist to support a very considerable amount of complementary empirical-statistical work. For example, the 1950 *Census of Population* reported the incomes of families and unrelated individuals, as grouped data by a combination of $500 and $1,000 class intervals up to a final open-ended class of $10,000 and over. Because of the open-ended upper class, more sophisticated measures of relative variation, such as the standard deviation or the Lorentz curve, must be abandoned in favor

[3] Department of Commerce, *U.S. Census of Population, 1960, General Social and Economic Characteristics, U.S. Summary*, Table 142.

of more primitive measures. A likely choice is the interquartile variation, $Q_3 - Q_1/Q_1 + Q_3$, where Q_1 is that item (household income)
one-quarter of the way up from the bottom of the (income) array and
Q_3 is that item three-quarters of the way up, or one-quarter of the
way down from the top.

A clearer idea of the nature of this index of income inequality and
some feeling for the range of income inequality between metropolitan
areas can be gained from the table shown below.[4] That household of
the Flint metropolitan area which is only one-quarter of the way up
the local income array receives roughly 32 per cent less (only 68 per

The Ten Metropolitan Areas with the Least and
Most Income Inequality, 1950

The Least		The Most	
Flint, Mich.	.323	Jackson, Miss.	.649
Akron, Ohio	.359	Montgomery, Ala.	.648
Detroit, Mich.	.366	Raleigh, N.C.	.646
Racine, Wisc.	.367	Austin, Texas	.644
New Britain-Bristol, Conn.	.370	Charleston, S.C.	.644
Youngstown, Ohio	.372	Baton Rouge, La.	.630
Lorrain-Elyria, Ohio	.379	Shreveport, La.	.622
Milwaukee, Wisc.	.388	Durham, N.C.	.609
Rockford, Ill.	.390	Columbia, S.C.	.607
Waterbury, Conn.	.396	Lexington, Ky.	.600

cent as much) income than does the median household and that household three-quarters of the way up the local income scale receives about
32 per cent more (132 per cent of the median), assuming that the distribution is symmetrical. In sharp contrast, in Jackson, Mississippi, the
range which encompasses the middle one-half of the households is
35–165 per cent of the median income of that area.[5]

[4] The metropolitan area, cross-section, income distribution analysis reported here
was drawn from a paper presented by the author to the Economics Section of the
Michigan Academy of Arts and Letters, Ann Arbor, Michigan, Spring 1954 (mimeo.).
The brief analysis of the *1950 Census of Population* income data which follows is
now being extended as part of a much broader-gauge analysis of the 1960 Census
data, scheduled for preliminary distribution some time in mid-1965.

[5] The interquartile variation is, of course, only one of the innumerable varieties
of this general measure of variation. If one preferred to measure the breadth of
variation between points farther out in the tails of the income distribution, the first
and fourth pentiles could be used or, farther still, the first and ninth deciles. In
the most generalized form, we can express the latter as the tenth and ninetieth
percentiles $(P_{90} - P_{10}/P_{10} + P_{90})$. If one wanted to study the relationship between city
size and income inequality, in line with the discussion opening this chapter,
the measure of inequality should also reach out well into the ranks of the very rich
and very poor, at least to the tenth and ninetieth percentiles. Fortunately, the 1960
Census has raised its upper, open-ended income class from $10,000-and-over to
$25,000-and-over so that P_{90} falls in one of the preceding closed classes and can be
estimated much more accurately.

Two threads of the urban income inequality pattern stand out clearly: industry mix and region. All ten of the areas with the least income inequality are heavily engaged in manufacturing and, with the single exception of Akron, are specialized in durable goods (e.g., automobiles, machinery and steel). Further, all ten of these metropolitan areas are in the North, just as all ten of the areas with the greatest income inequality are in the South. Let us pursue these findings a step or two farther for whatever broad perspective they may impart to suggested further analyses.

Almost one-half of the variation in income inequality between the 151 standard metropolitan areas was statistically "explained" by inter-area differentials in the proportion of total employment engaged in manufacturing. The greater the proportion in manufacturing, the greater the degree of income equality. That manufacturing towns should have a more equally distributed income than nonmanufacturing places is not too surprising in light of our deductive analyses above.

In the light of the high probability of a strong regional influence, the argument might be made that northern and southern metropolitan areas should be analyzed separately, else the risk be run that the purported correlation between specialization in manufacturing and income equality is really quite spurious—is really a regional cross-cultural effect instead. More precisely, the hidden snare is that southern towns have greater income inequality largely because of sharper occupational discrimination against Negroes, while northern towns are characterized both by less discrimination and fewer Negroes against whom to discriminate. In short, the observed differentials in income distribution might reflect primarily racial effects. But removing the South from the correlation only lowers the "explained" variance from 46 to 44 per cent.

One might argue in rebuttal, moreover, that if the South becomes more *economically* integrated and more egalitarian as it industrializes, and because it is industrializing, then the combined North-South correlation is not only valid but assumes a dynamic developmental quality. That is, if there is a legitimate cross-cultural content here then the analysis even takes on predictive qualities. The cross-section (static) regression functions could then be turned and projected in time to predict the rate at which urban income inequality will lessen in Southern towns as that region industrializes. One reservation to such a prognostication is that manufacturing is growing more slowly and automating more rapidly than services. This could turn factory towns into places of relatively high unemployment, producing thereby a countervailing force toward greater inequality.

None of this denies the powerful role of racial discrimination in income distribution. This same empirical effort found that by combining specialization in manufacturing with a racial variable (nonwhite as a proportion of the total population) the explained variance rose markedly from 46 to 61 per cent. The racial element in income distribution thus seems to have a basis in both the forces of demand and supply in semiautonomous urban labor markets. On the demand side, manufacturing provides practically the only mass source of high-wage employment for nonwhites; on the supply side, nonwhites seem to be relatively better off where they are least numerous. This tentative hypothesis is further supported by a second set of correlations drawn from this same study. The second selected index of income inequality is the ratio of median Negro family income to median white family income. This ratio of racial inequality was correlated with the same two independent variables, per cent of total employment in manufacturing and nonwhite as a per cent of total population. The explained variance was even higher, 64 per cent, with median Negro income rising relative to white income in urban areas of higher manufacturing specialization and relatively fewer nonwhites. Both variables were statistically significant, with the racial supply variable having the greater weight.

Public Policy, Opportunity, and Inequality

What are the important policy aspects of all this? While the study of urban income distribution is at much too early a stage of development to talk policy in any comprehensive fashion, a few general observations with research implications may not be amiss. First, the overall objective of our public policy should not be to reduce (before-tax) income inequality *per se,* at least at the local level. A one-crop farming area with uniform soil throughout, or a unionized one-industry town, such as Flint, probably exhibits the greatest income equality, but few would idealize either of these industrial structures. Rather we should recognize the metropolitan area as a diversified local labor market and act to enrich the opportunity for each and every worker in the area to exploit fully his productive (income earning) potential. Such a policy may well *increase* income inequality in areas where opportunity is currently limited. Of course, if the local developmental prospects are bleak, to prescribe action which enhances the

productive expression of local workers may bring local authorities to
the uncomfortable position of encouraging and facilitating net out-
migration, and this is usually a very unpopular and impolitic program.

Yet, there are many situations in which acting to increase opportunity will also serve to reduce income inequality, for example, reducing discrimination in the labor market. Reducing racial discrimination in employment will, of course, reduce white-nonwhite inequality.
But even here at least a temporary increase of income inequality among
nonwhites is likely, as the more talented and energetic nonwhites pull
ahead in the competitive race.

One might be tempted to leap to the conclusion that there is an
indirect approach to the alleviation of Negro poverty: foster more local
manufacturing employment by a vigorous industrial development
program. To take this position would be to ignore the hard fact that
the golden age of manufacturing, at least as measured in production
jobs, has given way to the service-centered, affluent society. To race
for manufacturing jobs in this era of automation is to swim against
the current, especially if it is unskilled and semiskilled jobs which
are sought. The early evidence from Detroit and Pittsburgh and similar
places is that it is the evaporation of manufacturing jobs which is
causing the alarmingly high level of unemployment among the low-
skilled, low-seniority Negroes in the great manufacturing centers—as
high as 30 per cent in recessions.

As Negro workers are displaced from factory work along with whites,
they must compete for jobs in the services industries, where they leave
behind, for the most part, paternal unionism. An interesting question
presents itself: Will nonwhites be afforded greater or less equality of
opportunity in the nonunion service industries than they experienced
in unionized manufacturing? Certainly, discriminatory practices by
unions have made some manufacturing work (and most construction
craft labor) virtually inaccessible.[6] But industrial unions have pursued

[6] The NAACP estimates that nationally less than 1 per cent of the apprentices in
the construction industry are Negroes. The National Urban League did not find a
single Negro apprentice in 17 out of 32 major cities, and only 100 in all 32 cities in
all fields. In the District of Columbia all of the 824 members of Plumbers Local 5
were white, as were all the apprentices. Similarly, all 500 members of Ironworkers
Local 5 were white, and all apprentices. Still, some slow progress was reported
among Bricklayers, Cement Masons, Carpenters, Rodmen, Machinists and Firemen's
Locals, with the Operating Engineers farthest along (200 Negro members and 15 or
20 apprentices). Ben D. Segal, "D.C. Paradox: Jobs Go Begging with 24,000 Idle," *The
Washington Post*, October 8, 1961, p. E2, drawn from his *Civil Rights in the
Nation's Capital: A Report on a Decade of Progress.* See also F. Ray Marshall,
"Racial Factors Influencing Entry into the Skilled Trades," *Human Resources in the
Urban Economy, op. cit.,* pp. 30–31.

many policies highly advantageous to Negroes: seniority rules, legal rights in grievance procedures, elimination of racial wage differentials.[7] In pushing for flat across-the-board wage increases, such as cost-of-living adjustments, unions have reduced the skill differentials in wage rates in relative terms, benefiting the lower-wage Negroes. While these policies were not aimed at helping the Negro, *per se,* that was their effect. This must, of course, be weighed against the amount of income inequality created by the exclusion of Negroes from certain work through closed unions, high initiation fees, and so forth.

The crucial question is whether nonwhites will gain or lose in the current shift in the structure of industry away from manufacturing and toward services. In places like Detroit and Pittsburgh where Negroes have enjoyed virtually equal access to manufacturing jobs for years now, the loss of union protection could be very damaging. What new socioeconomic institution could be developed to pick up the protective role played by a benevolent union, such as the United Automobile Workers? The function of the shop steward and the employment contract may become even more critical in the service industries where face-to-face contact in the daily routine intensifies the color barrier.

Another facet of the changing labor market deserves comment. The typical factory worker is accustomed to going to work without having to supply any of the capital requirements of his work—without even the carpenter's tool kit. If some of these former factory workers are to become cab drivers, small shopkeepers, television repairmen, and so forth, they will for the first time need modest amounts of fixed and working capital. Herein lies a challenge to our financial institutions, especially those most suited to making small business loans. The federal government has begun to respond to this challenge by establishing a Small Business Administration but this does not pre-empt the field. Nor should a program limited to direct business loans be thought sufficient. Personal financial aids to unemployed factory workers and new entrants into the labor force to enable them to acquire business training are prerequisites to a successful small business lending program. Somewhat more unorthodox, the local public authorities might experiment with some form of public or quasi-public small business forecasts designed to suggest new business opportunities and also to warn against already overcrowded fields. Such a service would

---

[7] See, for example, F. Ray Marshall, *op. cit.,* p. 30.

complement the Labor Department's *Occupational Outlook* studies.[8]
The care and feeding of the small proprietorship should become a
major concern of local government if automation is not to create a
dichotomy of ever-more-skilled princes and displaced paupers among
the erstwhile ranks of manufacturing labor. But let us return to these
matters at greater length in Chapter 6.

INTERGOVERNMENTAL INCOME INEQUALITY WITHIN METROPOLITAN AREAS

The basic degree of interpersonal income inequality in the total
labor market—the metropolitan area as a whole—may be blunted or
sharpened, in its social implication, by the internal spatial pattern it
assumes. Our purpose now is to compare and evaluate alternative
internal income spatial patterns, especially with reference to alternative
sizes of the various economic, social and political entities within which
urban life is organized. What impact does the pattern of residences by
income class—where the rich and poor live relative to each other—
have on urban efficiency, equity, and development?

Political Fragmentation, Income Inequality, and Public Services

Probably the single most pressing problem arising out of the typical
intrametropolitan area arrangement of income classes is that of financing adequate public services. One of the warmest current issues concerns the political fragmentation of metropolitan areas and the
virtues and feasibility of various forms of local political unification.
While *inefficiency* in public services under fragmentation is the evil
most often cited—the sacrifice of economies of scale and co-ordination
in water supply, sewage disposal, police and fire protection, and so
forth—the income distributive aspects of fragmented local government
are also of vital interest. "Income fragmentation" may well be the
stronger part of the case for metropolitan political unification,
especially as it leads to the *inadequacy* of public services in the less
affluent political subdivisions of the metropolitan area.

The size of the typical political subdivision is critical. If a metropolitan area is divided into many small political entities, then the

[8] U.S. Department of Labor, Bureau of Labor Statistics, *Occupational Outlook
Handbook*, 1961 (830 pp.).

distribution of income within each of these usually small areas will tend to be quite equal. People are inclined to group their residences by income and a small area can easily separate out and encompass the homes of just the very rich or just the very poor; a large residential area must almost of necessity mix the rich and the poor to some extent.

If, then, the existence of many small subdivisions permits sharp residential segregation by income class, per capita income will vary greatly between subdivisions. (This is especially true of those political subdivisions largely built up in the postwar period when builders put in place very large-scale housing developments in a very limited price range, and all built within a short period of time so that they aged together and retained their narrow range of original values.) Conversely, if the metropolitan area is broken up but little and then only into subdivisions that are large relative to the total urban area, each of these subareas will tend to average out interpersonal income differentials internally, and only a minor amount of per capita income inequality will be manifest between subdivisions. All of which leads to the overarching hypothesis: Variation in income level between subdivisions of a metropolitan area is a direct function of the degree of interpersonal income inequality that characterizes the area as a whole, and a direct function of the degree to which the area has been subdivided.

Insofar as per capita income by place of residence measures local tax capacity, when residential segregation by income becomes hardened and formalized by political fragmentation, the now classic local public finance dilemma is created: the divorce of public service needs from tax base. To the extent, moreover, that per capita public service needs are greater in low- than in high-income areas, the inequality of needs and means is heightened. The low-income subdivision both needs more and has less. It is useful in this regard to distinguish between the traditional general functions of local government, such as the provision of "collectively consumed" services such as public safety, justice, sanitation, and general administration, and the more obvious income redistributive activities of government, such as public assistance, free school lunches, summer camps for slum children, family counseling, and other public "social work."

These latter "welfare" programs were referred to as "the more obvious income redistributive activities" because a very substantial amount of income redistribution is carried out, less obviously, through the performance of the general functions of local government. The urban rich and poor are served by the same sewer system, fire and police departments, street cleaning trucks, and zoological park. To the extent that the tax system takes more dollars (not per cent of income) from the upper- than from the lower-income classes, some redistribution of income occurs, if the expenditure side of local public finance is considered. (This is usually not the case; typically we debate *tax* progression and regression.) The redistributive aspect of general governmental functions is far from trivial and increases with city size. In sharp contrast, the rural poor do not have as efficient and high quality a system of sewage disposal, transportation, or fire protection available to them as do their richer neighbors. One of the reasons why the poor rural migrants who settle in even the worst city slums seldom return to their home areas is the many superior public services afforded them in the city, either free or at much less than average cost.

Still, as in most subtle phenomena there are countervailing tendencies, and a net balance must be drawn. "Free" public services do not redistribute income toward the lower-income classes if the poor do not choose to consume the free service, and to the extent that they pay local taxes in any measure, these services would then redistribute income away from the poor. Urban acculturation and/or a substantial amount of formal education are prerequisite to the enjoyment of a number of local public services. Examples such as free public libraries and museums come quickly to mind.[9] Another significant group of public services requires an appreciable capital investment on the part of the citizen to complement the public capital; examples are public marinas and boat launching ramps, campgrounds reached only by automobile, and skiing areas. Most often, the local public economy cannot judge any particular public service on the basis of its independent impact on the distribution of income, so the vital question becomes that of the net income transfer from the many and diverse activities of local government.

[9] The relationship between the value of free museums and the cultural milieu has been neatly set forth by two sociologists in a different context than ours but one quite related and illuminating.

It is easy to dismiss many factors which are really life chances with the notion that the individual controls his own destiny: the statement, for instance, that class status influences one's chances to view fine art can be brushed aside with the retort that museums are free and that, if a person does not take advantage of them, it is his own fault. Such an attitude fails to take into account the power of subculture. A child reared in a slum area who does not even know about the existence of museums or who has been socialized to believe that painting is for "sissies" has different chances for art experience than one brought up in a wealthy home and taught that all respectable people know something about art.

Raymond W. Mack and Dennis C. McElrath, "Urban Social Differentiation and the Allocation of Resources," *The Annals of the American Academy of Political and Social Science,* Vol. 352, March 1964, pp. 29–30.

Urban life is much more complex and interrelated than rural life. Many functions which are performed individually in rural areas become communal functions in the city, either because they must carry coercive power to ensure that they are performed (e.g., waste disposal) or because the size and density of population affords internal or external economies of large-scale production (e.g., transportation). With local government a strong candidate for *the* "growth industry" of both the past and the coming decade, local public services bid fair to become the chief means of income redistribution in our economy. The primacy of local government in income equalization will become especially marked if large federal grants-in-aid are soon forthcoming to support both local welfare programs as such (e.g., public assistance, work relief, unemployment compensation, etc.) and the more traditional activities (e.g., education, urban mass transit, municipal water plants under the area redevelopment authority, hospitals and community health programs, and so forth).

Only if the many local governments of the metropolitan area can draw on roughly comparable tax bases can the growing need for public services be supported in each of the subdivisions at even the area-wide minimal levels that the citizenry would be willing to pay for *in toto*. And since local public services seem destined to become more and more the principal instrument for the redistribution of income, any metropolitan political fragmentation that threatens to create large per capita income disparities between local political jurisdictions should be "viewed with alarm." We need to know much more about the pattern of intrametropolitan area, intergovernmental distribution of income, tax base, and service needs. And we need also to know better the "impact and incidence" of public expenditures by income class.

Political-Financial Responsibility and the Division of Powers

While one might argue that political segregation by income is a well established fact of life in large metropolitan areas, to argue that the residents of the exclusive high-income suburb have by the very act of isolating themselves renounced any obligatory financial responsibility for the plight of the local poor is to fly in face of the fact that we have chosen as a nation to accept this responsibility. The only real question that remains is at what level of government this responsibility shall be met. The way that this question is answered has very important ramifications on the "division of powers."

The central city of the large metropolitan area typically encompasses the oldest housing and thereby serves as home for the elderly, retired, long-time resident, usually of low income, and others whose low income is a result of some disadvantage in the local labor market, for example, nonwhites, the physically handicapped, the uneducated-unskilled recent rural in-migrants. True, the wealthy suburbanite is spatially isolated from the urban poor, and by retaining local home-rule would seem to have divested himself of the welfare burden, a burden that is a clear responsibility of the whole labor market of which he is part. But the alimony enforced by the total body politic is still to come. By divorcing public service needs and tax capacity at the local level, the upper-income suburbanite has contributed to the erosion of the very foundation of local "home rule." Public welfare and other important redistributive functions of local government must eventually be transferred to some higher level of government that encompasses both rich and poor residential subdivisions—to the county, state or federal government. At least the financing must be transferred upward, the administration may be retained down below through grants-in-aid. Further, financial assistance from above may even be required to maintain adequate public service levels even in the more general public functions. More and more, the rationale of municipal government may be lost and the income-homogeneous residential enclave may come to be political in name only—confined to administering neighborhood playgrounds and residential building restrictions and planning the annual local fair. To argue otherwise is to imply that society will renege on its broad and growing welfare responsibilities, and do so in a devious way.

This is not to deny that a painful interim period of dereliction of duty on the part of government as a whole may not be in the offing, especially in pressing welfare matters. A coalition of rural and suburban legislators may stall state acceptance of the welfare responsibility and the federal government may move into the gap only very hesitantly. The relative merits to individuals and to society as a whole of, on the one hand, preserving income segregation as a residential amenity or, on the other hand, of preserving local government in a real and meaningful sense are certainly debatable and are likely to involve highly emotional value judgments. But a failure to recognize that these two urban goals are jointly incompatible and that, in the end, a choice must be made will lead to continued postponement of

120 GOALS AND PROCESSES

that decision, which is perhaps the greater evil. As in all first-rate
tragedies, a bit of wry comedy is manifest as those who are most responsible for originating and perpetuating the political income segregation cry out in anguish against the "dangerous trend toward the
centralization of government."

Repugnance to Madison Avenue values and techniques has dulled
the appreciation of economists and other social scientists for the fine
art of mass communication. And it is possible that the dissemination—
even the dramatization—of information is precisely what is at issue
here. Perhaps suburbanites do not fully realize, and have not been
forced to explicitly recognize, that their migration from the central
city has left that area with a residue of hard core unemployed, very
old and very young persons, social misfits and broken homes—in short,
an abandoned needy. Surely, they sense this vaguely but they have
never been personally and specifically confronted with the implications
of their action. Perhaps we need more to emulate than to decry powerful and persuasive advertising. Forcefully written urban poverty and
local public service findings may be every bit as critical as further
research. The degree of income redistribution is debatable, but the
proposition that the central city poor are the responsibility of the
whole local labor market of which they are rejects is not a moot point.
And this author finds it hard to believe that, under carefully docu-
mented presentation, suburbanites would explicitly renege.[10]

Typically, the affluent suburbanites are vaguely exhorted to do their
duty toward the central city poor but are not supplied with the

[10] Some indirect evidence that the well-to-do are not the ones who veto proposed
local government activities which would probably redistribute income away from
them toward lower income groups is provided by James Q. Wilson and Edward C.
Banfield in a recent empirical study, "Voting Behavior on Municipal Public Expenditures," a paper presented at the Second Conference on Urban Public Expenditures of the Committee on Urban Economics of Resources for the Future, Inc., at
New York University, February 21-22, 1964 (mimeo.).

In an examination of the voting behavior on 35 expenditure proposals passed
upon in 20 separate elections in 7 cities, they found that "the higher the income of
a ward or town, the more taste it has for public expenditures of various kinds. That
the ratio of benefits to costs declines as income goes up seems to make no difference." They recognize that "the diminishing marginal utility of money" makes tax-
paying easier for the richer taxpayer but they point out this still does not account
for the support given by the well-to-do citizens to expenditure proposals which confer only trivial benefits on them.

In an interesting extension of this work, they held homeownership, race, and
family income constant and found a negative correlation between foreign stock and
the support of public expenditures: "the percentage of Poles and Czechs is a more
important influence on voting than median family income, and is second in
influence only to homeownership."

numbers which document the case, and without these cost estimates they are free to fill the vacuum with extravagant fears about the cost of responsible action on their part. Little wonder that rejection or, at the very least, delaying tactics ensue. But with alternative welfare programs laid out and coupled with estimated budgets and tax levies per household, the fear of the unknown would be laid to rest. If all this seems naïve, one might try to answer this simple question: How much per household would a 50 per cent increase in welfare payments or a 50 per cent extension in coverage cost? Can we really assume that we are making state and local public policy on welfare matters from a base of knowledge? Economists have always been much too sanguine about the dissemination of critical information.

INTERPERSONAL INCOME INEQUALITY IN THE COMMUNITY

Residence, Education, and Economic Democracy

We now move from the metropolitan area as a whole down through the net of political subdivisions into one of its constituent municipalities. Our purpose now is to examine at much finer grain the implications of the typical clustering of residences by income class. Suppose our metropolitan area political subdivisions were large enough to mix the various income classes within them so that there was little variation in per capita income between the municipalities. With fiscal resources and public service needs roughly equalized, what further concern need we have for the spatial distribution of income?

James B. Conant has argued eloquently for the comprehensive high school that draws students from all income groups, as in the small town, seeing in it a powerful "instrument of democracy." Clearly, if a given political subdivision of a large metropolitan area is so small that it has only one high school, the full income spectrum is embraced within that school. The full spectrum, that is, of income groups residing in that political subdivision, but if the subdivision is small enough to have only one high school it may be small enough to have only a very narrow range of incomes, especially if the metropolitan area is large. This, then, is the dilemma of the large, politically fragmented metropolitan area. Only a large political subdivision will have a wide range of incomes contained within it, but a large political subdivision will have many high school districts and permits, thereby, income-segregated schools. Given American city dwellers' propensity to cluster their homes by income class and their preference for the neighborhood school arrangement, it is very difficult, in our largest urban areas, to carve out high school districts that enable our high school classrooms to remain "instruments of democracy."

If an income-mixed high school is hard to find in the large urban area, how unusual it must be to find an intermediate or grade school district that mixes income classes. Homeowners find it much easier to prevent houses of greatly different value from being sited within half-a-mile, that is, in the same grade school district, than they do trying to control residential values over the much longer reach of high school districts. Would a public policy aimed at achieving income mixing at the gross grain of the high school district be sufficient? Is finer grain income mixing worth the cost of upsetting traditional zoning and building practice?

The social gains from income mixing seem to be even greater at the lower grades than at the upper ones. Income mixing in most metropolitan areas becomes, in large part, racial integration, and in recent studies of school integration psychologists have almost invariably found that racial tolerance is much more readily learned early in life and that early-age integration experiences are very powerful in forming basic attitudes. This result stands in sharp contrast to the "reverse stair-step method" adopted to desegregate most school systems in the South, where the higher grades are desegregated first.[11] Also the grade school child probably travels farther to go to school than for any other regular purpose; the grade school district is his maximum "life space." This is much less likely to be true of the high school student. The grade school district would, ideally, bring variety to the young child, especially in the case of the slum child who has literally no contact with the mainstream of American culture if he attends a slum-only grade school.

Beyond this, the evidence is that children in slum schools drop behind at the rate of about one grade every three years. Graduates of slum grade schools are, therefore, ill prepared to mix with students from high-income neighborhoods in high school. An almost inevitable set of personal failure experiences is in store for the slum child as he moves upward in school into more income-mixed school districts. This paves the way toward despair and delinquency or, at the very least,

---

[11] See, for example, Robert Coles, *The Desegregation of Southern Schools: A Psychiatric Study,* Southern Regional Council and Anti-Defamation League of B'nai B'rith.

unemployability as a "drop-out." The current educational process is such that at least to some degree success begets success and failure leads to more failure; a bad beginning is not easily redeemed later.

Because Americans are such a long way from achieving income and/or racial mixing at the grade school, "neighborhood"[12] level or even at the high school, "community" level, at least in the larger urban areas the search for a viable short-range strategy sometimes approaches desperation.

Let us consider briefly the current "solution" of school busing between segregated neighborhoods to achieve integrated schools. The neighborhood school system is one of the most fiercely defended practices of primary education. Educators have long argued that the young pupil benefits from "the security that comes from learning and living in the same familiar environment" and they pay their respects to "the constructive community pressures on school administration." (There are others, Admiral Hyman G. Rickover for one, who are somewhat less enchanted by the typical PTA.) Even so, a number of educators who earlier criticized the busing of children to integrate schools have reversed their positions recently. James B. Conant, the dean of American education, recanted from the anti-busing position he took in *Slums and Suburbs*[13] and John A. Fischer, President of Columbia University Teachers College, shifted away from his earlier opposition to such "social engineering," arguing that while the neighborhood school should be preserved in principle it must be violated in practice "for now" to bring Negro children into the mainstream of our culture.[14]

But busing students to achieve income-mixed and ethnically mixed schools is probably not a realistic nor a comprehensive solution. We can hardly expect to bus thousands of slum children about throughout New York, Chicago, and Philadelphia, and it is often five to ten miles from the heart of the slums in these big cities to middle-class neighborhoods. Moreover, if the policy is pursued at all it is likely to be largely on a voluntary basis. Parents who will sacrifice to participate in busing are largely those who have already instilled higher aspirations

---

[12] To choose the elementary school district as the basic spatial unit of the city is, of course, quite conventional, dating back to its introduction by Clarence A. Perry in the famous Haig New York Study, *Regional Survey of New York and Its Environs, Volume VII*, Monograph One, "The Neighborhood Unit," pp. 34ff.

[13] James B. Conant, *Slums and Suburbs* (New York: McGraw-Hill Book Co., Inc., 1961), pp. 29–31.

[14] *The New York Times*, June 6, 1963, p. E-7.

in their children and have already created a good home life; voluntary transfers are more likely to help the slightly disadvantaged child than the greatly disadvantaged one.

We are a long way from solving the problem of segregated education. And since the high degree of segregation we know today is a phenomenon which has been in existence less than a generation, the long-run implications of this practice, so at variance with our socioeconomic institutions, are hard to assess. Furthermore, the possibilities of a trend toward even bigger cities and even more segregation can not be lightly dismissed.

Economists know that a large market permits greater specialization; conversely, specialization can extend the reach of the relevant market area. To cite an example pertinent to this study, the Bronx High School of Science draws students from a very wide area and was, in fact, changed from a comprehensive to a specialized high school to keep from becoming dominated by a single ethnic group in the school district.[15] Any large city might profit from the experience of this school and create excellent specialized high schools of natural science, social science, arts and humanities, and whatever else seems appropriate. These schools would be open to all residents of the city and to suburbanites (with modest tuition). Excellence of curriculum and instruction, carrying into freshman college courses, would almost surely compensate for longer bus rides to school, especially in this period of fierce scholastic competition (among parents!). Without denying the superiority of a school integration program which begins in the first grade, even a small step forward would be a welcome break in the rapid trend toward harder and narrower school segregation. And citywide high schools "segregated" by occupational interest should count as a giant step forward.[16]

---

[15] Dan W. Dodson, "Can Intergroup Quotas Be Benign?" *Journal of Intergroup Relations,* Autumn 1960, reprinted in *American Race Relations Today,* edited by Earl Raab (Garden City, N.Y.: Doubleday Anchor Books, 1962), p. 130.

[16] Gans believes that heterogeneous residential areas will produce neither a fuller democracy nor social interaction and understanding between classes. He argues that mixing different socioeconomic levels will effect, at best a "polite exchange of greetings" and that conflict is at least as probable as co-operation, and that when hard issues, like school expenditures, come up, the "fragile norms of democratic procedure sometimes fall by the wayside." But this dismal view is brightened by his own exceptions to this general position. He points out that students of social stratification "have found that ideas and values are diffused from one class to the one immediately above or below it" even if they are not transmitted over big social gaps. He also says that, while mere visual contact is of little or no value, playmates do transmit conceptions and attitudes.

It is not the intent here to probe deeply into the subtleties of residential patterns and educational policy, but only to go just far enough to suggest the relevance of socially significant questions to the economist *qua* economist at levels of areal disaggregation much finer than those to which he is accustomed. The linking of residential land-use patterns to politicoeconomic education for citizenship in a democracy is only a small part of the full case to be made for subgovernmental urban economic analysis.

Residence, Public Welfare, and Human Resource Development

Welfare policy is greatly hampered by income segregation. A good case can be made for the proposition that important progress toward resolving the problems of urban poverty—in contrast to alleviating some of their more obvious symptoms—must await a much more widespread understanding of the "culture of poverty" and that this is not learned at great distance, either social or spatial. Wanting to help is not enough, one must know how. Recent trends in public opinion on welfare questions suggest that even the present grossly inadequate programs of financial aid and counsel are in some jeopardy, largely because of the lack of any widespread first-hand knowledge of welfare problems, including the nature and needs of welfare recipients. And our current minimal programs of public assistance must become much more imaginative in long-range objectives of human rehabilitation and personal development. It is time to replace stopgap measures.

Perhaps we need to bring the upper-income classes that mold public welfare policy into closer physical proximity with the lower income classes that are the objects of that policy. The residents of the current day income-segregated large metropolitan areas probably know less about the weaknesses and potentialities of the local poor than did their parents who lived near them and mixed with them in small towns. Specifically, some questions that need testing are: Would the existence of submetropolitan communities with a wide range of in-

---

Gans' knowledgeable pessimism would not seem to undermine seriously our educational-residential strategy outlined above. Besides, our knowledge of the nature of cultural diffusion does not extend to the new programmatic situations with which we will almost certainly be soon experimenting. The impending crises of urban human resource conservation and development demand that we begin doing some of these things that can't be done. See Herbert J. Gans, "The Balanced Community: Homogeneity or Heterogeneity in Residential Areas?" *Journal of the American Institute of Planners*, August 1961.

come classes lead to more sophisticated public welfare programs that emphasized human rehabilitation and personal development? The image here is the community meeting in the high school auditorium that introduces, however nominally at first, the upper- and lower-income classes to each other. Again, if welfare families are to be judged on middle-class standards, must they not have easy access to a middle-class culture? If so, is not income mixing at the community level the *sine qua non* of achieving this exposure to expected performance?

But would a greater proximity of upper- and lower-income classes tend to reduce the tolerable level of income inequality—in a long-range developmental sense? Certainly, we cannot blithely presume a smooth transition from proximity to interaction. The very rich and desperately poor do live almost side by side in East Manhattan and along the Gold Coast in Chicago with slight salutary effect.

Yet, one can induce some inferential support for the existence of an "awareness effect." Our urban renewal program has a decided physical bias—we renew buildings to renew people, rather than the reverse—probably at least partly because the *sight* of slums offends the aesthetic sense of the upper classes as they commute through them between their suburban homes and central city workplaces.[17] (A number of observers of the cityscape have pointed out that we are in danger of losing even this mild effect, as our new depressed freeways are beginning to hide the dilapidated homes of the poor from the passing motorists.) A more intimate exposure to urban poverty would reveal the even uglier cases of tuberculosis and malnutrition hidden inside, or less dramatically just the almost invariably lower level of general health.[18]

---

[17] "While there is great variety in our city slums, most of them have one thing in common: they are eating away at the heart of the cities, especially their downtown areas. The slums would, in fact, be much easier for the cities to endure if they were off in the fringe areas." Daniel Seligman, "The Enduring Slums," *The Exploding Metropolis*, The Editors of Fortune (Garden City, New York: Doubleday and Company, Inc., 1957), p. 100. Perhaps we are fortunate that the poor are not tucked away in outlying slums, easily forgotten, until they erupt volcanically, as is true in many Latin-American cities.

[18] In a "secondary analysis" of civil defense survey data from eleven large cities compiled by the Survey Research Center of the University of Michigan, Schnore and Cowhig found the "perceived" (self-rated) health of an individual varied directly with socioeconomic status for both the 35–49 and 50 and over year age groups. The per cent of persons who reported only fair or poor health was well over twice as great in the under $3,000 family income group as in the over $5,000 group. Even greater variation was associated with educational level. Although the analysis was pursued under the implicit hypothesis that poverty leads to poor health, the authors

Perhaps if we were to drive through the houses instead—something our imaginative highway planners may yet arrange—a very real first step would be taken toward impressing the leading citizens of the metropolitan area that it is they who must ultimately assume the leadership roles if we are ever to have anything more than the superficial humanitarianism of an "urban farm policy."

With a better understanding of the nature of poverty among our community leaders our urban renewal programs might come to be coupled with a new set of welfare programs which strike at the basic problems of human rehabilitation and personal economic development, replacing current programs which merely spread cosmetic salves on these sores and soothe guilty consciences. The road to lasting slum clearance probably should begin with the physical and mental health of the slum-dwellers, proceed to education, productivity, and income, and end with grace and beauty.

This is not to deny that the heavy physical bias in our urban renewal program also follows from two hard facts of urban life and technics: first, the programs are still largely in the hands of landscape architect-city planners, and the civil engineers, who quite naturally stress the visual and engineering aspects of the problem; and second, our housing technology is so much more advanced than our human technology that we feel surer ground under our feet when we move in this direction. Still, a serious effort aimed at developing an incisive and perceptive socioeconomics of urban renewal would partly right the balance.

Unquestionably, residential proximity of a wide range of income classes will be looked upon by the affluent less as an opportunity to come to know the culture of urban poverty than as a threat to their physical safety or mental tranquility. Perhaps even more than the prospect of poorer schools, the prospect of greater exposure to communicable diseases and crime would stiffen the resistance of the affluent to even the most nominal incursions of the most impoverished group (i.e., welfare families) at the community level. It may be that the economist is poaching here on the natural hunting grounds of the urban sociologist, cultural anthropologist, urban geographer, city planner, community development specialist, and social worker. And

pointed out that a reverse causation may be just as defensible: "poor health—whether real or imagined—might so inhibit the individual's activities as to prevent the acquisition of further education and contribute to lower family income." Leo F. Schnore and James D. Cowhig, "Some Correlates of Reported Health in Metropolitan Centers," *Social Problems*, 7 (1959–60), Table 3 and p. 225.

then again, maybe the reason that fields like "housing and urban land economics" and "consumer economics" have never developed into strong academic or programmatic fields is that they never spanned a vital social content, and perhaps community-level, urban socioeconomics could open up whole new horizons to them.

Residence and Urban Economic Efficiency

The wealthier urban households tend to cluster for many reasons unrelated to local public finance. The most desirable locations, like hilltops and waterfronts, and those most convenient for commuting tend to command high prices and demand the erection of expensive homes. More commonly, income segregation is socially based as families choose their neighbors by using income as an index of desirable personal and social characteristics, and housing value as the surrogate for the unknown income. The chance that one may get a rich racketeer instead of a poor minister or professor for a neighbor is counted a small risk to run and a small price to pay for the easy applicability of the property value criterion.

A number of economies are achieved by creating residential subdivisions populated by similarly circumstanced persons. With similar incomes come similar tastes and similar consumption patterns. The relevant manifestation of this is that various shops and personal service places that cater to the "carriage trade" can be conveniently provided near the more exclusive residential areas. Specifically, urban efficiency in land use and transportation is served by clustering furriers, gourmet food shoppes, and musical instrument stores in one area, and ten-cent stores and work clothes stores in another. In personal services, the distinct clientele of tailors and pawnbrokers come to mind. These forces are mutually reinforcing. Good sites sell high, justify expensive houses with wealthy families, which in turn spawn luxury shops, all of which creates "addresses of distinction" that attract more affluent families.

This clustering to reduce the movement requirements of the household as a consuming unit is clearly consistent with the Hoyt "sector thesis"—is, in fact, a major expression of it. This thesis sees the city as a series of pie-shaped residential wedges centered on the central business district, each containing a distinct socioeconomic class. The high-income wedge, for example, holds families who cluster near each other and near their exclusive shops, clubs, private schools, and the like. The Hoyt sector thesis is, in large part, a transportation-land use model, in sharp contrast to the "concentric zone thesis" which sees the city as a series of rings, with socioeconomic class rising with each successive step outward. Since house-age decreases with distance from the core of the urban area, the concentric zone model is largely a residential depreciation model—older means poorer, newer means richer.

Accordingly, the net value of the gains in land-use-transportation efficiency that follow from residential segregation by income should be estimated to round out any judgment on the balance of total social benefits and costs associated with alternative spatial income patterns. If downtown is likely to remain the primary focus for household shopping for all income classes, the efficiency gains from income segregation will probably be negligible, but if an increasing proportion of shopping trips become local, then the advantages of having differentiated community shopping centers serving market areas with different income levels may be worth appraising with some care. In contrast, the probability of the recreation and amusement facilities of the upper income class remaining downtown is much greater—the cultural and theater districts have not shown anywhere near the same tendency to move outward. The recreation and amusement facilities of the lower-income classes, like movies and bowling alleys, may well continue to be ubiquitous or, as in the case of outdoor recreation, located outside of the built-up urban area. If recreation and amusement patterns continue much as they are now, then the efficiency case for income segregation would probably have to be made largely on retail trade and personal service grounds.

Finally, let us draw together three intraurban regions especially critical to income distribution, in descending order of probable optimum size: (1) the largest: the smallest area within which a reasonably wide range of local governmental functions can be efficiently performed (the indivisible public service efficiency unit), (2) intermediate: the smallest area within which a reasonably wide range of income classes is socially and politically feasible (the balanced income-mix unit) and, (3) the smallest: the largest area in which more than token interpersonal and social interchange can take place across culturally diverse income classes. Ideally, the third criterion would prevail in land-use planning and the first would prevail in the organization of local government, assuming that the minimum size public service efficiency unit is larger than the minimum size balanced income-mix unit. But the real need is to first quantify this or some similar set of urban organizational entities so that one can determine rough "optimums" and the cost of deviating from these optima, counting both the economist's private and social (money) costs and weighing the sociologist's pure social costs to the extent possible. Some additional background for this task will be provided in the discussions of public finance and of land use and housing in Chapters 7 and 8.

A NOTE ON PROJECTING
SPATIAL INCOME PATTERNS

A valuable analysis of urban income patterns that may prove to be reasonably operational is projection of the *coming* spatial pattern of income from *current* property values. By working methodically from the current values of the existing stock of houses to their likely depreciated values, say, ten years hence, we might infer the income of future occupants of that aged housing by applying customary home-value-to-income ratios. This would seem to be a reasonably attainable goal in all but the most rapidly changing places. Although boom towns could double or triple in size in ten years, the total stock of housing ordinarily grows very sluggishly. A gross addition to the housing stock of 2 to 3 per cent per year means that a ten-year projection begins with precise knowledge of about 70 to 80 per cent of the houses of a decade hence. The longer the time period encompassed by the forecast, the more the housing of the future date will consist of dwelling units not yet in place, and the more room there is for the current housing pattern to change, both in locational arrangement and structural characteristics.

The accuracy of housing value projections will vary widely between subdivisions of the urban area. A ten-year projection which encompasses a time period within which, say, 20 per cent of the housing stock consisted of still-to-be-built units, would be highly accurate out to the edge of the area built up at the time of the making of the projection and perhaps only barely acceptable beyond that point. Thus, it is not so much that the over-all accuracy diminishes with the length of the prediction period, but rather the area within which the projection is highly accurate (the aging structures) steadily diminishes in extent and the area within which the projection is quite tenuous (the newly built and rebuilt area) steadily increases as the time horizon is extended.

The validity of the property value projections depends primarily on the validity of the depreciation rates applied to the current values of the existing stock of houses. Recognition must be given to the construction characteristics of the houses, but perhaps even more critical and subtle is the problem of estimating the care and repair which will be accorded the various houses. A wood house need not be treated as a historic shrine to outlast a neglected brick house. Some attention must be paid to "neighborhood" characteristics and trends which would affect home maintenance through the pride of ownership and/or stability of tenure among the residents. (*The Decennial Census of Housing Characteristics* includes considerable data on a block basis.) In this regard, a rapidly growing urban area contributes a degree of uncertainty to our projections, apart from the fact that we have to deal with more unknown new additions and fewer known aging houses.

A booming urban area adds new dwelling units at a greater than average pace and thereby moves families from older to newer houses at a relatively rapid rate. (This assumes that the incoming families settle more than proportionately in the older areas.) The rapid turnover in neighborhoods, as families move outward, destabilizes social structure and probably weakens pride of homeownership and accelerates depreciation. Despite the uncertainties, a ten-year projection of the spatial pattern of residential property values seems, intuitively, to be a manageable chore. Even if we must be content with a simple ranking of neighborhoods by average property value, this largely accomplishes what we seek because we really need only describe the spatial pattern of income distribution by broad income classes. If we could just say that those households from the highest one-fifth of the income distribution will live in this area, ten years hence, and the next highest fifth in that area, and so forth, we would have achieved most of our purpose.

When we move from projected depreciated property values to projected household income levels, we need to integrate into our analysis some assumptions about trends in building and housing codes and their enforcement. Large single-dwelling units may be subdivided legally or "overcrowded" illegally, creating a neighborhood which has both more households and lower income households than "expected." Certain kinds of housing regularly develop in this direction, the aging mansion in the rapidly deteriorating neighborhood, for example. A special depreciation formula could be devised to handle this with some modest amount of empirical effort. But overcrowding is more characteristically a phenomenon of nonwhite neighborhoods, where discrimination and a perpetually tight supply of housing operate to produce a sharp jump in population density in the normal course of the filtering down of housing. Thus the forecaster of urban income patterns is ultimately forced into the new and certainly equally hazardous field of predicting trends in racial patterns in housing, a matter taken up in some detail in Chapter 8.

Today's public finance problems in the blighted central city may be tomorrow's dilemmas in many of the older and/or more hastily constructed middle-income suburbs, and these may be foretold in a projection of future spatial income patterns. Will not these suburbs, built up *en masse* in the early postwar period with $12,000 look-alike, frame and asbestos-siding houses, become the blighted areas of to-morrow (perhaps by 1975), and will not these same political entities be the ones critically deficient in public services, especially sorely pressed for public revenue because they lack the compensating rich commercial and industrial tax base of the central city? If the spatial distribution of income is of great social significance, especially in the politically fragmented large metropolitan areas, the great value of anticipating the changing spatial pattern of income is too obvious to labor—the lure of such an adventure in projection should be almost irresistible.

CHAPTER 4

Patterns of Economic Instability: Preventives and Cures

Economic instability manifests itself in at least three forms: seasonal patterns, business cycle fluctuations, and shifts in growth trends. Each is analytically interesting and distinctive in the urban context. Even so, the literature on urban economics exhibits a very uneven interest in them with the greatest attention focused on cyclical instability which is probably also the one malady of the three least susceptible to *local* treatment—most clearly a national-level problem and a federal responsibility. Accordingly, the lesser emphasis on seasonal and growth fluctuations in this chapter is simply a reflection of their relatively low stage of development, not an index of their relative importance.

These three distinct forms of instability carry very different policy implications at the local level; to complicate things further our analytical emphasis will shift back and forth between the export and local service sectors. Cyclical stability is linked to the export sector and treated as an income maintenance problem. Seasonal fluctuations in the local service sector are emphasized and analyzed as a critical problem in planning and administering the use of *existing* urban capital (social overhead). Growth instability is linked to the export sector but treated as a problem in planning *new* local service sector capacity—investment in social overhead.

"SEASONAL" PATTERNS

The seasonal pattern customarily encountered in the general literature of economics is an annual cycle largely founded on temperature variation and custom. The monthly sales curves of heating fuels and ice cream illustrate the former, the holly wreaths and firecrackers the latter. In urban economics our interest in the income generating stability of the export base serves to focus our attention on the seasonal patterns of the export products of the area. The seasonal variation in demand for the area exports may be greater than the cyclical fluctuation—tourist towns like Atlantic City and Las Vegas, for example, may experience off-peak declines in sales and employment of one-half or more. Even though it may be difficult to cite many large urban areas in which the seasonal fluctuation is comparable in amplitude to the business cycle, it is on grounds other than relative amplitude that the comparative neglect of seasonal fluctuations must be rationalized.

Urban seasonals tend to be accepted with equanimity partly because, deeply rooted in natural phenomena or basic custom, they seemed to be fixed parameters. In short, the seasonal fluctuation is seen as a fact of life. Seasonal dips in economic activity are, moreover, of short duration and the concomitant unemployment can usually be weathered by those most affected by some combination of personal savings, consumer credit, and government transfer payments (e.g., unemployment compensation, welfare). Of more recent vintage and less widespread, private *"supplementary* unemployment benefits" paid by the employer has further softened the financial blow of seasonal layoffs for those so protected. Thus, not only does regularity lend an aura of inevitability to the seasonal fluctuation, but seasonal dips are so brief and punctual that they are usually anticipated and planned for by the householder with a rationality not ordinarily characteristic of consumer behavior.

Idle Capacity and Efficiency

Even if seasonal instability were conceded not to pose a major income problem, the process of adjustment to seasonal variations may have very notable side effects. One can cite numerous examples of economic inefficiencies spawned by seasonal instability. The building trades, for example, present a classic case in both seasonal instability and in the variety of restrictive practices to which this instability gives birth. Efficiency in construction is hampered by apprenticeship fees and quotas which restrict entry into the union; efficiency is also heavily constrained by work standards which reduce workers' output and stymie technological progress, so that a given lump of work can be spread over a maximum number of workers. The effect of restrictive practices, partly induced by the heavy seasonal influence in construction, is to increase the cost of housing and lower the standard of living. Further, to the extent that an artificially high cost of housing hits hardest the lower-income groups, then the adverse effect on the *distribution* of *real* income—the slum creating force—of the construction seasonal may have even greater social import than its adverse effect on over-all economic efficiency (median income).

But the urban "seasonal" that is most dramatic is the traffic pattern. And this is, in large measure, a seasonal problem in that it is an extremely pronounced hourly fluctuation in the demand for intra-urban movement which is primarily responsible for the attack of vehicular indigestion which typically follows breakfast and precedes dinner. The hourly expression of the daily traffic pattern—using any sensible index of urban movement—is quite like the monthly expression of the customary annual seasonal pattern, especially in form and repetitiveness.

The efficiency problem generated by seasonal factors stems from the fact that heavy fluctuations in the use of fixed capital greatly complicate facilities planning. The shifts in demand that occur from day to day or hour to hour do not allow much time in which to make the necessary supply adjustments. We cannot, for example, tailor our central retail district to fit normal (October) usage and then expect it to handle the peak (Christmas) demand without suffering a substantial amount of crowding, irritating queues and other costly delays. And even if we could expand our basic retail capacity on short order in December to avoid peak inefficiency, we would still have to be able to liquidate, quickly and gracefully, the excess capacity in January, or bear the cost of carrying the maximum amount of overhead over into the slack periods. The dilemma is clear: either we must suffer inconvenience in time of peak demand to economize on capital and reduce overhead costs, or we must buy peak period convenience at the cost of maintaining capacity idle most of the year.

Stabilizing the Use of Urban Public Facilities: The Demand Side

In view of the intimate relation between seasonal variation and urban economic efficiency surprisingly little attention has been paid to the techniques and criteria of making seasonal adjustments in public capital. More explicit recognition of the need for greater flexibility in our public service facilities might serve as a catalyst to invention and innovation in this field. The current rethinking of the school year as it relates to maximum use of the school plant is at least a first tentative step in this direction. Witness the rapid growth of the "quarter" and new "trimester" systems at the college level.

The single biggest step toward breaking the traffic bottleneck might well lie more in the direction of flattening out the demand for movement than in adding to the supply of facilities to accommodate the peak movement—forever building more expressways. Certainly much of the resistance to staggering working hours is based on specious arguments. The obstacle here is partly lack of incentives; most of the benefit from your shifting your work day accrues to the rest of us. Certainly, it would be hard to argue against making a trial run with paper and pencil; juggling working hours for broad categories of employment into viable patterns, deriving the resultant new traffic "seasonal" pattern and calculating the transportation cost savings (including time) and balancing these against other losses sustained (e.g., the shortened hours of interpersonal communication for business and social purposes).

There are a number of other cases in which serious thought has been given to staggering demand or where administrative steps regularly have to be taken at critical periods. During the height of the summer drought and the peak of the seasonal demand for water (and the trough of its supply), restrictions on the use of water for inferior purposes are often put into effect; for example, lawns may only be watered after dark. Again, delayed motorists frequently and plaintively inquire why the Department of Public Works must make street repairs in the daytime during the traffic rush, when evening or nighttime repairs would achieve great savings, even at overtime wage rates if the delayed motorist's time cost is reckoned at even a fraction of its full value.

Jane Jacobs has provided us with an imaginative and challenging example of the interrelationship of urban land-use patterns and efficiency in the use of fixed capital and attending personnel. She argues for mixing primary land uses, at fine grain, largely on the grounds of creating interest, vigor and liveliness, but not without weaving economic efficiency into the argument. She cites the case of a lower Manhattan clothing store, ringed by big offices, which must do most of its business during two or three hours of the day and during only five days of the week. The image she conveys is of the sharp "contrast between the mob scene at lunch and the dullness at other times."[1]

[1] Jane Jacobs, *The Death and Life of Great American Cities* (New York: Random House, 1961), p. 155.

Again, land-use planning which leads to intense land-use specialization
—aloof culture centers, unadulterated business and financial districts,
theater enclaves and integrated shopping centers—also leads to extreme
"seasonals" in the use of streets and parking facilities.

> Downtown, the Pittsburgh Parking Authority garages are operat-
> ing at only between 10 and 20 per cent of capacity by eight o'clock
> in the evening, except for the central Mellon Square garage which
> may reach 50 per cent if something is doing at the hotels. . . . Mean-
> while the parking problem three miles from downtown in a section
> called Oakland is something fierce. . . . "It's a headache." It is also
> easy to understand. Oakland contains the Pittsburgh symphony, the
> civic light opera, the little theatre group, the most fashionable
> restaurant . . . major clubs . . . library . . . museum . . . art galleries
> . . . favorite hotel . . . all the major hospitals. . . .
> American downtowns are not declining mysteriously, because
> they are anachronisms, nor because their users have been drained
> away by automobiles. They are being witlessly murdered, in good
> part by deliberate policies of sorting out leisure uses from work
> uses, under the misapprehension that this is orderly planning.[2]

Thus Jane Jacobs argues that mixing land uses to stabilize the use of
urban capital facilities—churches abutting shopping centers to share
a common parking lot—is not just a matter of economic efficiency in
some narrow static sense, but is an integral part of an over-all strategy
for creating a viable city—a matter of *Death and Life*.

Once again, the admittedly inadequate outdoor recreation facilities
of the large metropolitan area never seem so pitifully inadequate as
on a summer week end. Given a continuing high rate of natural
increase in our population, its continued agglomeration in large
metropolitan areas, ever-increasing income and automobile ownership,
and a contracting workweek, real relief does not seem near at hand.
Yet it is not completely beyond the bounds of rationality to suggest
that some staggering of the workweek might be effected with careful
and thoughtful planning. Some businesses might experiment, at least
during the summer months, with Wednesdays off instead of Saturdays,
or Mondays off if the two-day week end is inviolable. The shortening
workweek opens new opportunities here. Certainly the problems of
co-ordination and of incentives are sizable; the only prescription sold
at this counter is for an intensive examination of the possibilities for

---

[2] *Ibid.*, pp. 170–71.

smoothing out demand (increasing the load factor) and some rough estimates of the costs and benefits which would probably follow.

Increasing the Flexibility of Urban
Public Facilities: The Supply Side

The urban managerial opportunities to achieve greater efficiency are not limited to the manipulation of demand. We have already had considerable experience in promoting greater flexibility in supplying seasonal demands for labor—high school and college students regularly clerk in department stores and deliver mail at Christmastime. Casual and part-time employment offices are to be found in most large urban areas, although this service is typically one of the less developed activities of both private and public employment agencies. Experiments have been made in smaller communities with combination policeman-fireman. While this literal "doubling in brass" is more an attempt to mesh random demand variations than true seasonal fluctuations, the objective is the same: to reduce idle capacity. This latter stratagem has been met with considerable resistance on the part of the affected employees, a quite normal human reaction to the demand for increased physical and mental effort on their part. But some extra incentive, like money, could be used to sweeten the "speed-up."

Public capital might also be made to double in brass. Greater imagination and administrative skill could turn the school plant into a much greater community asset: the high school auditorium could become a community center; the adult education curriculum of evening school could be greatly expanded beyond the typical cake decoration and millinery courses; and the high school gym could provide new adult recreational facilities and support physical fitness programs. The parks and recreation areas in the urban region are generally not outfitted for winter sports to anywhere near the degree possible. Skating rinks and toboggan slides should become as common in our parks as swings and baseball diamonds and tennis courts, with artificial rinks and snow, and hills made out of the expressway excavations,[3] if need be.

---

[3] A small "hill" of excavated earth has, in fact, become the recreational pride and distinguishing landmark of a Detroit suburb, and a playground which would otherwise be idle throughout the wintertime is now crowded with children's sleds. (Not to mention the convenience of dumping the dirt nearby the depressed expressway construction.)

LOCAL BUSINESS CYCLES

Whether a truly local business cycle of real consequence actually exists has still to be established—an autonomous local cycle, in contrast to a local reflection of the national business cycle. If the industry mix of the local economy were a mirror image, in miniature, of the national economy, we might expect their cycle patterns to be very similar, if not identical. Similarly, to the degree that the locality has a more than proportionate share of the more unstable industries, we might expect a more violent local fluctuation; to the degree that a locality has specialized in industries that lead at the turning points of the cycle, so we might expect that subarea to falter and recover first. One might argue that only if we corrected for the effect of industry mix on the local cycle might we expect to see the outlines of purely local phenomena if, indeed, any systematic residual does exist.

Whether the local cycle is or is not merely an industry-mix phenomenon, there is a local income maintenance problem of considerable social consequence. The depression phase of the business cycle, unlike the seasonal trough, persists much too long to expect the typical unemployed householder to bridge the gap by some skillful manipulation of personal finances. Cyclical instability will, therefore, be viewed here primarily as an income maintenance or poverty problem, even though the idle capacity which results—the counterpart to the unemployment—renders it analogous to the seasonal fluctuation as a source of economic inefficiency.

Alternative Concepts

Even casual reflection on the nature of the local business cycle suggests an industry-mix approach as a promising first approximation—analytically or empirically. One of the most thoroughly accepted structural characteristics of business fluctuations is that certain broad classes of industries are consistently more unstable than others—durable goods industries are more unstable than nondurables, producers' goods industries more than consumer goods—and, since the various industries are unevenly distributed spatially, we would be amazed if those areas specializing in steel, machinery, and automobiles were not considerably more cyclically unstable than those specializing in food, tobacco, and petroleum products manufacturing. The industry-mix frame of reference poses the business cycle as a national-industrial phenomenon, with the local manifestations predestined by the particular combinations of industries present.

Similarly, the export-base frame of reference also sees the local cycle as a reaction to an exogenous force. The export industries of the area import the national disturbance and transmit it to the local economy through their sales, production, and employment responses, translated into parallel fluctuations in local income payments. Obviously, the more sensitive the local export products are to cyclical swings in national expenditures, the more unstable the local flow of primary income from the export base. Thus, both the industry-mix and export-base formulations would seem to be saying, in chorus, that the local cycle can be simulated by aggregating the *national* cycle patterns of those industries represented in the local economy, weighted in proportion to their local importance (e.g., by income payments or employment).

But this inference would miss a significant subtlety. The industry-mix approach imputes to each local industry the national average decline in that industry, quite different from the export-base logic which holds that the export industries transmit to the local service sector cyclical impulses of magnitude roughly equal to the ones they receive. Assume a decline in national aggregate expenditures of 10 per cent which is reflected in a decline in local export sales of 20 per cent— because the local economy is specialized in producer durable goods, for example. The expected local slump, following the *industry-mix* approach, would be the weighted average of a 20 per cent decline in the export sector and a 10 per cent decline in the local service sector, or 15 per cent in the hypothetical local economy, as shown in the table below (column 3). The expected local slump following the *export-base* logic would, however, be 20 per cent as the local "multiplier" (= 2) spreads

Industrial Sector	National average decline in income generated (per cent)	Prosperity level of local income (dollars)	Expected decline in local income under: industry-mix logic (dollars)	export-base logic (dollars)
Manufacturing	20 ⟶	50 ⟶	10 ⟶	10 ⟶
Local service	10 ⟶	50 ⟶	5	10 ⟵
		100	15	20

the 20 per cent decline in exports throughout the whole local economy. That is, the 20 per cent cutback in manufacturing output and employment is translated first into a similar decrease in the income and spending of manufacturing workers and then into a parallel reduction in the income of local doctors, lawyers and merchant chiefs and subsequently into a similar reduction in their spending, and so on and on. In the end, everyone has received and spent roughly 20 per cent less than during the preceding prosperity peak.

In essence, the industry-mix logic imputes to the locality the national cycle patterns, industry-by-industry, with the local aggregate cycle being summed from these weighted components. The export-base logic, however, imputes to all local industries a cycle pattern which duplicates the *export* sector cycle pattern. Consequently, the export-base theory would predict greater over-all stability for an urban economy specializing in, say, cigarettes than would the industry-mix approach, and a greater aggregate instability for, say, a steel labor market. By casting the local business cycle as the lengthened shadow of the export industry, the export-base theory imputes a probable deviation from the national aggregate performance of greater magnitude than does the blander industry-mix concept.

City Size, the Multiplier, and Relative Stability

The relation between the size of the urban economy and its stability deserves careful review because a number of deductive traps are hidden here for the unwary. The economic-base theory, when used in a cyclical context, is a special application of Keynesian economics to a small-area, open economy, differing mainly in that the principal exogenous force which effects change is now exports, rather than investment.[4] The Keynesian analytical framework recognizes both investment and exports as exogenous, income determining forces, but the high degree of self-sufficiency of the large national economy, such as the United States, results in fluctuations in investment expenditures which far outweigh the amplitude of change exhibited by exports, when both are expressed in absolute terms. As the regional subdivisions of the national economy become smaller and smaller, regional investment

[4] The best conceptual and analytical work on the local multiplier has been done by Charles M. Tiebout and a decade of his work culminates in his excellent little monograph, *The Community Economic Base Study*, Committee for Economic Development, December 1962, Chapter 6. He has manipulated a much more complicated and realistic local multiplier than the one developed below. The choice was made here to pursue the nature and sources of local cycles in breadth rather than pursue the multiplier in depth, so Tiebout's recent study is complementary.

expenditures tend to average out to the national proportion, but with self-sufficiency diminishing, regional imports and exports take on greater relative importance. Exports probably account for as much as one-half of local economic activity in the smaller urban areas of, say, 50,000 population or less.

Since changes in exports come to greatly exceed (in absolute magnitude) changes in investment expenditures as we move down to the urban region, we come to think of local cycles more as export cycles, just as we think of national cycles more as investment cycles. Local investment expenditures, moreover, do not have a local income generating effect unless they are spent for locally produced capital goods. The tools and machines purchased by a local firm are probably supplied from external sources more often than not, especially in the smaller urban economies. (No such caution is needed in national analysis except for the minute proportion of producer durable equipment which is imported from abroad.) Local construction, however, can be netted down to local value added (local sales receipts minus material purchases from outside) with probably as favorable a ratio of local income generated to sales receipts as typifies local export products, on the average.

A local income (employment) "multiplier" can be computed which relates the change in the principal exogenous variable, export income (employment), to the derivative change in local service industry income (employment). In the national income model, the size of the multiplier is determined largely by the size of the savings "leakage"; the multiplier is the reciprocal of the "marginal propensity to save," where the latter is defined as the ratio of a change in saving to the change in national income that was necessary to produce that change in saving. In the export-based, small-area economy, the multiplier is again the reciprocal of the rate at which income leaks out of the internal circular flow of income and expenditure. In this latter case, however, the multiplier is largely determined by the reciprocal of the marginal propensity to import; for local imports, not savings, are now the important income leakage. (This simple model ignores all tax drains.) Reduced to its essence, the exports of the local economy pump in a flow of income (and thus provide jobs). This income, to the extent that it is used to purchase local goods, remains in the local economy for another round of spending and creates secondary income (more jobs) in the local service sector. To the extent that the export-derived net income is spent by employee-consumers for imports, the income flows back out of the local economy with no secondary or further effects. And an equilibrium level of local income is achieved when the rate of in-flow through the export pump equals the rate of out-flow through the import drain.

Imports constitute a leakage of income, which if retained would lead to further rounds of spending and income generation. Thus it appears that a *low* propensity to import would be in the local interest during periods of national expansion. On the other hand, a decline in local income is largely translated into a reduced rate of local spending on imported goods in periods of national contraction and declining local exports. Thus, if there is a *high* marginal propensity to import, the unemployment creating effect of the reduced local spending is more shifted onto outside business and less passed on to the local service sector—all to the good from the local viewpoint. All of this means that a low marginal propensity to import sets the stage for export impulses to ricochet, at length and in strength, around the local economy creating substantial cumulative, parallel changes in total local income and employment, both upward and downward—creating a high local multiplier. But does a higher local multiplier imply greater local instability?

In the first two chapters we noted that larger urban economies tend to produce a much richer range of goods for themselves as they achieve local markets whose size can support ever more esoteric products. In our present context, this can be translated into the statement that the marginal propensity to import tends to decrease with increased city size. From this one might quickly infer that the export multiplier would be larger in large urban economies and then, too quickly, further infer that a given cyclical fluctuation in the export sector would produce a greater derivative total effect in the large city.

The resultant of this deductive chain would seem to be that large cities should be more unstable than small ones. But this would contradict casual observation and common sense. A confusion between absolute and relative magnitudes must be carefully avoided. The multiplier effect does increase with increased city size, in absolute terms. A given absolute reduction in export income and employment in a New York metropolitan area firm would cause a comparatively large absolute amount of derivative unemployment because a large fraction of the reduced export income would lead to reduced consumption spending by New Yorkers for New York produced consumer goods and services. The amount of derivative unemployment produced in Binghamton by an equivalent absolute decline in export employment would be less because a much larger proportion of local consumption spending is for externally produced consumer goods (imports). But the counterpart of a lower propensity to import is a lower propensity to export—a smaller share of employment making export products. Moreover, under the simplest and most reasonable set of assumptions, the larger city's higher multiplier is *exactly* offset by a lower export orientation, to the net effect that a given proportionate change in the export base of large and small urban economies would effect exactly the same proportionate change in the total level of total activity in the two economies.

All this can be made quite explicit by a simple numerical example, as shown in the table below. The relationship between total local income (Y_L) and its allocation between local expenditures on locally produced goods and services (C_L) and local expenditures on imports (M) is given for three levels of local income. Turning first to the small urban economy shown at the left, we note that one-half of local income

Small Urban Economy (say, 50,000 pop.)				Large Urban Economy (say, 500,000 pop.)		
Y_L	C_L	M		Y_L	C_L	M
$110	$55	$55 million		$1,100	$825	$275 million
100	50	50		1,000	750	250
90	45	45		900	625	225

$$\frac{M}{Y} = .5 \text{ and } \frac{\Delta M}{\Delta Y} = \frac{5}{10} = .5 \qquad\qquad \frac{M}{Y} = .25 \text{ and } \frac{\Delta M}{\Delta Y} = \frac{25}{100} = .25$$

$$k = \frac{1}{\frac{\Delta M}{\Delta Y}} = \frac{1}{.5} = 2 \qquad\qquad k = \frac{1}{\frac{\Delta M}{\Delta Y}} = \frac{1}{.25} = 4$$

$$\Delta E \times k = \Delta Y \qquad\qquad \Delta E \times k = \Delta Y$$
$$-5 \times 2 = -10 \qquad\qquad\qquad -25 \times 4 = -100$$

a 10 per cent change in exports effects a 10 per cent change over all

$$\frac{-5}{50} = \frac{-10}{100} = -.10 \qquad\qquad \frac{-25}{250} = \frac{-100}{1,000} = -.10$$

is spent on local goods and services and creates new local income and one-half is spent on imports and leaks out of the local economy, at each level of income. That is, the *average* propensity to import (API) is constant at .5. Further, changes in local income of $10 million lead to changes in imports of $5 million, so that the community's *marginal* propensity to import (MPI) is also .5. The export multiplier (k) in this economy is 2; $1 in new income generated by increased export sales will create an additional $1 in income in the local service sector, or a total of $2 in new income.

Turning now to the large urban economy at the right, we note that a much larger proportion of local income is spent for locally produced goods and services (3/4), and a much lower proportion is spent on imports (1/4), on the average, reflecting the wider range of goods and services available locally in the large urban area. The marginal propensity to import is again assumed to be equal to the *API*, and the multiplier has now risen to a value of 4. Does this higher multiplier imply greater cyclical instability? No, because an interesting structural property, implicit in the assumption that $MPI = API$, operates to precisely counteract the rising multiplier with a proportionally declining multiplicand, nullifying the effect of city size. Specifically, as the urban area grows in size and becomes more self-sufficient, the propensity to import falls, increasing the multiplier, but the propensity to export— the orifice through which the cycle shock enters—also declines in relative size, decreasing the multiplier effect, such that the product of the two cyclical forces remains constant:

$$\frac{1}{\dfrac{M}{Y}} \times \frac{E}{Y} = \frac{E}{M} = 1 \ \ (\text{where: } \frac{M}{Y} = \frac{\Delta M}{\Delta Y} \text{ and } E = M)$$

The net result of the assumption that $MPI = API$ is that the per cent change in total income is identical with the per cent change in export income.

$$\Delta E \times \frac{1}{\dfrac{M}{Y}} = \Delta Y$$

$$\frac{\Delta\, EY}{\Delta MY} = \frac{\Delta Y}{Y} \ \ (E = M)$$

$$\frac{\Delta E}{E} = \frac{\Delta Y}{Y}$$

That is, a 10 per cent fluctuation in export income in either the small or the large urban economy effects a 10 per cent change in total income, despite the widely divergent multipliers, as shown at the bottom of the example above.

How reasonable is this assumption that the community's division of its next dollar between imports and local consumption is roughly the same as the division of all its dollars, on the average, up to its current level of income—the assumption that the average equals the marginal propensity to import? We can assume that during the period of a cycle lasting a year or so the population of the community is fairly constant and that changes in aggregate local income are largely changes in per capita income, rather than additions to the number of persons with income. We must be prepared to modify this position to the degree that a cyclical up-turn expands local income by putting the unemployed to work, but even here this previously unemployed group pre-existed in the community—occupied housing, absorbed school space and consumed local services of many kinds, out of savings, consumer credit and/or public assistance payments—so that this too is basically a per capita income change, albeit from a very low level. Again, to the degree that cyclical swings lead more to alternating periods of short workweeks and overtime earnings, our per capita income change assumption is even more valid. If, then, per capita income changes, more than employment changes, characterize a given local cycle, our inquiry should be directed to the relative income elasticities of demand for imports versus locally produced goods and services.

Are imports more the luxury or more the necessity goods? Or, perhaps more to the point, are imports more or less durable, on the average? Imports tend to be more income-elastic the more weakly felt the want for them and the more durable (postponable) they are. And the more income-elastic the demand for imports, the higher the cyclical marginal propensity to import and the lower the local multiplier. Are local imports, in fact, more income-elastic; is spending on imports subject to sharper and heavier cutbacks and surges over the cycle?

But deduction fails us here. For every income-elastic import (e.g., automobiles and tourism) one can cite, one can come up with an income-inelastic import (e.g., food, cigarettes, and fuel). And for every income-elastic local good or service (e.g., entertainment, restaurant dining, and home repairs), one can cite a likely income-inelastic one (e.g., rent, utilities, and local transportation). This is unlike the case of the Keynesian (national) multiplier, where we have a clear intuitive feeling, good deductive presumption, and some reasonably good empirical evidence that consumption (the counterpart to expenditures on local goods) is income-inelastic and savings (the counterpart to imports) is income-elastic. We cannot, therefore, have any sure feeling for the shape of the local-consumption-of-local-production function or the local propensity to import.

But perhaps we have pressed too hard and too far, for the local cycle is not purely an export cycle, as is developed in the appendix to this chapter. Let it suffice here that we have demonstrated that there seems to be no deductive presumption, via a *simple* Keynesian model, in favor of any systematic functional relationship between size and stability, despite the fact that the multiplier varies directly with size. The multiplier and the "base-to-service" ratio tend to cancel out, leaving the relative change in the base as a critical factor. If the relative stability of local exports is more the key to over-all local cycle stability, then analysis of the local export industry mix may be a more promising avenue of inquiry than the difficult task of quantifying the local multiplier. We turn now to the industry-mix factor, first in a general way, and then in more depth and detail.

City Size, Industrial Structure, and Relative Stability

Clearly, increased city size brings greater industrial diversification, but does diversification bring cyclical stability? A diversified or "balanced" industry mix has long been venerated as the key to economic stability, but whether this reputation is deserved has still to be established.

Economic fluctuations, as we have noted, can be classified as seasonal, cyclical, and growth instabilities. *A priori,* the case for industrial diversification as a stabilizing device would seem to hold varying promise. Seasonal patterns of the various industries are probably randomly distributed, that is, there are roughly as many seasonals with winter peaks as with summer peaks. The significance of diverse timing, if true, is that complementary industries are not hard to pair—meshing "coal and ice" businesses is a practicable planning goal. Even unplanned, random diversification is likely to effect a substantial reduction in local seasonal instability.

Industry growth trends are probably also randomly distributed in time. A narrowly specialized urban economy may be dominated by industries which are secularly young or mature or decadent. Accordingly, industrial specialization offers both the prize of maximum growth and poses the threat of local stagnation and decay, depending on time and the "luck of the draw." Or, if a given urban society has strong aversion to risk, it may, at least conceptually, compound an industry mix of complementary growth trends. Even random diversification becomes a form of long-range hedging; the more heterogeneous the industry mix, the more stable the industrial growth rate.

But cyclical instability seems to pose a quite different and more difficult planning problem. The cycle peaks and troughs of the various industries are not randomly distributed in time, instead they are quite similar in timing. Otherwise, of course, there could not be an aggregate business cycle. Therefore, any given urban economy is restricted to the limited choice of various sets of industries with aggregate cycle amplitudes of greater or lesser degree. Even this imputes to the local economy far too much free will in that many of the theoretically possible sets are incompatible with the indigenous economic environment; besides all urban areas cannot possess the relatively few stable industries. Industrial diversification, then, seems to be an averaging process which will better or worsen the cyclical stability of the local economy, depending on whether the cycle amplitudes of existing local industry are greater or less, respectively, than those of the industries to be added. That is, industrial diversification leads toward a cycle pattern approximating that of the national economy—an improvement for Detroit but probably not for Washington, D.C.

The tentative hypothesis, then, is that large urban economies tend to have diversified industrial structures and, therefore, tend to replicate the national degree of cyclical instability; the smaller urban economies exhibit a much greater range of cyclical instability, as some tend to specialize in the more unstable and some in the more stable industries. The expected relationship between city size and cyclical stability, assuming that size randomizes the local industry mix, is shown schematically in Figure 5.[5] (The curved regression line is explained on page 160.)

Figure 5. City size and cyclical stability.

[5] McLaughlin found no statistically significant correlation between local "industrial concentration" (percentage of value added by manufacture in the five largest local industries) and cyclical decreases in value added in manufacturing in the 1919 and 1921 recessions. Glenn E. McLaughlin, "Industrial Diversification in American

The Demand Side: Nature of the Cyclical Impact

The most direct way to evaluate the cyclical sensitivity of an urban economy is to study the character of the area's export industries. And the place to begin is with the dynamics of the demand for their products. If we accept the export-base theory, at least in a cyclical context, the local business cycle can be clearly traced to the instability of the external demand for area exports, and a familiar economic concept, income elasticity of demand, becomes the heart of the matter.[6] A product has an income-elastic demand if the quantity purchased varies more than in proportion to the change in the buyer's income, and the demand is income-inelastic if the change in quantity purchased is less than proportionate to the income change. Clearly, a local economy which exports income-elastic products such as automobiles, high-style furniture, and tourist services is likely to feel the augmented force of changes in national business conditions; a local economy which trades in income-inelastic goods such as tobacco products, staple foods, and space-heating fuels will probably ride out the storm in fairly good shape.

But this concept is little more than a tautology if we go no further than to say that a more than proportionate fall in local export sales causes a more than proportionate fall in total local income. What caused local export sales to be so sensitive to income changes? The "income elasticity of demand" can be traced back to a number of basic attributes which may or may not be relevant in any given case: (1) the quality or style line of the good, whether "deluxe" or "economy" model, (2) its durability in use and/or time, (3) its use, whether consumer or producer good, (4) its position in the stage of production, whether final or intermediate good.

The likely ramifications to a local economy of producing a high-style or deluxe-model product are obvious: the external demand for the good expands very rapidly during periods of cyclical expansion and falls off precipitously in periods of concentration, as "discretionary

---

Cities," *Quarterly Journal of Economics*, Vol. 45 (1930), pp. 131–49, especially pages 148–49. Rodgers also tested the relationship between degree of manufacturing diversification and cyclical variation for 12 urban areas in Pennsylvania over the period 1925 to 1950. The coefficient of linear correlation was .22, not significant. While both McLaughlin and Rodgers were forced to use very rough measures of cyclical variation and industrial diversification and their findings should be treated as preliminary, they do confirm our *a priori* expectation. Allan Rodgers, "Some Aspects of Industrial Diversification in the United States," *Economic Geography*, Vol. 33 (1957), pp. 16–30, especially p. 27.

[6] See Chapter 1, footnote 18.

income" undergoes its wide swing. The demand for the economy model neither expands nor contracts nearly so much in response to income changes, and in special cases sales of the economy model could even increase slightly in downswings, as demand shifts from the deluxe model.

The durability of the good is perhaps the most important characteristic of all. Durables such as automobiles, refrigerators, and furniture can always be made to last just a little longer with only a slight reduction in the efficiency with which they perform their services. To postpone the purchase of a bright and shiny new durable, and make the still-serviceable old one last a little longer, is probably the easiest consumption retrenchment that a consumer can make when his income declines. The fundamental concept here is that of inventory accumulation and depletion. During a period of national prosperity, the customer builds up his inventory of unused automobile mileage by trading in his old used car for a new unused car, and during depressions he draws on his inventory of unused mileage by running his car without replacement, or with only partial replacement in the form of minor repairs. The very pronounced durable good fluctuation is essentially founded on the ability of the buyer to bunch his purchases, in time, by manipulating his inventory of that good. And, of course, only goods which can be stocked—durables—can be so manipulated.

Shifting to budgetary constraints, one can argue, by looking to the likely pattern of consumer retrenchment, that durables perform most poorly relative to nondurables in recessions and not quite so badly in deep depressions. The first 5 per cent decline in family income may be taken largely out of savings, the next 5 per cent largely out of durable good replacements, but very shortly the point is reached where the next bite must come out of nondurables. If the average life span of consumer durable goods is, say, ten years (automobiles, furniture, appliances), about one-tenth of the total stock is normally replaced each year. The cutback in durable good expenditures, through postponements, could at the very most run to about 10 per cent of the value of the stock. Any declines in income beyond the amounts that can be absorbed out of savings and making do with existing durables must then be taken out of nondurables and services. This suggests that urban economies which specialize in durable goods should, other things equal, tend to show much sharper amplitude variations in recessions and be at a much lesser disadvantage in depressions, relative to those urban economies specializing in nondurables and services. Since, moreover, the true depression may well be a thing of the past and the "inventory recession" (including consumer inventories) the common current manifestation of the national business cycle,[7] the trend clearly favors the nondurable and service-oriented urban economies over the durable good specialists.

The first two points are additive. An urban area specializing in a nondurable necessity (e.g., canned foods) should be the most stable and an area specializing in a durable luxury good (e.g., ironers and outboard motors) the most unstable. The areas producing nondurable luxuries (e.g., entertainment) and durable necessities (e.g., washing machines) should fall somewhere in between.

We might also distinguish between local economies on the basis of whether their exporters' customers are households or other businesses. Business cycle literature has always emphasized the extreme instability of the producer durable goods industries, and by implication the areas that specialize in such products as steel, machinery, and instruments should be the most unstable. While a major element of this instability is the durable aspect, another major part of the explanation lies in the producer as the customer. The basis here is simply the much greater variability of investment expenditures. A decline in national income will prompt a cut in consumption expenditures of a somewhat lesser amount than the fall in income, the difference coming out of reduced savings and tax liabilities. On the other hand, gross private investment expenditures may be cut back, in relative terms, much more —even to zero. Investment decisions reflect anticipations which can fluctuate wildly. While such an extreme reaction is reserved for the deepest depressions (gross private domestic investment fell from $16 billion in 1929 to less than $1 billion in 1932), the relative variation in investment expenditure is typically two or three or even half-a-dozen times that for consumption expenditures.[8]

A second, probably less significant, facet of the distinction between consumer goods and producer goods lies in comparative inventory policies and source of supply patterns. If businesses, more than households,

[7] See the Addendum to this chapter, Table 4.1. The future role of inventories in business cycles is hard to assess: improvements in technology, especially in the speed of transportation (e.g., air freight) and in inventory control (e.g., electronic data processing), tend to reduce the size of stocks, while increasing affluence leads to more product differentiation and the need for larger stocks.

[8] See the Addendum to this chapter, Tables 4.1 and 4.2 and surrounding text. For an elementary discussion of the relative role of investment in generating business fluctuations, see any national income or business cycle text, for example, Wallace C. Peterson, *Income Employment and Economic Growth* (New York: W. W. Norton and Co., Inc., 1962), pp. 84ff and 216ff, and the *National Income Supplement to the Survey of Current Business.*

tend to reduce the impact of a cyclical change in their income by complementary accumulation or depletion of inventories, they do so only by transmitting a magnified cyclical impulse to their suppliers. Consequently, the sellers of producer goods would experience greater inventory cycles than the sellers of consumer goods. Conversely, if businesses are more inclined than households to speculate in inventories by buying in excess of current needs in periods of low prices (recessions) and unloading inventories when prices are high (prosperity), then businesses will tend to absorb cycle shocks more and soften those they transmit, such that producer goods sales would tend to be more stable than sales of consumer goods, holding durability and other factors constant.

Perhaps it is just as significant to distinguish the use to which the product is put as it is to distinguish the character of the buyer. For example, a good deductive case can be made for the likelihood of greater instability of those urban areas which export intermediate goods than those which sell final goods. (We will ignore the raw material case because urban economies perform very little extractive activity.) The argument hinges on two points. First, inventories of intermediate goods are likely to be larger because they are less subject to style and do not therefore pose problems of loss of value through obsolescence. And large inventories permit greater contractions in current purchases through inventory depletion. The confidence in this argument is somewhat shaken by the knowledge that style (product differentiation) may make it necessary to carry very large inventories of finished goods to be able to satisfy the variegated and less predictable demands. But a second point is less ambiguous. Intermediate goods—semifinished products—are often purchased by a few, large, final-product plants from a number of small suppliers, including one of their own divisions or subsidiaries. The big firm's practice of supplying part of its own needs—"tapered vertical integration"[9]—results in extreme instability for the small firms which supply the marginal portion of their customers' needs because, obviously, when the customer firm's sales decline the full cutback will normally be passed on to the outside firm, while output in the captive source of supply will be

[9] For an elementary and interesting account of "tapered vertical integration" in a particular industry, see Donald A. Moore, "The Automobile Industry," *The Structure of American Industry* (New York: The Macmillan Company, Revised Edition, 1954), pp. 297–98. Moore points out the value of this practice to the big automobile manufacturer in stabilizing his captive source of parts, but our interest lies equally in the fact that an augmented cycle impact is shifted on to the small independent supplier.

maintained. Urban economies based on marginal supplies, for what-ever reason, are in a cyclical position similar to the low seniority worker.

Market Structure of the Export Industries: Nature of the Cyclical Adjustment

Our demand analysis should be complemented with a dissection of the supply side of the export base.

In our analysis of the level of income in the second chapter, the degree of competition in the export product market was held to be a most important factor—oligopolistic export industries enrich the locality. Once again, the market structures of the principal export industries is a factor but more ambivalent now. The local impact on employment of a given decrease in demand for a local export may be a significant function of the degree and kind of competition that characterizes that industry. If the industry is highly competitive, the chances are that the product price will decline and this price decline will tend to take some of the impact of the decline in demand off of production and employment. Buyers will not cut back their purchases quite as much—in physical units—if the price falls appreciably. Con-versely, if the local export firm is an oligopolist and administers its price in tacit collusion with a few nonprice "competitors," a decrease in demand will most likely be met with rigid prices and the full impact of the decrease will be absorbed by a reduction in production and employment. Other things equal, local employment holds up much better in competitive industries than in oligopolistic ones, given parallel declines in demand for the two.

This conclusion has to be qualified by the assumption that the firm failure rates are approximately equal in both market structures. But the oligopoly is more likely to survive a protracted or deep de-pression, both because its price power probably enabled it to build up cash reserves in the previous prosperity period and also because it is typically bigger and has easier access to sources of credit in an emergency. In contrast to employment, the value of output (price times quantity sold) will probably fall less (assuming price-inelastic demand) if prices are administered. However, if the firm is largely absentee owned, value added and paid out locally will be confined largely to wages and salaries; the value of administered prices would then accrue mainly to the absentee owners, except again, to the extent that the avoidance of failure saves local jobs.

Generally, the oligopolist handles a larger and more diverse line of products than the smaller competitive firms, for a variety of reasons: (a) the big firm is often constrained to a self-imposed nonprice competition and this stimulates product differentiation; (b) the big firm can push research and development harder and typically is in an industry characterized by a complex and rapidly advancing technology; (c) the big firm, typically with a high rate of return, widespread share ownership and managerial control of dividend policy, has a large source of captive capital (still maintaining reasonable dividends) which is freely available for reinvestment in new fields; (d) the big firm more often gains tax advantages through mergers. To the extent that a number of the big firm's many products are produced in the local plant, local employees will find their employment more diversified and more stable.[10]

Does oligopoly in the export sector tend to stabilize or destabilize the local income stream over the business cycle? Some quantification of the forces described above, enough so that we might strike some rough net balance, would constitute a useful addition to our knowledge of local business cycles.

Structure of the Local Labor Market and Its Effects on Wage Policy

Like the national product markets in which the local export firms sell their goods, the local factor markets from which these same firms draw their productive resources, especially labor, may be classified by their degree of competition and price flexibility. A unionized labor market is typified by a rigid wage rate and a perfectly elastic supply of labor—"$2.50 per hour take it or leave it," with all the workers you want at that price and none for less. A priori, the effect of union-imposed wage rigidity on local employment over the cycle is not

[10] This assumes that labor mobility between industries (products) and occupations, within a given local labor market, is smoother and easier if accomplished within a single, large, multiproduct firm than it is if the movement must take place between different employers. Presumably, a single management is better able to anticipate changing skill requirements and to shift workers around strategically, including arranging the necessary retraining, than is society in some collective way, as through public employment agencies and public adult education programs. This question is pursued at greater length in Chapter 6.

clear. Certainly, unless wages fall, prices can fall but little, even without administered product prices. With profits typically accounting for perhaps 5 per cent of the sales dollar in prosperous periods, a slim and declining profit margin in recession leaves little room for price cuts. (A profit margin of 5 per cent on sales may, of course, yield a very handsome rate of return on investment, but price flexibility not firm profitability is the issue here.)

Wage rate and product price cuts, moreover, have an ambiguous effect on local employment. While purely local reductions might effect significant increases in output and employment, depending on the elasticity of demand for the local export product, such a case as can be made locally generalizes very poorly, as competing local economies match the local price cuts to regain their lost market shares. Viewed collectively, wage rates that are cut everywhere reduce labor income and purchasing power, thereby wiping out most of the consumption leverage households might have gained through lower product prices. The chief rebuttal one might offer here is that the purchasing power of accumulated savings is increased, but augmented "discretionary savings" are probably dust in the balance for the great majority of households; consumer surveys suggest that anticipations are even more critical, and consumers are most conservative in periods of high and/or rising unemployment. Thus local price cuts, like price wars in oligopoly, are usually futile expansionary devices and even the parochial case for them breaks down. Wage cuts in depression, once regarded as an integral part of any effective expansionary program, have not been seriously considered by economists to be promising or even rational for over a decade now,[11] not to mention the inescapable fact that such action is unrealistic under widespread and militant trade unionism.

The further possibility of labor cost reductions through increased labor productivity is, if possible, even less promising as a depression remedy. In the short run, increased labor productivity would probably have to come, in large measure, out of a "speed-up"—using the term without prejudice to the speed at which the employees were

---

[11] The great debate on whether the Keynesian underemployment equilibrium rests on wage (and price) rigidities and the efficacy of wage cuts as depression policy dates back to the prewar and early postwar period of the Keynesian Revolution. Great elaboration of minor technical points did little to dislodge the main point to be made, clearly stated from the beginning: "What is overlooked . . . is the fact that the wage reduction is a two-edged sword. On the one side it cuts down costs, but on the other side it equally reduces demand," Alvin Hansen, *Fiscal Policy and Business Cycles* (New York: W. W. Norton and Co., Inc., 1941), p. 334.

working previously. But a local increase in output per man-hour of, say, 10 per cent would lower the labor cost component by 10 per cent but total costs by only one-half that amount in most cases—material costs are a major item, interest is a contractual obligation, profits may have already been squeezed to very low levels or may be negative. With productivity up by 10 per cent, consumption of the good would have to increase by over 10 per cent in response to a price decline of, say, 5 per cent before any expansionary effect on employment would be felt. Demand elasticities of 2 and over (a 10 per cent increase in quantity purchased divided by a 5 per cent decrease in price) are probably not common.

The tentative conclusion is that a protracted analysis of the supply side of the local labor market is neither likely to yield rich insights into the foundations of local cyclical instability nor to guide the way to rational and effective local stabilization policy. This judgment stands out in clear contrast to the leading role accorded the study of the local labor market in the matter of the level of income (Chapter 2), and the dismissal here of the labor-wage factor in the analysis of local depressions does not extend to problems of local stagnation and the problems of "depressed areas" (Chapter 1). Other aspects of the structure of the local labor market, equally significant in depressed-area growth economics, are also of marginal importance in local cyclical analysis and policy. For example, out-migration, a prime policy option for a depressed area, is not a very real local option in time of depression—migrants must not only go *from*, they must also go *to*. Even in the absence of the customary provincial resistance to any program which would deflate the size of the local community, a policy of encouraging out-migration of the unemployed residents is stymied by the fact that nearly all areas are suffering unemployment.

The Organizational Characteristics of Local Business

The organizational characteristics of local export firms themselves, as distinct from the competitive characteristics of the supraregional product markets in which they sell, deserve careful attention. We might, among other factors, look into: (1) the relative age of local firms, (2) whether they are single-plant firms or branch plants of multi-plant firms, and (3) their financial structure.

Local firms may be among the most or least unstable within their industries, depending on their costs and customers. The hypothesis that older firms, with the marginal (high-cost) productive facilities, may be the most unstable has been advanced as a possible basis for predicting greater cyclical instability for the older industrial areas that host them (e.g., various subeconomies of New England). Presumably, the higher cost firms cut back production or close down first in recession and then rebound only after the recovery has proceeded far enough to raise prices high enough to cover their higher costs.[12]

The multiplant firm presents a greater range of local cycle pattern possibilities than does the single plant firm. A 10 per cent decline in production has a clear and certain impact on the latter, but the local representative of a multiplant firm might be the least efficient of, say, ten plants and be shut down, or be the most efficient and continue almost unaffected. Or perhaps the local plant produces the luxury line of the product and suffers the most, or produces the economy line which holds up well. The spatial position and relative transportation costs of the local plant may be all important in the role it is assigned over the cycle in the light of managerial considerations that are weighed outside of the local economy. Thus the range (and standard deviation) of cyclical possibilities is greatly widened for the urban economy which is based on multiplant export operations, even though the mean expectation may be very much like that for urban economies founded on single plant firms. We distinguish here, of course, from the much narrower range of cyclical amplitudes that would characterize the multiplant firm as a whole due to the hedging effect of geographical dispersal and product differentiation and diversification.

We argued above that large urban areas would tend to exhibit about the same average instability as smaller areas but a narrower range of instability (Figure 5). To the extent, moreover, that large urban areas have plants of both single-plant and multiplant firms, they will also experience more average cycles. Conversely, small places are much more likely to run the gamut of cyclical fluctuations by having only the most stable or the least stable plant(s) of a multiplant firm(s) or largely single-plant firms in the middle. In sum, then, the smaller urban places tend to have either the stable or the unstable industries

---

[12] This author's appreciation of greater cyclical fluctuation of the older, high-cost facility traces back to an article written a decade ago, Irvin Sobel, "Collective Bargaining and Decentralization in the Rubber Tire Industry," *Journal of Political Economy*, February, 1954. Sobel pointed out that in the rubber tire industry the Akron plants are, of course, the original facilities and a labor productivity differential in their favor of about 30 per cent in the twenties turned to a 10 per cent differential against them by 1947 so that increasingly "the Ohio plant capacity is treated as a cushion to absorb any seasonal or cyclical changes in demand" (p. 21).

and either the stable or unstable plants, while the large urban areas tend to mix both industries and plant types.

Finally, the financial characteristics of the local firms and the nature of the local financial industry must not be overlooked. The depression staying-power of a firm depends on both the capital structure of the firm and its access to sources of funds. The firm which is largely equity (stock) financed is least likely to go under in depression because dividends can be passed by, whereas interest on debt capital (bonds, notes, bank loans) must be met on time, regardless of earnings. Not only is a high proportion of equity capital an intrinsic source of strength, but it also provides a thick ownership interest as a protective cushion sheltering potential suppliers of emergency credit—unencumbered assets as collateral on which to borrow. What is the "local economics" of all this? The capital structure and viability of local firms is not fully fashioned by managerial attitudes and financial proclivities; local financial facilities and practices play an important role too. If local equity capital is relatively abundant, especially during the early precarious years of the firm's life cycle, local businesses will almost certainly grow up with better balanced capital structures. And it is the availability of *local* equity capital that is most critical to a new venture, almost totally unknown outside of the community. Well organized associations of wealthy residents may make significant contributions to the supply of such capital. In addition, later on, if local bankers are a little more venturesome than those elsewhere, local firms will be more likely to survive a depression than those in other places.

Size of firm also is relevant; the large nationally known firm finds sources of funds more easily and cheaply than the small firm known only locally and subject to a high load factor per unit of capital raised because of the small size of its borrowings or security offerings. Not only does the large firm achieve important economies of scale in the capital market but the simple momentum of the big firm, with the market power to recoup its losses when prosperity returns, conveys an aura of failure-proof perpetuity that lulls the capital contributor into a sense of security. All of which tends to lower the fixed charges, reduces the need to borrow in depression and increases the ease of borrowing.

The nature and cause of instability are further complicated by interactions between the forces at work. For example, there is some evidence that durable goods tend to be produced in rather broad industrial complexes—some combination of primary metals, metal fabricating, machinery, vehicles, and instruments—while nondurables are more often isolated in one-industry towns.[13] If the durable goods complex largely takes the form of vertical integration with only one or two end-products, then little if any increased stability is achieved by the mere addition of local firms and industries. But insofar as the growth of durables complexes proliferates end-products, even if they are all durables, the averaging effect will move the durable goods industrial areas away from extreme instability. Similarly, while towns with nondurable goods industries may be more stable on the average, a place which is highly specialized in the most unstable nondurable may approach or even exceed in instability the typical durable goods complex.

On the other hand, durable goods industries are more characterized by big firms and big plants and, given the size of the urban area, a nondurable goods town would tend to have more firms. And the sheer number of firms, even if confined to one or a few industries, tends to create some increase in stability. Number has an averaging effect which serves to protect the area against extremes in managerial incompetence, sudden shifts in consumer brand loyalty, and natural disasters (e.g., a devastating fire). Thus the nondurables may regain through the number-effect some relative stability, all adjusted for the market structure implications of firm size discussed above.

Further, if a tendency for durable goods industries to form broad industrial complexes does exist and if, therefore, durable goods areas tend to be bigger than nondurables—the larger the urban area, the greater the proportion of manufacturing activity in durables—this would obviously alter the hypothesized relationship between city size and cyclical stability (Figure 5, page 148), perhaps toward some slight positive slope—a general drift of the points upward and to the right. But then the very largest urban areas tend to have a very high proportion of activity in services because (a) they export services, (b) they draw persons with a strong taste for services, and (c) their residents

13 In a state level cross-section study of employment growth in the period 1947–54 at the two-digit SIC level, the coefficients of correlation associating employment growth in primary metals, fabricated metals, machinery, electrical machinery, transportation equipment and instruments were all remarkably high (ranging from .35 to .80, with a median value of .59), while the correlation coefficients interrelating nondurable growth rates were almost all statistically nonsignificant or negative (showing repulsion or at least incompatibility), with but three exceptions (food and apparel, food and leather, and paper and printing), three out of sixty-six. While this is only indirect evidence that durable goods tend to cluster more than nondurables, it is striking enough to warrant further inquiry. Wilbur R. Thompson and John M. Mattila, *An Econometric Model of Postwar State Industrial Development* (Detroit: Wayne State University Press, 1959), pp. 28–34.

have a higher than average income and the demand for services is clearly income-elastic. To the extent that services are more stable, we may find an inverted "U" regression line, showing the smallest and largest urban areas to be the most stable and middle size areas to be the most unstable. (See the curved line in Figure 5.)

GROWTH INSTABILITY

A third variety of instability remains to be considered: growth instability. While it is somewhat unconventional to extend the concept of instability to the growth trend, good cause can be elicited to support this extension, especially in the urban context. But before marshaling arguments to support this contention, an operational definition of the concept itself is offered.

The Concept

Ordinarily, we conceive of the business cycle as a more or less regular oscillation of business activity about a growth trend that defines the general direction in which the economy is moving and the time-rate at which it is moving in that direction. But trends in business activity are not inherently more immutable than cycles or seasonal patterns, especially at the local level. When, moreover, in the interests of simplicity and expediency, we approximate the "true" trend with a straight line—a "least squares" trend, for example—we do so with full knowledge that our linear approximation must be regularly revised. The frequency with which the "true" trend changes direction may be taken as a measure of the growth instability of the local economy, at least in its hazy perception by mere mortals.

A surer feeling for this concept may be gained from Figure 6, in which schematic time series for two hypothetical urban economies are compared. Area A exhibits very great stability in growth, with no revisions of the linear trend over the full period of six local business cycles, even though this same area displays a high degree of cyclical variation. Area B exhibits cycle amplitudes only a fraction as large as Area A's, but the former's growth trend must be revised twice in this short period of time. A simple but sensible classification of these two small-area economies might be this: Area A is characterized by cyclical instability

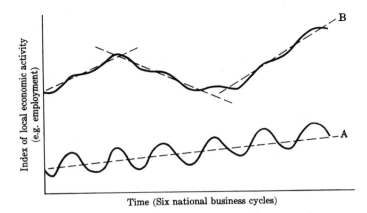

Figure 6. Contrasts in cyclical and growth stability.

and growth stability; Area B is characterized by cyclical stability and growth instability.

Since growth instability is essentially the phenomenon of changing rates of growth, the degree of instability (changeableness) might be approximated by the degree of the trend equation—or some comparable mathematical stratagem. If a second degree curve (polynomial) fits the data better than a linear trend, the time series exhibits some growth instability; if a third degree trend equation fits better than a second degree equation, then even more instability is evident. In addition to the frequency with which direction changes, some index of the sharpness of the breaks in trend is needed—the angle formed between successive linear trend approximations, for example.

If one objects to the use of the word "instability" in a growth context when it is customarily associated with business cycle movements, the term "predictability" might be substituted. The power to predict is precisely what is at stake here. Since the typical trend projection is linear in form, an area that is growing linearly will be highly predictable, even to the least sophisticated analyst. But the more that growth departs from this simple pattern, either in the frequency or the magnitude of directional change, the more likely the forecaster is to miss the mark, and to miss it by a wider margin. One might argue that, within limits, the degree of a polynomial which best fits the "true" trend which the local economy is riding is also a measure of the degree of sophistication called for in making area projections. A first degree (linear) trend is most easily seen; even if unappreciated, it still operates in such a way as to protect those who use the simplest techniques by validating their projections. The application of a second degree ("U" shaped) trend requires that the forecaster appreciate an imminent change in the life cycle of the local economy—some feeling for a sequence of growth stages. A third degree ("S" shaped) trend can probably be rationally founded only in the most sophisticated and finely spun growth theory, and even then it must be perceptively and delicately applied to the given local economy to synchronize timing and relative magnitudes.

The high durability—near permanence—of urban public and quasi-public capital necessitates a very long look ahead. One need only mention the huge investment in the street system to convey with force some idea of the lengths to which the community must lie in the road-bed that it makes. The more than ordinately vexing traffic problems of the pre-auto-age cities, with their narrow, tortuous streets, is illustration enough. To pick, at random, from the private sector's stake in urban trend predictability, consider the case of the privately owned and operated public utilities which must lay lines, pipes, and rails with multidecade time horizons. The intimate relationship between local growth stability (predictability) and urban land use and facility planning need not be labored.

Concocting a local industry mix of complementary growth trends is an attainable goal. In fact, a mix of young, mature, and decadent industries would follow almost inevitably from large urban size. Deductively, we would expect that the larger the urban economy, the more diversified its industry mix and the stabler its growth. The larger the urban area, the more it resembles the national economy in both growth rate and growth stability. Of interest to urban planners and administrators is the corollary that "nationalizing" the local growth pattern would render it more predictable.

Instability, Inefficiency, and Capital Planning

Urban seasonal swings, cycles, and the long waves of rapid growth and retardation present a number of interesting parallels and contrasts. All three present an efficiency problem in that each of them poses a Hobson's choice in capital planning: whether to economize on capital (e.g., street and store capacity) and suffer congestion and costly delays in periods of peak demand (e.g., Christmastime, prosperity highs, and epochs when the local industry mix is loaded with "growth industries"), or to splurge on capital to save on time and tempers and bear more costly idle capacity in the off-peak periods. The appropriate strategy in capital planning differs quite markedly, however, among the three cases.

While local business cycles waste productive capacity in depressions, the ineffectualness of local government in the face of nationwide fluctuations in aggregate spending leads to an attitude of resignation toward cycle-based waste and inefficiency. And the analysis of the relevant section of this chapter did more to cast doubt on the few home remedies that are in favor than to point the way to new ones— industrial diversification pursued directly or achieved indirectly through growth and city size was held out as a moderate stabilization hope only to the most unstable urban areas. While we may leave local cycle analysis with a clearer understanding of the processes involved, we have not changed the conventional feeling of local helplessness and the primacy of federal power and responsibility. The one bright spot is that the *national* business cycle may be diminishing in amplitude, even if not in frequency, with the apparent postwar transition to mild "inventory recessions." With little that localities can do to smooth the cycle, local planning is confined to developing as much flexibility in capacity as possible—expanding the range of adjustments that can be made on the supply side (e.g., facilities that can be conveniently shut down during cycle troughs). Thus, the local reflection of a national recession becomes largely a problem in income maintenance and the local public powers become largely confined to administering unemployment compensation and public assistance.

Seasonal and growth instability, however, offer a much greater potential for effective intervention, with strategies ranging from preventatives to cures. Seasonal instability and the resulting inefficiencies in the use of capital can be approached preventatively by smoothing the oscillations in demand (e.g., bus fares raised at rush hours and cut during slack periods), or curatively by increasing the flexibility of plant and equipment (e.g., baseball diamonds that double as skating rinks).

Tendencies toward great instability of growth may also be managed to a considerable degree, although the techniques are rather different from those applied to rationalize seasonal fluctuations. Rates of natural increase are very similar between urban areas, so that rapid growth is nearly synonymous with heavy in-migration. Since the new residents must be housed and serviced with additional stores, schools, streets, and utilities, capital shortages plague the community during the period of rapid growth. As with urban seasonal fluctuation, efficiency can be achieved either by dampening the basic instability or by increasing the area's ease of adaptation. Industrial diversification holds much more promise as a secular stabilization device than as a cyclical one, simply because a random mix of growth stages can be much more easily assembled than industries with complementary cycle patterns. Industrial diversification is, then, probably the most efficacious way to achieve growth stability, although this may require large city size in most cases. All urban areas could attain growth stability by growing only if small and medium size urban areas were consolidated or evacuated.

Growth instability differs from seasonal instability in that growth oscillations are highly irregular and unpredictable, at least in the present state of the art, in sharp contrast to the well-behaved seasonal. Because the period of the growth wave is so long, the response to changing rates of local growth could be made quite orderly and graceful, if we knew better the path we were taking.

With the seasonal pattern known, seasonal strategy should emphasize increasing the flexibility of capital because the speed of response is critical. With the growth pattern unknown, growth instability strategy might better devote extra effort and ingenuity to discovering the nature and processes of small area growth and development because, when the time periods are long, forewarned is forearmed. Our problem at present is that we seldom recognize the growth stage in which we are currently living, much less anticipate the coming order of things. While industrial diversification would help to stabilize local growth and thereby render it more predictable, really sophisticated long-range capital planning demands a much deeper understanding of the nature of the urban growth process. But this was the theme of the first chapter. We have come full circle.

Technical Appendix

CITY SIZE AND THE SOURCES OF CYCLICAL CHANGE

The argument above was that as we move from the national economy down to the local economy in income analysis, investment declines and exports rise in relative importance as prime movers of the relevant business cycle. Can we not deduce, in reverse, that, as the urban economy grows and becomes more diverse and self-sufficient, exports become relatively less important and investment comes to rival exports as an income determinant? And if we open the door to let in investment as a second autonomous local cyclical force, we might as well admit a third force, autonomous shifts in the "consumption function." This can all be quite explicit by a set of simple numerical examples.

Let us divide the *national* economy into two sectors, consumer goods industries (C) and producer good (or investment) industries (I), with consumption spending accounting for 80 per cent of total national spending and investment accounting for the remaining 20 per cent. For simplicity we will assume that government activity and national foreign trade activity are negligible. Let us follow the Keynesian orthodoxy by assuming that investment is the most volatile kind of spending and impute an autonomous reduction of 20 per cent from prosperity peaks to recession troughs. But let us also extend the Keynesian framework, in line with current practice, to allow for autonomous changes in consumption spending—"shifts in the consumption function"—of, say, 5 per cent.

Let it be clear that these are autonomous and not induced changes in consumption spending to which we refer. True, contemporary national income analysis still imputes to changes in investment the major blame for the national business cycle, with cutbacks in investment reducing first income earned and then derived consumption. But this analytical framework makes ample room for increases and decreases in consumption expenditures that cause, rather than follow from, changes in income. Households may cut back their consumption expenditures prior to any decline in their income. Consumer surveys have shown householders to be quite easily moved to postpone purchases of durable goods (e.g., automobiles, appliances, furniture) in anticipation of forthcoming layoffs. And, in a local cyclical context, we could experience a sequence in which the local service industries begin to sag first because of a downward shift in the local-services consumption function. This would be especially likely if the local export industries are among the more stable ones (e.g., tobacco products, staple foods, paper products).

If autonomous decreases in consumption of 5 per cent are as likely to occur as are autonomous decreases in investment of 20 per cent, then a $100 billion national economy could expect recession shocks of $4 billion to originate in either reduced investment (−.20 × $20 billion) or in reduced consumption (−.05 × $80 billion). Perhaps this illustration overstates the relative importance of autonomous changes in consumption, and then again perhaps the traditional emphasis on investment in business cycle analysis reflects a failure to appreciate fully the cyclical implications of the steady growth of consumer durable goods in our affluent society. Not only can spending on consumer durables be easily postponed but also successive additions to these hard goods satisfy ever more weakly felt wants. These figures are illustrative only, to suggest the framework for empirical effort which will establish their relative magnitudes with nicety.

Let us now construct a two sector local economy by reclassifying the consumer goods and producer goods into exports and local services. We mix both consumer and producer goods and services in each of these two local sectors, as an urban economy may produce for export either refrigerators (C) or lathes (I) and produce for home use either retail services (C) or the store buildings themselves (I). We then subdivide both producer and consumer goods into three varieties: (1) goods which can be economically produced at small scale and which tend therefore to be found even in the smallest urban economies (I_s, C_s); (2) goods which exhibit substantial economies of scale and which are subject to specialization and exchange among small urban economies but can be produced solely for local use only in large urban economies (I_l, C_l); and (3) goods which exhibit such great economies of scale (and other characteristics) that they are sold in national or at least very broad regional markets and are therefore largely export (and import) goods even in the largest urban areas (I_n, C_n).

If, in a small urban economy, one-half of total local activity originates in the export sector and one-half in the local service sector, as set forth in the table below, then one-half of the autonomous change would originate in each

Small Urban Economy
(approximately 50,000 population)

Sector	Income generated (millions)	Autonomous cyclical variation		
		Relative change (per cent)	Absolute change (millions)	Per cent of total change
EXPORT				
Producer goods (I_l, I_n)	$10	20	$2 ⎱	50 (Exp.)
Consumer goods (C_l, C_n)	40	5	2 ⎰	
LOCAL SERVICE				
Producer goods (I_s)	10	20	2	25 (Inv.)
Consumer goods (C_s)	40	5	2	25 (Cons.)
	$100		$8	100

of the two sectors. This follows automatically from the explicit assumption that the mix of producer and consumer goods is the same (1:4) in both the export and local service sectors (column 1) and from the implicit assumption that the kinds of producer goods exported and the kinds used internally have similar cycle characteristics. The same assumptions hold for the mix of consumer goods in the two sectors (column 2). We will expand on this somewhat subtle point below; here let us simply note that we have just created a local business cycle which may be characterized as a 50 per cent export cycle, a 25 per cent investment cycle and 25 per cent consumption cycle (column 4).

Now let us enlarge the local economy, assuming that with larger size the export sector shrinks relative to the local service sector. The urban area we shall now consider is ten times as big as the one we just left. Let us shift from the export to the local service sector those economic functions which can be supported by large local markets (I_l, C_l), cutting the relative size of the local export sector in half. Now we have a new distribution of autonomous cyclical impulses, as shown in the table below.

Large Urban Economy
(approximately 500,000 population)

Sector	Income generated (millions)	Autonomous cyclical variation		
		Relative change (per cent)	Absolute change (millions)	Per cent of total change
EXPORT				
Producer goods (I_n)	$ 50	20	$10 ⎫	25.0 (Exp.)
Consumer goods (C_n)	200	5	10 ⎭	
LOCAL SERVICE				
Producer goods (I_l, I_s)	150	20	30	37.5 (Inv.)
Consumer goods (C_l, C_s)	600	5	30	37.5 (Cons.)
	$1000		$80	100.0

With only one-quarter of total local activity originating in the export sector (column 1), only one-quarter of the cyclical impulse resides therein (column 4). Local investment fluctuations and shifts in the local-consumption-of-local-production function each account for three-eighths of the local cycle. Clearly, the "local" economy could be continually enlarged up to the point where it encompassed the whole country, with no export sector remaining and all of the cycle attributable to fluctuations in investment and consumption, given our simplifying assumption of no foreign trade. If, moreover, the proportions cited in this latter example understate the export sector's role in cyclical disturbances in a 500,000 population economy, we need only attribute the illustration to a 5,000,000 population economy or the 20,000,000 population New York-Northeastern New Jersey metropolitan area if need be. The principle remains.

Still, in our effort to deflate the naïve conception that the local cycle is almost purely an export phenomenon, we may have gone too far. The export sector may tend to be relatively loaded with producer goods and the local services may be heavily weighted with consumer goods. If we were to distribute producer goods activity so that three-quarters (rather than one-quarter) of it was sold in national markets (I_n) and fell in the export sector, and to balance the accounts we shifted consumer goods production so that only one-eighth (rather than one-quarter) of it was exported, then the local accounts would appear as shown in the table below. The export sector, still accounting for only one-quarter of total local activity, now originates almost 44 per cent of the cyclical shocks. The export sector is not dominant but it remains much more than proportionately the source of instability.

Large Urban Economy
(approximately 500,000 population)

Sector	Income generated (millions)	Autonomous cyclical variation		
		Relative change (per cent)	Absolute change (millions)	Per cent of total change
EXPORT				
Producer goods (I_n)	$ 150	20	$30	43.75 (Exp.)
Consumer goods (C_n)	100	5	5	
LOCAL SERVICE				
Producer goods (I_1, I_s)	50	20	10	12.50 (Inv.)
Consumer goods (C_1, C_s)	700	5	35	43.75 (Cons.)
	$1000		$80	100.00

Alternatively, and probably more realistically, we could restore some of the autonomous cyclical power of the export sector by assuming different rates of autonomous variability among various kinds of producer goods and among the various kinds of consumer goods and by assigning the highest rates of variability to export goods in both classes. Starting again with the assumed *average* rates of autonomous cyclical variation of 20 per cent in producer goods and 5 per cent in consumer goods, we might disaggregate these averages, as shown in the following table. How might we defend the assumption that national-market goods (both producer and consumer) are the most unstable, and that those goods produced for home use even in the smaller urban areas

Assumed Autonomous Cyclical Variation
for Selected Classes of Products

Producer goods			Consumer goods		
Market size class	Employment weight	Relative change (per cent)	Market size class	Employment weight	Relative change (per cent)
$I_{national}$	5	30	C_n	20	9
I_{large}	5	20	C_l	20	5
I_{small}	10	15	C_s	40	3
weighted average		20	weighted average		5

are the least likely to initiate a large cyclical impulse? Gross private domestic investment encompasses expenditures on producer durable equipment (tools and machines), new construction (factories, stores, and homes) and changes in business inventories (investment in building up stocks and disinvestment through selling, on net, out of stocks). Spending on producer durable equipment and on inventories would seem, *a priori*, to be more unstable than new construction. Construction activity is probably less speculatively motivated, at least in the context of the "minor cycle" of three to four years, both because the amortization period over which the new building must be paid for greatly transcends the cycle period and because the very building process itself is not flexible enough—cannot be started and stopped strategically—to be used as a speculative instrument. Conversely, the scheduling of investment in tools and machines and, even more, in inventories is much more flexible and potentially much more maneuverable. Changes in business inventories alone, in fact, accounted for about 80 per cent of the total decline in gross private domestic investment in both the 1949 and 1954 recessions and about 60 per cent of the investment slump in the 1958 recession.

Even casual recourse to the data supports this deductive position. In Table 1 below the per cent decline from peak to trough, as reckoned from the quarterly series of the National Income Division of the U.S. Department of Commerce, has been computed for each of the three kinds of investment for the three postwar periods. Clearly changes in business inventories are by far

Table 1. Peak to Trough Changes in Gross Private Domestic Investment in Three Postwar Business Recessions

Class	Absolute change (billions of dollars)			Relative change (per cent)		
	1948–49[a]	1953–54[b]	1957–58[c]	1948–49[a]	1953–54[b]	1957–58[c]
Change in business inventories	−11.2	−5.8	− 8.0	*	*	*
Producer durable equipment	− 2.6	−1.1	− 4.8	−13.3	− 5.0	−16.6
New construction	+ 0.6	+1.1	− 0.9	+ 3.3	+ 4.0	− 2.5
Total (GPDI)	−13.3	−5.8	−13.7	−31.4	−10.8	−20.2

*In all three periods the change in business inventories was from a positive figure (net investment through inventory accumulation) to a negative figure (net disinvestment through inventory depletion). A per cent change figure cannot, therefore, be derived.
[a]Peak: 4th quarter 1948; trough: 4th quarter 1949.
[b]Peak: 2nd quarter 1953; trough: 2nd quarter 1954.
[c]Peak: 3rd quarter 1957; trough: 1st quarter 1958.
Source: U.S. Department of Commerce, Office of Business Economics, *Survey of Current Business*, various issues.

the most volatile kind of investment spending. Purchases of tools and machines just as clearly outranked new construction as a source of instability in all three recessions.

Now if we could show that the production of coal, steel, cloth, garments, paper, and other business materials and supplies destined for stockroom bins and shelves, and also tools and machines for the production line have relatively concentrated locational patterns and hence are much more likely to flow in interurban trade, then these relatively unstable goods would predominate in the export sector of their home areas. And if we could show that construction activity is much the most likely of the three to fall under the heading of production for local consumption (which seems intuitively reasonable because production usually has to take place at the site of the consumer so that at least the payroll component of value added in construction goes to on-site workers within the local labor market) we would have succeeded in allocating the most stable kind of investment to the local service sector.

Turning now to consumption expenditures, we divide consumer goods into three classes: durable goods, nondurables and services. We argued above that durables tend to be more unstable than nondurables because the easiest retrenchment a consumer can make during a recession is to postpone replacing his aging automobile, appliances, furniture, and the like. And these are the very goods he is most likely to splurge on in the early stages of recovery and optimism. Nondurables and services cannot be postponed and accelerated speculatively to anywhere near the same extent, and this is borne out by the data in Table 2.

Table 2. Peak to Trough Changes in Personal Consumption Expenditures in Three Postwar Business Recessions

Class	Absolute change (billions of dollars)			Relative change (per cent)		
	1948–49[a]	1953–54[b]	1957–58[c]	1948–49[a]	1953–54[b]	1957–58[c]
Durable goods	[+2.8]	−1.2	−4.4	[+12.6]	−3.6	−10.8
Nondurable goods	−2.8	+0.2	−0.2	− 2.8	+0.2	− 0.1
Services	+3.3	+4.3	+3.4	+ 5.7	+5.3	+ 3.2
Total	+3.4	+3.2	−1.3	+ 1.9	+1.4	− 3.4

For explanation of notes, see Table 1.
Source: Same as Table 1.

In passing let us note that total consumption expenditures may actually remain steady or even increase in a recession or, if they should sag, the decline is small. With a growing population and a secularly rising per capita income we really should measure a recession decline from a rising trend line for proper perspective, but the purposes here are much too modest to warrant such statistical sophistication. The most obvious pattern to be found in the data is the sharp difference in the performance of durables relative to nondurables in 1949 over that in the other two recessions. We could with good cause delete the 1949 experience as being most atypical. The long war period so depleted the households' supply of automobiles, refrigerators, and furniture that purchases of these goods rose throughout 1949 despite falling incomes. If we segregate the 1949 pattern, at least the durables part of it, as a special case and concentrate on the two later recessions, we find their patterns are similar and as expected. Sharp jumps in instability occur as we move upward from services to nondurables to durables.

If we can show that consumer durables are produced under conditions of substantial large-scale economies that result in spatially concentrated production and much interregional trade, then the more unstable kinds of consumer goods would be found more than proportionately in the export sector of the local economy. Even more deductively appealing is the hypothesis that the services are the most localized of all—restricted to the smallest market areas (C_s). The localization of services follows from the high cost of transportation when persons must move to complete the transaction, whether the patient travels to the doctor or the doctor to the patient (and if the latter

illustration is obsolete, when the domestic servant travels to the household).
If, on the average, services are both the most stable and most localized of the
three classes, the export sector again rises as the main source of autonomous
instability.

We now can apply to our small and large urban economies the pattern of
differential variability hypothesized above and supported in a general way
by the empirical evidence of Tables 1 and 2. With the export sector still
held to 50 per cent of total activity in the small urban economy and to 25 per
cent of the total in the large one, we return to our original assumption that
both producer and consumer goods are allocated between the export and
local service sectors in the same 1:3 proportions.

When higher rates of variability are assigned to goods marketed in large
and national market areas, I_n, I_l, C_n, C_l, the export sector in the small urban
area rises to account for not 50 but 66 per cent of total autonomous cyclical
change, as shown in the table below. Similarly, the large urban economy now

Small and Large Urban Economies

		Autonomous Cyclical Variation			
Small		Income generated (millions)	Relative change (per cent)	Absolute change (millions)	Per cent of total change
Export sector					
National market	I_n	$ 5	30	$1.5	
goods	C_n	20	9	1.8	
Large market	I_l	5	20	1.0	
goods	C_l	20	5	1.0	
				5.3	66.25 (E)
Local service sector					
Small market	I_s	10	15	1.5	18.75 (I)
goods	C_s	40	3	1.2	15.00 (C)
		$100		$8.0	100.00
Large					
Export sector					
National market	I_n	$ 50	30	$15	
goods	C_n	200	9	18	
				33	41.25 (E)
Local service sector					
Large and small	I_l	50	20	10	
market producer	I_s	100	15	15	
goods				25	31.25 (I)
Large and small	C_l	200	5	10	
market consumer	C_s	400	3	12	
goods				22	27.50 (C)
		$1000		$80	100.00

exhibits an export sector which accounts for only 25 per cent of total activity
but which is responsible for over 40 per cent of the autonomous cyclical
variation transmitted to the local economy.

Thus we may impute to the local export sector cyclical shocks more than proportionate to its size either by assigning to exports a more than proportionate share of producer goods or by assuming that the more unstable varieties of both producer and consumer goods are exported. In either case, the export sector is presumed to have a mix of relatively unstable industries. We could, of course, have combined the effect of both factors by assuming that the export sector has both a larger proportion of producer goods and the more unstable elements of both producer and consumer goods.

But nothing should be more apparent than the fragile character of this largely deductive *tour de force*. This extended set of interrelated hypotheses can only be justified as a stimulant to further analysis and empirical reformulation. We need both a better theoretical conception of the local business cycle and its application in some good operational econometric models. While we always need better data, pilot econometric models of local business cycles can be built on existing data, and preliminary empirical experimentation is a partial prerequisite to specifying more precisely what "better data" we do need.

CHAPTER 5

Interactions among Goals: Opportunity Cost at the Policy Level

SUBSTITUTABILITY AND COMPLEMENTARITY IN URBAN ECONOMIC GOALS

The literature of urban economics is remarkably free of any discussion of the mutual compatibility of the goals discussed in the first four chapters, nor is any notable amount of analysis of their interrelationships much in evidence. To the extent that any particular couplet of goals are incompatible, then the pursuit of one has as its "opportunity cost" the sacrifice sustained by not emphasizing the other one instead. While the term, opportunity cost, is customarily employed in a much more prosaic context—the amount of "butter" that must be foregone to have more "guns" as resources are shifted from one industry to another—the concept is equally valid and powerful at the very highest levels of policy. It is true, however, that the lines of decision making and the identity of the decision maker are not nearly so clear with public policy as with marketable goods.

The matrix of goal associations may reveal at least an equal number of positive correlations—conjoined, consistent goals. This latter situation might seem, on first blush, to connote the best of all possible worlds—to be able to have one's cake and eat it too. But the darker side of each picture still remains. Stability has its counterpart in instability, growth faster than the national average implies that somewhere there must be less than average growth or even decline, and a higher than average income in some places leaves the poor agglomerated elsewhere. Thus a rash of positive correlations between urban economic goals may mean the compounding of good fortune one place and ill fortune another. For example, if the rapidly growing areas are

173

also the most stable, then the stagnating areas are doubly cursed by having heavy cyclical unemployment piled on top of heavy structural unemployment—not too inaccurate a description of a distressingly large proportion of the local economies in Pennsylvania and West Virginia. And if the high-income areas have relatively little income inequality (e.g., an automobile manufacturing city like Flint, Michigan), then the low-income areas, with what little income they do have distributed very unequally, struggle with the most dire poverty.

Certainly, much empirical work is needed here and a considerable amount is possible with just the existing data. Still, if we now slice through the material already developed in this study, first one way and then another, we should gain some feeling for complexity of interactions between goals as well as a heightened sense of appreciation for the difficult social and economic choices involved. Also even the most tentative and limited deductive sorties into this new frontier provides more intriguing hypotheses per page than any other subject matter this author has ever encountered. There are, in his considered opinion, at least a dozen and probably two dozen worthwhile doctoral dissertations in the next twenty pages, both implicit and explicit, awaiting only the magic touch of imagination, enthusiasm, and energy.

Growth and Income Level

Traditional economic analysis has more to say on the interaction of growth and income level than any of the others. Areas with higher wage rates and per capita incomes tend to attract labor force and population from areas of lower wage rates and income. Since wages are notoriously sticky downward, wage differentials usually manifest themselves as growing gaps between areas of slowly and rapidly rising wage rates. While the relative availability of jobs is probably more directly relevant than relative wage rates, the two phenomena are highly correlated as growth brings labor scarcity and rising wage rates, and stagnation brings stable ones. The point was made in the second chapter that the migration response to relative wage rates may be asymmetrical, at least as seen from the vantage point of a given small area. High wage rates and/or labor shortages serve to expand a local economy more easily and quickly than low wage rates and/or persistent unemployment serve to contract it. In-migrants are drawn from all over and are the most mobile elements of the population. The potential out-migrants are the currently unemployed. They usually comprise disproportionately large numbers of the elderly, handicapped, and impoverished, who find migration the most physically, psychologically, and financially taxing.

Further, when unemployment is nationwide and chronic—and this seems to be both the order of the day and the threat of the coming decade—local unemployment provides, at most, only the motive to move from an area, without providing a destination. Moving to an area with a lesser rate of unemployment still does not provide a job. From the national standpoint, differential regional unemployment does not function well as a labor allocating device during periods of substantial aggregate unemployment. Of course, in depression, those few areas with labor shortages become beacons made even brighter by the surrounding darkness. Thus, either recurrent national depressions or an inadequate rate of national growth (secular stagnation) tends to intensify the income-migration asymmetry, with the market price mechanism feeding booming areas much more efficiently than it empties out the depressed ones.

High wages and high levels of local income generate local growth in another way, as they create a rich local market and draw market-oriented industries. A number of empirical studies have shown market-oriented industries to constitute a large and rapidly growing proportion of all manufacturing industries.[1] The best employment estimating equations derived from an analysis of the 1947–54 state data contain a size-of-the-local-market variable in one form or another (e.g., population, personal income, number of households) for at least half of the twenty Census two-digit manufacturing industry groups (e.g., apparel, furniture, paper, metal products, machinery, automobiles, etc.).[2] And an indirect market linkage through these industries to many of the remaining ones could surely be traced.[3]

[1] See Harvey S. Perloff and Lowdon Wingo, Jr., "Natural Resource Endowment and Regional Economic Growth," Joseph J. Spengler (editor), *Natural Resources and Economic Growth* (Washington: Resources for the Future, Inc., 1961), pp. 203–04.

[2] Wilbur R. Thompson and John M. Mattila, *An Econometric Model of Postwar State Industrial Development* (Detroit, Michigan: Wayne State University Press, 1959), Table 10, p. 51 and Table 12, p. 68; and John M. Mattila and Wilbur R. Thompson, "The Role of the Product Market in State Industrial Development," *Papers and Proceedings of the Regional Science Association, 1960*, pp. 87–96.

[3] Interindustry growth linkages might be traced not only via static input-output linkages, usually set in a spaceless context, but also by cross-section correlation of interindustry, interarea growth patterns. Interstate differentials in employment growth may be correlated between each possible pair of industries, indicating the

A reverse relationship running from growth to the level of real income has been suggested at various points above, especially in the first two chapters. The tendency for larger size to widen the range of choice open to both consumers (variety of goods) and producers (occupational choice) was developed at some length. The counter-argument was advanced that growth (and size) tends to produce external diseconomies of scale in public services, if it leads to political fragmentation (as it almost always does), or if internal diseconomies of scale arise due to the limited expansibility of the urban managerial factor. Thus the net effect of growth and size on real income is not deductively apparent, and depends on individual tastes—the degree to which one is a confirmed urbanite.

Perhaps most significant of all is the likely effect of the current trend of population to congregate more and more in a relatively few very large urban areas which have relatively similar median incomes. The logic here is parallel to that advanced in Chapter 4 to relate cyclical stability to city size. Just as small cities tend to specialize in either (not both) the stable or unstable industries, so, too, small cities tend to host either the high paying or the low paying ones. And just as size brings a mixture of stable and unstable industries, so, too, it surely blends high and low paying industries into a bland average wage rate. But more about this below.

Growth and Income Stability

One might begin a deductive analysis of the relationship between growth and stability by recalling that construction activity is one of the more unstable industries and that a rapidly growing area would normally have a relatively large proportion of total activity in construction. The upswings, therefore, would tend to be sharp as the construction of factories, houses, stores, and schools boom, and the cutbacks could be equally sharp and sizable. Thus we might expect a rapidly growing area to have a local cycle of relatively large amplitude.

Still, one feels intuitively that a rapid rate of aggregate growth in an urban area could foster local cyclical stability, if for no other

possibility of interindustry *spatial* linkages, originating in physical input-output ties, complementary labor market demands, associated technologies, by-product relationships and so forth. See Thompson and Mattila, *An Econometric Model* . . . , *ibid.*, pp. 28–34.

reason than that growth would swamp the local cycle. This hypothesis gains stature if linked to the conviction that modern fiscal and monetary policies have greatly softened the national cycle, with national depressions a relic of the past. The resolution of this seeming paradox would seem to lie in a subtle measurement problem. While the amplitude of the local cycle in a rapidly growing area may be rather large when measured around the trend (with trend removed), a cycle trough that is barely lower than the preceding prosperity peak is a "depression" in only a very special sense of the word. The concrete manifestation of such a "depression" is probably a reduced rate of in-migration of labor, with local employment holding steady.

This peculiarity of cycle pattern—heavy local cycles but little or no trough unemployment—can only be obtained in a context of very rapid growth. The average annual rate of growth must nearly equal the annual rate of cyclical decline in the downturn, a situation highly unlikely at the national level but literally true for total manufacturing employment in both Los Angeles and San Diego in the 1953–54 recession.[4]

There are always cross-currents, so one can easily construct situations in which rapid growth could lead to cyclical instability. Let us imagine, for example, an area which introduces a new durable good which catches the public's fancy and produces very rapid local growth. Local service business, typically small in size, will press local financial institutions for both short- and long-term loans. By some combination of reducing excess reserves and secondary reserves (government obligations) to a bare minimum and soliciting outside depositors with the lure of higher interest rates, local commercial banks strain to respond to local needs. Other financial institutions in the area, such as building and loan associations, follow the commercial banks in loading up on local business' notes and mortgages. All in all, with local rates of return high, lending to local businessmen is not only public-spirited, it is profitable. But a sharp national recession may strike this durable-good producing town especially hard, and, even if none of the local

---

[4] In the 1954 national recession, total manufacturing employment fell by about 3 per cent, nationally, but actually increased by 0.7 per cent and 1.8 per cent in the Los Angeles and San Diego metropolitan areas, respectively. These were local "slumps" only when compared to their phenomenal manufacturing employment growth rates of 7.1 and 11.6 per cent, respectively, as measured from a linear logarithmic trend line fitted to annual data for the period 1947–60. Estimates derived from an empirical study of local cycles currently being conducted by John M. Mattila and the author sponsored by CUE-RFF, drawing on data from the various *Censuses and Surveys of Manufactures*.

financial institutions fail, local credit will be unusually tight during the local depression. In short, a national recession could produce a local depression. The experience of the Detroit area economy in the thirties resembles, more than a little, this hypothetical model: automobiles boomed in the twenties and collapsed in the thirties, and the Detroit banks were the first to close in the Great Depression.[5]

The relationship between rapid aggregate growth and *growth instability* is quite different. A rate of growth fast enough to swamp the local reflection of the national business cycle may sweep a local economy smoothly upward for a decade or so, through perhaps two or three "minor cycles" in national business activity. But rapid rates of growth are very hard to maintain; usually they are built on the stage of most rapid growth of a single industry. Now growth in one industry may well develop the industrial base which spawns another, but the probability is that the new industry will not develop at a rate which will exactly absorb slack created by the maturing of the original economic base. In short, there are transitional pauses in which gains are consolidated in even the most vibrant local industrial areas. A tentative hypothesis is that a rapid rate of aggregate growth tends to create growth instability. Large size may bring growth stability, as argued in Chapter 4, but achieving that size rapidly may be temporarily destabilizing.

Growth and Income Distribution

Rapid urban growth serves to reduce impoverishing cyclical and structural unemployment in a number of ways. The point was made above that, in a booming local economy, a local cycle trough may be no more than a brief pause in the steady climb of employment, rather than the typical period of heavy unemployment. Again, "hard-core" unemployment which otherwise would crystallize when structural shifts in taste patterns and technology close up local business firms and close out various occupations yields to the powerful solvent of replacement job opportunities in the local growth-industries. Changing jobs need not also entail changing place of residence. In a booming local labor market, moreover, the less skilled workers are upgraded to high-wage work especially rapidly, almost under forced draft. Thus the

[5] See Patricia McKenzie, *Some Aspects of the Detroit Bank Crisis of 1933*, a doctoral dissertation submitted to Wayne State University, May 1963.

weight of evidence from the labor market seems to be preponderantly on the side of linking rapid aggregate growth with income equality and stagnation with income inequality.

The only cause for some hesitancy in tentatively associating rapid growth with income equality is the side effect that rapid growth attracts the rural poor; persons lacking in both assets and urban-industrial skills pour into the tight job market. A reservoir of near-indigent families in the urban hinterland (e.g., underemployed farmers on marginal land, itinerant laborers in stagnant small towns) awaits only some sign of a tightening in the major local labor market to enter the big city. The steady influx of low-skilled labor tends to perpetuate the existence of a sizable group with a very low income and to retard the trend toward greater equality. But migration is sluggish, so this is not cause enough to reverse the impression that vigorous growth brings greater income equality, only that in-migration is a partial offset in an open economy.

Rapid growth, with its attendant influx of the rural poor, combines with large urban size to intensify another form of income inequality, intergovernmental inequality. The rural in-migrants usually settle in the core of the central city because it contains the oldest and shabbiest housing in the area with a concentration of furnished rooms and rental housing that most fits their needs. If the in-migrants are non-white, the core area is probably the only area open to them. Since these people are new to urban living they often have not yet acquired an urban culture, even in such simple matters as the proper disposal of wastes, and it is not surprising that their arrival tends to set off a wave-like motion of residential displacements, with each income class pushing outward and upward to better housing, to hold their place in line.

While the growth may not change the basic concentric spatial pattern,[6] in which income and wealth vary directly with distance from the central city, the fact that political boundaries are usually fixed, especially those of the central city, means that rapid growth can impoverish the central city. To oversimplify and exaggerate, when the central city accommodated virtually everyone, it mixed the rich and

[6] For a reinterpretation of Ernest W. Burgess' concentric zone theory in a growth context, similar to its use here, see Leo F. Schnore, "On the Spatial Structure of Cities in the Two Americas: Some Problems in Comparative Urban Research," Philip M. Hauser and Leo F. Schnore (editors), *The Study of Urbanization*, The Committee on Urbanization of the Social Science Research Council (New York: John Wiley & Sons, Inc., 1965).

the poor. Today, with about one-half of the metropolitan area population living outside the central city limits in the typical large area, the central city struggles with the lowest one-half of the income earners of the local labor market. And in a decade or two the central city may be left with the lowest one-third.

Further income segregation occurs in the suburbs as the middle- and upper-income classes separate into little homogeneous residential enclaves which become hardened and formalized by political boundaries, as noted in Chapter 3. Growth, size and politicoeconomic inequality form a tight complex.[7]

The distinctive residential and political spatial patterns formed as the urban area grows to large size not only hamper the redistribution of income through local public services, they also hobble further economic development, both local and national. Even though residential segregation by income class may be practiced no more strictly in large urban areas than in small ones, sheer size itself may create a difference in kind. In a large urban area the slum section may be so extensive that the slum child may almost never participate in or even witness bourgeois socioeconomic phenomena. His counterpart in the small town at least occasionally plays with the children of the middle- and upper-income classes and regularly attends the same comprehensive high school as they do. Some of the cultural advantages of a superior home environment may, therefore, be acquired indirectly by the slum child as he is exposed to experiences which may both implant higher aspirations and, by providing good examples, show the way. Conant[8] has written persuasively on the value of the small

---

[7] But the "complex" is complex. We argued that rapid industrial expansion of a metropolitan area would tend to increase the income gap between the central city and its suburbs by attracting large numbers of jobless low-skilled labor from outside, and the impoverished newcomers tend to locate in the central city, physically pushing and socially driving higher-income households outward. Thus we might expect a negative correlation between the growth rate of an urban area and the ratio of central city income to the income of the full local labor market—the metropolitan area or urbanized area. But we might also expect a very slow rate of local employment growth or absolute decline in local job formation to depress central city income *relative* to the suburbs, as chronic unemployment and dire poverty are especially characteristic of the marginal workers of the central city—the old, handicapped, nonwhite, and uneducated. Over all we probably should not look for a linear relationship between urban growth rate and the central city-suburban income gap but a concave curve reaching a peak at an employment growth rate somewhere near the natural rate of increase in the local labor force, and dipping downward in both directions, at higher and lower rates of growth.

[8] James B. Conant, *Slums and Suburbs* (New York: McGraw-Hill Book Co., Inc., 1961), p. 4.

town comprehensive high school as an instrument of democracy, and it is emphasized here as a tool of human resource development.

The parents of the slum child, as less productive members of the labor force, might receive more sympathetic and intelligent treatment if they were not so spatially isolated from the social, economic, and political leaders of the community. This unfamiliarity leads both to a lack of interest in their plight as well as to a stereotyped image of their characteristics. And on their part, tighter and tighter ghettoes produce a smoldering sense of injustice, persecution complexes, and mental illness—"mere" inhumanity and inequality of opportunity evolve into "social dynamite."

When the leaders of an affluent nation such as ours call for greater economic growth surely they must mean the expansion and extension of the opportunity for creative expression and personal achievement, and not merely some undifferentiated increase in gross national product—not just a bigger pile of automobiles and refrigerators. So as long as the more marginal members of the labor force remain "out of sight and out of mind" and as long as slum children can encounter only other slum children no matter in what direction they reach out, human resources are being wasted and human beings treated shabbily. Thus the boundless metropolitan areas we have created may be economically, socially, and politically fragmented as never before, hobbling local, and, therefore, national economic development. Have we, too, built a "wall" seriously hampering social interaction and human progress in our rapidly growing and proliferating giant metropolises? From urban growth to great city size to great residential segregation and economic isolation and back to the waste of human resources, the key to rational social "growth."

Income Level and Distribution

The most obvious tie-in between the level and distribution of local income is found in the local industry mix, particularly the degree of specialization in manufacturing. Manufacturing areas are generally high-wage labor markets; perhaps as much as 30 per cent of the variation of median income between metropolitan areas is statistically "explained" by the proportion of employment in manufacturing.[9]

[9] The coefficient of correlation between 1949 median family income and per cent of the local labor force engaged in manufacturing in 1950 for the full 151 Census standard metropolitan areas is .55 (an explained variance of $.55^2$ or 30 per cent).

The typical industrial city also tends to be highly egalitarian in income distribution, as noted above in Chapter 3, where evidence was introduced to show that as much as one-half of the variation in income inequality among metropolitan areas is inversely associated with manufacturing specialization.

A third factor, unionized manufacturing activity, tends to reinforce these effects. Therefore we should expect to find high levels of per capita income associated with a greater equality in income distribution—a pleasant companionship. Our feeling for this tentative hypothesis is strengthened when we recall that the durable goods manufacturing tends to be both higher paying and more unionized than the nondurables.

Operating in a complementary way is another force, structural unemployment. The depressed area, the home of structural unemployment, is characterized by heavy chronic unemployment, and a large proportion of perpetual welfare families may both lower the local per capita income and produce a high coefficient on inequality. This may not be merely a statistical freak inherent in the mathematical characteristics of the indexes used, but rather the meaningful finding that a community is most unlikely to have extreme poverty and still exhibit over-all affluence, even if one uses an "average" in a spurious context (i.e., in a bimodal distribution). Again, the presence of a large proportion of nonwhites may operate similarly to both lower the average income and increase the degree of income inequality. (An exception is the smaller depressed area which has been stagnant long enough so that many of the more talented residents have left the area, reducing both the degree of inequality and the over-all level of income—equality in poverty.)

Empirical support for the deductive position that affluence and egalitarianism go hand-in-hand is offered by the close association found between median income and income inequality. An analysis of the 1950 Census data revealed that about 69 per cent of the interurban variation in intraurban income inequality is associated with differences in the level of family income between urban areas—the higher the median family income of an urban area, the less the income inequality between families within that area.[10] Here, then, we have a strong

---

Derived from the *1950 Census of Population*. However, the correlation between 1959 median family income and per cent in manufacturing for 135 SMSA's dropped sharply to .36 (explained variance of 13 per cent), suggesting that specialization in manufacturing is no longer the key to affluence it once was.

[10] See Chapter 3, footnotes 4 and 5.

presumption of "joint products"; the twin blessings of relative affluence and equality, or the twin burdens of relative poverty and inequality. But the evidence is limited and the tentative conclusion little more than a fortified hypothesis.

One might continue this investigation by considering other industrial characteristics relevant to the pattern of local income distribution; for example, big versus small plants, strong versus weak unions, locally owned versus absentee-owned business and specialized versus diversified production. From these purely illustrative four couplets one might form as many as sixteen distinctive subsets of local industrial attributes. Of these, only a few are probably sufficiently common (or, in the more normative planning context, feasible) to be worthy of note. For example, the subset: big plants, strong unions, absentee ownership and specialized production combine to describe the automobile town of Flint, Michigan, a small metropolitan area which has a very high per capita income and very low degree of income inequality. Perhaps the performance of the Flint economy could have been predicted from its attributes: a strong union leads to an aggressive wage policy; large plants, oligopoly, and firm control over price enables local firms to buy industrial peace with product price increase without sacrificing profits; industrial specialization narrows the range of occupations, and unionization further constricts wage differentials on ideological grounds; absentee ownership reduces the role of property income as a local source of income—a kind of income usually disproportionately realized by the upper income groups. All of this combines to produce an economy which has a high average income and a very low degree of income inequality.

Conversely, the diversified economy of small locally owned plants and weak unionism (no unions or company unions) could probably be characterized by low wage rates, constrained by active competition from other areas, and large elements of property income, especially profits. This combination of low wages and a large profit element in local income would produce the reverse case: a relatively low per capita income relatively unequally distributed. Whether or not these two industrial syndromes can be empirically tied, in significant degree, to the two income patterns described will require much more than a quick deductive effort and some casual illustration. But therein lies the challenge: to identify alternative urban structural patterns that characterize alternative urban economic performance patterns.

Perhaps one of the most powerful interactions between income level and income inequality occurs in an *intra*metropolitan area context.

A rising money income enables central city residents of middle income to buy new homes. These usually are in suburban communities because the central city has little or no vacant land left. This money income effect is supplemented by a real income effect as the middle class aspires to escape the dirty, aging central city and the poor who are captive therein. But the higher real income that the middle class enjoys by this social separatism is extended to financial separatism through political fragmentation of the large metropolitan area. Unless the state picks up the lion's share of the financing of public assistance, public health, education, and so forth, the redistribution of income through the public sector will be greatly reduced. Thus, while the middle-class suburbanite may find his real income rising even faster than his money income, as he escapes financial responsibility for the poor, a member of the central city lower-income class finds his real income position deteriorating rapidly.

Still, the satisfaction that people derive from living in a given urban area may be appreciably reduced if extreme poverty exists. A great urban slum may endanger health, cause a nagging guilt feeling, offend one's aesthetic sense, endanger property values and in other ways detract from the total utility extracted from a given money income. Just how much people are willing to pay for relief from this detracting element is, of course, the public welfare equation. While the magnitude of this presumed urban poverty depressant poses a measurement problem surpassed by none heretofore mentioned, perhaps some rough outline of its dimensions can be sketched. After all, income redistribution decisions have to be made on some basis.

Income Level and Stability

A priori, at least a weak case can be made for the proposition that a high level of income is likely to be associated with income instability. Approaching the question from the vantage point of the local industry mix, we can eliminate two of the most unstable industries from consideration: construction because it is a ubiquitous activity that employs a similar proportion of the labor force everywhere, and extractive industries because they are predominantly nonurban in character. This leaves us with manufacturing as the major suspect in the case of the local business cycle. Adopting, instead, an economic base approach would have led us to a similar conclusion. Manufacturing is the primary export industry of most areas and, if the local business cycle is an exogenous phenomenon produced at the national level and then transmitted to each area through its interregional trade linkages, we would expect to find that an area is only as stable as its manufacturing export industries. The expected tendency for the higher-income areas to be more unstable is then deduced from the fact that the durable goods industries tend to be both higher paying and more unstable than the nondurables. Moreover, durables and nondurables do tend to cluster in separate urban areas, largely because most of the nondurables cannot compete in the same local labor market with the high-wage durables.[11]

Now if it could be shown that those service industries which are significant exporters (e.g., state government, tourism, amusement and recreational services, and central offices of nationwide corporations) are even more stable, on the average, than nondurable manufacturers, export activities might be arrayed in descending degree of instability: durables, nondurables, export services. And if it could be shown that the pay scales run downward similarly, then one need invoke only the most general application of the export-base logic to assemble both a deductive and empirical case for the low probability of a high level of income coupled with a high cyclical stability. While it is highly unlikely that such a simple, unequivocable case can be made to stick— the world is never that simple—one might establish a *tendency* toward the mutual exclusiveness of these two goals within a much broader and more subtle complex of forces.

While cyclical stability may not be associated with a high level of money income, both cyclical and seasonal stability do tend to raise the real income of the community by promoting urban efficiency. Stable levels of production and employment, both month-by-month and year-by-year, permit urban capital facilities to be tailored more precisely to business and household demands. In Chapter 4 we discussed the tendency for heavy seasonal fluctuations in demand to create alternating periods of shortages and idle capacity; although the analysis was oriented to shorter time periods than those which concern us here, the arguments are similar. Under heavy oscillations

---

[11] The average annual change in employment, 1947–54, by states, in each of three nondurable industry groups generally characterized by low wage rates, tobacco, textiles, and leather, is negatively correlated with employment growth in each of seven high-wage, durable goods industry groups, ranging over metals, machinery, vehicles, and instruments. While the coefficients are not all statistically significant, the pattern seems unmistakable, nondurables and durables do not live easily together in the same local labor market. Thompson and Mattila, *An Econometric Model . . . ,* *op. cit.,* p. 30.

in demand, capital facilities planning becomes a kind of Scylla-and-Charybdis navigating between too little capacity, with congestion and delay in the peak periods, and too much capacity, with its burden of heavy overhead charges intensifying the fiscal problems of the trough periods. Stability economizes on capital without sacrificing efficiency, thereby raising local living standards in real terms.

Income Stability and Distribution

A deductive approach to the interrelationship between stability of local income and inequality of its distribution is sufficiently inconclusive to again point up the need for empirical work. The most obvious and perhaps the dominant force at work is the poverty creating effect of cyclical unemployment. Frequent periods of pronounced local unemployment would surely seem to have an unequalizing effect. Still, we are reminded from the analyses above that it is the highly unionized, durable goods industries which tend to be the most unstable, and a tool or die maker in the automobile industry may be unemployed for three or four months during a recession year and still end up with an annual income that at least equals that of a textile worker or hotel clerk who works the year around. Similarly, if we regard the high hourly wage in the building trades as a device to equate these workers' *annual* earnings to other occupations, seasonal instability need not create annual income inequality, only high hourly wage rates and low average workweeks.

Not only is seasonal and cyclical unemployment often recouped through higher wage rates, but manufacturing employment, the largest unstable group of jobs, is also the most unionized of all work and therefore exhibits the most egalitarian pay schedules. The high-wage, highly unionized durable goods towns may well exhibit no more income inequality, in annual terms, than the more cyclical stable nondurable or service industry centers.

Even when unemployment does not hit the head of the household it displaces second earners, such as working wives, who come more than proportionately out of the lower income families. A highly unstable economy would seem, then, likely to oscillate between greater equality in booms when its labor market would become especially tight and productive of "second jobs" and greater inequality in recessions when its especially slack labor market produced very few jobs for wives and minors from poor families.

A further note of ambiguity is introduced when one looks to the future rather than the past. The trend in highly automated plants is toward a much more fixed input of labor—a consequence of fixed proportions of labor and capital. If one man must always observe a given set of dials and gauges, regardless of the rate of flow of output, fluctuations in production over the business cycle are not as faithfully translated into parallel fluctuations in employment as they once were. But perhaps even more important is the growing tendency to supply the higher levels of output demanded in prosperity periods by working the current labor force overtime, rather than by rehiring the workers displaced during the previous slack period, or those displaced by recent automation. Thus, while those still at work in the steadily automating plants are employed more regularly than before, a chronically unemployed group of displaced workers accumulates.

The combination of automation and unionization may well be giving rise to local labor markets in manufacturing areas in which the "average" amount of income inequality will be roughly comparable to that found in the nonunion, nonmanufacturing areas, but the former "average" will be blended out of a greater inequality at the lower end of the income spectrum (chronic unemployment) and a lesser inequality at the upper end (a narrow range of high wage rates). If the urban areas now most heavily specialized in manufacturing come to be the areas of chronic unemployment (though they also may well have high "average" incomes) they may combine the worst features of inequality and equality: extreme poverty without a local wealthy class from which to draw economic leadership. The service city, in this prospective golden age of the service industries, is more likely to provide many unskilled jobs that may be only modestly paid (even poorly paid by manufacturing standards), but which are sufficiently numerous to avoid the crushing poverty of chronic unemployment.

A corollary conjecture is whether the blue-collar egalitarianism that has so narrowed wage rate differentials will come to include a sense of responsibility for the chronically unemployed manufacturing worker. Union leaders and labor intellectuals aside, casual observation does not suggest any rapid development of *noblesse oblige* on the part of even the highest paid production workers. Tool makers, machinists, electricians, and the like, still tend to regard themselves as the exploited and underprivileged, and still look to "the rich" to carry the burden of unemployment and welfare. The question that may soon loom large is how to impress on the employed manufacturing worker, who becomes increasingly well paid with each technological advance, that *he* is "the rich" and that his technologically displaced and impoverished "brother" is not *a* shame but *his* shame.

While it is true that the more unstable employments and occupations are often those in which bargaining power has affected some compensating adjustment in the hourly wage rate, it is also true that those who are the first to be laid off in any given employment are usually those least able to afford it and least able to make any compensating adjustment. Typically, they are the marginal members of the labor force—the least productive or most subject to discriminatory treatment. The physically handicapped, mentally deficient, nonwhite, elderly, less-educated, or female are likely to have both the lowest pay rates and the least seniority. Therefore, any slackening of business activity is likely to cause unemployment first among the lowest income groups in the metropolitan area, compounding the poverty problem. The problem is compounded because these very groups are the ones most likely to be concentrated in the central city—the one political area probably least able to finance even the normal welfare demands, not to mention the heavy depression loads. But let us reserve more careful treatment of intrametropolitan area patterns for Chapters 7 and 8.

THE NATIONAL INTEREST AND THE FEDERAL ROLE IN URBAN-REGIONAL DEVELOPMENT

The urban goals matrix sketched out above is unabashedly provincial. The national interest is, at best, only implicit in the analyses above and then only to the extent that it emanates more or less automatically as a by-product of enlightened local self-interest. And perhaps the general welfare of the nation is advanced, more often than not, by enlightened local self-interest and ethical interurban competition, much as we trust the "invisible hand" of interfirm and interindustry competition to generate economic progress. Still, we might pause here and consider quite explicitly what the national interest and federal role might be in the processes of urban-regional growth and development and in the national urban pattern to which the federal authorities fall heir.

Allocation of Aggregate National Growth
between Urban Regions

Explicitly and implicitly, through free market mechanisms, plan and chance, the nation distributes and redistributes a couple of million people among the various urban regions each year. To the extent that we wish to plan, or at least to anticipate and prepare for, the interregional allocation of this growth in population and the labor force, we should clarify our interest in and position on: (a) the preferred rates of growth of urban areas under various conditions of size, location, and so forth, (b) the preferred size distribution of urban areas, and (c) the preferred spatial pattern of these urban areas.

We do have some dimly discernible national policy in these matters. Federal area development policy is oriented more toward increasing job opportunities in the depressed areas than toward moving people out. This is tantamount to setting the goal of a rate of employment growth in each region approximately equal to the natural rate of increase in the local labor force.

This is not, of course, a completely inflexible objective to be achieved at all costs. We are probably quite clear about the desirability of stimulating out-migration if a locality lacks the economic potential ever to provide enough jobs to go around (e.g., cut-over forest areas and depressed coal towns) at wages substantially in excess of the legal minimum wage. But it would be hard to argue that we are pursuing the less compelling objective of encouraging out-migration from areas of below national average wage rates (or median annual family income) to areas of higher than average wage rates (income), until interregional variations in per capita (or family) real income are nominal. Although we do have an Area Redevelopment Administration vaguely encharged with bringing industry into depressed areas, we have no programs to help redundant laborers move from looser to tighter labor markets.

If these indeed are our national objectives, are we clear on what they mean? Perhaps a very useful service would be rendered if the full implications of this position were spelled out so that we might review this implicit national decision.

Next, it may not be obvious that a national policy on urban-regional growth has locked into it a corollary position on city size. To promote area development in the characteristically small-town depressed areas implies a judgment that small isolated towns are economically viable in the latter half of the twentieth century, a doubtful position discussed at some length in the first chapter. Perhaps even more significant is our implicit position on the large metropolitan area. When the federal government actively promotes policies which discourage the out-migration of the unemployed in the Detroit or Pittsburgh metropolitan areas, or implicitly approves the continued growth of New York and Chicago by not moving to contain their further growth, the national position can be read that we anticipate and approve of the growth of our metropolitan areas at an over-all rate equal to their natural rates of increase plus the current rate of net in-migration. Can we say that our national policy is to provide for an average annual increase of, say, one and one-half per cent in our large metropolitan areas? This would seem to be a corollary of our current lack of interest in interregional growth patterns.

Extrapolating the size of existing urban areas by their expected natural increases—corrected for a declining rate of rural to urban migration as the rural areas and small towns empty out—has further implications for the future spatial pattern of our urban areas. On first blush, it might seem that if the existing city sites remain fixed, so will the urban spatial pattern. But as cities grow in size their relative spatial position changes. The most spectacular example of this condition is the new phenomenon of the almost endless strip city—"megalopolis." The filling in of the interurban open spaces between Boston and Washington may greatly alter the spatial pattern and the urban characteristics of the Atlantic seaboard. But less dramatic alterations in pattern occur even in isolated urban areas as the countryside recedes and outdoor recreation slips away, and water supplies falter and sewage disposal costs mount. Interregional transportation changes in its character and cost as trunk line surface routes, largely subsidized by the federal government, become more heavily travelled (probably leading to economies of scale and lower land travel costs) and air corridor congestion mounts (probably leading to diseconomies of scale). Finally, little has been written, at least for public consumption, on the national defense ramifications of continual population concentration and megalopolitan growth, especially since the advent of the hydrogen bomb and widespread fallout discouraged the early advocacy of industrial dispersal.

Let us now take notice of a potential structural change which will bear heavily on regional growth patterns, an economic transformation that provides the recurring theme for the remainder of this chapter. With aggregate growth and increasing size, the urban areas of the country will probably assemble ever more diversified industry mixes.

The blending of young, mature, and decadent industries should stabilize local growth and force it into rough conformance with the national rate of growth. If employment in each of our large metropolitan areas comes to grow at roughly the national rate, local population would also tend to grow at the national rate, all over. If we further assume that the natural rate of population increase would be everywhere about the same (and there is little reason to expect significant regional differentials in birth and death rates) we would expect to find a system of cities developing in which few would need to move to find a job. We assume here that the national rate of change in job opportunities keeps pace with the national rate of increase in the labor force. Moreover, not only would large urban areas grow steadily at the "right" rate to absorb natural additions to the local labor force, in aggregate, but these large local labor markets would offer the variety of jobs necessary to match occupational preferences. The implicit aggregate growth goal uncovered at the beginning of this section would be realized—the minimization of involuntary migration.

If the trend toward very large urban areas were to narrow interregional growth rate differentials, interregional migration would not cease, certainly not in gross terms and not even in net terms, as reasons for migration other than economic would persist. The need for variety and the search for greener pastures would still impel the young to move about and the elderly would continue to move South. But this migration would surely be less a social welfare matter. The need for federal leadership in arranging for a better exchange of labor market information between the many semiautonomous local labor markets would come to be less critical than it is right now. The federal role in migration could diminish before it is responsibly assumed.

Interregional Redistribution of Income

An important function of the federal government from its inception has been to arrange for the interregional redistribution of income. In the national interest, the East was called upon to subsidize the opening of the West as federal services were provided long before they were economical, for example, mail service, railroads, military protection. In this century, the regional redistribution of income has run more from North to South, as an excess of federal tax payments over federal expenditures in New York and Michigan finance a favorable balance of federal expenditures over tax payments in Alabama and Mississippi,

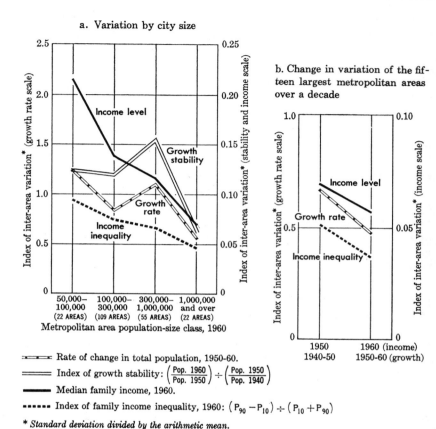

a. Variation by city size

b. Change in variation of the fifteen largest metropolitan areas over a decade

Rate of change in total population, 1950-60.

Index of growth stability: $\left(\dfrac{\text{Pop. 1960}}{\text{Pop. 1950}}\right) \div \left(\dfrac{\text{Pop. 1950}}{\text{Pop. 1940}}\right)$

Median family income, 1960.

Index of family income inequality, 1960: $\left(P_{90} - P_{10}\right) \div \left(P_{10} + P_{90}\right)$

* *Standard deviation divided by the arithmetic mean.*

Based on data from the Decennial Census of the United States, 1950-60.

Figure 7. Variations in the rate and stability of population growth and the level of distribution of family income within different size classes of metropolitan areas. *The Chart, based on data from the Decennial Census of Population, suggests that large urban areas are more like each other in the rate and stability of growth and the level and distribution of income than are small ones. It shows the degree to which cities in the same size class resemble each other. Furthermore, urban areas in the largest size class seem to be growing more alike over time.*

lifting the latter states toward parity in hospitals, roads, rural electrification, and so forth.[12]

But in Chapter 2 we saw how interstate differentials in per capita income, ranging as high as 2½ to 1, are reduced to interurban differentials of only 1½ to 1 or so. Thus what we have long come to know as interregional income differentials turn out to be largely urban-rural differentials. And as state after state empties out its rural areas leaving only the more productive and affluent farmers behind, our highly urbanized states will surely come to exhibit much more uniform per capita incomes.

A trend toward diminishing interregional income differentials among the large metropolitan areas is already noticeable. The coefficient of variation of median family income among the fifteen largest metropolitan areas fell from .069 in 1950 to .057 in 1960.[13] While careful empirical work is needed here, there is good reason to believe that as the metropolitan areas of the country grow ever larger and able to support an ever more diversified mix of industries they will come to exhibit increasingly similar per capita incomes. This is not to say that every metropolitan area will produce everything, and that regional specialization and interregional trade will cease, only that each of these metropolises will produce many products and that even random industry mixes, if large enough, will tend to produce average performance characteristics.

A diversified industry mix not only blends high and low wage rates but also mixes labor demands by sex, age, color, and education to achieve similar labor force participation rates between urban areas. Not just wage rates but family incomes are thereby pulled closer together, as developed in some detail in Chapters 2 and 3. Simply said, Boston, Baltimore, and Birmingham will all come to have a similar mix of rich and poor.

[12] The staff of the Upper Midwest Economic Study estimated that Alabama received back in federal expenditures about 45 per cent more than it paid in federal taxes for the year 1960, and Mississippi received back about 58 per cent more than it paid into the federal treasury. In contrast, New York and Michigan received back from the federal government about 20 per cent less than they paid in. *The Geographic Impact of the Federal Budget,* Technical Paper No. 3 (Minneapolis: University of Minnesota, October 1962). Table 1, p. 6.

[13] The particular coefficient of variation employed was the one most commonly used, the standard deviation (of the fifteen median incomes) divided by the arithmetic mean (the average of these fifteen medians). The source of the data was the 1950 and 1960 *Censuses of Population.* Washington, D.C., was excluded because it is clearly unique and not subject to the hypothesized trend toward an average industry mix.

A trend toward a similar mix of rich and poor in the very large urban areas does not imply any lessening of the degree of interpersonal income inequality within them. Such a trend would create a situation in which each large urban area would experience about the same welfare need per capita and have about the same per capita income and wealth out of which to meet it. Local government could be hamstrung in its efforts to tap its potential tax capacity by lack of access to the more powerful tax instruments, such as state limitations on the use of personal or corporate income taxes, or through fear of using these taxes, due to interarea competition for industry and wealthy residents. But at least the financial potential would exist at the local level with which to solve each community's own welfare problems. There is some evidence that the largest urban areas are coming to have more similar degrees of interpersonal income inequality. The coefficient of variation of the interquartile deviations of family income for the fifteen largest metropolitan areas fell from .076 in 1950 to .065 in 1960.[14] That is, the variation *between* very large urban areas in the degree of variation in income *within* them decreased over the past decade.

Certainly, we would expect some differentials in money income to prevail to offset differences in the local cost of living and in local amenities. Further, warm climates attract the older people on low retirement incomes, leaving Tucson and St. Petersburg with an age distribution of population weighted toward the lower incomes. Still, one might hazard the guess that a decade or two hence, with most of the population living in large diversified urban areas, there will be less need for interregional income transfers and the federal role in urban affairs will turn largely on other matters.

Regionalism in National Stabilization Policy

A trend toward population concentration in a relatively few, very large metropolitan areas could also act to homogenize local business cycles. As metropolitan areas pass the million population mark they begin to exhibit highly diversified industrial bases. Glaring exceptions such as Detroit and Pittsburgh may or may not occur again. The spectacular decentralization of the cyclically sensitive heavy industries

[14] For a brief description and rationalization of the interquartile deviation as a measure of interpersonal inequality see Chapter 3 above. Washington, D.C., was again excluded for the reason given in the preceding footnote and the source of the data was the same.

which once were so highly concentrated and so heavily dominated their host areas—automobiles, steel, machinery—is one main element in the hypotheses that local business cycles are becoming less distinctive.

Probably just as critical is the continuing national shift from manufacturing to service activity. Since services must often be rendered through face-to-face contact and demand the most expensive kind of movement—the carriage of persons, where time cost adds to direct costs—their market areas are relatively small. With a growing part of the local labor force producing services for local consumption, and with consumption patterns highly similar everywhere, it is difficult to see how the business cycles of the large metropolitan areas could fail to lose much of their distinctiveness over the next decade or two. It was, after all, the rise of manufacturing for national markets which turned the relatively standardized trade and service centers of the nineteenth century into the highly specialized manufacturing cities of the twentieth century. Smelting, canning, wood products manufacturing and other resource-based industries may continue to locate near their raw materials sources and dominate small towns. But under continuing automation, processing of raw materials will use and affect ever fewer (though higher paid) workers, and pose more of a capital planning problem to its managers than a human welfare issue to society.

Another factor tending to homogenize local business cycles is interregional convergence in the age distribution of capital. The national business cycle strikes some urban areas harder than others because the older, high-cost facilities are cut back first and most and brought back to high levels of operation last. Thus the older industrial areas are more vulnerable in cycle fluctuations. Manufacturing activity was spawned and clustered in the "American Ruhr" stretching from Boston to Chicago and has recently moved to the South and West, partly in pursuit of markets. Northern cities entered the postwar period with a relatively old age-distribution of industrial facilities and the South and West were relatively favorably situated with modern, low-cost capacity. But little by little successive additions and retirements of capital with heterogeneous life spans have randomized the age distribution of capital in the older and newer areas.

Finally, with large urban areas all growing at similar rates, their construction industries would be of roughly comparable size and impart roughly the same cyclical impulses to their local economies. Increasing city size tends to produce local business cycles which mirror the national pattern. The spatial pattern of industry may re-form over the next decade or two in such a way that need for a regional approach to business stabilization may wane before the federal government has managed to introduce important elements of regionalism in its cycle policy.

The hypothesized homogenization of industry mixes should also blend fast growing, slow growing, and declining industries in the large city-states-to-be so as to narrow their interregional growth rate differentials and stabilize them. If, in fact, the growth rates of very large urban areas do tend to become more alike and more stable, as argued in Chapter 4 and as indicated by preliminary empirical work,[15] construction activity would also show similar time patterns in the various metropolises.

Urban Experimentation: Efficiency, Choice, and Progress

Suppose population concentration does continue and we do become a nation of a relatively few, very large metropolitan areas, each with widely diversified industrial structures, and suppose that this diversification is random enough to mix rich and poor in roughly equal proportions everywhere, and to mix stable and unstable industries in roughly equal proportions, effecting thereby very similar local business cycles. Suppose, further, this greatly reduces the need to employ the federal authority to redistribute income between urban regions or the need to regionalize anticyclical fiscal and monetary policy. What then would be the federal government's role in urban affairs?

The federal government might still have to concern itself with urban-regionalism to achieve its own primary goal—national economic growth. The compilation of summary national aggregate accounts, such as gross national product, should not obscure the fact that production takes place in actual factories located on very specific sites, drawing on laborers living nearby, served by the local schools and transportation systems, and managed by executives who draw more or less intellectual and creative stimulus from their immediate environment. Unless the federal authorities' call for "growth" is pure exhorta-

[15] The coefficient of variation of percentage change in population from 1940 to 1950 for the fifteen largest metropolitan areas, excluding Washington, D.C., was .66; the coefficient for the fifteen 1950–60 changes fell sharply to .48. Granting that the first of the two periods includes the very substantial war dislocations, even so the decrease is still arresting. The 1950 and 1960 Censuses of Population were the source of the data.

tion or purely for political purposes, national policy must percolate down into localities and help create an environment in which economic productivity will flourish; that is, it must foster urban efficiency. Granting the role of fiscal and monetary policy in insuring that growth does not lag due to inadequate aggregate demand, the supply side of growth—upgrading of labor skills, the nurturing of entrepreneurship, the supply of low-cost, high-quality business services—would seem to require a more searching look at the federal level. A responsible program of national growth should look not only to the quality of local schools, local government, and public utilities, but also to labor and capital markets and even to the urban amenities which stimulate a feeling of well-being and stimulate creativity.

The indispensable role for the federal government may come to be that of fostering the growth of knowledge about the nature of the urban "production function," the relationship between urban size and urban form on one hand and urban productivity on the other. Are there "U" shaped cost curves in *public* services which favor some intermediate size urban area, much like those on which firm and industry theory is built? Does increased size in a city offer better private and public services and facilities and better forums for the exchange of ideas and other external economies up to some optimum point, and beyond that are any further economies of scale more than offset by powerful diseconomies (e.g., high land rents, traffic congestion, and higher labor cost to cover these increased living costs)? Is there, in other words, an optimum city size considering both public and private costs—or more realistically a number of different optimum sizes relevant for various industries or complexes of industries—larger for finance, smaller for textiles? To what extent should industrial specialization in urban areas be encouraged or discouraged for national purposes—"comparative advantage" versus "balanced growth"?

In sum, can we achieve *both* the big plants which enhance productivity *and* local industrial diversification for stability and choice by creating a nation of giant metropolises? And can we do this without sacrificing important political and social values? For instance, recent evidence of callousness bordering on inhumanity in New York City streets has raised nagging doubts about the quality of life in the "great city."

Beyond serving as a catalyst for increased local productivity, the federal authority may fill a critical role in acting as the sponsor of invention and innovation designed to make cities better places in which to live—the real income side. We might see each of our giant metropolitan areas as "experimental stations." We borrow a phrase long used to describe the advantages of our political system which provides for a division of powers between a strong (though limited) central government and semiautonomous states, free to compete with each other by experimenting with new political institutions— Nebraska's unicameral legislature, Georgia's lowering the voting age to 18 years. The interstate competition did, of course, occasionally become destructive, e.g., the steady whittling away of inheritance tax rates in competition for wealthy retirees. Still, the federal government was not without corrective power: a federal estate tax was enacted with an 80 per cent credit for state inheritance tax liabilities, forcing state rates back up.

Federally-sponsored experimentation is especially important because of: (a) the limitations of purely deductive analyses of a phenomenon so subtle and complex as a large modern metropolis, (b) the frustration of a comparative empirical effort when there can be no data on untried new forms, and (c) the dilemma of unaided local experimentation when the full cost is borne by the locality while the pay-off of a successful new device is available to all other cities and a failure saves *them* money—social invention without patent protection. The federal role, then, would be to employ outright grants, grants-in-aid, and long-term, low interest rate loans to encourage controlled efforts to create interurban differentiation. Rather than supply each urban area with its pro-rata share of highway money and deny each area mass transit money, the federal authorities would finance automobile freeways in some places (e.g., Detroit and Los Angeles) and mass transit in others (e.g., New York and San Francisco). Funds for slum clearance and outdoor recreation facilities and indirect subsidies such as FHA-insured mortgages could also be varied in form to encourage innovation in urban form: high-density, stellate, mass transit cities; sprawling, flexible, automobile-oriented cities; loose networks of federated cities, such as could develop in North Carolina; and so forth.

The purpose of encouraging interurban differentiation would be partly to build urban pilot plants and then to be able to replicate the more efficient forms and discard the inefficient, but only partly. In many, if not most cases there are no better or poorer forms in any universal sense but only designs which appeal more to some and less to others. To at least an equal degree we would be providing variety and increasing consumer welfare through enlarging effective choice. We witness daily the retired New Yorker migrating to urbane Miami and the retired Iowan choosing folksy St. Petersburg instead. The very fact of a Los Angeles and a San Francisco in the same state, and both growing rapidly, provides convincing testimony to the sterility of protracted argument about which form is better. Still many city planners do seem intent on determining the nature of the ultimate in urban form—their eternal verities.

If very large urban concentrations do develop throughout the nation, permitting local residents to find work at home whatever their vocational interests, as suggested above, distinctive styles of life in the various urban areas could become the main desiderata of residential choice. That is, a Los Angeles resident graduating with a degree in chemistry could stay at home and work as a chemist, but he would be free, if he chose, to exchange his present decentralized automobile-oriented urban life for the more centralized, mass transit-oriented environment of a San Francisco or New York. Interregional migration could become much less involuntary, in response to money income differentials and job opportunities, and much more oriented toward personal tastes and urban amenities—oriented toward "psychic income." Thus the federal role would be to increase range of choice by fostering nationwide variety in living arrangements—product differentiation at the gross grain of whole cities.[16] This would all be in addition to the residential variety offered within the "fragmented" large metropolitan area, discussed in detail in Chapters 2 and 7.

What is proposed here is simply that Americans explicitly recognize legitimate variations in urban form and exploit them in such a way as to improve them and learn from them. Federal financial aids could and probably should be used to enhance urban differences both to achieve the short-run (static) end of greater choice and the long-run (dynamic) end of progress through experimentation. Both of these ends can be achieved only in the nationwide context of a system of cities and by dipping into the federal purse. Perhaps only the integration and co-ordination of the many federal urban programs would permit the comprehensive planning and the complex strategy implied, but we leave others to make a careful case for a "Department of Urban Affairs."

[16] Federal encouragement of interurban differentiation in living styles may become even more critical in the near future if the impressions of William H. Whyte, Jr., as set forth in *The Organization Man* (New York: Simon and Shuster, 1956) and John Dyckman, as set forth in "The Changing Uses of the Central City," *Daedalus*, Winter, 1961, p. 119, are shared by many, if not most, of the people. They argue that one can move among the cities of the United States and experience little or no significant environmental change—have little or no consumer choice in residential arrangements.

PART II

PRESCRIPTION:
Problems and Policy
in the Urban Economy

CHAPTER 6

Urban Poverty: Employment, Employability, and Welfare

There is no need to marshal elaborate argumentation to justify discussing unemployment policy under the rubric of urban economics; the urban economy is first a labor market. And in an era characterized more by depressed areas than by depressions and more by chronic unemployment of the few than by periodic mass unemployment, the local labor market assumes new importance and local government new responsibilities. The argument of the first part of this chapter is that the change from a heavy national business cycle to a checkered pattern of poverty amidst plenty shifts responsibility for maintaining full employment from an almost unadulterated federal responsibility to a federal-state-local partnership.

Heavy local unemployment, especially the chronic variety that does not just temporarily depress living standards but impoverishes households, destroys housing, and contaminates neighborhood environments, plays havoc with local government budgets and otherwise bedevils urban public administrators and city planners. The local labor market is a (perhaps *the*) main arena in which urban economic issues must be resolved. To rest easily on a rising per capita income— "economic progress"—as the salve which will remove the blemish of slums may be to ignore an insidious tendency for a small group of chronically unemployed to lag far behind, as automation destroys low-skill jobs, as discrimination against nonwhites and older workers distorts employment patterns, and as personal "failures" occur for a variety of reasons.

Ambitious physical slum clearance efforts can be futile and frustrating when chronic unemployment and crushing poverty create new slums at an even faster rate. Urban managerial economics seems destined to become heavily involved in labor market analysis and manpower planning, the perfunctory role accorded to it at present notwithstanding. The second section of this chapter will, therefore,

203

emphasize the strategy and tactics for achieving a more efficient local labor market, especially with reference to employing the least employable members of the local labor force.

Finally, a significant, if unknown, share of our adult population is temporarily or permanently unemployable, for reasons of education, age, physical or mental health, or whatever. We must distinguish the employable from the unemployable on our public welfare roles and put the former to work or into vocational training or general education programs so that they can make the contribution to our national product of which they are potentially capable. This is very important for at least three distinct reasons. First, the potentially employable need the self-respect of doing useful work; there is much useful unskilled work to be done cleaning up our cities so that there is no need of resorting to make-work projects. Second, we need an educated citizenry in a democracy, so that education is an end in itself. Third, the taxpayer surely will be more willing to support adequate levels of public welfare if nonwork relief payments are clearly going only to those who cannot work or should not work. Accordingly, in the third section of this chapter, we will consider the strategy and tactics of making public assistance payments to accomplish these ends. Special attention will be given the problem of the multigeneration welfare family, that is, the need to begin now working on the employability of the next generation of welfare families—the slum children.

THE CHALLENGE OF STRUCTURAL UNEMPLOYMENT

The Changing Nature of Unemployment

Just as the decline of the farm and the rise of the factory as the center of employment forced a great relocation and retraining of the labor force, the current shift from a manufacturing to a service economy is making large demands on labor. And the technological revolution now in progress is perhaps destined to be an even greater disruptive force. This brings us to what is almost certain to be the great *domestic economic* issue of the sixties, employment and manpower policy.

Briefly, we may distinguish two types of unemployment: cyclical unemployment due to periodically inadequate aggregate demand (too little spending) and structural unemployment due to an insufficiently flexible supply of productive resources, under which there can be substantial unemployment at the same time there are labor shortages. Since the great work of John Maynard Keynes, the demand side of employment analysis has been in fashion. Keynes depicted and dissected the aggregate demand basis of economic fluctuations so neatly and incisively as to make the allure of his system of thought irresistible —except to Congressmen. Keynesian economics characterizes the economy as a circular flow of income from business to households (in wages, interest, rents, and profits) and back again (in consumption spending) and around and around. Savings are seen as a drain from the hydraulic system and investment as a recirculating pump, and full employment equilibrium is attained when investment fully absorbs and returns to the income stream the very high level of savings (leakage) generated by a full employment level of national income.

Not only did the New Economics have an undeniable simplicity and grace to it, it also gave rise to crisp and clean policy dicta. Since the government, conveniently, straddles the circular flow with its own drain (taxes) and pump (public expenditures), it could serve as an equilibrating mechanism. If the economy were suffering from too little spending (deflation-depression), the government could transfuse the economy by running a deficit—spending more than its tax receipts. Alternatively, if total spending were excessive and inflation threatened, government could either raise taxes or cut its own spending and, by running a surplus, bleed the patient.

Cyclical unemployment has always been diagnosed as a national malady calling for federal treatment. If fluctuations in national aggregate demand are the principal cause of unemployment, only a political entity big enough to change total spending by at least a per cent or two (e.g., $5 to $10 billion) can rise to the occasion. Local governments, moreover, are not able to influence the rate of spending even within their own local economies with the same leverage that the federal government can exert on the national economy because of two hard constraints. First, only the federal government, with control over the money supply, can purposefully and with near impunity run the large and continuing deficits needed to transfuse a depressed economy with new money and new spending.

Second, any fillip to local spending achieved by chancing a hazardous *local* public deficit of substantial magnitude would be quickly dissipated throughout the whole national economy as a large part of the new money left the local economy to pay for imports. The local

multiplier is much lower than the national multiplier, probably ranging from a value of perhaps one-half as large in a million plus population urban area down to perhaps one-quarter as large in an urban area
of 50 thousand population. Unlike the national case where the multiplier must be at least one and is probably rarely less than two, the
local multiplier could easily be less than one. To illustrate, a (deficit-
financed) depression public works project (e.g., a new civic auditorium)
might cost one million dollars but over one-half this amount might
be lost to the local economy immediately through the purchase of
imported building materials, and the one-half that remained in (construction worker) wages and (building contractor) profits might be
re-spent in such a way that less than one-half added to wages and
profits in the local service industries in each ensuing round of re-
spending. The local multiplier would then be less than $\frac{1}{2} + \frac{1}{4} + \frac{1}{8} +$
. . . , or less than one, a very expensive way to buy local recovery. In
sum, the local public economy cannot cope with the problem of a
deficiency in aggregate demand.

All or most localities, acting in concert, could of course achieve a
multiplier effect equivalent to that of the federal government, as
the individual local import leakages cancel out, leaving only savings,
taxes and imports from abroad to dampen the multiplier effect. But
such harmonious action is quite unrealistic, besides, the federal government is, essentially, the agent for concerted action on a national
scale.

But the nature of the unemployment problem seems to be changing.
For some years now, Keynesians have been haunted by the paradox of
rising prices (too much spending?) in periods of unemployment (too
little spending?)—one cannot transfuse and bleed simultaneously.[1]

An even newer development further muddies the waters of Keynesian fiscal policy. Each postwar recession has left us, on recovery,

---

[1] While the economics of full employment without inflation is a national policy
question and will not be treated here, this dilemma of fiscal-monetary policy is
relevant in that only if we are able to reduce cyclical unemployment to a near
zero level by manipulating aggregate demand, via the Keynesian-type and other
remedies, is it likely that structural unemployment can be successfully treated. The
serious student of local structural employment policy, our primary interest here,
should be reasonably conversant with the main ideas and issues of national fiscal
policy. A standard principles of economics text, such as Paul A. Samuelson, *Economics, An Introductory Analysis* (New York: McGraw-Hill Book Co., Inc., 1961),
Chapters 11–19, or George Leland Bach, *Economics, An Introduction to Analysis
and Policy*, Fourth Edition (Englewood Cliffs, New Jersey: Prentice-Hall, Inc., 1963),
Chapters 5–16, would be a good place to begin. Any one of a number of collateral
readings books designed for the first course in economics would then flesh out the
bare bones of the textual treatment.

with a higher level of residual (hard-core?) unemployment than did the preceding one—prosperity *with* unemployment. We seem to be struggling with a situation in which a 2 or 3 per cent increase in spending (in either the private or public sector) might cut unemployment back a per cent or so, from the disturbing level of, say, 6 per cent back to the uneasy level of 5 per cent. But further increases in spending could easily spend their force in raising prices and/or give overtime to the already employed, without much reducing unemployment.

All this suggests that the aggregate demand approach so appropriate to cyclical unemployment needs to be complemented by a new emphasis on the supply side of unemployment—"structural" unemployment. Structural unemployment can be exemplified by a sixty-year-old coal miner with a sixth-grade education who has lived his whole life and owns his own home in a West Virginia mountain town. Structural unemployment is symbolized by the company pension plan which discourages the employment of older workers, and by racial discrimination in hiring and in union membership, and, unfortunately, so on and so forth. The treatment of structural unemployment clearly requires a reconversion of the labor supply through retraining and relocation programs to fit changing patterns of occupational, industrial, and spatial demand. Increasing aggregate demand, in some undifferentiated way as through a federal budget deficit, is a grossly inefficient way to fit square pegs into round holes.

But there is no real cause for quarrel, in public policy, between the Keynesian who emphasizes the demand side of unemployment and the "structuralist" who emphasizes the supply side; an adequate level of aggregate demand is the *necessary* condition to full employment. The first step in the treatment of widespread unemployment is the use of the federal government's fiscal and monetary powers to raise total spending to the point where the labor market is under gentle pressure, as evidenced by more than occasional labor shortages in specific skills or areas. Nothing is more pathetic than the sight of different state and local industrial development commissions scrambling during a recession for a grossly insufficient national total of jobs. Until the total demand for pegs has been raised to a level which will absorb the full supply, retraining programs which knock the corners off redundant square pegs will only succeed in making redundant round pegs.

Still, there is a point beyond which the pressing need is to adjust the supply of skills and places of residence to match new patterns of consumer demand, new industrial processes and new industrial locational patterns. A full-scale attack on the supply side adds the *sufficient* condition to full employment policy. And at this point local government becomes a full partner in employment policy for the first time.

Even the principal tool of the federal government for combating unemployment, a budget deficit, can be used in ways that have greater or lesser leverage. To run a federal deficit by cutting taxes (the current fashion), attacks unemployment on only one front, aggregate demand, and even if the relieved taxpayer does spend most of the tax cut (questionable, depending on whose taxes are cut), his spending may give overtime work to already employed automobile or furniture workers rather than create work for the marginal labor supply. To argue that, ultimately, some of this new spending will reach the pockets of the unemployed, roundabout through an upgrading of the employed labor force which opens up jobs at the bottom, is to depend on a "trickle-down" theory of employment stimulation. Forced upgrading may well be the key, but probably only if approached powerfully from the supply side simultaneously.

Conversely, a budget deficit incurred to finance new retraining and relocation programs for unemployed workers in declining industries and depressed areas attacks the problem on two fronts, aggregate demand and labor mobility. The demand-multiplier effect would be at least as great and probably greater because the marginal propensity to spend of the structurally unemployed is almost certainly greater than that of the average relieved taxpayer. Moreover, the unemployed would be made more employable and hence more competitive with overtime labor. And the enhanced employment leverage goes hand-in-hand with what most would agree is a better, more humanitarian income distributive effect. Thus, a federal deficit designed to reduce cyclical unemployment could be structured in a way which would help local government treat chronic unemployment.

Frictional-Structural Unemployment: Displacement and Transition

The rapid rate of technological change over the past decade[2] has revived fears of technological unemployment, especially in light of

---

[2] Commissioner Ewan Clague and Leon Greenberg of the Bureau of Labor Statistics set the over-all increase in output per man-hour for the period 1950–61 at between 2.7 and 2.9 per cent per year, as compared to the long-run average rate of

the fact that *peak prosperity* unemployment has risen steadily from less than 3 per cent of the labor force (Third Quarter 1953) to over 4 per cent (Fourth Quarter 1956) to over 5 per cent (First Quarter 1960) to a currently sticky level of around 6 per cent.[3] A decade of growth in hard-core unemployment presents a perplexing and serious social problem that is highly relevant to our interests. What is the nature of the relationship between technological change and unemployment and how does it relate to urban economics?

The current international competition for industrial and technological leadership of the world, interregional competition between states for the new technology-based industries, and the substitution of quality for price competition in oligopolistic markets have all combined to produce a quasi-official, national crash effort in research and development. This apparent acceleration in the growth of technology is more than just another happy fact of our materialistic life; it is also a serious challenge to our powers of social invention. The brightest of us, urged on by appeals to patriotism along a way paved with lush financing, have succeeded in displacing the dullest of us from accustomed work at a surprisingly rapid rate. With a growing stream of displaced workers floundering in an inefficient labor market, local labor market planning and policy could easily come to comprise the very heart of "urban managerial economics"—its virtually complete neglect in the urban planning and public administration literature notwithstanding.

Thus is the specter of technological unemployment raised again, after having presumably been laid to rest so many times in the past. How serious is it? On the bright side, one can cite this country's long history of technological progress with rising levels of employment. And the historical evidence can be supported with a deductive effort. New jobs, it is argued, are created for making the very machines that displace workers, although it must be conceded that the number of

---

2.4 per cent per year for the 1909–61 period. Ewan Clague and Leon Greenberg, "Employment," *Automation and Technological Change*, The American Assembly, Columbia University (Englewood Cliffs, N.J.: Prentice-Hall Inc., 1962), p. 116.

[3] The National Planning Association would set frictional unemployment at about 2 per cent of the labor force and characterize the remainder of the "prosperity" unemployment as chronic unemployment: from a small percentage in 1953 to 2.2 per cent of the labor force in 1956 to 3.2 per cent in 1960. National Planning Association, *The Rise of Chronic Unemployment* (Washington, D.C.: NPA, April 1961), p. 7. They attribute this rising "structural" unemployment more to structural weaknesses in aggregate demand than to occupational or spatial labor immobilities. Whether they believe the standard Keynesian-type fiscal policies would eliminate most of this "structural" unemployment is not clear; in our view it would not.

jobs created is smaller than the ones eliminated, otherwise no over-all labor (cost) saving would be effected by introducing the new technology. More new jobs, however, are created in filling new demands generated by the savings accruing to the consumer from lower prices for the now more efficiently produced goods—new demand generated by the very productivity increase that was needlessly troubling the pessimist. The term "technological displacement" should in this view be substituted for "technological unemployment."[4]

One might harbor a reasonable doubt, however, about the adequacy of this sanguine rationalization. Granting, for the sake of argument, that the workers displaced by a given set of technological advances will eventually be absorbed—and this is a bit too strong a concession to make, considering the inflexibility of the older and less educated workers—still the frequency of these displacements and the length of time required to effect the transition remain to be considered. In any interval of time, the number of job displacements (due to technological change, shifting demands or whatever) plus net additions to the labor force (due to population growth or changing labor participation rates) may be exactly equal to the number of new jobs created, but this alone tells nothing about the size of the unemployment "float." The float of unemployed workers, the number of workers between jobs, is a function of the rate of displacement and the average length of time spent in transition between jobs.

Structural unemployment can increase even if workers are reemployed at the same rate that they are displaced. If the monthly displacement rate should rise from $\frac{1}{2}$ to 1 per cent of the total labor force, with the average duration of transition between jobs remaining the same at, say, six months, and with the rate of reemployment rising

---

[4] "To the extent that there are real problems of unemployment associated with automation, they are problems of dislocation . . . it does not follow that automation has caused unemployment, but only that it has changed the occupational distribution of the labor force. . . . When some of those automated out of their jobs do go through a period of unemployment, the explanation is always something other than automation: that the economy is not at "full" employment, for example, or that people are reluctant to move their homes . . . the same as . . . a shift in consumer demand." W. Allen Wallis, "Some Economic Considerations," *ibid.*, p. 111. Wallis seems to prefer to set up a norm of perfect occupational and spatial mobility of labor and then to see job dislocations that turn into temporary unemployment as caused by the failure of the market mechanism to work perfectly, rather than by the fact of the dislocation itself. In his view, it is the imperfect mechanism not the unanticipated impact which is responsible for the unemployment. Which blade of the scissors does the cutting? What we argue here is simply that a period of transitional unemployment does occur—due both to "structural" changes in labor demand and "structural" immobilities of labor supply.

in parallel fashion from ½ to 1 per cent six months later when the first new higher crest of higher unemployment completes its period of transition, then the economic system will settle down to a new higher rate of unemployment exactly double the earlier level.

Again, the rate of reemployment may equal the rate of displacement ("everyone who wants to work will find a new job") but if the time required to retrain or relocate the displaced worker increases—possibly because of the growing complexity and skill requirements of the new jobs—then the proportion of the labor force unemployed would also increase proportionately. If, for example, 12 per cent of the labor force must change jobs during a given year with an average of 13 weeks of work (one-quarter of the year) lost in transition, this is equivalent to an annual rate of unemployment of roughly 3 per cent (12 per cent × ¼ year), but if the transition time grows to 26 weeks of work lost (one-half of the year), the annual unemployment equivalent is 6 per cent of the labor force.

In its simplest terms, this technological-frictional unemployment can be seen as a labor market queue waiting to be served with new jobs. The length of the queue depends on the frequency with which the average worker enters the line and the speed with which the line moves, assuming that a new job is always provided in due course for everyone in line. It is not enough, then, to debate the question of whether our economic system can provide, ultimately, enough new jobs for the technologically displaced worker; the hard questions seem to be: how often is this readjustment demanded and how long does it take?

The impact of technological change (or any other labor displacing shock) on frictional-structural unemployment, as described above, can be expressed in simple algebraic form as shown:

$$U = dl \quad \text{when: } d = r$$

where: U = number of workers unemployed at any point of time (a limiting valve achieved in equilibrium)

d = number of workers displaced per month

l = time lag from displacement to reemployment, in months

r = number of workers reemployed per month

If two workers are displaced each month and the time lag to reemployment is three months, then the equilibrium level of frictional unemployment, due to whatever shocks are causing the displacement, is six workers. The sense of this formulation is that two workers are displaced in January and are reemployed in April, two more are between jobs from February to May and two more from March to June. Thus, in March we have two workers who have just been laid off, two who have been unemployed for one month, and two unemployed for two months.

If automation and other rapid technological changes tend to demand less specialized skill and more general education, retraining time may be reduced because machine-tending exhibits substantial similarity among products and processes. It may come to be easier to shift from being an efficient welding machine operator to being an efficient plastics molding machine operator than it is now from being an efficient welder to an efficient molder. Easier, that is, given a good basic education in English and mathematics which enables the worker to read a technical manual, write a report, and handle the quantitative aspects of the new job. The displacement time for the educated, skilled workers may decrease in the current stage of technological progress.

But the low-skilled worker who, when displaced, finds he must go back to school and pick up more general education before he can even begin learning a new skill, will certainly find the transition period longer now as he shifts, for example, from a drill press in a dirty shop to a cash register in a spotless department store. Thus even if machine displacements were to occur at the same rate among the various levels of skill, the longer transition periods for the unskilled and semiskilled would threaten greater frictional-structural unemployment for them. The clear fact, moreover, that the simpler processes are most easily automated certainly threatens that the lesser-skill jobs will be subject to a higher rate of displacement as well as a longer period of transition. In sum, the more skilled worker becomes subject to the inconvenience of frictional-structural unemployment, while the less skilled worker becomes subject to the heavy burden of chronic structural unemployment.

While this illustration was cast in terms of technological change, any other set of labor displacing shocks would have served equally well, such as drastic shifts in consumer taste patterns or a sharp relocation of industry.

By breaking down frictional-structural unemployment into two elemental and complementary factors, the job displacement rate and the length of the transition period, a new role for local government in manpower planning and employment policy becomes evident. Since the rate of displacement is largely attributable to changes in technology and spending patterns in a national market, the local role in altering this factor seems modest at best. Local instrumentalities can best be brought to bear on the length of the transition period, such as through stuffing more basic education into the locally controlled school curriculums to increase the students' adaptability to new kinds of work in the event that their former work is automated. It is to this matter that we now turn.

A Growing Role for Local Employment Planning

Structural unemployment is just as much a national phenomenon as cyclical unemployment in that structural changes in taste patterns and technology are nationwide manifestations of a common industrial culture. A crucial distinction, however, arises in the fact that structural unemployment accords to local government, for the first time, an important role in employment policy and manpower planning. When the point is reached at which increases in aggregate demand (total spending) are reflected more in price increases than in increased production and much of the increased production is achieved by overtime employment rather than through new hirings of still unemployed workers,[5] the remaining unemployment may be characterized as largely structural. Here, the local government controls the major instrumentalities that bear on the supply side of labor markets. When more spending leads to overtime for Cleveland machinists while barely touching the plight of unemployed West Virginia coal miners, counseling, retraining and relocation become the mainstays of a new employment policy.

The art lies, of course, in determining about when this point has been reached. As an aid to such determinations, excellent data on

---

[5] An excellent illustration of the way in which increased spending can lead to overtime for the already employed rather than to work for the unemployed can be dug out of a recent statistical report on the Detroit metropolitan area economy. Total manufacturing employment in the Detroit area fell from the depressed level of 474,000 in the national recession year of 1958 to 450,000 in 1961, while average weekly hours were rising from 38.8 to 40.3 hours. The revival of the local economy between 1961 and 1962 saw manufacturing employment return to just short of its 1958 level (472,000), with the average workweek now up to 42.3 hours, 9 per cent above 1958. Throughout this whole period, except for the final year, 1962, Detroit area unemployment was running at two to three times the national rate. In short, prosperity seems to manifest itself more in overtime work for the high-seniority employed worker than in jobs for the unemployed at least in an automobile economy. The Detroit Area Economic Forum, *The Detroit Area Economic Fact Book* (Detroit Branch, Federal Reserve Bank of Chicago, March 1963), pp. 8, 9, and 14.

the length of the average workweek and the level of unemployment as well as the consumer price index are reported monthly by the Bureau of Labor Statistics.[6] A careful reading of the relative movements in just these three indexes could nearly suffice to establish the point at which cyclical unemployment has largely disappeared and hard-core structural unemployment remains to be treated from the supply side. This is not to say that we could not profit from some careful quantitative expression—tabular, geometric, or algebraic—of the "normal" interrelationships between these three indexes at different phases of the cycle and a suggested interpretation of their implications for public policy. For example, the combination of a one-half percentage point fall in unemployment and a two percentage point rise in the consumer price index and/or the lengthening of the average workweek by an hour might signal the advent of minimum feasible cyclical unemployment (consistent with some specified degree of price stability) and a preponderance of structural unemployment. The implication would then be that public policy should turn from fiscal-monetary measures to structural adjustments and from federal dominance to a federal-state-local partnership.

The treatment of structural unemployment rests on three basic tactics: information, retraining, and relocation, all of which deeply involve local government. In the depression phase of the business cycle when the problem is too little spending, nationwide, the principal function of the local public employment offices throughout the country is to pass out unemployment compensation checks. The understaffed employment offices are so busy processing unemployment compensation claims in recessions that they literally do not have time to disseminate information, counsel, and otherwise create an efficient local labor market.[7]

[6] The Bureau of Labor Statistics compiles monthly data on national average unemployment (Table A-1), weekly hours of production workers by industry for mining, manufacturing, wholesale, and retail trade (Tables C-1, C-2), and also average overtime hours of production workers in manufacturing (Table C-4), the latter two series at roughly the three-digit SIC level of industry breakdown. The consumer price index is also reported on a monthly basis for the nation and for twenty selected cities (Tables D-1, D-2), Department of Labor, Bureau of Labor Statistics, *Monthly Labor Review* (Washington: U.S. Government Printing Office).

[7] Apparently neither state nor private employment agencies are now regarded by displaced workers as an important instrument for locating a new job, at least by professional and skilled workers. None of the 157 newspaper employees thrown out of work when the Detroit *Times* folded found new jobs via public agencies and only one of 88 editorial and 6 of 69 commercial employees were reemployed via private agencies. A similar pattern has also been found in studies of job dislocation among industrial workers. In his studies of the ex-*Times* workers and of the literature of

With the elimination of cyclical unemployment these offices can concentrate on the function of matching changing labor demands with the traits of a steady stream of workers displaced by changing product demands and the automation of their work. If the sixties do prove to be a decade of structural unemployment, the local public employment office could become the nerve center of unemployment and manpower planning operations.

Retraining of displaced workers is a logical extension of the traditional local responsibility for education in general. With machines constantly expropriating ever more complex manual and clerical skills, the worker of this day will need more to be sophisticated and adaptable than to be narrowly skilled and efficient. Consequently, additional *general* education of displaced workers may well come to be more important to placement in a new job than the more traditional vocational retraining. Since it is doubtful that private business will assume much more than token responsibility for even vocational retraining, business almost certainly will not assume any substantial responsibility for teaching English, mathematics, basic science, and similar academic subjects to displaced workers. With displaced older workers having to compete with ever more educated new entrants to the labor force, with excess capacity inherent in a public school system which usually operates only one shift a day, with the community college system spreading out so fast that some at least minimal public facilities for higher education will soon be within easy commuting distance of almost every worker, local government is in a position to enter the adult education field on an unprecedented scale. The demands on the local public purse would be sizable, although it is quite likely that federal and state aid would be forthcoming, but the penalty for not performing well in this task is harsh. To harbor a growing group of chronically unemployed workers, with ever more obsolete skills and ever less financially able to migrate, is to create even more insatiable demands on local public revenue, plus all the nonpecuniary costs originating in impoverishment and slum formation. Vocational

---

the field in general, Ferman notes "a general tendency for the worker to emphasize the unemployment function of the state employment service and to have little knowledge or interest in the job referral function." Louis A. Ferman, *Death of a Newspaper: The Story of the Detroit Times,* The W. E. Upjohn Institute for Employment Research, Kalamazoo, Michigan, April 1963, p. 29. The three principal sources of new job leads for the ex-*Times* workers were: friends or relatives (30 per cent), direct application to a prospective employer (28 per cent) and contact of worker by employer (21 per cent); reemployment four-fifths by informal processes.

adult education—broad-gauge occupational retraining—must become a central preoccupation of local government.

Finally, though federal government money is almost sure to enter the picture sooner or later, most of the planning and administration and much of the financial burden attendant on the relocation of displaced workers must be borne by local government. The depressed urban area exporting population must face the problem of spreading heavy social overhead costs over fewer and fewer taxpayers while struggling to contract its public plant in an orderly fashion. At the same time, the booming urban area importing population faces the problems of shortages and congestion in school plant, street space, water and sewage systems that are at least as grave. Indeed, from a social standpoint, housing shortages are even more undesirable than high vacancy rates, and half-day school sessions even more undesirable than empty classrooms. The problems of adjusting a sluggish public plant to the changing needs for public services falls largely on the local public authorities. So, while cyclical unemployment may be passively regarded by local public officials as an exogenous evil to be endured with patience and treated only with palliatives, as federal officials scurry about seeking the right lever to pull, structural unemployment places responsibility squarely on local officialdom. Local government seems on the verge of becoming as important to full employment as full employment is to the local economy.

None of this denies the supporting role of the federal government. Federal funds will be most appropriate to arranging interregional income transfers, as one locality is called on to retrain redundant workers for new jobs in another. Also, only the federal government can tie the local labor markets together into a rational national labor market by facilitating interurban communication and financing retraining and relocation that otherwise would unrealistically ask one community to pay the costs of services that redound to the benefit of another. Nevertheless, most of the actual managerial work must be performed on the spot. To take an extreme but very significant example, we have the case of the chronically unemployed elderly worker whom we would almost certainly not ask to migrate, and who therefore is most clearly a local responsibility.

The sheer size and scope of a comprehensive retraining and relocation effort would almost surely prevent the creation of anything more than a nominal direct *local* role for federal personnel. The federal role seems best confined to research, general guidance, and financing through some special organization, parallel to the Area Redevelopment

Division of the Department of Commerce, lodged perhaps in the Department of Labor. Because almost every locality would prefer to import needed industry rather than export redundant workers, the co-ordinating services (and funds) of the central government are indispensable to harmonize conflicting objectives and effect national economic efficiency in the location of population and industry. But the attack on structural unemployment must be quite unlike our more monolithic fiscal policy in that the former calls for very personalized and highly differentiated treatment across a very heterogeneous country and across differently circumstanced households. A sophisticated response to structural unemployment requires, moreover, a bit of meddling in the lives of people, in contrast to the relatively impersonal federal deficits prescribed for cyclical unemployment. And "meddling" is best done at the local level.

Chronic Structural Unemployment and Urban Slum Formation

For years we got along on just two concepts and classes of unemployment: (1) "frictional" unemployment due to the normal process of adjustment of a specialized labor force reacting to the changing demands of a dynamic economy, a problem in microeconomics, specifically the efficiency of local labor markets, and (2) "cyclical" unemployment founded in changes in aggregate spending, a macroeconomic problem of national proportions. Frictional unemployment was written off lightly as unavoidable and even beneficial. People are always changing jobs: looking for greener pastures; moving between seasonal jobs in agriculture, construction, and the tourist industry; moving upward as they acquire skill and experience.

To these we have recently added "structural" unemployment which, on first impression at least, seems to be merely an extension of the concept of frictional unemployment. Long lags between jobs, occasioned either by the need to make a greater adjustment in skill or location or by a greater reluctance to adjust, transform frictional into structural unemployment. Trends toward heavier investments in very specialized skills, extension of homeownership to lower-skilled (lower-income) workers, the spread of unemployment compensation, and other developments which serve to reduce the occupational and spatial mobility of labor have combined forces to raise "frictional" unemployment to worrisome levels. Six per cent unemployment can hardly

218   PROBLEMS AND POLICY

be lightly disposed of as mere friction in a dynamic system. Structural unemployment is the term coined to categorize frictional unemployment which: (a) requires a basic adaptation on the part of the displaced worker, (b) tends to persist much longer, and (c) poses a graver social problem.

The taxonomy of unemployment has become so sophisticated and so widely popularized today that newspapers refer familiarly to a fourth variety of unemployment, "chronic," in which unemployment becomes concentrated on a small proportion of the labor force. The chronically unemployed class find their lot only slightly improved during business recoveries (a little part-time work to do) and only slightly worsened by recessions (you can't fall off the floor). Chronic unemployment, largely insensitive to our new and improved and definitely milder postwar business cycle, can be characterized as another variation on the theme of structural unemployment, at the opposite end of the scale from frictional. Structural unemployment, then, would range from minor problems in labor market efficiency (frictional) to major problems in social welfare and urban poverty (chronic unemployment). But the analytical kinship between structural and chronic unemployment needs to be established more surely.

Let us consider an economy in which unemployment oscillates between 3 per cent at the peaks of prosperity and 7 per cent in the recession troughs. A highly simplified but reasonable breakdown of this unemployment would assign between 0 and 4 per cent to the business cycle and the residual 3 per cent to frictional-structural causes. We would classify the full 3 per cent as frictional-structural unemployment if the full unemployed "population" were turning over continually so that no worker lingered in the unemployment pool more than, say, twice as long as the average transition period. At the other extreme, if there were no turnover at all among this unfortunate group, that is, the same workers always comprised this 3 per cent residual unemployment, we might reasonably assign the whole group to chronic structural unemployment.

While chronic unemployment is the very antithesis of cyclical unemployment and depends on structural phenomenon for its perpetuation it can originate in either structural or cyclical change. For example, a worker may be laid off either because aggregate demand falls (a recession) or because demand shifts away from the product he is producing (structural change). But this worker will remain chronically unemployed only if some structural force comes to bear, such as the fact that he is an older worker and employers discriminate against his class in hiring, or that he lives in a declining area and resists migration. Cyclical unemployment can, by definition, become chronic only by being transformed into structural unemployment. Using a hypothetical arithmetic model built on structural discrimination against older workers, a closer examination of the mechanics by which structural unemployment is transformed into chronic unemployment provides a useful introduction to various associated urban problems, slum formation for example.

Suppose we divide the labor force into two classes, younger workers and older workers and that we assume, quite realistically, that employers prefer younger workers to older ones and discriminate accordingly in their hiring practices. Suppose further that structural changes displace workers randomly so that roughly the same proportion of workers in each age group are laid off in each time period. The failure of a firm with the consequent release of all its workers would be a good example of such a random discharge of labor. One might argue that older workers typically have more seniority and higher skills, protecting them in cases of less sweeping layoffs, but older workers would also tend to have more obsolete skills and less general education and work in the older, more stagnant industries (e.g., coal, textiles, steel), exposing them more to displacement. (Here we have a question of fact which would be well worth the price of some preliminary inquiry.) If, then, in each time period, a random age mix of workers were added to the stockpile of the unemployed and a similar number of mainly younger workers were taken off the pile, in time, the pile would consist entirely of older workers, chronically unemployed, as the younger workers slide quickly across the top of the pile to reemployment.[8]

[8] The use of older workers as the disadvantaged group was, of course, purely illustrative. Nonwhites, uneducated workers, or new entrants into the labor market could have been used instead, for all of these groups show rates of unemployment about double the average rate. Seymour L. Wolfbein, "Counting the Employed and Unemployed," *Michigan Business Review*, March 1962, pp. 4–5. Mr. Wolfbein also sets long-term chronic unemployment at 1.2 million out of total unemployment in December 1961 of 4.1 million, or a little less than the one-third we assumed in our highly oversimplified model. Again, Mueller and Schmiedeskamp in a study designed to get away from the "snapshot data" gathered in one point of time surveys and to get at *recurrent* unemployment (each spell of which might be fairly short), asked their respondents to give the *cumulative* duration of their unemployment during the preceding twelve months. They found that "27 per cent of family heads who suffered any unemployment between mid-1960 and mid-1961 were unemployed for more than half of the time during those twelve months. This is equivalent to about 3.5 per cent of all family heads in the labor force." Eva Mueller and Jay Schmiedeskamp, *Persistent Unemployment, 1957-1961*, The W. E. Upjohn Institute for Employment Research, Kalamazoo, Michigan, November 1962, pp. 9–10.

We could have assumed instead that the shock was specifically technological change and that, while a wide mix of skills was displaced, the higher-skilled workers were reemployed more quickly than the lower-skilled ones. The main point to be made is that the growth of chronic unemployment originates in an asymmetrical pattern of job displacement and rehiring which in turn reflects a combination of factors such as discrimination in hiring, differential degrees of adaptability of workers to change and problems in industrial relocation and labor migration. Moreover, with enough asymmetry in displacement and absorption patterns, the transition periods of unemployment may vary so widely between the favored and disfavored in the labor market that a bimodal distribution of structural unemployment will form. In that event a very deceptive average period of transition is concocted out of a combination of inconvenient frictional unemployment for some and calamitous chronic unemployment for others.

Unemployment and Renewal: An Imbalance of Power

An appreciation of the relevance of chronic unemployment to urban blight and renewal begins with the simple statistic that unemployment in big city slums seldom runs as low as 20 per cent. If frictional and cyclical unemployment pose significant fiscal problems for the city, chronic unemployment with its much greater and more prolonged loss of income is a near catastrophe for urban planning and management, given our current goals and tools. In the urban planning and housing literature, urban blight and renewal stand out as the main source of concern and hope for the future of our cities, and in the reading one gets the impression that slums are a product of a too high population density (rural slums notwithstanding) and/or a poor physical design. Urban blight is customarily quantified in such terms as persons per square mile or persons per room or per cent of dwelling units without indoor toilets. Unemployment, if it enters the discussions at all, is regarded as a regrettable complicating exogenous force which has something to do with poverty and slums.

Slums could just as easily be characterized as the place where the very poor live—the weaker, duller, lazier, as well as widows and victims of discrimination and other unfortunates—and be identified by various income measures. Glibly, one might even identify the slums as the home of the chronically unemployed and the unemployable—persons who are not physically or mentally able to perform useful work or who need much industrial acculturation to compete successfully. But while economic surrogates would be every bit as defensible as the typical physical-housing characterization used by the planners, the implicit economic determinism of urban slums is just as intellectually offensive. The urban sociologist might just as defensively describe slums as the home of socially maladjusted persons who are escaping responsibility or rebelling against the existing order. And psychologists have pointed out the existence of some who simply prefer or need the slum culture.[9]

The fact that urban blight is described much too narrowly in physical terms is much less serious than the apparent transfer of this inadequate characterization into policies and programs. The current program of urban renewal heavily emphasizes physical correctives to the slum problem—new buildings for old as the answer to slums. City planners and housing people have frequently been accused of blithely assuming that housing renewal automatically (by some undefined mystique) effects human renewal—a new and better home is the elixir of physical and mental health, leading to better jobs and higher income. Surely, these people are sophisticated professionals who recognize the slum syndrome as a complex one that calls for treatment beyond the remedies applied by architects and contractors.[10] But, anxious to get started someplace, they quite naturally chose to begin on their home grounds, site planning and housing design.

[9] "There is security in crowding and closeness to people with similar religious views, values, recreations, family patterns. Ghettos are made by both the oppressors and the minorities themselves. . . . For some people the design of a clean new city may mean not peace and serenity but boredom, a lack of color and vitality that old cities have provided in chaos. . . . The importance of a house close to other houses, gregariousness, an apparent absence of privacy, and the presence of noise are but some of the needs of these people. . . . This does not mean slums must be preserved, but rather that new cities must find ways of responding to the needs of all segments of our population." Leonard J. Duhl, "The Human Measure: Man and Family in Megalopolis," *Cities and Space: The Future Use of Urban Land,* Essays from the Fourth Resources for the Future Forum (Baltimore: The Johns Hopkins Press, 1963), pp. 137–40.

[10] The new criticism reflects in part the disillusionment of liberals who expected too much of public housing. "Once upon a time," says a close student of New York's slums, "we thought that if we could only get our problem families out of those dreadful slums, then papa would stop taking dope, mama would stop chasing around, and Junior would stop carrying a knife. Well, we've got them in a nice new apartment with modern kitchens and a recreation center. And they're the same bunch of bastards they always were."

It is now recognized that housing is far from decisive in the making of good citizens. Very few students of the subject now believe that the slums create crime and vice and disease; it is now considered more likely that the slums simply attract problem families. And their problems will not be erased by putting these families in a public-housing project.
Daniel Seligman, "The Enduring Slums," *The Exploding Metropolis,* The Editors of Fortune (Garden City, N.Y.: Doubleday Anchor Books, 1957), p. 106.

Even if we do not join in the current sport of belaboring the urban renewal planners and administrators for a naïvete of which they probably are not guilty, the fact remains that the contemporary massive urban slum clearance programs do presume that a significant amount of human rehabilitation will follow from the housing improvements—by plan and not just as fortuitous and incidental by-products. To assume otherwise would be to reduce urban renewal to unadulterated urban aesthetics, a return to the late and unlamented "city beautiful" phase of city planning. Considering the size of the public subsidies involved and the opportunity costs of those funds in vocational training programs, mental hospital construction, and outdoor recreational facilities, the whole urban renewal program becomes a highly dubious venture without a very substantial rationale in human development. On viewing all this, the economist feels more than a little uneasy because, on his home grounds, one does not plant better houses and neighborhoods to grow better households but rather one implants better skills, aspirations, and opportunities to grow better houses and neighborhoods.

Recognizing the myopia common to all disciplines, especially in a question so broad as the nature and causes of urban slums, no attempt is here made to push some oversimplified model of economic determinism. But the suggestion is offered, deferentially, that a program of urban renewal can attain a high order of efficiency and success only if it draws on a number of supporting socioeconomic programs. The current program of urban renewal, without a strong program in employment counseling, vocational retraining, and general adult education, is not only unlikely to raise the socioeconomic level of the slum dwellers in significant amount, but is almost equally unlikely to even keep pace with the prospective rate of blight formation.

True enough, the physical planners and housing experts do appreciate that we are moving more slowly than the treadmill on which we are running, as depreciation and obsolescence and mistreatment of the existing stock of housing dwarfs renovation and rebuilding in the older areas of our cities. But what they have missed is the threat that the current high rate of chronic structural unemployment will hold for the net rate of slum clearance over the next decade—even with urban renewal budgets doubled or tripled. If some combination of automation, shifting spending patterns and labor immobilities dominates the labor markets of the sixties, creating levels of unemployment that rarely dip below 6 per cent, even the most optimistic projections of the likely size of our urban renewal budgets over the next decade are dust in the balance compared to the slum generating power of 6 to 7 per cent unemployment rates—rates, moreover, which puff up to twice that figure (and more) for Negroes living in the central cities and other marginal workers residing in the main blighted areas. A powerful and sophisticated local labor market and manpower program is not merely a complement to an urban renewal program, employment policy is the senior partner in any realistic joint venture in slum clearance.

If the sequence depicted—from cyclical unemployment to structural unemployment to chronic unemployment to destitution (amidst plenty) to accelerated slum formation—is at all probable, then the highest priority should be accorded to a careful quantification of the relevant magnitudes involved. Estimates should be made of: (a) the income distribution implications of various mixes of cyclical and chronic structural unemployment, (b) the translation of family income levels into slum formation potential (racial discrimination in housing considered), and (c) the appropriate depreciation schedules for the existing stock of housing. By bringing together unemployment, income, and depreciation data and projections, we would gain a clearer perspective on the net progress in slum clearance that seems most likely over the next decade. The net rate of slum clearance would, of course, vary substantially between localities.

If the implications of the persistence of the current level of unemployment to urban blight programs are made explicit, those who are responsible for the various programs which bear on hard-core unemployment—officials in charge of education, welfare, public works, employment agencies, and the like—will be forced to give the problem of chronic structural unemployment much more serious attention than they now do. Studies which show that the great bulk of the American workers have never had it so good and that "it" is getting better are correct, but this may be largely irrelevant to the urban slum formation problem—at least unless there develops among the employed majority a strong sense of responsibility for the plight of the unemployed minority.

BUILDING AN EFFICIENT LOCAL LABOR MARKET

The number of pages written on cyclical versus structural unemployment suggests that we are slowly awakening to the new employment problem. But the discussion has leaned heavily toward diagnosis rather than specific prescription. If a thorough understanding of the nature of our unemployment malady were an indispensable prerequisite to prescription, one might argue forcefully for delaying treatment until we learned more about the relative importance of technological change, taste changes, and affluence. But aside from the almost insuperable problems of isolating these joint factors, there is little to indicate that our society intends to stay or divert these forces appreciably. At most, we would only loosely hobble the rate of innovation, lightly constrain free choice of consumers, and/or probably not slow at all the rate of increase in income. If the more appropriate response is to increase the mobility of laborers and the efficiency of labor markets, irrespective of the precise cause of unemployment, we can move directly to consider the strategy and tactics of reemployment. If, then, our goal is to reemploy workers not prevent their displacement, the fact that "we really don't know to what degree our current unemployment is technological"[11] is, in large measure, academic. The next part of this chapter is directed, therefore, to concocting prescriptions of general enough nature to be largely independent of the precise cause of the structural unemployment.

Dissemination of Information

Good lines of communication are a prerequisite in building an efficient local labor market. Economists habitually underestimate the importance of the dissemination of information in markets, concentrating instead on ease of entry and exit, ease of substitution between products and services, and on size and market power. The impression is created that some way or other news gets around. Even in labor

[11] See the dissenting comments of Arthur F. Burns and Henry Ford II in *Automation: The Benefits and Problems Incident to Automation and Other Technological Advances*, The President's Advisory Committee on Labor-Management Policy, January 11, 1962 (Washington: U.S. Government Printing Office, 1962). Both are skeptical that rapid technological change has been a major cause of unemployment, deny it is accelerating, and decry "exaggerated fears." Their view is quite contrary to that of the majority of the twenty-three-man committee. At the other end of the spectrum, Donald N. Michael argues in *Cybernation: The Silent Conquest* (Center for the Study of Democratic Institutions, Santa Barbara, California, 1962) that automation and computers, leaving manufacturing unemployment in their wake, are moving rapidly into the service trades and threatening even the jobs of middle management and mediocre professionals (teachers, doctors, scientists). His is a most pessimistic view of automation and unemployment.

markets, where some notice is taken of the inadequate dissemination of information, the overriding impression is that, while communication may lag a little the resulting frictional unemployment is of only minor magnitude and of only passing interest.

Any realistic policy designed to reduce unemployment to the lowest possible levels must not depend on the individual to actively seek information about job opportunities, but instead must bring such information to his attention forcefully—perhaps even forcibly. When a worker's job has been eliminated by a shift in demand away from the product he was producing or the substitution of a machine for his labor or for whatever reason, his discharge constitutes a message or directive from the economic system, *specifically addressed to him,* advising that his old services are no longer required and that he must develop some new service that is needed and demanded. The problem is, however, that there is no specific and personalized affirmative counterpart to the discharge. The worker is quite clearly informed as to where he *is not* wanted but not clearly informed as to where he *is* wanted. We cannot and should not impute to the labor market an alertness and opportunism on the part of the participants comparable to that which we depend on to produce a "close and quick" stock market. The stock market is a speculative market, one which screens the whole population to assemble the most alert and agile opportunists, while the labor market obviously includes roughly everybody.

Job counseling, therefore, becomes a key instrument in any realistic unemployment program but a *pro forma* provision of the service is not enough. The workers must be gently coerced into consuming the service. We should not underestimate the typical lag in the recognition of the need to readjust one's labor service (skill) to changing conditions nor the complementary reluctance to begin the readjustment itself (e.g., enrollment in a trade school) once the need is clearly seen. A quite natural human inertia operates to perpetuate the illusion of eventual reemployment in an old trade long after the futility of such wishful thinking is apparent to an impartial observer. An unemployed tool or die maker in the automobile industry can and does delude himself about the temporary nature of his unemployment as an escape from the fears and insecurities he feels whenever he contemplates changing occupations and/or geographical locations.

What needs to be done is much more apparent than how to do it. Clearly, the preliminary signals emitted by our sometimes too subtle free market price system could be made more obvious, especially the first warnings. Straws in the wind—more frequent and longer layoffs, shortening workweeks, highly automated pilot plants and other such developments—should be sharply articulated and widely publicized, not be just ominous portents secretly shared by labor leaders and personnel directors. Complementarily, lengthening workweeks, current or imminent labor shortages, and other good omens (lures) should be brought to the attention of all workers. Bulletin boards in unemployment compensation offices and government pamphlets available on request do not constitute dissemination of labor market information in any realistic sense.

A general approach to the problem is suggested by two quite distinct illustrations. First, a regular newspaper column devoted to both the more general and more specific aspects of the labor market outlook could be initiated, with the space donated by the newspapers as a public service—one which would almost certainly more than repay itself in increased circulation. On alternate days, the column might swing back and forth between quite general discussions of major labor trends (e.g., the current shift from manufacturing to service employment and from blue- to white-collar work within manufacturing) to very specific information on the local job market (comparative wage rates, workweeks and employment trends that are as detailed and precise as ship arrivals and departures). Or maybe television would reach this audience more effectively, the illiterate portion in particular.

Second, we might quite rationally (and paternalistically) make attendance at job outlook conferences compulsory as a condition to continued eligibility for unemployment compensation, after some reasonable interval of unemployment. Nominal appearance at the employment office to establish availability for work is not nearly enough. Workers who have invested heavily in a specialized skill which is becoming obsolete because of a changing demand for their product or the mechanization of their jobs, must have the fact of their growing redundancy in the labor market drummed into their heads. A purpose is served by just making them sit still long enough to contemplate the full implications of trends in their trade, under the guidance of an informed, articulate, and dispassionate observer. Comfortable myths, created and nurtured within the guild, die hard. Only face-to-face contact in this new personalized labor market—symbolized by the employment counselor—will insure that information is really disseminated, that is, transmitted *and received*.

If our times are destined to be an era of heavy and widespread structural unemployment, we are almost certainly spending far less on job counseling than we should on economic grounds alone, even ignoring the more important humanitarian considerations. The marginal expenditure on another job counselor (e.g., $20 per day) may be less than the direct saving in unemployment compensation alone (e.g., $40) achieved by channeling a displaced worker into a new job one week earlier than would have resulted from the impersonal working of the market forces. To make the *public sector* accounting more inclusive, we might add the tax gain extracted from one extra week's pay check (e.g., $20). Thus, in our hypothetical case, the expenditure of one man-day, the counselor's time, returned the equivalent of two counselor man-days (the $40 saving in unemployment compensation) on the public expenditure side and the equivalent of one counselor man-day (the $20 tax yield) on the public revenue side, for a threefold return to the public economy.

The accounting could be made even more inclusive by simply comparing the increased income to the worker from making the job transition one week earlier than otherwise (i.e., the addition of five man-days of output to social product and income) to the one man-day of counselor (labor) input, for a fivefold *total social* return. This latter ratio assumes that the worker who returns to work a week earlier is indifferent to whether he is at work or at home, apart from wage considerations, for we have not counted the loss of his involuntary leisure at any cost. The illustrative magnitudes may be grossly overstated (and, again, they may not), but the point is that we have not even attempted to measure the marginal productivity of employment counselors and, consequently, we are in no position to make good social judgments on the social cost of frictional unemployment or the efficiency of local labor markets as currently constituted.[12] The possibilities for some extremely valuable cost-benefit analyses of local labor market instrumentalities are readily apparent in the simple job counselor illustration used above. Analysis in much greater depth could pay enormous returns because the subject matter is so unexplored and the magnitudes

---

[12] In the context of comparing private and state employment agencies, to the detriment of the latter, a female clerk-typist remarked that she "waited half a day before seeing anyone. Then they didn't get me a job." If this experience is at all typical, then the marginal productivity of job counselors may indeed remain quite high over a very substantial addition to their ranks. A second reaction that "private employment agencies . . . are better than the state employment service because they get your first pay and therefore will work hard to get you a job," reintroduces an old problem of creating incentives and evaluating performance in public service. Interview remarks quoted in Ferman, *op. cit.*, p. 29.

involved—the loss of social product and income through frictional-structural unemployment—are so enormous, and growing larger.[13]

Finally, no account has been taken here of the operation of a multiplier effect. The structural adjustment which reemploys a worker earlier than otherwise increases his income and spending, helping thereby to absorb whatever *cyclical* unemployment still persists. Just as a high and rising level of aggregate demand tends to make structural adjustments easier, structural adjustments speed re-employment, increase income, and act thereby to wipe out whatever residual cyclical unemployment remains. While most of the employment multiplier effect is lost to the local economy, through import leakages, as discussed in earlier chapters, the locality's loss here is the nation's (some other locality's) gain and, in effect, constitutes a kind of a *quid pro quo*. Ideally, imaginative and sophisticated local public policies in many localities, primarily designed to reduce structural unemployment, would as a by-product create an environment conducive to minimizing national cyclical unemployment. An enlightened federal fiscal and monetary policy, primarily designed to reduce national cyclical unemployment, would as a by-product create an environment conducive to minimizing local structural unemployment.

The Role of the Job Counselor

The job counselor faces many difficult decisions, for example, whether or not to recommend to an unemployed worker (and his family) that he migrate to another area. The capacity to provide good counsel on such matters would not be easily achieved; still, the job specifications here do not seem to be appreciably higher than those we have set for the social case worker: some specialized knowledge, part of which comes only with experience; interest in and liking for people; and only an average level of intelligence but a better-than-average measure of common sense. (We do, of course, greatly underestimate and grossly underpay the better-than-average social worker.) In time an experienced and perceptive job counselor would develop a flair for detecting the workers who could move easily—the ones who can best

---

[13] For a recounting of the day-by-day experiences of a social case worker which suggests the high likelihood that welfare, and by analogy employment counselors, have a marginal value product which exceeds their wage rate, see Edgar May, "A Way Out of the Welfare Mess," *Harpers*, October 1961, p. 41.

assimilate change and have the capacity to benefit by trading an old routine for a whole new life and fresh outlook.[14]

As much as anything, a reasonable degree of professionalization and *esprit de corps* is needed among job counselors. We see the lack of this all too often in what may be the most critical role of all: the high school vocational counselor. This position has often been awarded to a promising young administrator as a step toward the position of school principal or as a safe place into which an inadequate teacher can be "promoted." Only recently has the vocational counseling work been widely seen as a career in itself.

The serious charge might be made that the job specification beginning to take shape calls for a quality of personnel and a pay schedule considerably above that which is likely to be accorded this work—the civil service pay constraint. Also the amount of time that would have to be spent with each unemployed worker might seem more in line with psychiatric services than what is being passed off as job counseling. The answer is that the upgrading of industrial social case work may in itself be counted a social contribution in a society which is on the verge of disgorging vast numbers of moderately well educated persons into a labor market in which machines are

[14] The key role of the employment counselor is highlighted in Research Report No. 1 of the Detroit Area Manpower Development Pilot Project conducted by the Michigan Employment Security Commission (mimeo.). This report details the results of a "longitudinal approach" to the study of the characteristics of 5,000 hard-core unemployed workers in the Detroit area, defined as persons unemployed twenty-six weeks or more. Three-quarters of this group had less than a high school education and 40 per cent had elementary school education only. Two-thirds of the workers were unskilled or semiskilled.

Project field workers made over a thousand personal visits to the homes of the unemployed. The initial interviews averaged two and one-half hours a piece and the subsequent interviews averaged thirty-five to forty-five minutes each. Many of the respondents stated that this was the first time that anyone had sat down and listened to their problems.

One of their more interesting findings was that on the usual basis of a formal application card, which many workers do not have the ability to fill out informatively, and on the basis of the typical hurried interview, information was missing that would have greatly facilitated the applicant's reemployment. Most notably, second skills are not mentioned. In one case a young man, coded as a machine operator only, an unneeded trade, also had training in meat cutting and on the basis of counseling sessions that uncovered this and also improved his job-hunting technique, he was placed in the meat department of a food store chain.

The Report concluded that "past emphasis has been placed on perpetuating the job-seeker's last regular occupation. . . . In face of the increased rate of technological change and the growth of hard core unemployment, a worker's last occupation could very well be the worst classification to assign." While this may be an overstatement, the value of interviewing and counseling in depth seems to have been well illustrated by this project.

performing most of the material handling and processing functions and encroaching on the simpler personal services as well. In essence, the creation of useful semiprofessional work could become almost an end in itself. Beyond this, one does not have to strain the imagination too much to foresee the time when we will need to have almost as many persons planning the assignment and reassignment and retraining of workers as there are persons actually performing work on end products.

Many of these job counselors would have to assume positions roughly comparable to that of the personnel director of a small firm or of a senior rank technician in the personnel department of a large firm. But we do, presumably, prepare students in our university business schools for executive level personnel placement work in private business. Therefore, either the business school or the department of public administration or the school of social work or some combination of these educational entities should be cued on the vacuum that exists in what seems destined to become the biggest arena of all in person-nel-placement work—*inter*firm, *inter*occupational, and *inter*area placements through public and private employment agencies. The universities might do well to recognize this trend by instituting the appropriate curriculum to supply the needed specialists. A more respectable body of knowledge than now exists would be needed for teaching under the new curriculum. But under private grants or public subsidy, an accelerated research program could fill the gap reasonably well within a few years.

Many, probably most, of the job counseling positions would, however, not demand a higher level of basic intelligence nor a longer period of specialized education than has long been demanded of the skilled blue-collar worker (e.g., electricians and machinists), differing only in that job counseling would draw more heavily on general education and less on vocational training. This would be quite in line with the educational background of the current crop of high school and college students. Further, these second echelon, semiprofessional job counselors would not need to be intellectually superior to their clients (the displaced workers) in the general way that social workers are usually intellectually superior to their clients. The "customers' man" in a broker's office need not be a person of greater mental capacity than the persons he is advising. Similarly, society could be well served in job counseling by the lower run of college graduates and the middle-run of high school graduates, if these persons of medium ability and mental capacity were well fortified with good information (up-to-

date data) and well coached in the application of sophisticated formulas and other devices useful in making the critical decisions and in
formulating good advice. This is where urban research enters the
picture again.

Considering the acute shortage of highly skilled people in all fields
and the salary schedule constraints that are almost certain to be imposed on job counseling positions, the best strategy seems to be to
substitute skill in research for skill in administration wherever possible. To the extent that research can lead to a partial automation
of the decision-making process in job counseling by devising good
rules-of-thumb and simple procedures that enhance the skill of con-
scientious but of only moderately talented counselors, research will
serve to economize on scarce talent. Research grants, moreover, usually
allow greater flexibility in remuneration than is common to civil
service salary schedules. Thus unusual talent is more accessible at
the research level for pecuniary as well as the obvious nonpecuniary
attractions of research work.

Some examples of the kinds of policy-based research that would
fortify a slightly shaky administrative staffing will illustrate the leverage of investment in research. A research group might formulate a set
of tables showing the present discounted value of various kinds of
income betterment to be gained by making a move: the present value
of earning $.25 per hour more or of a given probability of working
ten more weeks per year or of gaining a second source of income for
the family at the new location. A second set of tables could estimate
the present cost of making a move for families subject to different sets
of circumstances. These latter calculations might range from such
simple matters as schedules of the cost of moving household furnish-
ings and the cost of selling a home and of buying a new one to more
subtle ones such as the financial leverage operating against the owner's
equity when a heavily mortgaged home is sold at a capital loss. And
capital losses on housing are the rule in the depressed housing market
of a declining area, the kind of area from which out-migration is
usually being contemplated and perhaps generally being recommended
by our job counselors. Even more subtle, careful note must be made
of and computational adjustment made for the expected working life
of the worker to whom a major change is being recommended; a 55-
year-old man has only about ten years in which to recapture the cost
of making a change.

There are analogies in the world of financial and investment analysis. The financial analyst has a whole drawer full of helpful ratios and

indexes—the "current ratio" (current assets to current liabilities), "times interest earned" (earnings to interest charges) and so forth—which have been devised by students of financial management and, with the proper *caveats,* are placed as tools in the hands of semi-professional consultants. Perhaps an even closer analogy is that of the actuarial tables that transform an insurance agent who has trouble with his son's arithmetic homework into a powerful mathematician. These ratios and tables would not be generically different from the machine tool that enhances the productive power of the blue-collar worker. The marginal value product of some extra research effort on some new tools for the social case worker would almost certainly exceed the cost of that research. A job counselor, armed with guides to rational action on problems of migration and retraining and the correction of detrimental personal habits and whatever else seems appropriate, would be as useful to the worker shopping for a new job as the (semiprofessional) real estate agent is to the lay buyer or seller of housing. We need a good handbook in vocational economics and a cost-benefit "slide rule" for our job counselors.

Policy-based research in job counseling could begin with taxonomy. Job counseling becomes, in part, a classification activity as the frictional unemployment which can be eased by better dissemination of information is separated from that structural unemployment which requires the more drastic surgery of major occupational and location readjustments. A number of unemployment classifications might be set up based on overlapping groups of unemployed workers:

1. Self-sufficient unemployed: those willing and able to find new jobs unaided;

2. personal placement problems: those with low intelligence, poor work habits (e.g., absenteeism, rebelliousness), alcoholics; part-time jobs for working mothers with little or no skill;

3. information problems: those unrealistically holding out for jobs that do not exist, jobs that have ceased to exist, or jobs that they could never get;

4. occupational placement problems: those with highly specialized skills and advanced age, where replacement without substantial downgrading will be difficult because an equivalent amount of occupational training in a new skill is impractical.

5. retrainees, vocational: divided between those whose retraining requirements are minor and could be handled by the potential em-

ployer and those who need a new or first skill imparted under a major (public) training effort;

6. retrainees, general education: those who must undergo substantial (public) education in English, arithmetic, and so forth before they would qualify for a private apprenticeship program, for example, rural in-migrants and long-time residents of urban slums;[15]

7. victims of discrimination: Negroes, females, school drop-outs, and older workers illustrate social groups which constitute more of an employer than an employee problem; these three groups are distinctive in that reconversions on the supply side are impossible, the pattern of demand must be changed; our knowledge here should include the effect of firm size and the nature of the industry on the willingness to employ these groups;

8. new entrants: the recent graduates and especially the school drop-outs; the problem of identifying the kinds of jobs that not only do not require experience but also produce experience—enrich the worker;

9. the locationally mobile: bachelors and renters and others for whom the job market is truly national; the group is especially valuable in adjusting total supply in the local labor market;

10. high-level reconversions: professional and technical workers who are either unemployed or more likely underemployed in jobs less demanding than their capabilities justify and who pose problems in advanced education, such as aeronautical engineers who need post-graduate university work in mathematics and physics to qualify for missile work.

[15] In the most widely publicized private retraining program to date, Armour and Company offered 433 displaced meat packing workers an opportunity to learn new skills (of other industries). Of the 170 who applied, aptitude tests eliminated 110 who presumably lacked either the intelligence or general education to benefit from the training. In Cleveland, Thompson Ramo Wooldridge, Inc. tried to train twenty long-term unemployed workers as semiskilled machine operators. But the Cleveland Electric Illuminating Co. had to step in and finance a short course in elementary mathematics—fractions and decimals prerequisite to blueprint reading—before the retraining could proceed. "The Hard Realities of Retraining," *Fortune*, July 1961, pp. 242 and 246. This latter case is an excellent example of what the combined effort of a private competitive firm, a public utility sheltered from competition, and a public school system can accomplish. But we are a long way from institutionalizing co-ordination across so wide a spectrum of interests and roles.

The most recent federal manpower development and retraining programs do put first things first by emphasizing basic literacy. After learning to read and write, the trainee is transferred to vocational courses, such as automobile repairing and meat cutting.

In the process of continually refining our classifications, we will begin
to see patterns and interrelationships that may grow into whole analytical structures. Only the thinnest of lines separates taxonomy from
analysis.

The Role of Vocational Education

Retraining technicians poses different problems. The U.S. Department of Labor estimates a current demand for 100,000 new technicians
per year, rising to double that by 1975. We are not spending enough
on vocational education, considering our growing need for skilled
technicians and the fact that 80 per cent of our population does not
go on to college. But unlike the situation for university training of
high-level professionals, merely to spend money within the present
framework of vocational education, may not help much. In addition,
we face some difficult political problems in the rural versus urban
orientation of vocational education.[16]

Federal grants-in-aid for state programs in vocational education go
back to 1917 and have altered little since then. In 1961, federally
supported, half-day high school programs had 25 per cent of their
enrollment in agricultural programs and 53 per cent in home economics. In the complementary extension programs, designed for
adults and high school drop-outs, agricultural courses accounted for
17 per cent and home economics 32 per cent of total enrollment. Thus,
in an economy in which the proportion of total employment in
agriculture has fallen to about 8 per cent, one-quarter of our federally
supported vocational education is designed to produce farmers; one-
half is designed to produce housekeepers in a passing rural tradition.
Considering that only about one-tenth of the farm youths can look
forward to full-time farming and that only about 35 per cent of the
high school graduates of the vocational agricultural programs have
gone into farming, the misallocation of federal vocational education
money is obvious.

By contrast, about two-thirds of the vocational education programs
that receive no federal help teach construction trades and office
occupations. There are no federal grants for training in clerical

---

[16] The following discussion of vocational education draws heavily on Sar A.
Levitan, *Vocational Education and Federal Policy*, The W. E. Upjohn Institute for
Employment Research, Kalamazoo, Michigan, May 1963.

occupations, despite the fact that a high rate of female labor turnover
in this work opens up about 400,000 jobs annually just for replacement, and clerical work is a growing sector. A powerful coalition of
rural Congressmen and the thirty-thousand-member American Vocational Association (dominated by teachers of agricultural and home
economics courses) have been able to prevent any modernization of
the program.

Another problem may be that some appreciable consolidation of
programs in the larger towns and small cities is required to gain the
scale needed to justify the expensive shop and laboratory equipment
consonant with today's technology. Until the urban areas and the
parents of the rural youth see their own interests here more clearly
and raise their voices, vocational education will continue to emphasize, not what students will need to know in the future, but rather
what their instructors learned in the past. And all the recent House
and Senate bills to increase the vocational education programs preserve, in large measure, this archaic structure.

One point of educational research strategy and one of political
strategy are suggested here. First, the fact that the graduates of secondary technical schools and high school vocational programs have
exhibited early career unemployment rates of less than one-half of
their contemporaries who elected general education curricula has
often been cited as striking evidence of the superior marketability
of vocational education. This may be true, but the acid test is the
long haul. If specialized education does ensure quick placement but
also threatens early obsolescence, then displacement and frictional
unemployment may be the ultimate price. Does vocational education
lead to more frictional unemployment than does a good general
education? And can the best of the two be combined? Can, that is,
general mathematics be made more attractive to the pragmatic student
by using appropriate applications and can English be taught more
in the context of work report writing?

Second, one reason why federal grants-in-aid of vocational education
have not gone to support office training programs is simply because
the private business schools have lobbied effectively against such
programs. If greater enrollment in business education courses is clearly
desirable, this opposition must be either overcome or appeased. Federal money could, for example, be used to pay the tuition at private
business schools as well as to establish public school programs in this
subject. There is nothing radical or even novel here; we have had a

long history now of paying the tuition of war veterans at private colleges. A compromise might be worked out in which the private business schools gave their blessing to federal support of high school programs in office work, in return for a program of federal scholarships for high school graduates at private business "colleges" of their own choice.

As we probe deeper, we will gain not only an appreciation of the needs and limitations of various groups of workers but also some sense of which existing or new social institutions can best perform the requisite reconstructive surgery on these obsolete workers. Universities will almost surely be called on to take the lead in making the high-level occupational reconversions mentioned above. The city university, in particular, is well suited in time and place to turn the middle-aged and younger aeronautical engineers into missile scientists, draftsmen into designers, tool makers into computer technicians, accountants into business economists and econometricians, and so forth.

It has been suggested that technically obsolete engineers and scientists be accredited to teach; their knowledge of basic mathematics and science is obviously not obsolete.[17] This might be not only to provide jobs for displaced professionals and help relieve the teacher shortage, but also provide part-time employment for those who seek to stay in their professions while they are attending university postgraduate courses in the new technology.

A real need exists to experiment—even with just paper and pencil— on the programming, financing, and phasing of postgraduate adult technical education. The low priority that tight budgets have forced most urban universities to place on educational programs for non-matriculated students (usually part-time, night-school students not working for a degree) must either be reversed or new institutions must be created to offer this advanced applied education. Otherwise, a callous waste of human resources and productive potential will haunt the next decade, to say nothing of the immeasurable human loss in frustration and self-respect.

Not only does adult education at the graduate school level contribute to full employment by increasing labor mobility, but in this age of technology it is hard to conceive of any urban area competing effectively for new firms and new industries without having a local educational complex that provides for continuing technical education of

[17] The author is indebted to Professor John Dyckman for this thought, expressed at an Urban Policies Conference in Norfolk, sponsored by the Brookings Institution.

all kinds.[18] By providing the opportunity to pursue advanced education on a continuous part-time or intermittent full-time basis throughout life, an urban area both attracts the most rewarding new jobs and
also helps their more able displaced workers to qualify for them. The
encouragement of advanced adult education would seem to be an
extremely important manpower planning program at the local level.
This is especially convincing when one recalls that many semiskilled
and unskilled jobs follow in the wake of professional work.

LOCAL GOVERNMENT EMPLOYMENT POLICY

*Public Discrimination as an Antidote
to Private Discrimination*

A substantial residue of very hard-core unemployment would almost
certainly persist despite the most skillful dissemination of information,
personalized counseling, vigorous enforcement of fair employment
practices, vocational retraining, and financial assistance in relocation.
At this point the government's role would seem to become a more
direct one. An imaginative use of either public employment or subsidies has great advantage over the humanitarian, but essentially de-
featist, policy of quick and easy resort to indoor relief. In current
practice, welfare payments have become a premature last resort.

Those hardest to make employable under aggressive and enlightened
public policy are far from homogeneous and we would do well to
identify a number of distinct groups which call for distinct treatment.

We have the elderly and handicapped workers who may not be less
productive than competing workers but who are the victims of irrational employment practices, such as an unsubstantiated belief that
these workers are more accident-prone or subject to greater absentee-

---

[18] The critical role of higher education in area industrial development is nicely
illustrated by the recent experience of Lewiston, Maine.

What looked like a major breakthrough came in 1960 when the Raytheon
Company leased a community-financed plant in Lewiston to manufacture semi-
conductors. But the company has begun to close down production and will eventually leave 1,500 workers jobless by the end of the year.

Raytheon attributed its decision to abandon Lewiston to the competitve nature
of the industry. But some sources feel that a lack of nearby facilities for giving
its promising technicians postgraduate education probably was a factor.
Special report by John H. Fenton to *The New York Times*, July 21, 1963, p. 111.

ism. Even a skillfully conducted information program will take us only part way here. Again, the reluctance to hire the elderly and handicapped may stem from institutional frictions, such as private pension plans which make the hiring of an older worker, close to retirement, significantly more expensive. Unions can be expected to resist any scheme for providing a lesser retirement benefit for this group for fear that this might become the means of breaking the basic retirement provision.

Because local government is free from the competitive pressures which make experimentation difficult, even dangerous, for private firms, the public sector will probably have to assume a leadership role in employing the elderly, the handicapped, and other hard-to-employ groups. Much public employment is clerical work and could be arranged so as not to make excessive physical demands. Further, state and local government employment has the added virtue that, unlike most federal employment, the work to be performed is conveniently located. The spatial pattern of local public employment, in particular, so closely coincides, by broad labor markets (metropolitan areas), with the residential pattern of elderly and handicapped workers that these relatively immobile people would only rarely have to move to accept the work.

We do not suggest that local government might staff-up with the elderly and handicapped in key positions, only that it use the hard-to-employ in routine operations. One could, in fact, make a good case that the critical personnel problem of local government is their over-representation of persons of average ability, where they would do much better to emphasize the extremes more. Our cities would probably be better planned and administered if two $10,000 salaries were combined to create a new $20,000 position to compete with private business for the most talented professionals. None of this weakens our main point: the need to use local public employment as *one* means of employing certain marginal workers.

A careful accounting of state and local government clerical jobs, by skill requirements and location, would be a very useful task, especially if this information could then be collated with an accounting of the skills and educational background of elderly and handicapped workers, also by location. The current rate of employment of these groups in the especially suitable jobs might then be compared with the potential for their employment. We might then examine the effect of a statute or administrative rule that only in special cases could a worker under forty years of age be hired for a clerical job in certain government offices, or perhaps we might adopt the more indirect expedient, used in the case of war veterans, of automatically adding a given number of points to the job-qualification examination scores of persons over forty or handicapped.

The suggestion that the appropriate employments and favored applicants be specified by location originates in two considerations. First, the use of aggregates would tend to overstate the degree to which public employment might absorb these workers if an excess of job opportunities marshaled in a given area (e.g., a state capital) could neither be relocated to where a job shortage exists nor the unemployed (elderly and handicapped) workers induced to migrate to the place with a surplus of jobs. Second, even within an easy commuting range (a given metropolitan area) public employment would almost certainly have to be broken down by political subdivisions because it is highly unlikely that municipal employment in one city would be available on a preferential basis to the elderly workers residing in some other city within that metropolitan area. It would be hard enough to wrest from the spoils system jobs that have traditionally been used to buy political patronage or to sequester jobs previously subject to the wide open competition of civil service examinations without trying to transfer them to nonresidents. Since the older and handicapped workers reside predominantly in the central city, the need for the data disaggregated by political subdivision is especially great.

A second possibility, almost as promising as direct public employment, is the sequestering of certain private jobs for certain disadvantaged classes of workers. This can be accomplished only where local government exercises some control over the work. A good example would be the licensing of taxicabs and operators. Here we have work which is well-suited to the typical older worker with a poor education and too "set in his ways" to be retrainable. In fact, one of the few transferable skills for many displaced older workers is the ability to drive a car and some knowledge of the local street pattern. Just as certain local government clerical jobs could be reserved for older workers with better-than-average education, so we might reserve all or a large proportion of taxi licenses for some select class of workers, for example, persons over forty years of age with less than a high school education and a good driving record or some similar set of qualifications.

Permits for selling door-to-door or for operating sidewalk stands or other concessions could be examined for similar potential in attacking the hard-core unemployment problem. Again, the favored class for whom work is sequestered could be Negroes or female heads of families or other special cases judged deserving of special treatment. Certainly, some very considerable dangers are inherent in fostering antidotal discrimination—political patronage and a new spoils system, for example—but in an economy that has become increasingly rationalized on the basis of countervailing power, an imaginative and honest creation of a *limited number* of noncompetitive local labor markets is surely not beyond our capabilities.[19]

The number of jobs that might be rationally sequestered by local government through hiring and licensing powers might not prove to be large. But then the number of workers with whom we are concerned in this regard is also modest. Further, the number of jobs at stake might turn out to be considerably greater than imagined as a result of related urban developmental strategy. To illustrate, suppose one appropriate tactic for relieving core area traffic congestion is to substitute, on a wholesale basis, oversize taxicabs (as well as buses) for privately operated motor vehicles. A host of new cab drivers would be needed, enough to make a very sizable dent in the chronically unemployed older worker group, especially if older workers were favored in licensing and also if we were simultaneously siphoning off those older workers who have better-than-average educations into local government clerical work especially set aside for them.

To take a significant step toward meeting both the hard-core unemployment problem and the urban traffic problem would require more careful thought than can be given here. But even this single illustration of taxi-licensing strategy suggests a considerable potential inherent in the *existing* powers of local government for attacking hard-core unemployment. The missing element is some policy-based re-

[19] In the Spring of 1962 the U.S. Senate considered the implications of a trend in the opposite direction: automatic vending machines are displacing blind vendors in federal buildings throughout the country. At a Senate Governmental Operations Subcommittee hearing, headed by Sen. Edmund Muskie (D-Maine), Sen. Jennings Randolph (D-W.Va.), who co-sponsored the original act of twenty-six years ago which put blind vendors into federal buildings, said he had received complaints that the intent of the Act was not being complied with and was prepared to amend it to protect the stand operators. If the full social costs of displacing these blind vendors were charged to the automatic vending machines, it is very doubtful that the automatic machines would be cheaper, and 2,332 persons at 2,174 stands throughout the country, with an average net income of $3,900, are involved. *Operation of Vending Stands for the Blind in Federal Buildings,* Hearing before a Special Subcommittee on Government Operations, U.S. Senate, June 26, 1962 (Washington: U.S. Government Printing Office, 1962), pp. 7–11.

search to detail the appropriate strategy and tactics and to lend credence to these speculations.

Subsidization of the Low Productivity Worker

When we turn to the case of persons who are not and cannot be made very productive, the case for public employment becomes even stronger. There are at least two noteworthy possibilities for employment of this low productivity group. First, the public economy may employ these workers at wage rates above their productivity and rationalize this action as economic, as well as humanitarian, if the wage payment minus the value of the workers' output (e.g., $60 per week minus $40 per week) is less than the public assistance payment (e.g., $30 per week), in return for which no product is received. To this reckoning, the social worker would want to add the psychic gain of personal dignity through useful work. Action that would be uneconomic for the individual firm becomes economic for the public economy when the cost of public assistance is brought into the economic calculus.

As long as the public employment remains within the bounds of economic activity which would have been carried on by local government anyway, no defense need be made of this strategy against the charges of "creeping socialism," bureaucracy, or "make-work programs." Care must be exercised, however, in extending this technique into pursuits traditionally reserved for private enterprise. Subsidized, low productivity workers might be accepted in the automobile license bureau, but not be so welcome as public parking lot attendants to either business or labor.

An alternative to public employment would be government subsidies to private employers who hired submarginal workers. In the beginning, this would be manageable probably only on government contracts where the subsidy could enter implicitly through the cost-plus provisions. We are not suggesting that the hiring of low productivity workers be forced on precision missile or instrument contractors; it would be enough to evaluate the potential for limited gains among suppliers of more mundane products such as printed forms, janitorial supplies and the like.[20]

[20] Seymour Wolfbein, head of the Labor Department's newly created Office of Automation and Manpower, cites the case of workers with I.Q.s of around 68 who were successfully trained by a restaurant chain to wipe lipstick traces off glasses. But

What is the potential scope for private employment of the elderly, physically handicapped, uneducated, rural in-migrants and other possibly submarginal workers in firms supplying materials to local government, under the stimulus of either direct subsidies or the indirect subsidies implicit in cost-plus contracts? How many workers and at what costs per worker? Exhortations for new public policies designed to stimulate public and private employment of the less productive worker are not likely to be effective unless through careful quantification we can clearly show that work relief can be handled so as to increase the overall efficiency of the local economy and/or to economize in the public economy, and in significant magnitude.

Of the two possibilities, direct public employment is surely of much greater quantitative importance. There may be a chance here to kill two birds with one stone: hard-core unemployment and urban blight. An increasingly glaring paradox of urban life is the existence of perhaps two million unskilled but able-bodied men standing idly in city streets ankle deep in trash, leaning against dilapidated buildings, behind which rat-infested alleys menace health.[21] Chronic unemployment in the midst of urban blight and drabness is an indictment of our vaunted Yankee ingenuity. The simplest solution would be to revive the old WPA of the thirties and dispatch work gangs through the city cleaning, painting, repairing, and gardening as they go. Apart from political resistance to work-relief projects from conservative quarters, the problem of financing arises. Deficit financing would not be widely popular at this time because we are not burdened with a deflation which might justify the new money that a public deficit

---

one wonders what will happen when the automatic dishwashers are improved to where they can remove lipstick, especially if we extend the minimum wage law to cover this group. At that point, public subsidies to private restaurants, in amount equal to the cost differential between the better machine and the cost of the current equipment plus the wage paid these men, would be necessary to keep them employed. "The Hard Realities of Retraining," *Fortune*, July 1961, p. 246.

[21] A large number of city departments (e.g., Public Works, Education, Parks, etc.) in Detroit employ a hundred relief claimants or more, typically for janitorial duties and ground maintenance. Under State of Michigan welfare regulations relief personnel cannot be used to replace regular city employees, therefore "these jobs are 'extra' jobs resulting in more custodial work than before. Because of the relatively 'free' labor made available to city departments through the work relief program, it is possible for schools, hospitals, city offices, parks, and recreation centers to be much cleaner than they would be otherwise. Such work is capable of almost unlimited expansion." Edward D. Wickersham, *Detroit's Insured Unemployed and Employable Welfare Recipients: Their Characteristics, Labor Market Experience and Attitudes*, The W. E. Upjohn Institute for Employment Research, Kalamazoo, Michigan, April 1963, p. 26.

creates. While only mild inflationary pressures are currently at work, our present adverse balance of international payments also operates as a very heavy constraint on new spending, reinforcing the conservative opposition to public deficits.

The most hopeful approach and one which demands thoughtful research is to go back over the "list" of the many local public projects that have been rejected, explicitly or implicitly, and determine whether a recalculation of associated benefits and cost might not open up some new possibilities for economic work-relief. The chances are that, if the relevant prices applied are revised a bit to reflect the social costs of unemployment, a number of "profitable" new public projects will be turned up. The cost of public projects which can make use of the kinds of labor that are chronically redundant—largely unskilled or semiskilled at best—could be recalculated using the differential between the potential employees' current unemployment compensation or public assistance payment and the wage that would be paid for his labor under prevailing standards. Moreover, a particularly close inspection might be made of those public projects which confer some identifiable and separable *private* benefits so that special assessments or user charges might be levied on the recipients of the benefits, to cover part of the total benefits.

With the, say, $1.60 per hour wage rate for common physical labor reduced to a real net cost to government of only, say, $.80 per hour because of the saving in welfare payments, and with user charges, fees and special assessments on the beneficiaries covering, say, one-half of that reduced amount, the net social cost of a previously rejected project is only one-half as much and the charge against net cost to the public economy is only one-quarter as much as originally estimated. The new and much higher benefit-to-cost ratio of this work-relief project may push it above some current local expenditure that uses labor much less intensively or uses a higher grade labor employable elsewhere, and thereby yield a net employment gain to the community. An even more appealing case could be made if the user charges were sufficient in themselves to cover the welfare-cost-reduced wage rate ($.80 per hour) so that many such projects could be initiated out of a small revolving fund.

It is hard to believe that there is not a whole host of potential public works projects drawing on the very kinds of labor that are chronically unemployed which would become "profitable" to society to undertake, at wage rates which were properly reduced by the cost to society of these men *not working* plus the values that could be recovered with various charges on the beneficiaries. The need is to track down these projects and to specify quite precisely the private and social benefits to be gained and the legitimate social costs of production and the proposed financing of the projects.[22] The physical rehabilitation of our cities will probably have to be carried on in important measure with the labor of displaced workers and the economic rationalization of this work will demand a more sophisticated and broad-gauge system of accounting than we now practice.

In the course of developing a strategy for rationalizing the local labor market to minimize the level of unemployment, we should take care that we do not allow labor downgrading to force us into a position of greater than necessary unemployment among the lowest skill groups. Public employment which requires only low-grade manual labor should not be filled with workers who can perform superior work unless that higher grade work is almost certain not to be forthcoming. For if potential clerks are working on the demolition projects, leaving able-bodied but illiterate workers in the labor pool, the local manpower planning group may find itself forced to rationalize inferior projects which can absorb the redundant manual laborers, while passing over superior projects requiring clerical skills. The job placements should be tailored to (a) provide employment for the less employable workers, (b) foster pride in the work by offering work as consistent with the worker's potential as is possible and (c) maximize the value of productivity of these workers. These are very close to being mutually consistent objectives, not unlike the results that a perfectly competitive labor market would achieve, differing mainly in that our efforts are designed to supplement the incomes that these workers would receive to raise them to "decent" levels.

Efficient management of public employment strategy would call for the creation of some kind of system of accounts which would bring together (a) an inventory of skills possessed by the chronically unemployed workers in the local labor force, (b) the relevant opportunity costs of employing these workers or supporting them in idleness under the current welfare schedules, and (c) the identifiable and separable

---

[22] "The Detroit Lighting Commission employs a crew of relief claimants to strip insulation from scrap wires. The salvage value of these scraps is substantial but not great enough to hire full-time employees to engage in the salvage work." Wickersham, *ibid.* But the salvage value may well exceed the cost of hiring relief claimants at the legal minimum wage minus their normal welfare payment (i.e., the true incremental cost of the work), not counting the hard-to-measure value of personal dignity associated with earning one's own keep.

private benefits that can be captured through user charges or special assessments to reduce the charges against the general fund and (d) the social benefits that can neither be precisely quantified nor neatly allocated but which can still be judged. This only partially quantifiable system of simultaneous "equations" must be sensibly and sensitively handled if structural and frictional unemployment is to be minimized.

LOCAL GOVERNMENT WELFARE POLICY

We began our analysis of employment and manpower planning at the national level, looking first to the federal government's fiscal and monetary powers to ensure adequate aggregate demand. Without enough total spending even the most sophisticated and energetic local planning can come to little; but even with enough total spending, we would still need to build better local labor markets. Only a close federal-state-local partnership can get at both cyclical and structural unemployment.

Here we are concerned with the poverty that arises not out of unemployment but out of *unemployability*. A comprehensive antipoverty program cannot rest on even the most ingenious employment strategy, as many of the poor cannot or should not work. Examples are: the severely handicapped, both physically and mentally; the elderly (but not everyone over 65 years of age and some younger); and mothers of large, young families, especially if competent relatives are not living-in to manage the household and mind the children. Over one-third of the 47 million families that earn $3,000 or less have a family head 65 years of age or older, and one-third depend on a female head of the household; thus a full half of our poverty originates largely outside of the labor market and must be treated outside of it.

Let us distinguish from employment policy the term "welfare policy": measures taken to relieve that poverty which originates outside of the competitive labor market. While we have accepted, with only minor reservations, the proposition that the federal authority has the main responsibility to control cyclical fluctuations in income and employment, we argued strongly for a major local role in manpower planning, in general, and in reducing structural unemployment, in particular. We turn now to argue for a major local role in income redistribution, outside of labor markets, through welfare policy.

Toward Consistent Multilevel Social Planning

Under current public policy, income redistribution is not confined to the federal government. Substantial income redistribution occurs through local public services, as noted in Chapter 3. The growing importance of such redistribution is partly of institutional origin—a political legacy of the "division of powers" and of "states' rights" tradition that has reserved many important social services for state and local government—and partly an economic phenomenon resulting from the *income-elastic demand* for most of the traditionally local services, such as education, recreation, and public health and hospitals. That is, for reasons buried in the past, local government has reluctantly accepted socioeconomic functions destined to be growth "industries" and to be extended to those who could not pay for them. But we will argue below that local government should be in the business of redistributing income for another reason: as leverage to change behavior patterns in a way which will promote human resource development and, ultimately, lead to greater income equality. Local government should get into the income redistribution business today, in good measure, to get out of it tomorrow.

However, the first bold strokes in social welfare planning should be taken at the national level. Granting this, an economist's first reaction might be to wonder what need there would be for *local* welfare work, if we had a well developed set of national welfare policies.

Suppose, for example, our national social security system did really provide a decent minimum retirement benefit. Suppose, again, the heavy health and hospital expenses which often accompany old age and wipe out what seemed to be provident retirement planning were fully insured against. Suppose we had family allowances and college scholarship programs on the national level which equalized opportunity, or at least closely approached the ideal of achieving a fair competitive race. Suppose, that is, we were to begin from a position of comprehensive national social-welfare planning (without digressing here to argue for or against such a policy). What would remain for the local authorities to do?

The first and easiest response is to suggest a supporting role: local government should take great care not to undo the welfare-redistribution work of the federal authorities by pursuing various *contrary* taxation, zoning, housing, urban renewal, and transportation policies.

This is not trivial. Heavy local residential property taxes to finance ever more ambitious educational programs can cut heavily into otherwise adequate retirement allowances. Zoning and housing policies that confine racial minorities to small areas and raise rents to double their normal level by concentrating housing demand can wipe out family allowances of any likely size. Urban renewal programs which replace tenements with luxury apartments and do not provide for rehousing the slum dwellers displaced can neutralize national social planning. Local policies which favor the automobile over mass transit to the point where the places of both employment and enjoyment are inaccessible to the poor or elderly (e.g., suburban factories and parks) redistributes income toward greater inequality. We could, of course, have inverted all the examples above to illustrate the power of local government to complement national social planning with consistent, rather than countervailing policy. Local government engages in social planning, explicitly or implicitly, constructively or destructively.

Toward a Constructive Public Welfare Program

The following three chapters take up local public services and taxes, housing and land-use, and transportation in detail. Let us focus here on that facet of social-welfare planning which is most identified with the term welfare: public assistance. What are and should be the criteria for distributing money income outside of the labor market, especially as this problem concerns local government in urban areas?

Local welfare policy should seek to identify those who could become permanently employable, even though considerable personal development might be necessary. Raising a welfare recipient to full or partial self-support should be a prime goal in any general human resource development program for reasons of both humanity and economy. But beyond this, the whole public assistance program can be endangered by the "discovery" of a few malingerers. Perhaps we should even be sure to arrange some *quid pro quo* for most welfare recipients, some not too onerous tasks to assure critics that irresponsibility is not to be rewarded.

The welfare check could be made conditional on prescribed behavior, for example, in payment for attending "night school." Recently the Cook County (Chicago) Department of Public Aid began requiring basic and/or vocational education of 16,000 able-bodied men and 34,000 mothers on its relief rolls, threatening to stop welfare checks as a penalty for missing classes.

In the case of the able-bodied males and some of the females, the clear objective is to increase employability and reduce relief rolls in the near future. A recent study by the Chicago Department of Public Aid revealed that more than one-half of the adult relief recipients were functional illiterates, unable to read want ads or fill in job application forms. Since, however, we wish to concentrate here more on the "pure" (more permanent) welfare case, let us consider the rationale of requiring education or other prescribed performance of the welfare mothers in the group. (Ideally, these able-bodied males would be covered by unemployment compensation and the appropriate strategy in their case would come within our labor market-manpower discussion above.)

The major purpose of making the welfare payment to mothers contingent on attending school should be to operate on unemployment and unemployability in the next generation, specifically to improve the households and neighborhoods in which the coming additions to the labor force are being raised. At least in theory, education is contagious, so that more educated parents should be more likely to rear more educated children. Or it could be that simply by setting a good example parents create new respect for themselves and new pride in their home, and the children become less rebellious and/or less nomadic.

While the broad strategy is clear, much remains to be done in devising good tactics. At present the instructors are "moonlighting" public school teachers; more specialized skills may be needed. Because baby-sitting is a problem, some experimentation with television is being considered. While it may be easier and probably cheaper to bring one instructor on a screen into a thousand homes than to bring a thousand students into contact with fifty instructors, the relative effectiveness of the two educational processes must be weighed. Motivation is especially critical and the early reports are that, because the very poor in big cities are socially isolated, these people, desperate for companionship, have found the classes to be a major social occasion and presumably a major socializing experience. They may, that is, go to the schoolroom but would not study at home.

Both direct controls and pecuniary rewards and penalties can be used to stimulate socially desired behavior. The next generation is also served by inducing parents to manage their households more efficiently, providing cleaner, neater homes and better diets. The New York City welfare investigator must give a prescribed budget to each family but the family does not have to follow it, although the investigator will check rent and utility receipts at each visit. Some local welfare programs already require that everyone on relief rolls must use the Food Stamp Plan, although the federal government does not require this of participants in the federally-financed Aid to Dependent Children program.

The Cook County Department of Public Aid has initiated another interesting experiment in programs designed to improve the environment in the welfare home and the behavior of its occupants. In October 1961 they introduced a two-week program training single women who were general-assistance clients as housekeeping teachers. These women are taught how to demonstrate these skills to others. Those chosen to receive the instruction of the new teachers are ones whose housekeeping has disturbed social workers or ones whose children come to school dirty or ill-fed. The objective is not only to get the children better housed, clothed, and fed but to develop a sense of achievement and pride in the home and, in turn, even higher aspirations, in both the parents and the children. Clearly, there is a valuable joint product here. The Chicago welfare department has not only moved to clean up its slums in a way much more meaningful than the usual bulldozer method, but also turned single welfare claimants into trained domestic service workers, a skill in short supply in the Chicago suburbs. This strategy should tend to reduce welfare claims in both the near and distant future—claims of both this and the next generation.

A number of different tactics could be employed to induce welfare families to use such services, ranging from the most drastic one of denying welfare checks to those who do not co-operate to the milder one of paying small rewards to those who do. We could begin with the least coercive tactics, say, informing the welfare housewives of the existence of the free housekeeping course and that free samples of various housekeeping supplies, e.g., brooms, soaps, disinfectants, would be given away—after class. But more powerful incentives such as higher support payments may be necessary. In all probability, the basic public assistance payment could not be stopped to penalize nonperformance so the activating mechanism will almost certainly have to become not the choice between the carrot and the stick but rather between two carrots and one carrot.

Dual Economies: Carrots and Sticks[23]

Will not the charge of undue government interference be levied against the introduction of a system of rewards and penalties in welfare programs—government dictation of both the family's spending patterns and in the use of their time? The implicit philosophy, critics will charge, is that low-income families do not know what is best for them.

Proponents of public welfare incentives might readily admit the existence of elements of both compulsion and paternalism in the programs outlined above, but defend them as being integral parts of our economy and society. Price compulsion is, after all, the main mechanism of control in the private market sector of our economy. Consumers "coerce" entrepreneurs to shift from low-price to high-price goods and consumers coerce workers to leave low-wage for high-wage work. Still, merely because the inhabitants of the poverty-welfare public economy cannot compete with the more talented and aggressive persons in the harsh free markets of the private sector, they need not be fully isolated from the discipline of the incentive system.

In effect, completely separate price systems could be used in each

---

[23] None of this endorses in any way the roughshod tactics used in Newburgh, New York, to reduce public assistance; this writer categorically rejects the punitive spirit in which that action was taken.

In late 1960, the new city manager of Newburgh, Joseph M. Mitchell, received nationwide attention by moving to crack down on local welfare recipients. According to the best newspaper and magazine reports, Mitchell greatly overstated local welfare costs in public statements and was prevented from indiscriminately slashing welfare rolls only by the counter-action of the state Social Welfare Department's area director. Despite the fact that both federal and state statutes had long existed denying assistance payments to any employable person who refused to register with the nearest local employment agency or who refused to accept work for which he was fitted, Mitchell dramatically proposed this as a revolutionary new idea. Again, the New York law declares ineligible for home relief any person who refuses to perform work assigned by a public official. Despite this fact, "the idea that Mitchell had invented a way to get a large and lazy labor force back to work persisted even after he was able to find only one employable man in July to put to work for the city."

"It is clear from the letters that have flooded local newspapers on the subject that Mitchell has tapped a deep reservoir of popular emotion that extends all across the nation. Among the 'Thank Gods' and 'God blesses,' there have been many demands for further humiliation of welfare recipients, apparently based on a strong conviction that the poor are carrying out some sort of deliberate conspiracy in a depressing world where vast numbers of chiselers and slug-a-beds buy not only whiskey but automobiles with their relief money and women conceive and bear illegitimate children for the sake of acquiring nineteen dollars a month. . . ." Meg Greenfield, "The 'Welfare Chiselers' of Newburgh, N.Y.," *The Reporter*, August 17, 1961, pp. 37–40.

sector of this dual economy, with a very basic difference. Individuals in the protected public sector would not be asked to compete with each other directly, merely required to meet prescribed norms of behavior. These norms would be set and revised partly on the basis of the performance of other welfare sector participants, but this indirect competition would be much more loosely linked and much more tempered. While it is unlikely we could or would cut the current basic level of welfare payments to recalcitrant claimants, we could certainly pay more to those who did co-operate rather than less to those who did not. The consumer (society) has a decided preference for an educated, clean, energetic populace and is prepared to pay for this behavior.

A fuller use of rewards and penalties to allocate welfare-sector "labor" between the home and the schoolroom, between teaching their own children and learning more, in response to the needs of society would be, in effect, a carefully modified extension of our value system from the private economy into the public economy. Ironically, we are now implicitly using the price system to encourage antisocial behavior. By cutting off welfare payments if an able-bodied father is in the home, we reward desertion.

The charge of state paternalism could be accepted as an ever present phenomenon and a case made for a more explicit and incisive paternalism. Society has assumed responsibility for its "children" in many ways, with government acting as its agent. We take children away from cruel parents and we order surgery for children whose parents believe in faith-healing. And where childhood (the need for protection) ends and maturity (self-reliance) begins is not a single, simple point in time. Our slums are filled with persons adult in years who need guidance in their work habits, their consumption patterns, their techniques of homemaking and budgeting. Education, our biggest and fastest growing industry, is in large measure an expression of enlightened paternalism. We lead students, coercing them with grades and job prospects, toward new behavior patterns quite paternalistically and with a much stronger hand than we exercise in our welfare work.

When we conclude that welfare families are spending too much of their income on entertainment and too little on food and books, we can convert this from a subjective value judgment into an objective development strategy by adding: more than they should allot to entertainment to get their families off welfare in this generation or the next. If we can bring ourselves, without major moral qualms, to subsidize middle-income youths to go to college, we might, if we tried hard, learn to accept paying subsidies to welfare parents or their children to induce them to finish high school.

The interest of society in all children, but especially in the children of the poor, is paramount and patent. Many of the heads of slum families have already failed as parents acting on their own. We need to develop ways of revitalizing their performance as parents, or at least enlivening them as agents of a society which can and will assume the more demanding parental functions. We "socialized" one-third of the child's life when we transferred the principal responsibility for his education from the home to the public school. (Even the private school institutionalizes education.) We may soon see fit to extend the influence of society into some aspects of home life in the slums by bringing various socially determined rewards and penalties to bear.

Most of the educational psychologists who have dealt with the slum education problem believe that only by getting to slum children during the pre-school years can we make major headway in school. If this judgment is at all accurate, a strategy for dealing with the "permanent welfare family" clearly requires social intervention in the home. The challenge is how to insure that society will lend a helping hand to, not lay a heavy hand on, these deprived people.

Some Economics of Tutoring

An appreciation of the need for a much expanded program of educational services for poor families, especially those living in slum ghettoes lacking in community pressures for education, suggests the possibility of "tutorial stamps." We could give welfare families *part* of any further increases in public assistance payments in the form of tutorial stamps—tied money—which city-approved tutors could turn in for cash, much as the grocer turns in food stamps. Unlike food stamps, these might have to be given free without any requirement that the recipient's "own" (welfare) money be added to them, because most of these parents probably do not place any significant value on tutorial services for their children.

The proposals advanced in recent years to help families bear educational expenses by means of tax deductions have emphasized *higher* education and the federal personal income tax. But nothing inherent in the idea would prevent its application to lower level remedial education paid for out of, say, local property tax credits. Substantial local property taxes are paid down to income levels much below those subject to significant federal income tax liability. Because a large proportion of the very-low-income groups are renters rather than home owners, we would have to substitute tutorial (stamp) payments for tax credits, with formulas to approximate the property tax component in their rent payment (at, say, one-third of the total). Local government is, therefore, in a strong position to induce the least-educated, lowest-income families to buy more educational services.

A program of subsidization of remedial-education tutoring could become integrated with the currently proposed "domestic peace corps." The Northern Student Movement and like groups which have mobilized significant numbers of college students to tutor slum children for little or no pay have performed a heroic labor. But purely or largely voluntary efforts tend to falter in time and, in any event, the small number of dedicated volunteers is wholly out of proportion to the immensity of this task. Money incentives are needed and wholly justified for this very important work.

Seldom do so many favorable factors reinforce each other as would do so in this projected work, if its strategy were well designed. By drawing mainly on college students, certified by the local Department of Public Welfare and/or the local Board of Education, we could accomplish several aims:

1. Because this almost must be part-time work, after school and on week ends, student labor is especially well suited, and this prime talent is available at a relatively low price. The slum children will get the best (except in experience) for their money, and in a time of shortages of talented labor.

2. Part-time jobs for college students are almost always in short supply and the imminent sharp increases in the number of college students promises that the part-time job problem will become desperate very soon. This proposed project would, therefore, be almost as socially valuable as a means of investing in the talented as in the impoverished.

3. Student-teaching is not the typical restaurant "bus boy" experience; this could be a very enriching contact with another world—the "culture of poverty." The teacher may learn as much as his pupil and the building of a citizenry which understands, a little, the nature of poverty could be the most valuable product of all in the long run.

4. Further, to the degree that college students vacate "bus boy" jobs, they open up this work for the "drop-outs" or, better still, those who would have had to drop out of school if these part-time jobs had not appeared. And in the long run by graduating from college and working

as engineers they leave open machinist jobs they would otherwise have filled. Because unemployment is so much more characteristic of the lowly skilled, full employment policy requires a manpower planning which forces upgrading whenever possible.

5. Finally, to the degree all of this works as outlined above, it tends to pay for itself. In the short run, higher tuitions may save taxpayers almost as much as they would pay out to the student tutors. (There really is no reason why college students should not pay a larger part of the cost of their education, especially if we were to provide them with the means to do so.) In the long run, the higher incomes and tax payments of a more educated work force and the lower social costs of public assistance, police protection, and prison maintenance could justify the investment many times over.

With imaginative design, dedicated management, and a little luck, we could kill at least three birds with one stone—and even get the stone back. (The author appreciates that there may be a little double counting in this example, but he believes that even the most conservative social benefit-cost accounting would turn up a tidy profit here.)[24]

[24] Perhaps this program can even be extended to high school students with reasonable success. Professor Richard A. Cloward, Columbia University School of Social Work, conducted a "home-work help" demonstration program for a juvenile delinquency agency operating on the Lower East Side of New York. He found that underprivileged high school students, doing only average work, employed as part-time tutors, helped underprivileged fourth- and fifth-grade pupils improve their reading skills by 40 per cent. Beginning in Fall 1962, 240 high school students were paid $11 for two hours of training under a professional teacher and six hours of tutoring each week. They tutored the 600 elementary students one at a time in two hour sessions twice a week (in the successful arrangement—once-a-week contact did not raise reading levels appreciably). The original plan called for matching the social, economic, and ethnic backgrounds of tutor and pupil but the lack of qualified Negro and Puerto Rican tutors forced use of Jewish and Italian youths, but ones from the same or similar neighborhoods. "The research center now is studying the effect of the program on the high school students to determine if their own performance improved, if they are motivated to stay in school or if, perhaps, they were inspired to become teachers someday." Reported in *The New York Times*, August 30, 1964, p. 55.

CHAPTER 7

The Urban Public Economy:
Problems in Scale and Choice

Boundaries between areas of thought are never neat, and this is especially true in the no-man's land between the young and still amorphous field of urban economics and the much older but still haphazard conglomerate loosely referred to as local public finance. Neither of the two fields has claimed the attention of more than a handful of outstanding economists—and seldom the undivided attention of these few. Witness the fact that no comprehensive textbook has yet been published in either field. Since neither urban economics nor local public finance has established its character so clearly that their interrelationships can be cleanly defined, the lines of mutuality and complementarity suggested below are obviously very tentative.

URBAN ECONOMICS AND
LOCAL PUBLIC FINANCE

A first approximation of the potential contribution of the urban economist to an understanding of the urban public economy can be gained from reviewing the local public finance literature—the appropriate chapter or two in any introductory public finance textbook or the more detailed state-and-local tax study report.[1] A careful reading of this scattered literature will acquaint the urban economist with what is known and suggest what still needs to be known. For maximum

[1] These latter contract research efforts—command performances at state capitols—are often strictly for the political record or contrived as a subtle legislative delaying tactic, but so poor an environment has not prevented many of them from growing to greater stature than the rival literature in the field. See for example, *Report of the Governor's Minnesota Tax Study Committee, 1956* and *Michigan Tax Study Staff Papers*, Legislative Committee, House of Representatives, Lansing, Michigan, 1958. Professor Harvey E. Brazer was research director for both efforts.

gain our work should pick up about where theirs leaves off; a rough complementarity of interest and effort should exist.

The standard format in research and writings on local public finance is to briefly outline the statutory provisions of a particular tax, identify its impact, trace through its probable course of shifting and final incidence, classify the tax according to some accepted standard of taxation (e.g., ability-to-pay, benefit theory), and finally consider the economic effects of the tax. The analyst then repeats the operation with each alternative tax in turn. The objective of such an analysis is usually to achieve equity in taxation, constrained by the array of tax instruments within reach of the local authority; that is, subject to administrative capabilities, statutory limitations, and political considerations, and to the public body's *given* need for revenue. On this latter score, the literature of local public finance almost invariably disposes of public expenditures in a simple descriptive fashion, perfunctorily apprising the reader of what it is that local governments do. ("Police and fire protection account for 10 per cent of total local expenditures, up slightly; health and hospitals account for . . .") Literally, public expenditures and public services are typically cast as exogenous variables—even as constants—that are extraneous to the proper study of local public finance.[2]

Our interests could easily come to center more on the level and efficiency of local public expenditures (services) than on the equity of local taxes. We might, on the one hand, tentatively identify local public finance more with such questions as whether the property tax can be justified on either a benefits-received or on an ability-to-pay basis; whether a sales tax with a food and drug exemption ceases to be a regressive tax; whether industrial real property (plant and site) should be distinguished from industrial personal property (machines and inventories) in local property taxation under a benefits rationale—all primarily equity questions. We might, on the other hand, tentatively identify urban economics more with efficiency in the production and financing of urban public services, especially as a function of the size of local government. And, as we shall see, scale in the local public economy becomes a study in spatial patterns of economic activity,

[2] There are a number of very notable exceptions to the generalization that public finance has been heavily preoccupied with the revenue side, to the virtual neglect of public expenditure theory. At the federal level we have the balanced, comprehensive work of Richard A. Musgrave, especially his definitive piece, *The Theory of Public Finance* (New York: McGraw-Hill Book Co., Inc., 1959). At the state and local level, more relevant to our interests here, we have the work of Brazer, Hirsch, Margolis and a few others on urban expenditures, cited below.

quite distinguishable from the functional preoccupation of a local public finance concept that up to now has been largely spaceless.

Where the interests of local public finance and urban economics join (and overlap) is at the point of consideration of the economic effects of taxation. Usually studies in local public finance give at least passing attention to the possibility that the local property tax rate may drive out manufacturing plants to nearby tax havens in the same metropolitan area or, less likely, out of the region altogether. While the specter of industrial flight is almost always raised, a more general analysis of industrial mobility is almost never considered relevant; industrial mobility enters the analysis largely as an implicit limitation on property tax rates, rather than on its own merits. If the effect of local business taxation on local industrial development is weakly handled, the impact of local taxation on *intra*-area spatial patterns of economic activity is almost totally ignored. Questions about the effect of property taxes on slum formation, urban sprawl, and the value of downtown real estate are seldom discussed. Almost categorically, one might say that traditional local public finance has emphasized revenue at the expense of expenditures, and equity at the expense of efficiency and area development.

Where local public finance studies, especially those commissioned by existing political authorities (e.g., the state legislature), are usually content (or constrained) to rationalize the existing set of local political entities, we are committed to a critical examination of the current political arrangement—often "fragmentation"—with an eye to re-arrangement. Accordingly the case for and against "METRO" and other political inventions and experiments is very much a part of our work. Our own simplification of leaving equity-in-taxation questions to the local public finance analyst does not, of course, relieve us of the heavy moral obligation to integrate their findings into our analyses. Let us turn now to scale and efficiency in the local public economy: first, the way in which the size and number of political subdivisions in a metropolitan area affect the cost and quality of local public services, and then to efficiency and equity in their financing.

SCALE IN PUBLIC SERVICES

No phrase in urban affairs is encountered more frequently than "political fragmentation." One interpretation is that the local public economy is made less efficient by being divided into too many political subdivisions too small to capture the many potential internal and external economies of scale. Water and sewage systems are either too small or, if of optimum size, are underutilized; police communication systems and street networks are unco-ordinated across a maze of city boundaries. The presumption is that the case for larger political scale is obvious and overpowering, so much so that only apathy, vested interest, or plain cussedness could account for opposition to enlarged local government—ideally metropolitan-area-wide "local" government. What is usually absent is any quantification of the purported economies foregone and/or the public service quality presumably sacrificed by retaining fragmented local government, and this is a gap in the case for bigness because political consolidation cannot rest easily on some trivial gain in scale economies.[3] A small sacrifice in efficiency will

[3] A number of statistical cross-section studies of city expenditures have failed to reveal significant economies of scale but Brazer, the author of one of these, argues that this by no means indicates that they do not exist. "Larger cities do not spend less, per capita, for police protection than smaller ones, but this is very likely a consequence of the fact that economies of scale may be offset by the performance of more sub-functions under the 'police protection' heading." Harvey E. Brazer, "Some Fiscal Implications of Metropolitanism," *Metropolitan Issues: Social, Governmental, Fiscal* (Syracuse University, February, 1962), p. 63, n. 2, and his *City Expenditures in the United States* (New York: National Bureau of Economic Research, Inc., 1959), pp. 25–28. Of the eight public expenditure functions tested, Brazer found a statistically significant association between population size and per capita expenditures for only one, police protection, and even in that case population size was the least important of the four independent variables in the police protection equation (had the lowest beta coefficient).

On the basis of both deduction and the evidence of a cross-section analysis of 149 government units in the St. Louis metropolitan area, Werner Hirsch concludes that public education, police and fire protection, and refuse collection, a group accounting for approximately 80 to 85 per cent of total local public expenditures, are furnished in horizontally integrated service plants probably subject to constant costs per unit. For these services Hirsch believes that additional output merely calls for replication of identical service plants. Hirsch believes that only water and sewage service, accounting for only 8 to 10 per cent of total expenditure, are rendered in vertically integrated plants and exhibit important falling unit costs up to very large size. In his empirical tests, none of the partial correlation coefficients between population size and per capita expenditures on police protection, fire protection, refuse collection and public education was statistically significant. Hirsch concludes:

Efficiency considerations, thus, do not appear to warrant across-the-board consolidation of metropolitan area governments. Consolidation of water services and sewage services, preferably into a multi-purpose district, can be a move toward greater efficiency and lower expenses. Otherwise, economic efficiency may be highest in medium-size communities of 50,000–100,000 residents.

Werner Z. Hirsch, "Expenditure Implications of Metropolitan Growth and Consolidation," *The Review of Economics and Statistics*, August, 1959, p. 240. Still, we cannot be sure that Hirsch has not assumed away an important part of the problem when he is forced to assume that "services of equal quality are rendered regardless

not offset a strong need or preference for either personalized political participation or intimate political control. At the moment we are not able to say with any assurance whether our pattern of political fragmentation in metropolitan areas is due to the fact that substantial economies of scale (a) do not exist, (b) are thought not to exist, (c) have not been thought about by the electorate, or (d) are not large enough to exchange for the luxury of retaining intimate small local government.

Political Fragmentation as Monopolistic Competition

Under the harsh discipline of pure competition, if a large mill can grind wheat into flour more cheaply than a small mill, large mills will survive and ultimately dominate. In the politically fragmented metropolitan area, local governments compete for residents, even though the inconvenience of moving one's household may make it a sluggish market. Will not the optimum size local political entity (least cost-producer of public services) also ultimately dominate? But an analogy couched in terms of pure competition is misleading. This is the age of affluence and, in public goods as well as private goods, product differentiation is the characteristic form of competition— "monopolistic competition." In general, utilitarian efficiency criteria do not dominate in our markets and the deluxe model outsells the standard model across the board from automobiles to aspirin.

Residents of large metropolitan areas have, in effect, chosen to devote part of their rising incomes to the luxury of buying small local government. And even if they were made fully aware of the relevant costs of this choice—knowledge we do not have—we have every reason to believe that urban residents would still elect to have local political entities appreciably smaller than the least-cost local government, although perhaps not quite so small as many now are. Small local governments offer some very high style features, such as easier political participation by the citizens and greater responsiveness of the public officials to the desires and aspirations of the local residents. Should we really be shocked by a prevailing preference for high-cost, small

---

of the scale of operations" and Brazer's *caveat* from above that a seemingly innocent category, like "police protection," may broaden in coverage with larger city size applies here too. In sum, we are still a long way from any sure feeling for the nature of the public service cost function.

local government over low-cost metropolitan government? Political participation may, like quality in general, be income-elastic, so rising per capita incomes would increase the preference for small local government with each passing year.

In a large metropolitan area one can choose to reside in an industrial enclave with ample, even lush, public services and very low tax rates (partly capitalized into higher land prices), if the unaesthetic wrapper on the package does not offend too much. Or one may choose a low density suburb of oversized lots and undersized public services, where fresh air serves to dispel the odors emanating from drainage ditches fouled by private septic tanks. Or one may choose the crowded, dirty, noisy and, to some, exciting and culturally rich central city, convenient to work, stores, theaters, museums, as well as to skid row and high crime-rate areas. Political fragmentation increases the degree of residential differentiation by piling heterogeneity in public services on top of variation in private features. Moreover, as per capita income rises and local government is called upon to perform ever more kinds of activities, product differentiation in public services is almost sure to be both more sought and more supplied.

The analogy between differentiated products in the market place and differential political subdivisions suggests the applicability of the concept of monopolistic competition to the large metropolitan area. Charles M. Tiebout was the first to apply, in a formal way, the theory of monopolistic competition to the politically fragmented large metropolitan area. In a highly imaginative, and to his critics heroic, attempt to rationalize political fragmentation, Tiebout saw the consumer-voter

> picking that community which best satisfies his preference pattern for public goods. . . . The greater the number of communities and the greater the variety among them, the closer the consumer will come to fully realizing his preference position. . . . Moving or failing to move replaces the usual market test of willingness to buy a good and reveals the consumer-voter's demand for public goods. . . . Such studies as have been undertaken seem to indicate a surprising awareness of differing revenue and expenditure patterns. The general disdain with which proposals to integrate municipalities are met seems to reflect, in part, the fear that local revenue-expenditure patterns will be lost as communities are merged into a metropolitan area.[4]

[4] Charles M. Tiebout, "A Pure Theory of Local Expenditures," *The Journal of Political Economy*, October 1956, pp. 418, 420, 423. While Tiebout carefully spelled out the assumptions of his admittedly highly simplified model—residential mobility,

The ever greater range for creative design in local public services is obvious in the extension of the local responsibility from primary education to new excursions into adult education; criminal and civil courts are now being supplemented with family guidance clinics as society enters preventive social medicine; utilitarian bus and railroad depots are supplemented with elaborate complexes of jet airports and connecting rapid transit systems. Not only does the urban resident have the traditional utilitarian choices to make—private septic tanks or public sewer, big backyards or public parks—but all of this is inextricably enmeshed with a complex quality choice. Thus, one does not simply choose to substitute taxes for private expenditure on land when one votes for public recreation space or chooses to live in a community that has authorized public recreation expenditures, one must also select the most appropriate recreation model: fewer large playgrounds or more smaller ones; emphasis on organized group recreation (baseball diamonds) or unorganized individual activities (golf). With rising per capita incomes and the growth of the local public economy, local government is supplying ever more highly styled goods and services. Local government, operating in a fragmented metropolitan area, produces a highly styled product, and if the area is growing rapidly in population, so that there is continual entry of new political subdivisions, the analogy is clearly much more that of monopolistic competition than of pure monopoly or pure competition.

To create an image of the political subdivisions of the large metropolitan area as engaged in monopolistic competition for houses (and plants) is to run the risk of misinterpretation. Even though the context here is clearly that of *public services only* and not the total living environment which a family buys along with the house (and a business firm buys along with the store or plant), care must be taken not to give the impression that public service differentials within the metropolitan area account for most of the elements of distinctiveness between resi-

---

knowledge of intergovernmental differences, wide range of choice, negligible cost of job commuting, and no external economies or diseconomies—his thesis has been heavily attacked for lack of realism and relevance, that is, that he assumed away the problem at issue. Small contiguous political subdivisions cannot avoid heavy spillover effects as people live, work, and shop in different communities, and consequently pay taxes and give rise to public service costs in diverse proportions, freeloading in some places and overpaying in others. Again his critics have pointed to racial segregation as a denial of his fundamental premise of mobility. But even if Tiebout's model be regarded as merely a *first* approximation of residential choice of *white* residents from among a limited range of relatively *small suburban* communities, we are unquestionably richer for his insight and dramatization of a facet of political fragmentation that too often escaped notice and evaluation.

dential subdivisions, or even the major part. Indeed, neighborhoods within large cities exhibit such substantial variation that their very names tell the story: Greenwich Village, Georgetown, Gold Coast, Chinatown. These examples, in fact, suggest that the most distinctive residential areas compound their distinctiveness largely out of various "private" factors, such as architecture, culture, race, and topography, rather than out of the quantity or quality of public services consumed.

Moreover, variation in public services can be observed within the city limits, as gravel roads remain in the less densely populated neighborhoods long after most city streets have been paved, snow is cleared from the mayor's street first, and the newer (richer) residential areas have newer school plants and better teachers than the older areas. Still, one has to struggle for good illustrations of intracity variations in the quantity and quality of public services, while intercity examples abound. And if much, even more, of the variation in the total living environment of the many residential subdivisions is attributable to private factors, still public service differentials between political entities are surely of notable proportions and figure significantly in selecting a home site. Similarly, to the business firm, water and sewage disposal, police and fire protection, transportation, and education are factors of production, directly or indirectly, and the tax rate is their price. Surely, intercity comparisons are made by business firms selecting a location for a new plant or store, not just on a price basis, but also to find the most appropriate mix of public services for a particular operation. The primary metals producer may look more to water and sewer facilities, the insurance company to mass transit facilities for its clerks and secretaries, and the research laboratory to the quality of the nearby schools (assuming some preference on the part of the employees to live near their work).

But differentiating public services between the various political subdivisions of a large metropolitan area has some very subtle and pervasive social ramifications. Many local public services are critical to creating an environment of equal opportunity for the next generation (e.g., education, libraries, museums, recreation) and should perhaps not be allowed to vary too greatly because of differences in the education, income, or taste patterns of the parents. The invariable rejoinder to this position is that the general social welfare requires only that some basic minimum level of public services be provided to all. But the meaning of a "basic minimum" education as preparation for a life-and-death contest for relative position in the labor market is a very slippery concept. And how does this square with the professional judgment that slum area schools should be spending much more per student to give their students even a fighting chance in competition with the youth of suburbia? Critical social goals, such as equal opportunity, become expressed in urban public services, so we must take great care that some easy market analogies between the private and the public sectors are as socially responsible as they are analytically intriguing.

Balancing Service Quality
against Cost Economy

Product differentiation in local government, to retain the phrase borrowed from price theory, may originate in (a) a preference for private over public sources of supply, or the reverse, (b) differences in taste patterns for public services or (c) desire for intimate control over the processes of government. The fragmented metropolitan area may sort out citizens so as to bring together in a given municipality a group who would minimize the public sector in their everyday life, with a volunteer fire department, self-provision of garbage disposal and outdoor lighting of their own property, and dependence on personal libraries. Alternatively, another like-minded group of residents may prefer to substitute "free" municipal swimming pools and golf courses for the more common "free" paved streets (by retaining dirt roads). A third group may be less distinctive in matters of the quantity or mix of public services than in their desire to exercise close control over the local government that produces these services. This latter group may feel that "bureaucracy" (diseconomies of scale in administration) more than offsets various economies of scale in production and finance, and so this might be an economy-in-government group. But more likely, this latter group wants *very* local government for its own sake; they want to feel important, as when they personally know their councilman, or they want to play politics for self-expression or just the fun of it, or otherwise personalize their local government. In this impersonal age of automation and the narrowest occupational specialization—this age of creative frustration for many people—the need for political participation may not be trivial and the trend may even be strongly upward.

The trick is to find the net balance of these two sets of countervailing forces, the cost economies of large scale and the preference for the personalized styling and control which comes with small scale, so as to be able to identify the level of government most appropriate, public service by service. Some public services display a set of attributes that clearly fall at one end of the spectrum or the other. Compare sewage disposal and storm drainage systems at one extreme with neighborhood playgrounds at the other. In sewage and drainage the internal economies of scale are considerable, especially for those communities far from the river or other place of final disposal. The external economies of scale are even more critical; one community's sewage can pollute another community and one's storm run-off can flood basements in another.

With cost heavily favoring the organization of sewage disposal and drainage at a gross grain of local government, we turn to quality considerations and find only the weakest force of attraction toward finer grain local government. Sewage disposal and storm drainage are not functions which admit of much styling to reflect local tastes. Once the decision to convert from private septic tanks and catch basins to public sewers has been made, the pipes must reach all the way and need reach no farther. Certainly, the rural-urban fringe areas will have fought the central sewer authority as long as it was at all possible for them to retain their individual household disposal systems, but once conversion to public facilities is forced on them (by the laws of nature and/or man) the routine administration of this activity could probably be lodged at the county or metropolitan area level with relatively little local resistance.

Compare the sewer system case to that of neighborhood playgrounds. Internal economies of scale are nominal; additional swings, tennis courts and baseball diamonds are added at nearly constant unit costs. If anything, larger tracts of land are harder to locate in urbanized areas and will tend to come at higher prices per acre than smaller tracts. Moreover, the probability of park users travelling from outside the taxing jurisdiction that supports the playground probably increases with the size (diversity) of the facility. Thus small neighborhood playgrounds do not confer important benefits without costs nor inflict sizable costs without benefits on neighboring political subdivisions, while big ones may.

Finally, not only is there little if any cost advantage to be gained by organizing this activity at any local governmental level higher than the very lowest, but a modest element of product differentiation is evident in playgrounds. In densely populated central city neighborhoods, playgrounds would normally have swings and sandboxes in profusion and these playgrounds would normally be both smaller and more frequent. Conversely, in suburban areas where private swingsets and sandboxes fit easily on large lots, the aggregation of many small play areas into fewer but larger areas capable of supporting football and kite flying might be preferable. Moreover, the playground is an extension of the home and school that reflects community values. The recreation programs might stress fencing, model airplane building, or basketball, depending on local values and aspirations, reflecting in turn local educational and income levels. While varied recreational programs could be instituted from a high central office, to fit the different needs and wants of the various subdivisions of the urban area, the decentralization of neighborhood playground administration would seem to be rational if any positive value is placed on having intimate local government and easy political participation.

The risk of generalizing broadly about gross aggregates of public services, such as "recreation" or even "outdoor recreation," is illustrated by a comparison of the neighborhood playground case with the nature area which would provide facilities for hiking, boating, camping, and similar outdoor recreations. Economies of scale in nature areas are striking when we recall that these parks are used less frequently than playgrounds and must be much larger in size. A hiking trail long enough to serve its purpose and a body of water large enough to accommodate fishing or water skiing would typically accommodate many more persons than reside in a single municipality in a politically fragmented metropolitan area. The sheer size required, and the relative infrequency of use, demand that the nature area accommodate a very large population if expensive idle capacity is to be held to tolerable levels. Externalities enter the picture too because residents of *noncontributing* political subdivisions would be willing to travel from nearly every corner of the metropolitan area to enjoy the use of the facilities. User charges might be used selectively to ration and finance certain kinds of equipment (e.g., boats and horses) but these could hardly make the park fully self-liquidating. In many cases, however, it would be difficult or very expensive at the least to exclude people who did not pay the charges voluntarily. Otherwise, it might very well be argued that the activity could have been left to private enterprise in the first place.

Hence, the nature area resembles sewer and water services in that substantial large-scale economies await exploitation by a larger local government, but the opportunity to achieve a considerable amount of distinctive product design complicates the nature area case. The wealthier political subdivisions of the metropolitan area would prefer more horseback trails and boat launching sites and the poorer ones would make more use of picnic grounds, hiking trails, and beaches. But since a park authority administering many parks could easily be big enough to accommodate all of these activities, is it not possible to have our cake and eat it too—to have economy *and* variety at large scale, as in automobiles? What further analogies can we draw from the market place?

To review briefly, the proponents of "METRO" see local government as a decreasing cost industry—a "natural monopoly"—which can be efficient only by encompassing the whole metropolitan area economy. The argument for metropolitan government to rationalize unco-ordinated, duplicative, and otherwise generally inefficient local public services is remarkably parallel to the traditional arguments for creating regulated monopoly as a means of eliminating wasteful competition. Moreover, the industries in which "destructive competition" was replaced by regulated private monopoly—the "public utilities"— are largely ones in which very substantial economies of scale are inherent and in which the product is highly standardized, for example, electricity, gas, telephone communication, and transportation—industries very similar to our sewer and water example from the public economy. At the other end of the spectrum, neighborhood playgrounds were likened to monopolistic competition, where product differentiation and the lack of substantial large-scale economies combined to create conditions conducive to the proliferation of many small suppliers of these governmental services. To complete the market analogy, the nature area may be likened to heterogeneous-product oligopoly.

The large automobile oligopolist produces only a very few basic body shells and engines common to all its models, and then allows relatively autonomous divisions of the corporation to ornament these common components so as to appeal to different tastes. The objective is to achieve large-scale economies *and* range of choice. Whether this industrial parallel is a strong or a weak analogy, the inference is clear that, ideally, we would selectively consolidate those public services or those of their components which can be standardized and subjected to mass production efficiencies, leaving the lower level governments to ornament the basic product. Quality variations can be hitched on to large-scale production economies at either higher or lower levels of local government. We can visualize a case in which a metropolitan area educational authority supplies (the funds for) a basic school building to each of its political constituents, and then swimming pools and driver training facilities are added at local option, financed out of local supplemental tax rates or user charges.

One of the biggest steps we could make toward economic rationalization of the local public economy would be to disaggregate important public services into (1) those components which are sufficiently standardized and/or sufficiently free of local possessiveness to warrant centralized production if economies of scale so warrant, and (2) those which are not. We would need to add understanding of efficient strategies for combining the two parts, the basic and ornamental, to produce a final product that did not look like a camel.

The Concept of Efficiency
in Local Public Services

The local public economy, especially in the large, politically fragmented metropolitan area, can be seen as a collection of separate economic entities (e.g., municipalities, "authorities," and "special districts") in both complementary and competitive interaction that are in many ways analogous to the private market place. Elements of monopoly, monopolistic competition, and oligopoly pervade the market in public services, affecting both the cost functions and product characteristics. Apparently, then, efficiency will be as difficult to define and quantify in public services as it is in the variegated private sector. Accordingly, we should not expect to be able to neatly define a public service cost function and then proceed unerringly to identify the least cost output and thereby the optimum size "firm" (local government) and the optimum number of these public service firms. At least we should not expect to proceed so surely in large aggregates to some quick and easy over-all judgment on optimum political size. About the best we can hope for is to achieve some technique with which to identify certain standardized components of public services and, through some rough quantification of the economies or diseconomies of scale in producing these components, to estimate the cost of choosing to operate at other than the least-cost scale.

How much does it cost to carry on public functions at the "wrong" scale of local governmental operation? Ideally, in estimating cost functions the quality of the product is held constant, but in practice this is often difficult or impossible. A metropolitan police force is a very different product from a complex of autonomous, semico-ordinated municipal police forces, not just a cheaper (or more expensive) service. The case for bigness in public services probably rests more on quality than on cost: an area-wide police force is better co-ordinated for traffic control and hot pursuit, and big enough to afford scientific crime detection facilities and specialists in juvenile and racial problems. Similarly, the case for smallness in local political organization hardly ever rests on grounds of economy, but rather on greater control over the style and production of the services, elements of quality.

Another complication that arises in formulating and quantifying public service functions lies in the tendency toward substitution of public for private costs with increased government size. The purpose of enlarging local government is usually to internalize external economies and diseconomies that plague small government under political fragmentation. If bringing a number of separate political subdivisions into a common drain authority reduces the *private costs* of flooded basements by more than the increase in taxes needed to finance the storm drains, then bigger local government is more economical, all costs considered. To the extent that METRO can internalize externalities, it is a device to enlarge the public sector, not to economize within it, in the interests of over-all economy.

Since the most highly developed part of the field of economics is value theory, the study of efficiency in the allocation of resources—producing the right goods at the least cost—we have a clear call to bring this rich tradition in value theory to bear on allocation in the public economy. There often will be less need, however, to apply the more elegant allocation theory of pure competition and pure monopoly than to adapt our limited successes from the fuzzier world of imperfect competition. The appropriate level of local government to best develop the potential of the public economy is every bit as much a question in oligopoly theory, concerned with research and development and product promotion, as it is a question in competitive theory, concerned with cost minimization and optimum plant size.

To suggest an analogy with oligopoly in the public economy, the urban traffic problem may ultimately require a mass shift from the private automobile to mass transit, but this will almost certainly not come about because of lower costs and fares, automatically achieved simply by juggling transit authority boundaries. Only when and if we have created a transit authority of such scale and organizational characteristics that it resembles today's aggressive oligopolist are we likely to effect any radical change in modes of urban travel. Only when a transit authority is operated by managers who are as creative and as aggressive as their counterparts (and rivals) in the automobile industry will the market rivalry here be fought out on roughly equal terms. Only when a transit service much superior to the one already offered is thrown into the competition will the fight be a fair contest for the consumers' favor—air-conditioned buses, with lounge seats and smoking privileges, running much faster because of fewer stops and charging *higher* fares.

The failings of the local public economy may be traceable less to inefficiency, in the restricted sense of failing to achieve minimum cost of production, than to a deficiency of true entrepreneurship. The local public economy, under present management and existing organization structure, is often just too stodgy to compete effectively. The strategy and tactics of cost minimization are often not appropriate in our affluent society with its rapid technological change. It is very hard to believe that the consumer-taxpayer will opt for utilitarian public goods to substitute for or complement his high-style private goods.

Further, judgments on optimum scale in local public services must be made in a dynamic context in which *demands are created* as well as supplied and in which rising per capita income is constantly altering consumption patterns. Local government is in active competition with the private sector for the new business generated by a rising per capita income and government has a number of very income-elastic products to sell: education, outdoor recreation, social welfare services, treatment of mental illness, and so forth. And these services do not sell themselves—over the din of Madison Avenue. Perhaps we would do better to emulate, rather than to decry, the merchandising methods of the private sector, both in product development and advertising, if we truly do have a "starved public sector."

In sum, the consumer-taxpayer clientele may favor either big or small government in different sets of circumstances but in almost every case affluence, technological change, and product development greatly reduce the predictive value of either the competitive or pure monopoly models. While a statistical cost study can make a valuable contribution to judgments on the economic rationalization of the local public economy (e.g., the average and marginal costs of a "unit" of fire protection at various levels of output and various scales of local government), informed decisions will almost certainly have to lean at least as heavily on dynamic demand analyses. Moreover, the evolution of some taxonomy of imperfect competition relevant to the politically fragmented metropolitan area market for public services seems to be a prerequisite to making any really big gains.

Perhaps a moral for urban economics is to be found in the experience of political science in the field of local government. Wood[5] has pointed out that the municipal reformers ran into trouble by over-

---

[5] Robert C. Wood, "The Contributions of Political Science to Urban Form," *Urban Life and Form*, Werner Z. Hirsch (editor), (New York: Holt, Rinehart and Winston, Inc., 1963), pp. 107–8.

emphasizing efficiency, neglecting the fact that public service outputs are more the residue of hard bargaining between groups with very different values and needs than they are the simple production of collectively consumed ("public") goods, or a process of rational investment in social overhead. He goes on to argue that political scientists labored too long under a "grass roots democracy mythology" and have seen social choice too naïvely; most people expect nothing of government and a few expect everything. While we may hope to improve on this pattern, we must be quite clear in our models of the rational public economy on the difference between what is and what ought to be.

Again, we must take care not to define local government purely in terms of the public services it performs because "government" is essentially a framework of social control, not a means of production. We must ask not just about the shape of the cost curve of the "X" public service, but also about the "shape" of the regulatory function of local government, as a function of city size, population density, degree of political fragmentation, and whatever else is most relevant. The optimum spatial pattern of local government in a large metropolitan area could turn more on efficacy in social control than efficiency in production. Finally, we must see local government in a dynamic role as a social entrepreneur because a country which has institutionalized research and development, as we have, places progress ahead of efficiency.

SCALE IN PUBLIC REVENUES

*Scale and Differentials in Fiscal Capacity
between Political Subdivisions*

The typical metropolitan area, as we saw in Chapter 3, is subdivided into many residential neighborhoods most of which house a highly homogeneous population, much alike in education, occupation, and, especially, income level. If we were to place a fine mesh grid over the urban area, we would find great disparity in income level between the cells of the land grid. As we slowly enlarged the mesh of the grid, we would begin to mix neighborhoods of diverse income level, and differences in average income between the cells would diminish. How many steps upward in mesh size are required before we achieve subdivisions of the metropolitan area in which most of the interarea variation in per capita income will have been removed? Or, in a public policy context, how few in number must the political subdivisions of an urban area be in order to equalize fiscal capacity (tax base) between subdivisions? ("Fiscal capacity" could be interpreted as income or wealth or sales or any stock or flow of value that is presently taxable or could reasonably be subjected to taxation or special assessment.)

The general configuration of the pattern can be easily deduced, as depicted in panel A of Figure 8 below. The interarea variation in

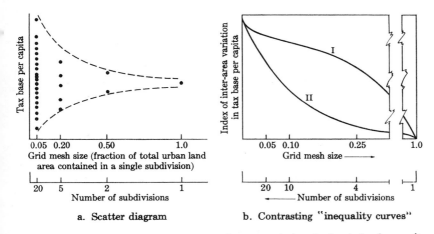

a. Scatter diagram   b. Contrasting "inequality curves"

Figure 8. Relation of political fragmentation to variation in local fiscal capacity.

tax base is largest when the subdivisions are most numerous and that variation narrows as the number of the subareas decreases (and their size increases), converging on the area-wide average when the subdividing ceases. What we do not know, and would much profit from knowing, is the precise shape of the curve shown schematically in panel B. This latter figure has been so constructed that when the urban area is most finely subdivided (the left side of the horizontal axis), our index of interarea tax base variation (e.g., the standard deviation, or, perhaps if the number of observations is small, the range or interquartile variation) is at a maximum. As we successively enlarge the grid mesh, the curve will fall until we have only one area remaining and, of course, no variation, the point at which the curve touches the horizontal axis.

The terminal points (the intercepts) of the curve are trite; it is the slope of the curve through the intervening portion that deserves attention. If an empirically based curve behaves as shown by the higher of the two curves (I) in panel B, the interarea equalization of fiscal capacity proceeds very slowly with increasing area size, superficially (mathematically) because income and wealth levels vary only modestly between adjacent "neighborhoods" and even between adjacent political subdivisions. Only when land area has been aggregated into a monolithic totality does the last remaining *large* element of interarea income inequality disappear. The lower of the two curves (II) depicts a sharply contrasting situation in which the rich and the poor "neighborhoods," standing side by side, are quickly merged by an enlarging mesh size and only a very nominal amount of interarea inequality persists when the subdividing has been reduced to a quartering of the total urban area.[6]

The implications of these two curves to the problems of scale in the local public economies which they represent are arresting. The urban area represented by curve I faces a spatial pattern of taxable income and wealth so distributed that no amount of political amalgamation short of metropolitan area government would serve to equalize the per capita tax base between subareas. Minimal levels of local public services can probably be financed only by metropolitan-area-wide government or by various fiscal subventions from above (e.g., grants-in-aid from the state or federal government). The urban area represented by curve II describes a quite different spatial pattern of

[6] A further technical point may have considerable practical importance. The amount of interarea variation in fiscal capacity exhibited at any given degree of political subdivision (mesh size) is not single-valued, as the curves of panel B portray, but depends rather on the precise geographical position of the grid. If one were to superimpose a grid of *fixed* mesh size a number of times, at random, on an urban area, at least slightly different values of interarea income inequality would result, as sometimes a grid line would fall close to the boundary between an upper- and lower-income district and sometimes a grid line would cut across homogeneous districts and average out differences. For each given mesh size, a frequency distribution of the interarea variations could be generated, with the lowest value representing the greatest interarea equalization of tax base that could be achieved at that level of areal subdivision. If all the observed inequality "coefficients" were plotted, for each of the mesh sizes used, the thin curves of panel B would appear as broad bands, darker along the center line (where the points are more dense) and lighter at the edges (where the extreme values occur). In a statistical sense, our curve could be seen as the centerline of the many frequency distributions—a locus of all the means. Alternatively, a more normative interpretation could be made by seeing the bottom edge of the band as the greatest degree of spatial equality of income and/or wealth that can be achieved at each mesh size by jockeying the grid into a position where the maximum income mixing occurred.

income and wealth and holds a different political moral. This latter urban area could be subdivided ("politically fragmented") into as many as four separate local public economies without effecting any substantial disparity in local fiscal capacity or public service capabilities. Rephrased, the case for metropolitan-area-wide government in this latter area would have to be built on grounds other than fiscal capacity —perhaps efficiency and economy in expenditures—although public revenue considerations would support holding the number of political subdivisions to four.

Since the ideal number of political subdivisions, on public revenue criteria, was derived as a spatial abstraction—without reference to existing political boundaries—these idealized local governments would have to be created *de novo*. The analysis could be made more pragmatic by using fewer and more irregular mesh sizes in the grid, corresponding to existing political boundaries in a typical metropolitan area. We could begin by comparing the per capita taxable income and wealth of the existing political subdivisions, usually municipalities and townships, and then move to the next higher level of existing local government, the county, at least for the multicounty metropolitan areas. Perhaps, some intermediate level of spatial aggregation, standing about midway between the existing municipalities and the counties, could be fabricated with reasonable boundaries. A set of such intermediate areas might be delineated with reference to the existing trade and service hierarchy of the metropolitan area. The trading areas of the major regional shopping centers that stand one rank below the central business district may give some guidance here. From even so limited a comparison as could be made from this three-step mesh size graduation—(1) existing municipalities, (2) subcounty sets of consolidated municipalities, and (3) counties—some feeling for the public revenue implications of political fragmentation could surely be gained. The analyst would also gain some sense of the degree to which aggregation of local governments could equalize local political fiscal capacity and public service capability, short of going all the way to metropolitan area super-government.[7]

---

[7] An empirical application of this analytical tool was made, using 1960 *Census of Population* data on median family income for the Detroit metropolitan area. The hierarchy of subdivisions used were: (1) the SMSA as a whole, (2) the three counties that made up the SMSA, (3) 14 subdivisions of approximately 12 square miles, formed out of 1-square-mile townships, plus the even larger undivided central city, (4) 54 subdivisions of approximately 6 square miles, plus the central city and, finally, (5) the 117 existing political subdivisions. Interarea income inequality at each of the five levels was expressed with Lorentz curves and the related coefficients were de-

The base to which fiscal capacity was related above was population —tax base per capita—but the use of other common denominator may also be instructive and in some cases perhaps even more relevant While many, probably most, urban public services are rendered t people and cost is therefore principally a function of the number o people in the political subdivision, some local public services ma well be more a function of area.[8] While driver training and licensing may be largely a function of total population, traffic control may be more closely related to population density, and police patrolling may be more a function of sheer area than any other single factor. Ac cordingly, a near equalization of tax base per capita between politica subdivisions may fall short of resolving the local public finance prob lem if greatly differing population densities cause wide disparities in expenditure requirements per capita. (Intuitively, one can easily imagine a "U" shaped public service average cost curve in which the cost of local government per family is greater at very high and very low densities than in the intermediate range.)

One might resolve this complication by devising a composite index of fiscal capacity which blends tax base per capita with tax base per acre, using weights which best reflect the relative importance of these

---

rived. Interarea income inequality, so expressed, was estimated at 0, .025, .074, .088 and .090, respectively, at the five levels described above. The conclusion was that most of the income inequality under current political fragmentation (.090) is elimi nated by the time areal aggregation has progressed up to the county level (.025); the Detroit area inequality curve resembles curve II in Figure 8, panel B. In the Detroit metropolitan area, county-level government would match tax base and revenue need so as to leave only moderate inequalities. The estimates are from Mindaugas F. Petru lis, *Local Public Revenue Considerations in a Politically Fragmented Economy,* Master of Arts essay submitted to Wayne State University, 1964, prepared under the direction of the author.

[8] Seymour Sacks has expressed both police and fire protection expenditures of the various political subdivisions of the Cleveland metropolitan area in "expenditure density" maps. Those two local public services are especially intimately related to real property and sheer space. His maps exhibit a striking concentric pattern with expenditures per acre falling steadily from the core area outward. See Seymour Sacks "Spatial and Locational Aspects of Local Government Expenditures," *Public Expenditure Decisions in the Urban Community,* Howard G. Schaller (editor) (Washington: Resources for the Future, Inc., 1963), pp. 188 ff. While a number of public policy questions might be well served by a formulation of the police and fire expenditure equations in acreage terms (e.g., the economics of residential lot size, open space and urban sprawl), the more generalized value of a spatial analysis of public services might be through the refinement of space as an independent variable for those per capita local public expenditure equations in which space is relevant. Ultimately all local public expenditures must be adjusted at the margin by the consumer-voter so that the value per dollar of another unit of each of the many private and public goods and services is roughly equal, and this requires that local public expenditures be expressed in per capita terms.

two variables in determining the level of local public expenditures. If, for example, a careful multiple regression analysis of aggregate local public expenditures turns up population coefficients that are twice as large as those for area, we might then manipulate our variable-mesh grid to equalize an index compounded out of two parts tax base per capita and one part tax base per acre. And since the tax base is itself a composite of property valuation, income and sales, and whatever else is locally taxed, with weights proportionate to the average tax rate on these bases, it is clear that this simple construct can be endlessly complicated to accord more closely to reality.

In place of juggling city sizes so as to reduce the *relative* variation in fiscal capacity between political (taxing) jurisdictions to some given low level, an alternative criterion would be to adopt some *minimum absolute* level of fiscal capacity for each jurisdiction. Thus, if the political subdivisions were enlarged until each area had sufficient income, wealth, and sales to generate, say, at least $200 per capita or $5,000 per acre in revenue out of some given tax structure, then that degree of agglomeration could be deemed sufficient to ensure minimum public service levels without undue financial strain on any group, even though substantial income and wealth inequalities still persisted between political subdivisions. To sum up, the number and size of political subdivisions should be treated as variables in the study of the local public economy and the precise form of this approach is a matter for much experimentation and even more local adaptation according to needs and objectives.

Scale, Taxpayer Flight, and Latitude in Tax Rates

An exercise devoted to identifying the "proper" size of local government as a revenue raising instrumentality would miss the mark if careful attention were not given to the impermanence of locational patterns. A *spatial long run* does exist, conceptually analogous and complementary to the *functional long run* of classical economics, during which period capital can be recovered in liquid form (buildings converted into cash) and factories, machinery, and houses can be relocated. To set this more ominously in the present context, those businesses and wealthier residents who contribute a net surplus to local government by paying more in taxes than they require in public services can flee to a tax haven—or can be coaxed to one by a political subdivision so desperate for tax base that it would be satisfied with a smaller net surplus (possibly even through ignorance offer tax concessions or special services which produce a negative balance for the public fisc). Thus, if we aspire to balance the boundaries of the many political subdivisions in a metropolitan area so that tax base and public service needs are distributed as rationally as possible, our idealized spatial pattern must reckon with taxpayers' reactions to changes in the local public economy. Consideration should also be given to the depreciation and obsolescence of structures as capital wears out and filters down to lower uses—the wealthy build new houses and a whole chain of lower-income classes moves up one rung on the housing ladder. This will be considered in the next chapter.

The head of a household or a business faces a local government that is a monopolist of public services rendered over a unique piece of the earth's surface. The degree of monopoly power wielded by that local government depends on the substitutability of other political jurisdictions in the urban area as sites for a given household or business. And the substitutability of other sites depends in turn on the spatial extent of the political jurisdiction in question. The ease with which a household or business may pack up its tax contribution (and public service requirement) and transfer it to another political entity depends on both the absolute physical (land) size of the local government "monopolist" and also on its fractional share of the total urban area—the number of political subdivisions with which it competes.

The effect of absolute land size is easy to appreciate. Even those business activities most constrained in their choice of site can often move a block or two to cross a city limit, a neighborhood hardware store, for example. A shopping center is relatively free to choose a site with a mile or two of leeway, even half-a-dozen miles leeway in the case of the very large regional shopping center. And enlarging local government to the county level would not necessarily lock-in a manufacturing plant which sells primarily outside the metropolitan area and engages a work force that commutes from all corners of the urban area and even from without. In fact, the manufacturing or service establishment that sells in a regional or nationwide market is usually free to choose between whole metropolitan areas, even states, when selecting a location, and firms selling in foreign markets can institute overseas operations and escape even the federal taxing authority.

In general, the closer the relevant political boundary, the easier flight can be accomplished or threatened as a bargaining weapon against tax exactions by the local government monopolist. But at each higher stage of government the number and variety of firms that can resist the quasi-monopolist of public services diminishes and the relevant public legislative body need pay less and less attention to consumer (taxpayer) resistance. In a metropolitan area, the nearer one gets to the city limits, the weaker is the taxing power of local government. In this regard alone it is clear that metropolitan area government would be able to concentrate more on questions of tax equity and less on the adverse effect of taxes on industrial location, in contrast to the reverse emphasis which plagues the small local government. Moreover, if we accept as proven the charge of a "starved public economy"[9] to strengthen the local tax power through rendering escape more difficult would be to take a giant step toward redressing the balance between public and private goods.

Thus, enlarging the size of local government serves to equalize tax bases and public service needs between political subdivisions of an urban area and also tends to strengthen their collective tax gathering power by reducing tax avoidance. This latter conclusion is reached despite the frequent though misleading charge that resort to a higher level (spatially larger) government to solve a revenue problem is a kind of dishonest legerdemain perpetrated by centralists. Nothing, it is argued, is added to public revenue raising power because the highest government merely squeezes from residents of lower level governments revenue which could have been tapped by the latter, and then returns the same money *less a brokerage charge,* contributing in the process to the decline of home rule and fiscal responsibility. But the case has been made here that higher levels of government do have superior revenue raising powers, insofar as larger size progressively dampens interarea competition for industry and discourages flight to tax havens.

There is some evidence, moreover, of a growing tendency toward increased economic self-sufficiency of the full metropolitan area economy, compounded perhaps out of a steady shift toward market orientation as the dominant locational factor and a tendency for metropolitan areas to increase in population faster than the average optimum scale in plant size, so that at least the larger areas can absorb nearly

[9] For a balanced presentation and sophisticated critique of the purported imbalance between the private and public sectors, see *Private Wants and Public Needs,* Edmund S. Phelps (editor) (New York: W. W. Norton and Company, Inc. 1962).

the full output of an efficient plant. If this does come to pass, the case for a metropolitan-area-wide taxing authority would become more persuasive because, with intermetropolitan area competition and flight dwindling, a METRO taxing authority could concentrate almost fully on equity and efficiency in the design of tax structures, largely ignoring the disturbing influence of threatened flight.

However, we know very little about the way in which the *absolute* size of a political subdivision and/or its size *relative* to the total metropolitan area affects the latitude with which it can vary tax rates. The challenge of quantifying the percentage change in tax base induced by a given percentage change in tax rates—the elasticity of investment in plant and residence in response to changes in the tax rate price—has yet to stimulate some econometrician to action. In common with all elasticity measurements, there is a time dimension here: the longer the period of time, the greater the expected change in tax base in response to a tax rate change, i.e., the greater the opportunity for flight. Any careful expression of the relationship between tax rates and tax base would have to be expressed in a context of time as well as of space.

Scale, Skill, and Choice in Revenue Administration

There is a third way in which the revenue raising power of government varies with size. Size brings with it a public purse large enough to pay for the professional skill necessary to administer more complicated taxes. A large political fragment (a suburb) may be able to administer a complicated value-added tax on business or an even more subtle capital gains tax on increments in land values which a smaller city that encompasses the full urban area would hesitate to try. A capital gains tax on land is an especially good illustration because a political fragment of a large metropolitan area need not worry that this tax will reduce its own tax base through flight of *rentiers* to a neighboring municipality which lacks the tax—nothing is so locked in as land and capital gains therefrom—therefore absolute size (the sum budgeted for revenue department staff) is controlling. This contrasts with the single local government of the small metropolitan area which turns because of unskilled staff to the simpler real property tax, pushing rates higher and higher with relatively little fear of flight; flight is open only to another urban area or to a rural fringe area deficient in pipes, wires, streets, and other near indispensable paraphernalia of modern industry and living. Thus, while exclusive political jurisdiction (monopoly power) permits greater latitude in tax rates, sheer governmental size opens up new revenue possibilities.

Small local governments must make do with so few employees that they are forced to hire general practitioners in public administration. Not only does a small staff lack tax specialists but it also probably lacks the superior organizer who can devise ways to bridge this gap— a bright, versatile executive is skilled at picking the brains of experts at the token cost of a free lunch. All in all, the choice of tax instruments available to the small local government is restricted to the more easily administered ones. The principal defense of the real property tax, which accounts for about 85 per cent of local tax revenue, is its adaptability to financial home rule. But a tax, such as the real property tax, which can be administered by small, moderately skilled tax staffs is characteristically overworked; what may be an equitable (well, at least tolerable) tax at low rates may become cruelly regressive or otherwise inequitable if pushed to very high rates. Retired people with low current income, but still in possession of real property conforming with their income prior to retirement, are subject to a harsh claim on their meager earnings by a local government which renders them fewer services than it did prior to their retirement. By inciting practically the whole elderly community to tax rebellion, too heavy reliance on the real property tax works against good government and especially against good schools.

We can weave together the arguments of the last few pages at this point with a few strategic quotes from the work of Harvey Brazer:[10]

> [While] Philadelphia and Pittsburgh or Los Angeles and San Francisco can well afford the administrative machinery requisite for the efficient administration of virtually any tax the states might or do impose . . . the major restraint . . . is that the geographic boundaries of the taxing jurisdiction are not co-terminous with those of the economy of which it is but an integral part. Thus with goods, people, and capital free to flow back and forth across city borders . . . the competitive position of the tax imposing city may be endangered and the effectiveness and equity with which taxes can be applied may suffer . . . [But] wide taxing powers that permit a broadly diversified tax system to provide the needed revenues with

[10] Harvey E. Brazer, "The Role of Major Metropolitan Centers in State and Local Finance," *The American Economic Review*, May 1958, pp. 309–10.

comparatively low tax rates are likely to produce fewer deleterious effects than would one or two major taxes imposed at higher rates.

Thus, large city size not only makes flight of taxpayers more difficult, because the havens are farther away, but also reduces the incentive to flee by making it possible to raise adequate revenue without pushing any given tax too hard. Tax equity and tax yield interact and improve with city size.

Even the largest cities of the country have been timid about experimenting with new taxes,[11] allowing for the fact that state legislatures have been heavy-handed in constraining cities in such adventures. The decided advantage in tapping new revenue sources that comes with bigness should be quantified. A much surer feeling is needed for the range of tax instruments open to political subdivisions of various size (and exclusiveness), with particular reference to the administrative skills required and the costs of collection at various scales of operation. Local public finance has been slow in handling its subject matter in a context in which the scale of local government is a key variable. Urban economics can move in to fill this void. Ideally, information on the relationship between both the absolute population size and the relative spatial coverage of a local political entity and the range of revenue sources open to it should be presented to the electorate at the time of public debate on political fragmentation and proposed consolidation.

The Special Case of User Charges

The effect of local government size on the professionalization of public administration and thereby on local revenue raising capability may be nowhere more significant than in the efficacy of user charges

---

[11] Students of local public finance are, in general, quite bullish about the future of nonproperty taxes as a source of local revenue. A recent study in local public finance trends estimates that the proportion of local tax revenue accounted for by nonproperty taxes will rise rapidly from the current 13 per cent to 25 per cent by 1970. That this is a sanguine view of nonproperty taxes is attested to by the fact that the nonproperty tax proportion rose very slowly during the preceding decade from 11.8 per cent in 1950 to 12.5 per cent in 1959, as derived from data compiled by the U.S. Bureau of Census, Summary of Government Finances, and reported by them. See Eugene A. Myers and Randall S. Stout, "Recent Trends in Permissive Local Taxation," *Michigan Business Review*, June 1961, p. 38 and Table I, p. 35. Of especial interest is the authors' judgment that it is the larger cities which will make most use of new tax sources.

as a source of public revenue. To exact additional financial support for local government by setting prices on selected public services almost surely would demand a degree of managerial finesse considerably greater than that called for in the levying and collecting of the current assortment of local taxes, fees, and special assessments. User charges carry the presumption that the beneficiaries of the public services are being called on to support these services by making direct, voluntary payments in proportion to benefits received, instead of compulsory exactions levied according to ability to pay or on some rough presumption of benefits received as very imperfectly measured by the ownership of real property. If benefits are measured by the cost of the services performed, the administration of user charges will require a much more sophisticated public cost accounting than has been practiced to date. To illustrate, the joint cost of interest and depreciation on school buildings must be allocated between school taxes and user charges levied on enrollees in adult education courses using the buildings at night—an operation which is further complicated by the fact that the latter use is an off-peak use of what would otherwise have been idle capacity. Similarly, user charges for street space and bus seats should be set to reflect on- and off-peak use. Ideally, bus fares would be varied through the day and over the week end to discourage and encourage demand strategically, reducing idle capacity and economizing on plant and equipment.

If the urban public managers wish to integrate a set of public services into the private market system, they would be called on to perform much more discriminating cost accounting than they perform at present, and in many cases more sophisticated accounting than they are now trained to perform. Even if we prefer to partly subsidize a public service, the demands imposed on the public administrator are not much lessened; subsidized user charges would still be related to costs and much of the same information must still be assembled. Moreover, if one prefers to use prices on public services as a means of social control—charges in excess of cost on the operation of private cars, coupled with bus fares below cost, to "educate" the public on the advantages of mass transit when almost everyone else is using it too—the degree of economic sophistication required would be greater still.[12]

---

[12] Price cuts designed to increase demand—shift the whole demand schedule by changing tastes rather than just increase the quantity demanded at a lower price—are referred to as "promotional pricing." The price cuts may even go below cost in the expectation that the increase in demand and output will so lower unit costs that profit margins will be reestablished, applying then to much greater outputs for

The economic planner, in this latter case, would be forced to estimate price elasticities and cross elasticities of demand for various modes of urban transportation (e.g., how drivers would react to higher automobile tolls and to lower bus prices, respectively) and the long-run effects on the land use pattern across the whole urban area. One need only recall the tremendous amount of economic, engineering, and accounting research that has been devoted to the gasoline tax and motor vehicle license fees—public revenue measures which come close to being user charges for streets and highways—to appreciate the sophistication demanded by user charges.

Ability to administer user charges could easily become a very important attribute of local government in the coming decade. These public levies have the virtue of reaching previously untapped income; for example, fees for the use of swimming pools, tennis courts, camping sites, and other outdoor recreational facilities would fall partly on the increasingly affluent teenagers who make perhaps the greatest use of these facilities but ordinarily escape local taxation. Also a widespread net of user charges catches the growing group of transients who live in trailer camps, largely avoiding the real property tax, and tourists who pay only the local sales taxes, if any.

By tapping new sources, user charges permit existing local taxes to be saved for the support of public services that cannot be handled in a fashion analogous to the workings of the market place. Government cannot rationally or efficaciously put prices on justice or police protection and sell these public services to the citizens at large. Not only are those collectively consumed public services from which noncontributors cannot be excluded beyond the pale of public pricing, but many local public services are quite frankly designed to redistribute income—exact payments from one group for the benefit of another group. One cannot finance public welfare by levying taxes on the recipients. Accordingly, to the extent that those activities of local

---

larger total profits. A considerable literature exists on this variety of promotional pricing; see, for example, any good text on public utility economics, such as Emery Troxel, *Economics of Public Utilities* (New York: Rinehart and Co., Inc., 1947). But less has been written on prices designed to discourage demand for the obvious reason that such tactics play a relatively small role in the private sector. Still, the use of selective excise taxes on goods temporarily in short supply (e.g., during wartime) as a device for reducing demand might be cited as an example. If, moreover, the strategy is to magnify a bit the scarcity of some critical public facility in order to force marginal users of it to develop substitutes which could, in time, become preferred to the original scarce facility, then we might have a truer analogy to promotional pricing.

government which border on the "proprietary" can be financed by user charges, precious mills of the local property or income tax rate can be saved for some public function that is performed for society as a whole.

Pricing Central City Services to Suburbs

One special set of user charges deserves much more attention than it has so far received. Central cities of large, politically fragmented metropolitan areas frequently sell public services to other smaller units of local government, with the latter governments redistributing the services to their residents. Central city water supplies extending outward to the suburbs and sewage disposal and storm drainage trunk lines coming back inward from suburban feeder lines are among the more common of such intergovernmental service arrangements. To the existence of this physical-economic interrelationship, we add the fact of strained relations, even bitter conflict, between the central city and its suburbs over who is beggaring whom on tax base and public service needs. The suburbs claim that they must bear the cost of educating the lion's share of the area's children and schools are the most costly commitment that local government must undertake, while the central city argues that they have most of the urban poor, left behind in the flight to the suburbs, and the noise, dirt, and congestion brought in by the commuter. On the revenue side, the suburbanite points to the rich tax base of the central city's business district and the central city dweller points to the suburban manufacturing plants and the homes of the wealthy.

This confused imbalance of externally inflicted costs and externally expropriated benefits poses a very real threat to rational resource allocation. Political pressures seem bound to produce a distorted set of relative prices on intergovernmental exchanges. Central cities, finding it administratively difficult to recapture the cost of accommodating the automobiles of commuting suburbanites, are becoming more and more irked by the steadfast refusal of these "free-loaders" to tolerate some inconvenience by shifting to mass transit. Central cities may well be on the verge of attempting to recoup this loss by overcharging suburbanites for water supplies and sewage disposal—services for which collection is administratively feasible and for which the suburban demand is highly price-inelastic. In substance, water rates and sewage disposal fees may be raised to cover the cost of free traffic control, parks, and museums.

This scattershot tactic of placing monopolistic surcharges on any or all intergovernmental services on which they will stick may help the central city solve its fiscal problem and might even achieve some kind of rough equity in the aggregate—in the distribution of aggregate public service costs and benefits between the central city and suburbs. But a set of relative prices distorted to reflect the degree of monopoly power wielded by the central city supplier would reduce the total real income of the whole urban area by causing a misallocation of resources. If water and sewage disposal services are overpriced, too little of that service would be consumed by suburbanites, especially relative to their overconsumption of free street space. The traffic situation can, in fact, be characterized as a disorderly market: an excessive demand for space within which to move and park cars generated by too low prices—a too long queue behind the "free" counter.

Even if the demands for water and sewage disposal services are highly price-inelastic—that is, higher prices do not much reduce consumption —inefficiency and inequity still trouble us. The water-sewage surcharges become imposts that *are* paid (not avoided by turning to other goods and services, thereby distorting one's expenditure pattern) and the volume of water-sewage purchases then become the criteria for determining the amount one should pay to support ("free") urban transportation services. The suburbanite who does not commute to downtown or rides the bus can be excused his reservations about the equity of this tactic. Moreover, while the amount of water and sewage disposal services that a household consumes may well be highly inelastic *for all interconnected* households, the underconsumption problem may be a very real concern to the community at the time and stage of first connection. Typically, the newer residential subdivisions on the periphery of the urban area tend to cling to private wells and septic tanks much too long, lowering the amenities of living in these places during the later stages of transition when water supplies are erratic and fouled, and streams and ditches become polluted. Further, external diseconomies in both public health and outdoor recreation may be imposed back on the central city through stream pollution, and the delay in construction of suburban storm drains may flood basements in the central city.

Just as a too high price for sewage disposal services may occasion delay in the construction of inevitable sewer plant on the urban-rural fringe, so also a too low price for urban street space for moving and parking privately operated vehicles may delay an inevitable reconversion of central business district land and buildings to new and more economic uses. Downtown traffic congestion may be reduced either by converting commuters to mass transit or by discouraging those with less important business to transact from entering this already over-crowded area. If, instead of subsidizing automobile transportation into the core area with surcharges on water and sewage service, we introduced user charges on automobile movement to and from downtown, automobile drivers in some unknown proportions would become bus riders or refrain from entering downtown. The merchants whose trade would suffer first and most would naturally resist this cure as worse than the disease. But the central city would gain a strengthened public economy if the savings in public services because of reduced traffic congestion and other associated factors plus the user charges collected from the motorists amounted to more than the property and sales tax revenue lost by the loss of some part of the downtown retail trade.

The well-entrenched dogma that downtown congestion must be relieved without diminishing the number of visits is unsound. The vitality and value of the core of a metropolis to the whole city region that it serves is much less a matter of the quantity of visits it accommodates and much more a matter of the quality of those visits. Downtown's primary function is to be unique and esoteric. As the apex of the pyramid of urban services, the central business district of a growing urban area must delegate inferior functions. If the core of the metropolis performs its function well, the fiscal problems of the central city public economy should yield to imaginative and professional management, without sacrificing over-all urban efficiency. But economic warfare with the suburbs can only balance the central city's budget at the expense of efficiency.

Looking ahead, the central city seems destined to remain the heart of the transportation and communication and utility system of an extended city region and our urban life seems virtually certain to become increasingly dependent on the flow of people, goods, messages, water, and power. The quantity and quality of utility services are an even more critical locational factor to the automated manufacturing plant than they were to its predecessor, so the central city may well acquire even greater bargaining power, with the suburbs—its service satellites—all desperately vying with each other for industrial tax base. While the central city may lack the vacant land to attract the new plants and gain taxable property, it would seem to be improving its position to extract some of the politicoeconomic rent from industrial land use through its strategic role as the node of the industrial environment—the network for distributing all manner of goods and services. This all assumes that manufacturing plants do yield more in tax revenue than they require, directly or indirectly, in public services. And the modern, neat, automated plant with its very high capital-to-labor ratio fits this description more often than not.

The local public finance problem of the future could just as easily turn out to be that of restraining the central city monopolist from exploiting its satellites (through user charges), as the reverse. A decade or two hence may well see the central city with much new housing and many suburbs with much old housing; the urban poverty problem, with its rapacious demands on the public purse, will not be confined to the central city. (For some reason, few anticipate the day, not too far off, when much of the present suburban housing will be decrepit and of necessity will house very low-income families.) If the central city of a decade or two hence not only has much new housing and many high-income families but is also the message and movement center of a highly automated, urbanized society, the suburbs may be the underdogs in matters of public finance. Whatever the future may bring, a good rate of return can be realized now from an investment in research into intrametropolitan area, intergovernmental economic relations, ranging from questions of fact and equity, such as the balance of external costs and benefits between political subdivisions to questions of policy and efficiency, such as the economics of pricing intergovernmental services.

RECONCILIATION OF EXPENDITURES
AND REVENUES

Except in the most unlikely event of a perfect matching of revenue and expenditures, local government by government, emphasis on scale in raising and spending money poses a financial dilemma: the level of local government that is of optimum size to perform some given set of public services may not be of optimum size to finance them, at least from the preferred revenue sources. If the most efficient expenditure district tends to be small relative to the most efficient revenue district, then the smaller political subdivisions would need heavy financial subventions from above to balance their budgets. If, probably less likely, the preferred expenditure unit is larger than the preferred revenue unit, then financial contributions must flow upward. If one seeks to attain efficiency in both local public services and revenue administration, then a complementary analysis of alternative ways of arranging the balancing intergovernmental fiscal transfers is a serious responsibility.

Fiscal Subventions: Central Control or Local Choice?

The most common method of effecting intergovernmental transfers is through "grants-in-aid," through which higher levels of government with superior taxing power finance public services rendered at lower levels. The advantages of centralized revenue administration are coupled with the advantages of decentralized performance of public service. But often more is at stake than internal economies of scale in tax administration and internal diseconomies of scale in public service performance. Grants-in-aid often influence the way in which the lower levels of government spend their money, in fact they are usually designed to do just that. Grants bias local choice by changing the relative price structure as seen by the municipal manager. A 50 per cent matching grant from the state for a local public health program alongside a 75 per cent state contribution for acquiring sites for out-door recreation facilities creates a situation in which $1 of local money spent on health buys only half as much as $1 spent on recreation but twice as much as $1 spent on unaided activities. A dollar just isn't a dollar. Local choice may be further shaped by imposing performance standards, such as by setting the qualifications of local public employees who render the supported service or by imposing acceptable salary schedules.

Because the grant-in-aid can be used to ensure minimum levels and standards of performance, it can be especially useful in the case of public services which have significant external benefits (e.g., education), or external costs (e.g., dumping untreated sewage in a common river). In general, one might argue that public services which show no significant *internal* economies of scale, or show diseconomies, should and can be performed at a lower level of government, even though the taxes most suited to finance them are best administered at a higher level of government. But, if these public services also confer on neighboring communities substantial *external* benefits or costs than can be accounted for and controlled only by imposing performance standards from above (e.g., sewage treatment), then these services would seem to be tailor-made for grants-in-aid financing *with strings attached*.

Social case work with juvenile delinquents might be used as an illustration of a public service which may have internal diseconomies of scale (i.e., should be kept close to home) but which has very considerable external implications to nearby communities. Even if efficiency did not require that the preferred source of revenue to support this activity be imposed and administered at a higher level of government, the broad area interest in having this function performed at some minimal level and performed well in each of the political subdivisions almost dictates that at least some of the financing come from above. Only then could local decisions on this matter be constrained to serve some larger social interest, as decided at some higher level of democratic decision making.

Consider, next, the case of a public service which also is subject to internal diseconomies of scale and has a substantial element of product differentiation, but which does not give rise to any important external benefits or costs. This public service should also be performed at the local level but, with no externalities involved, the quantity and quality of the service should be left entirely to local discretion. If the preferred source of revenues is, again, a tax best administered at a higher level of government, then some locally levied but centrally collected tax could be used. The most common such device is the "shared tax" in which localities have the option of loading supplemental tax rates on to a tax structure administered at the state level, for example, supplemental local millage on a state sales tax or a local surtax added "piggyback" on to a state income tax schedule. About nine-tenths of California cities have locally imposed but state-administered sales taxes.

The suggestion was made above, in the somewhat different but related case of coupling economies of scale to product differentiation, that the basic school plant might be supplied by the state from state-levied-and-collected taxes, with whatever educational "frills" the locality chooses financed with supplemental tax rates, levied at the local level but collected and rebated by the state. Just as grants are suited more to intergovernmental transfers when local choice should be constrained, so shared taxes are more appropriate when local choice should be unencumbered.

To sum up, a number of concepts must be brought together to rationalize the local public economy: internal economies of scale, product differentiation, external costs and benefits, and the character of intergovernmental fiscal transfers. Expenditure analyses in terms of internal economies or diseconomies of scale and product differentiation help us place each public service at the proper level of local government; integrating this analysis with the scale effect in revenue administration determines whether an intergovernmental transfer is indicated. If so, a determination must then be made as to whether grants-in-aid with strings attached or shared taxes without strings are more appropriate to the situation, and this in turn depends on whether any significant broader social interest is involved—whether there are any substantial external benefits or costs associated with the local public services in question. From these and other pieces, a full blown general theory of the efficiency and equity conditions in the local public economy awaits formulation. Enough has been written on these matters and enough experience in intergovernmental fiscal relations has been accumulated to make a major step in the desired direction quite possible, albeit demanding of specialized skill and knowledge.

Intergovernmental Equity: A Pragmatic Approach

A second kind of intergovernmental transfer must be considered: *involuntary* transfers arising out of external costs and benefits. These transfers, unlike the planned and fabricated set described immediately above, are destructive of efficiency and equity. Indeed, the irrationality of the metropolitan area public economy that attracts the most attention is the intergovernmental transfer of real income which occurs when one political entity passes off on another the costs of some activity from which it benefits. The central city accuses the suburbs of beggaring it by using its streets, traffic control facilities, museums, and so forth free of charge while holding its residential property (tax base) out of political reach. The suburbs rejoin with the complaint that they must educate the children of the area without having tax recourse to the rich commercial and industrial property of the central city. A few attempts have been made to find the net balance of these involuntary transfers of costs and benefits but, while the preliminary results seem to find for the central city as the net loser, the definitive work has still to be done.[13]

---

[13] Margolis, in a study of 55 city governments in the San Francisco-Oakland metropolitan area, attempted to get at the balance of external costs and benefits flowing between business and dormitory cities through statistical inference. He concluded:

The suggestion here is not that we should attempt some full-scale assault on the question of the net balance of these external costs and benefits so capriciously spilled in and out across central city and suburb boundaries, certainly not activity by activity. The bulk of this chapter has, in fact, argued for the more direct and pragmatic approach of identifying the most appropriate governmental level at which to administer each source and use of funds and then to arrange for *planned* intergovernmental transfers to balance budgets and rationalize benefits and costs. But because this suggested approach is so highly normative (and perhaps, to some, much too academic) an alternative and more pragmatic approach to rationalizing the total local economy of a politically fragmented metropolitan area is also offered. Instead of searching for efficiency (and that will-of-the-wisp, optimality) so intently, one might take a very narrow view of what is politically feasible and work toward some rough equity within this narrower framework.

We might begin by tentatively identifying a few local public services which probably account for a major part of the involuntary intergovernmental transfers that should be rationalized. By experimenting with different combinations of municipal, county, multicounty, and state responsibility for these functions, we would attempt to determine whether most of the externalities could be eliminated, or offset so as to leave only very minor net transfers between political subdivisions. Specifically, rather than run the risk that attempting to optimize public services and revenue administration will degenerate into a kind of

---

The findings of this study cast doubt on the rationality of a program of encouraging industrial and commercial land use for suburbs. They suggest the hypothesis that accompanying the business use of land there will be a change in the nature of residential uses and an expansion of public services so that the tax costs per dollar of property value will increase. The findings are consistent with a suburban-exploitation-of-central-cities hypothesis. . . .

Julius Margolis, "Municipal Fiscal Structure in a Metropolitan Region," *The Journal of Political Economy*, June 1957, p. 236.

Brazer differs sharply with Margolis on the importance of commercial and industrial property as a fiscal aid, but agrees with him that the evidence supports a suburban-exploitation-of-the-metropolis hypothesis. Brazer, however, draws on a study by Amos H. Hawley and one of his own showing that "the proportion of the metropolitan area's population that lies outside of the central city is closely associated with the per capita expenditures of the central city. Both sets of findings reflect the fact that the number of people for whom the city must provide services is the sum of its resident population and the nonresident or contact population which spends time in the city in the course of the working day, shopping, pursuing recreation, and so forth." Harvey E. Brazer, "Some Fiscal Implications of Metropolitanism," *op. cit.*, pp. 76–77.

precious overanalysis leading to highly unrealistic political implications, we might try to resolve the whole issue with one bold stroke. First, we might calculate the fiscal implications of transferring the local welfare function, wholly or in major part, from the municipal level to the county or a multicounty metropolitan area authority or to the state. This would reflect a strong impression that the principal source of the adverse fiscal balance against the central city is the extraordinarily heavy public assistance and public health demands made on it. Since the care of the poor is clearly an obligation of the whole local labor market—the whole metropolitan area—would there be any especially notable central city fiscal problem left if just this one major area-wide financial obligation were borne area-wide?

After carefully pricing out the implications of shifting welfare to the metropolitan area or state level, a second step could be taken in the same direction if a sizable residual net balance were still felt to exist. The costs of streets and traffic control throughout the whole urban area might then be considered a common cost of all and financed accordingly. In this latter case, some experimentation, both conceptual and empirical, with user charges might be introduced as the means by which some of the urban transportation burden is shifted from the taxpayers of the central city on to motorists throughout the urban area.

And then again, the rapid growth of "reverse commuting"—central city males moving back and forth to suburban factories and central city females to suburban homes as domestics (see Chapter 10, page 365, and footnote 5)—could reduce the net balance of commuters to near zero in the not too distant future, by balancing large gross flows of commuters between central city and suburbs. The bringing together of home and work to reduce gross flows is a more distant prospect at best. But reverse commuting *could* produce a near zero net balance in movement which yielded a near zero net balance in intergovernmental costs and benefits, although probably not within a decade.

Quite possibly, some *ad hoc* combination of fiscal devices, such as a metropolitan area welfare authority financed by an area-wide income tax, coupled with an area-wide transportation authority financed by user charges and the state administered gas tax, would so reduce the probable magnitude of the remaining net intergovernmental fiscal transfers that the question would lose most of its social significance. And not only might the *net* balance of the many and sundry intergovernmental external costs and benefits become negligible, satisfying the equity objective, but the major individual transfers might also become greatly reduced, satisfying the efficiency condition.

The great complexity of the metropolitan area market in public services, the powerful vested interests in being, and the sheer inertia that must be overcome if government is to be restructured in these political mazes, all strongly support the wisdom of hedging the risky normative analyses with some such pragmatic inquiry. A substantial effort should perhaps be devoted to inventing some relatively simple approximate solution to the efficiency and equity issues raised. Even if it be only a holding operation while a more elegant and intellectually satisfying solution is being worked out, the possibility of going most of the way toward achieving equity and much of the way toward efficiency in urban public services in our politically fragmented metropolitan areas with but a few well-delivered blows is much too intriguing to ignore. And the gamble of achieving the impossible with a modest effort (and luck) makes some such pragmatic, aggregate, inferential resolution almost irresistible.

CHAPTER 8

Housing and Land Use Patterns: Renewal, Race, and Sprawl

The urban area is more than a local labor market and a public service area; it is also a local housing market. The labor and housing market viewpoints are closely interrelated: workers must live near their jobs and they prefer to keep employed where they live. True, there is a growing group of superprofessionals who function increasingly in a national labor market made possible by the jet aircraft.[1] But we cover the living patterns of the vast majority of the population by assuming that local labor markets and local housing markets are roughly coincident, as a first approximation.

Three housing questions are treated in this chapter, one from each of the most distinctive residential areas of the city: the core, the "great gray area," and the urban-rural fringe.

Because cities grow centrifugally, more or less, the core of the urban area is ordinarily the oldest, ugliest, and unhealthiest residential area—preponderantly the slum area. In those parts of the core area so deteriorated and/or so homely that custom renovations are simply out of the question[2]—where mass demolition and redevelopment is the

---

[1] For a provocative argument that a truly national labor market is coming into being see the work of Melvin M. Webber, for example, "Order in Diversity: Community Without Propinquity," *Cities and Space*, Lowdon Wingo, Jr. (editor) (Baltimore: The Johns Hopkins Press for Resources for the Future, 1963). Webber's thesis is, essentially, that advancing technology has narrowed professional specializations, making it necessary to interact with fellow professionals on a national scale. Increasing airplane speeds and growing affluence has, moreover, made such a national intellectual community both technically and economically feasible.

[2] A number of critics of our current practice of demolishing whole blocks or more without regard to individual structures have written most eloquently on the charm and livability of piecemeal renovations versus the depressing monotony of large barracks-like housing projects. But the issues seem to revolve more about aesthetics and sociology than economics. Moreover, the small number of "Greenwich Villages" and "Georgetowns" deserving renovation and the small number of people who can afford this creative experience (hobby?) would seem to limit the application of custom renovations. How much of the core of Baltimore, Chicago, and Detroit is worth saving at costs per square foot fully as high as new buildings? For an eloquent and spirited brief for piecemeal renovation rather than wholesale renewal, see Jane Jacobs, *The Death and Life of Great Cities* (New York: Random House, Inc., 1961).

only realistic course of action—the critical *economic* problem becomes efficiency and economy in urban renewal, with due regard for the people who are forced to move. Because the cost of urban renewal is so great relative to our meager current budgets for that purpose, the inexorable process of aging is creating new slums faster than we are removing the old ones. A strategy to achieve the greatest possible leverage in slum clearance for each dollar spent—the relatively narrow problem of economy in urban renewal—is, therefore, neither a trivial nor demeaning question.

Then we will turn to what is probably the single most bedeviling problem in that great gray expanse of housing that stretches from the core area slums to the pleasant lands of suburbia—racial segregation in housing. Humanitarian considerations aside, urban residential *apartheid* has pervasive and detrimental socioeconomic impacts, on both private and social values. If at the first signs of neighborhood invasion by nonwhites, the white residents flee *en masse,* substantial and regrettable private capital losses in real property values may be sustained by people who can ill afford to lose. From a welfare point of view, that they would not have suffered these losses if they had not sold in panic is small consolation. But even more basic and lasting in effect are the social costs which are left in the wake of massive, abrupt population shifts within neighborhoods. Mass flight, for example, demolishes neighborhood conservation programs, the indispensable complement to an effective urban renewal effort.

Finally, we shift the housing focus outward to the edge of town where the problem of urban "sprawl" is encountered. This, too, is an efficiency problem in that the principal *economic* crime attributed to sprawl is the increased costs incurred (public plus private) in servicing a larger-than-necessary land area—streets, pipes, wires, and personal contacts are strung out farther than they "should" be. One form of urban sprawl, the postwar phenomenon of ever greater lot sizes, may be viewed as a problem in consumer economics, an irrational purchase of too large a lot through lack of information. Or oversize residential lots may be seen as the product of a distorted set of relative prices, where land prices and/or taxes are set too low to reflect various social costs they impose on the community at large. Finally, the question is raised as to whether a second form of urban sprawl, leapfrogging over vacant tracts, may not be "inefficient" only in a static context and may often (not always) become a blessing in disguise in the unpredictable long run by introducing an element of flexibility in land-use patterns.

Is by-passed vacant land a squatting frog-prince awaiting the touch of change—or just a homely old frog?

URBAN RENEWAL STRATEGY

Occasionally, housing and urban renewal people push themselves back from the details of their work and regard the over-all rate at which blighted areas are being renovated, whether by massive public renewal or piecemeal private renovation, relative to the over-all rate at which new blighted areas are being created by the inexorable process of aging. An overpowering feeling of despair usually follows, for new blight is forming faster than it is being eliminated in most, if not all, cities.[3] To some extent, growth in the absolute amount of urban blight is the natural product of the growth in absolute size of the urban area, and one would have to show that the relative amount of blight is also growing to conclude that we are losing the race against slums. But even the most optimistic urbanists would not argue that we have turned the tide and are now beginning to win the slum battle. Apparently, national growth has succeeded in raising the living standard of all but the lowest tenth.

Renewal programs are, moreover, up against the hard fact of a fierce competition for public funds with other powerful contestants, such as public health, juvenile delinquency, vocational retraining, general education, urban transportation, outdoor recreation, and other high priority programs. With much enlarged urban renewal budgets hard to win, any new over-all strategy or set of tactics that might exact

[3] The relative magnitudes of our stock of slums and the rate of new slum formation, on the one hand, and the current rate of renewal, on the other, are so disparate that even the roughest estimates suffice to give a fair general picture of the losing battle we are fighting. The CED, updating figures from Dewhurst and Associates, *America's Needs and Resources: A New Survey* (1955), estimated the current (1960) costs of replacing 6.9 million substandard dwelling units and rehabilitating another 2.0 million units, plus supporting facilities, at about \$120 to \$125 billion. At another point, they estimated that obligations for urban renewal are being assumed by the federal government at an annual rate of approximately \$300 million per year. At that rate we will work off the current stock of slum dwellings in 400 years (\$120 billion $\div$ 0.3 billion per year). Assuming fifty years as the average life span of an urban house, by that time we would have added to the stock of slum dwellings an amount equal to 8 times the current stock. Straight-line projections for such ridiculously long time periods, have, of course, no real meaning, except for dramatic effect. But they do convey the proportions of the problem. *Guiding Metropolitan Growth* (New York: Committee for Economic Development, August 1960), pp. 36–38.

more renewal leverage for each public dollar spent would be most welcome. The challenge to the urban economists, then, is to reexamine most critically the current approach to urban renewal, with particular reference to economy and efficiency.

Slum Clearance and Public Housing

The principal means by which the housing occupied by the lowest income class is upgraded is not through new public housing construction but rather by "filtering." As the middle-income class moves into new small houses and larger houses discarded by the upper-income class, they pass their discarded houses on to the poor. The lowest income class progresses, of course, only if the filtering down process is proceeding faster than the aging of the relevant houses—if the typical family in a blighted area "upgrades" their living abode by ten years only every ten years, they move to stand still. Any tendency or public policy that speeds the rate of construction of new housing, and thereby increases the rate of turnover at the top, raises housing standards all down the line. Granting that a high rate of new starts in housing is the most powerful medicine of all in the treatment of slums, it is still worth our time to examine briefly the current urban renewal programs of subsidized housing. While our urban renewal program is small relative to private residential construction, it is a direct approach to slum clearance and has its champions who would greatly expand it.

Typically, we purchase the highest density slum properties, simply because they are usually the worst offenders in matters of health, welfare, and aesthetics. But the densest slums are also usually the ones which generate the highest rents and (via capitalization of net earnings) the highest property values per acre. We pay dearly to raze those areas. Not only do our current urban renewal budgets shrink distressingly in real purchasing power but, by having to evict large numbers of people, we force mass migrations into nearby neighborhoods. Thus we overcrowd the contiguous residential ring, precipitate its early deterioration, and commit future funds to the purchase of similarly overpriced slum properties in the next round. We set up one round after another of expensive condemnations by shoving ahead with brute force, compressing evicted populations ahead of us as we go—a kind of human bulldozing.

Enough examples have come to light of families who have been forced to move repeatedly to make way for one land redevelopment after another to suggest that we have created an identifiable population group whom we inhumanely dislocated continually. On careful study we might even find that these involuntary urban gypsies have become the pawns of the same set of slum landlords who move outward with them, and in effect sell them to the housing authorities over and over again through the enhanced property values that their overcrowding creates. We could hardly concoct a worse urban renewal strategy if we had set out to be diabolically clever. Small wonder that our very limited urban renewal funds have hardly made a dent in the urban blight problem, while the programs themselves are creating new enemies faster than new friends. ("Urban renewal is Negro removal.")

Students of housing have long appreciated that if, instead, we were to unload population from these slum areas first and then purchase the properties when they are partly vacant, we would be able to buy slum acreage at much reduced figures. Perhaps we should approach slum clearance from a housing supply vantage point first, and then after we have lowered slum housing densities appreciably we may find the goal of "city beautiful" to be within the limits of our purse. Our current approach may, too much, reflect revulsion against the way slums look—an ugly blot on the landscape that offends the aesthetic senses. A more roundabout but much more efficient, economical, and humane strategy would begin by building new low-income housing on peripheral vacant land, but still close to core-oriented public mass transportation. We could still put the highest priority on the rehousing of the inhabitants of any particular slum area by offering space in the new low-rent buildings first to the current residents of the worst slum areas.

By building on vacant land we could get core area slum dwellers into better housing earlier and with less discomfort than by cutting houses out from underneath them, especially if they could and would move to the urban fringe. And even if some would choose to remain in a central location they would still have the same option of crowding in on the inhabitants of adjoining neighborhoods, with less crowding than if all were forced to do just that. Finally, new low-income housing could be built on the cleared central site when the depopulated slum properties are bought and demolished, even if these new centrally located units would lag a little behind their time of construction had we begun by cutting them out from under their present inhabitants.

The relocation of the slum housing families to new housing units in the suburbs would provide an opportunity to enforce building and housing codes much more strictly throughout the slum areas, especially codes applying to density of occupancy. The resulting combination of spreading out and higher vacancy rates would be almost sure to greatly reduce the net earnings and condemnation prices of slum properties. In the "short run" (which is quite long in the housing market), the supply of housing is highly inelastic (almost fixed in supply regardless of rent levels), so even a relatively small decrease in demand for core area tenements could convert a grave housing shortage, with crushing rents, into a substantial redundancy of housing, bringing rents tumbling down. If we would but contain our revulsion against the ugliness of decrepit buildings and dirty environments and refrain from sweeping the mess away (into the neighboring residential areas) long enough to increase the total supply of low-income housing units to the point of slight redundancy, we could effect great economies in our urban renewal efforts and at considerable gain in human values.[4]

Perhaps some variation on this theme would be even more in harmony with our social goals, but in any event we cannot rationally continue along the present path. Most of all, we need some numbers here to judge the width of the margin between a low-income housing shortage, with overcrowding and exorbitant rents and land clearance costs, and a slight housing redundancy which gives both room to maneuver and stretches the renewal dollar much farther. We may find that nothing would be so good a buy for the public economy as a few "too many" low-income housing units. Maybe we just need to learn how to play "musical houses," with one extra house.

---

[4] A considerable body of literature has accumulated on the strategy of using vacant peripheral land to increase the supply of low-income housing units prior to reducing their supply through demolition. The problem of political fragmentation has been sloughed over here. Renewal is usually in the hands of city housing authorities and they are confined to land within the city limits, little or none of which is vacant. County housing authorities would not be so confined but county government is notoriously inefficient and ineffectual at this time, and suburban political influences would almost certainly add to the delay. (It is hard to imagine suburbanites subsidizing the encroachment of the very neighborhoods that they have just fled.) For a brief discussion of the increase-supply-first strategy see Webb S. Fiser, *Mastery of the Metropolis* (Englewood Cliffs, New Jersey: Prentice-Hall, Inc., Spectrum Books, 1962), pp. 97, 134–35.

Housing Market Indexes as a
Guide to Public Policy

Housing market analysis and housing programming might be greatly facilitated by some set of simple devices which together would constitute an analytical system or model by which the current state and trends of the housing market might be assessed. The devices need not be complicated or esoteric. The financial analyst often works with a number of simple ratios—profits to net worth, current assets to current liabilities, profits to interest charges and so forth. Separately used and in inexperienced hands these are highly ambiguous and dubious indexes, but in experienced hands and used in concert they often become powerful tools of analysis. It may well be that some similar set of ratios expressing vacancy rates in rental housing, persons per room, family size, discretionary income, and other relevant variables might be combined and recombined in such a way as to form useful leading series that facilitate prediction, even if the precise lines of causation are not fully articulated. Certainly, predictive devices are far more satisfying and dependable if they are rationally founded, but a period of experimentation in which empirical success precedes strong deductive rationalization should not require elaborate apology.

For example, a rule of thumb guideline could provide that if the housing-stock-to-household ratio should drop below some local historical value and/or some regional or national comparative figure, slum clearance projects which involve demolition of houses would continue only if accompanied by a rate of new construction in excess of family formation. The proper amount of disaggregation of the relevant ratios would be necessary to reflect noncompeting or weakly competitive housing submarkets, so that a surplus of suburban housing, for example, could not become the justification for the destruction of core housing if the latter were in tight supply, or big, old, four-bedroom houses that fulfill the needs of low-income large families might not be demolished because of a small surplus in the supply of medium and high price two-bedroom apartments.

Accelerator Effect of Public Investment

Urban renewal policy and programming need not only a micro-economic strategy which relates number of households and housing stock to slum density and condemnation prices, but also a microspatial strategy built on an appreciation of the critical point at which neighborhoods change basic character. Grodzins[5] and others have elaborated the concept of a "tipping point," the point at which a neighborhood under nonwhite "invasion" converts quickly and irreversibly to an all nonwhite population, as the whites flee *en masse*. Is there some analogous tipping point at which public renewal sparks private efforts and a chain reaction results, perhaps bringing a mass return to the core of the central city instead of mass flight? Suppose we take, illustratively, an isolated slum area, bounded by a railroad, a depressed expressway, a park, and a river. What proportion of the property must be renewed to change the ecological balance enough to make it profitable to rebuild the remainder of the area speculatively, and/or to rekindle pride of ownership in those older, owner-occupied houses which are worth renovating? For the public authority to redevelop more than this minimal amount is wasteful of scarce public funds, but to build less than the minimal amount would be to risk loss of the whole, too small investment. This is a very real and important issue.

We need to identify and quantify some cumulative external-economies function that produces a kind of "accelerator" effect, where public investment in new housing and parks and other public works so changes the environment that it induces private investment in new housing, stores, and other private facilities. That an accelerator effect does actually exist is undeniable; even if it takes $4 of public investment to evoke a $1 response in private investment we have an accelerator effect of 1.25—$4 gets you $5. The subtlety of the renewal process almost certainly is such that no single coefficient can express this accelerator effect under various sets of circumstances. For example, the spatial form of the public investment may change the amount of investment required to achieve a given effect. A site plan which maximizes the periphery of the renewal project and thereby its contact with surrounding properties might have the greatest leverage effect. Or perhaps, a periphery of intermediate length, retaining a moderate amount of massed impact, would still have many points of uplifting contact without dissipating its effect by spreading its force too thinly. An example would be the open pincer form from military tactics— renewal in the rough shape of a "C."

[5] Morton Grodzins, *The Metropolitan Area as a Racial Problem* (University of Pittsburgh Press, 1958), reprinted in *American Race Relations Today*, Earl Raab (editor) (Garden City, New York: Doubleday Anchor Books, 1962).

The renewal-accelerator function is almost surely a stochastic one in which there is a set of probabilities associated with various site plans and one can play for a higher probable leverage on private investment only by running a greater probability of failure—loss of the public investment. For example, an "L" shaped project would have greater leverage (private response) *if* it "took" and the "L" were filled in, completing the square. An "O" shaped project is more conservative in that the fully encircled area is much more likely to be rebuilt than is the only partially encircled area inside the open "L," but while the probability of success is higher, the probable gain is smaller. While the plan which offers the highest (weighted) probable pay-off is clearly a prime candidate among the many alternatives, there are other possible strategies which cannot be rejected offhand, such as the minimization of total loss with some given level of leverage. The "O" shape might promise modest leverage with minimum probability of failure, analogous to a minimax strategy in game theory.

What may seem, at this point, to be a highly complex and even overly ambitious objective becomes much more manageable if plans can be changed along the way. If, once a project is begun, no changes can be made there will be a strong tendency toward conservative design, filling in the renewal area solidly for fear of failure if part of the environment is left unchanged. "Better to lose a little potential 'capital gain' than to lose the 'principal'." But suppose that a once-and-for-all commitment is not binding and, like the old cook, we can keep adding a pinch more at a time until a self-regenerative process takes hold. Under these conditions there is little excuse to overinvest with public money; public subsidized housing should be cut back as soon as private housing has been stimulated and the remaining funds should be transferred to a new slum area as seed money to begin again. We may, in time, learn site plan tricks which save as much as half of the funds now used in our typically blanket coverage public renewal programming. But the physical planner must be willing to give up a deeply cherished (self-bestowed) prerogative: complete and detailed power over the whole project. He must be content with planning only the broad skeletal form which natural organic processes then complete. From a "super-block" mentality to shepherding growth—from paternalist to promoter—is a big step.

Irregular shapes may increase various initial construction costs, especially utility costs as pipes and wires must run farther, but even here adequate existing utilities are often available in these older parts of the urban area. Team research seems especially appropriate because the question cuts across matters of physical site planning, community development and cost-benefit analysis. If the judgments of experienced urban planners, sociologists and economists could be integrated, some radical changes in our urban renewal microspatial strategy might result.

Some feeling for the breadth of the grand design needed can be conveyed by returning to the educational-residential strategy of Chapter 3. One of the most critical problems in urban renewal is that of providing good schools for the middle- and upper-middle-income families lured back to the central city. Because the first redevelopment projects will be small islands in a sea of slums—much smaller than a typical elementary school district—the first question will be whether to subsidize small and inefficient "country schools" restricted to the housing project families or to bus the project children to distant schools. Almost certainly, nearby slum schools will not be acceptable. But even if contiguous projects expand the redeveloped area to school district size and eliminate this problem, we are back to a suburb in the city and have done little more than rearrange the urban furniture. Perhaps the renewal projects should grow no bigger than, say, two-thirds the size of an elementary school district, leaving unrenewed areas (lower-income families) between them. A policy of creating mixed school districts is, moreover, the natural complement of the strategy outlined above of interspersing new housing amidst the old so as to encourage private (nonsubsidized) renewal.

Firm Size, Product Development, and Filtering

One of the more intriguing possibilities in the fight against urban blight is the promotion of greater research and development in housing technology. To the extent that new housing technology can lower the cost of shelter, a direct contribution to reducing urban blight would result as new houses become available at lower prices and through competition reduce immediately the price of the whole low-income housing stock. The lower price would induce low-income families to upgrade their houses. Less obvious is a second possibility that arises out of technological advance that improves quality rather than lowers costs. Product improvement, even if initially confined to upper-income housing, would contribute to an upgrading of housing all the way down the line, not just among the higher-income buyers of the new and improved units.

The automobile market offers a good example of how this works. Rapid product improvement has made new cars become out of date very quickly, thereby inducing higher-income households to trade in their "new" car on a newer one frequently. This has put a large number of only slightly used secondhand cars in the hands of lower-income families, cars which they never could have afforded without the value-deflating force of rapid technological and style changes. A substantial gain in real income accrues to the used car buyers over what they would have enjoyed if the product changes had been slower and the cars held longer by the initial buyers. Forced obsolescence and conspicuous consumption of automobiles by the upper-income households have produced a substantial redistribution of income and greatly improved the transportation position of the lower-income classes.[6]

By analogy, if we could stimulate an increase in the demand of the well-to-do for new houses, we would, in effect, increase the supply of used houses available to lower-income groups, and lower their prices. To say this, of course, is to formulate a durable goods/product-improvement variant on the "trickle-down theory" of income distribution. The opprobrium with which this patronizing rationalization of current income inequality is traditionally received does not obviate the force of income redistribution that does occur by this path. But one must be careful to count the social cost involved in any policy of forced obsolescence. One could argue that the premature discarding of housing might result in the overallocation of resources to housing construction relative to alternative uses. We might, instead, upgrade our schools and mental hospitals. If the housing "improvements" become primarily ostentatious and faddish we would be guilty of encouraging a tail-fin consumer psychology in housing.

Still, the social benefits to be derived from the filter-down effect of forced obsolescence in housing may well be as large as any resulting from any other directions our conspicuous consumption is likely to take. (And conspicuous consumption is almost unavoidable in an affluent society.) If the increased spending on updating housing were to come out of what would have been additional tax money, then the

[6] An important qualification here is that the very lowest income class which cannot afford to own and operate even the oldest car may become worse off in a mass automobile society because the nonmotorized public may become too small to support good public mass transportation. Hence, the very poorest may be left without any decent supply of urban transportation. But this qualification does not carry over to housing because no external diseconomies comparable to poor bus service are inflicted by the upper- on the lower-income groups.

income redistributive effect would probably be inferior to that achieved through additional public services. But it is much more likely that the housing expenditures would be at the expense of automobiles and clothing, and an increased supply of good, used housing is to be preferred over increased used supplies of either of the latter goods. And if the updating of housing were to cut in more on nondurable goods or personal services (for which there can be no used-product market), the gain to the lower-income group through the trickle-down effect would be even stronger and more sure.

Granting the potential of a rapid rate of product development in the residential construction industry, the actual methods by which that might be accomplished are less than obvious. Even at first glance, however, the relationship of firm size to research and development in this industry stands out as a prime point of inquiry. Since the residential construction industry is characterized principally by small firms and easy entry into and exit from the industry, the typical firm lacks both the capital resources and the extended life expectancy prerequisite to a serious research and development effort. And the spectacular success, or at least reputation for success, of the large corporation in research and development—electronics, aircraft, automobiles, metals, chemicals, petroleum, and so forth—strongly suggests applying the lessons learned about the relationship between firm size and product improvement in those industries to the housing industry. Moreover, the fact that the housing industry is widely regarded, fairly or unfairly, as an industry of slow technological change[7] strengthens the feeling that firm size is our best point of entry into policy-based research on residential construction.

In housing, the relationship between firm size and product development is not nearly so direct as in the heavy industries mentioned above. The size of the research budget as such—laboratory space and equipment and salary schedules of scientists and technicians—is not the main issue. The reason for this lies in the nature of the product. Housing as a product can be defined very elastically to include much more than the physical house itself—to include the whole neighborhood, the whole community. The typical individual builder experiments with very modest changes in the design of individual houses; the larger private developers exercise product control over residential

[7] See Richard B. Andrews, *Urban Growth and Development: A Problem Approach* (New York: Simmons-Boardman Publishing Corporation, 1962), Chapters 6 and 7, for a detailed discussion of the housing industry.

subdivisions that often encompass a number of blocks or even as much as a quarter of a square mile; seldom will the design of as much as a square mile be under unified direction.

The character of a residential community—the house as a family living experience—is intimately related to the physical form of the surrounding area for a mile or so in every direction. That is, the form of the residential (and related) developments over a surrounding area of at least four square miles is an important attribute of the individual house as a marketable product. Only a very large private firm (or a well integrated and highly structured joint venture on the part of many smaller firms) could command the financial resources and assume the risk of so big a project.[8]

This is not to argue that the piecemeal development of residential areas may not turn out well under nothing more than the customary negative zoning ordinances and building codes. They have. Nor is it to argue that large-scale housing projects are necessarily better sited or more aesthetic than neighborhoods that grew piecemeal. They are often dreary and monotonous. But the current range of choice is limited to those residential forms which can be accomplished under the present institutional arrangements: small-scale private builders, negative zoning and building controls, and controls couched in structural rather than performance criteria. While the consumer enjoys a wide range of choice as to the design of the house itself—colonial, ranch, split level; brick, frame, asbestos siding—he faces much less choice in neighborhood or community form.

The argument for bigness in the residential construction industry is that external economies and diseconomies abound in housing, relative to other products. While we try to cope with the problem of spillover effects—benefits here which impose costs there—with zoning ordinances and building codes, these negative local public controls are more likely to minimize external costs than to produce external benefits, and least of all to encourage creativeness and experimentation

---

[8] The location of the National Aeronautics and Space Administration's new Manned Spacecraft Center on a site near Clear Lake, Texas, will lead to the construction of the "largest and most unusual completely pre-planned community in the nation." This full-scale city will, over the next 15 years, grow to cover nearly 24 square miles, house approximately 140,000 residents in some 40,000 homes, complete with a 365-acre town center and 1,000-acre research park. The site is a former ranch purchased by the Humble Oil Company in 1938 as an oil property investment and the "New Town" is a joint promotion of Humble and the Webb Corporation, a large building firm. "The Birth of a City," *The Humble Way*, Vol. II, No. 4 (Fall 1963), pp. 1–3.

in housing and community design. Phrased again, negative controls are more likely to achieve short-run (static) economic efficiency than to stimulate the changes—the breakthroughs—which produce economic progress. Perhaps only a General Motors in the residential construction industry can continually titillate the blasé house buyer with some novel feature, for example, access to a village green, as optional equipment. Even radical changes in the physical form of the house itself are more likely to evolve out of industrial bigness—radical new design in both house and community, in matched set.

Again, the argument is not that the product offered by a very large-scale residential builder would be superior to that now being marketed, either intrinsically or when neighborhood and community also are considered. The brief goes no farther than to point out that the range of choice in housing would be extended over that which now prevails and that radical change in product would come about much faster, both because of the greater resources devoted to research and development and the greater control exercised over the product in its fullest sense. Further, as we have noted earlier in this chapter, a forced rate of product change fosters early obsolescence and the quick filtering down of good used products.[9]

These speculations about the housing industry's role in slum clearance deserves, at this stage, no more than careful critique, and only after that, perhaps, should come the painstaking empirical work which could give it substance and reality. But the firm size/product development/filter-down housing equation formulated above seems quite consistent with the rest of the consumer matrix in our affluent society. In sum, the residential construction firm appears to be a retarded competitor for the consumer's dollar in the high pressure world of giant oligopolies and Madison Avenue. To argue for its conformance is neither to bless nor curse the current industrial culture but merely to argue, in earlier Galbraithian terms, for balance through counter-

---

[9] Professor Max R. Bloom has pointed out to the author that a policy of forced obsolescence could have some very troublesome by-products.

Where we have high loan-value mortgage loans, the equity tends to be thin. Rapid obsolescence might result in market values dropping below the outstanding mortgage loan balance. This, to put it mildly, would disturb the property owner, the mortgage lender, and perhaps a few government agencies which insure and guarantee mortgages.

Quoted from a letter to the author, dated February 19, 1963. A quick answer might be that our rapidly rising incomes could be used to purchase new houses with larger down payments and faster write-offs. The upper-middle and upper-income classes who buy most of the new houses will be able to afford to pay for their houses in ten instead of twenty years.

vailing power. (All without denying that the "starved public sector," of a later Galbraithian period, may rate an even higher social priority.)

Nonresidential Renewal: Key to Residential Renewal?

Urban renewal also has its nonresidential side. While public housing programs have the sole purpose of improving the housing of the poor, renewal is, in part, a program through which the central city mayor-legislator-planner group hopes to increase tax base and reduce public service costs. Deduction and casual empiricism suggested that upper-income families yielded a net public budget surplus. The well-to-do live in dwellings with high assessed valuations and pay high local property taxes. They have fewer children to educate and even then often send them to private schools, with little or no expense to the city. True, they are articulate and demand good police and fire protection but, all in all, they pay in more than they cost.

But any realistic grasp of the relative magnitudes involved served notice to the central city public officials that not nearly enough well-to-do persons could be attracted to new core area housing developments to fill the vast areas of blight that they wished to clear. And so a search was begun for nonresidential land uses which might be attracted, which would also yield a net budgetary gain. If it is only a slight exaggeration to characterize current core area urban renewal programs as devices to improve central city public finances, what are the prospects for this strategy when directed toward nonresidential land uses?

The total amount of retail trade activity in the core area of the central city probably will not change appreciably. The reach of central business district retailing is limited to an absolute radius, for all but the most esoteric comparative shopping goods. As the metropolitan region grows the CBD does increase its sales a little by selling to the retreating urban-rural fringe but this is about counterbalanced by the lower sales per family it experiences in the central city, as the more affluent residents move out and poor in-migrants flood in. Manufacturing, with its continuing shift to more and more space per worker and to one-floor plants, is unlikely to demand much high-cost space in vacated core areas. With only a few manufacturing industries such as printing, baking, and brewing that are still able to compete while housed in multistory plants (whether or not they prefer them), the redevelopment authorities have begun to look elsewhere. If anything, the razing of cheap manufacturing loft space serves to eliminate the small job shops and the shaky new businesses that have long been a staple of core manufacturing activity.[10]

The current consensus seems to be that the rapidly growing professional and personal services offer the best prospects for nonresidential renewal. The prospect for the Detroit metropolitan area, for example, is that professional services will account for about as many new jobs between 1960 and 1975 as will manufacturing, and that finance, insurance and real estate, business services, and other core-oriented activities will account for perhaps two-thirds as many new jobs.[11] All in all, if the CBD can retain its traditional attraction for services, core renewal has found a strong nonresidential support.

The new professional, financial, and business service firms cannot be counted on directly to fill up the cleared land areas—office buildings tend to cluster in the heart of downtown and pile up floor space through height, to conserve on the scarce, prime land. But keeping these service activities downtown provides a powerful incentive for professionals to live near downtown—in the new expensive, redevelopment areas, for example. And as the metropolitan area grows and traffic congestion gets worse, the lure of living near work grows stronger. The more professionals that can be lured in to live, the more reason there is for placing the new office facilities in the core. Home and office interact to generate a cumulative mutual attraction that could produce core growth and development.

Further, as the core area professional residential population grows, CBD restaurants, theaters, museums, night clubs become revitalized. This attracts even more of the metropolitan area's sophisticated, affluent population to town houses. It also attracts convention and tourist business, one of the lush plums for which every local economic development group is reaching. The dynamics of urban redevelopment are such that we may find, when looking back on this frantic period of city planning from the vantage point of 1980, that our many downtown redevelopment efforts did not assume a normal distribution in degrees of success. Rather, a decided bimodal distribution could be seen, with some cumulatively progressing to clear success and others

[10] See, for example, Raymond Vernon, *Metropolis 1985* (Cambridge, Massachusetts: Harvard University Press, 1960), reprinted as a Doubleday Anchor Book, especially Chapter 5, "External Economies."

[11] Wilbur R. Thompson, "The Future of the Detroit Metropolitan Area," *Michigan in the 1970's: An Economic Forecast,* University of Michigan Bureau of Business Research (Ann Arbor, 1965).

cumulatively retrogressing to dismal failure. A corollary of this would, then, be that the worst projection we could be making now about our "downtowns" is the balanced, moderately conservative kind. Downtowns may be destined to either come back in a burst of new glory or slowly die—Manhattan or Los Angeles?

RACIAL RESIDENTIAL PATTERNS
AND HOUSING CONSERVATION

A few students of urban problems have been so impressed with the primacy of the race problem in urban development, especially in the context of the politically fragmented metropolitan area, that the reader is almost left with the feeling that metropolitan area problems are essentially racial. We do not need to overstate the importance of racial considerations to appreciate the many facets of race in urban affairs. We choose only one for discussion here: the pattern of expansion of Negro population and the effect of this pattern on neighborhood conservation programs. This material supplements the preceding discussion of urban renewal, for a comprehensive attack on urban blight requires powerful neighborhood conservation programs to lessen the crushing financial requirements of renewal.

Because good planning should be built on good projections, we begin by trying to devise a means of anticipating the racial residential patterns of a decade or two in the future. While these are perhaps more difficult to anticipate than the future income pattern (a projection outlined in Chapter 3), one can still set up a small number of fully operational models built on extreme assumptions and thereby box in the likely range of future possibilities. By specifying the range of alternatives the community is forced into conscious choice, and every community does choose its racial-residential pattern, implicitly if not explicitly.

A Segregated Housing Model

The most obvious and, unfortunately, probably the most realistic place at which to begin racial-residential spatial projections is with a segregation model, positing a concentrated, contiguous expansion of nonwhite housing. Here we would assume that under pressure of the growth of the Negro population, both through natural increase and net in-migration, the Negro-white residential boundary would be pushed farther and farther outward from the core of the central city. Assuming strict residential segregation, the physical expansion of Negro neighborhoods across the land space of the urban area could be mapped with almost as much accuracy as the population growth could be forecast. A ten-year projection of Negro household formation out of the current resident population is one of the simpler demographic exercises, especially with the 1960 *Census of Population* in hand.

This complete count of the population stock out of which the households of the coming decade will be drawn, roughly the 10- to 20-year-old age group, provides the upper limit of household formation from current residents. The actual rate of household formation may be somewhat lower than the potential, especially if high rates of local unemployment prevail, discouraging family formation and/or encouraging doubling up in housing. And so a local labor market forecast would have to be integrated into this analysis to arrive at an estimated household formation ratio to apply to the population figures. A labor market forecast is even more crucial to the second part of the population supply estimate, the rate of net in-migration. A depressed local labor market would greatly discourage net in-migration, restricting growth of the local Negro population to natural increase and the ten-year household formation to the fixed and known existing stock of teenagers. An expanding local economy forces the analyst to estimate the net in-migration of Negroes and also the age structure of the in-migrants.

Clearly, the rate of net migration of Negroes to the urban area is the principal element of uncertainty in the Negro household-formation equation, and this is further complicated by the likely existence of a strong feedback effect at this point. To the extent that the urban area provides a relatively elastic supply of residential land for the Negro—to the extent that the white population falls back promptly and easily (if not gracefully)—overcrowding is reduced and living conditions generally raised for this minority group. Such residential amenities undoubtedly serve to enhance the drawing power of job opportunities, in fact, housing conditions are probably second only to job opportunities as a force of attraction. Thus we might construct some simple model in which the rate at which the Negro-white residential boundary moves outward is a function of, among other factors, the rate at which net Negro in-migration occurs, which latter is itself a function of the rate (better, the ease) with which the boundary moves outward, as measured by density (overcrowding) and relative rents for housing of given quality.[12]

Having projected the number of Negroes who will reach the age of family formation within the coming decade and having translated this into the expected rate of separate household maintenance by adjusting for income distribution trends (e.g., the degree of unemployment and underemployment), the next step is projecting the physical extent of the amount of contiguous expansion necessary to house the projected additional households. By assuming contiguous residential expansion, we almost know the very houses into which the Negroes will move, the full relevant housing stock is in existence now and subject to complete count and description. Correcting for a small amount of housing demolition (for expressways and the like) and for some subdividing of the larger dwelling units and trends in the expected level of enforcement of building and housing codes, we know the holding power of the land into which this expanding population will be moving. The chances are good that we could come very close to pinpointing the precise neighborhoods into which this minority group will flow.

Granted, the contiguous expansion will tend to move outward in solid fingers of advance more than in perfect concentric circles and so it could prove to be a neat trick to site, in advance, protrusions and interstices. But to be cartographically precise in timing at such fine grain is more an academic exercise than a substantive consideration because the interstices tend to fill in rather quickly. An exception is a first- or even second-generation ethnic ghetto. Such a place will exhibit far more resistance to a Negro advance than a heterogeneous population. Clearly, it is difficult for such a community to relocate *en masse,* especially without sacrificing substantial social capital (e.g., schools, churches, halls). But the major value of the work resides in tracing the general outlines of the advance, not in precisely timing the stages of development of specific small areas.

[12] The Advance Mortgage Corporation has issued a special report, *Midwestern Minority Housing Markets* (Detroit, Michigan, December 1, 1962), in which they compare changes in the pattern of nonwhite occupancy between 1950 and 1960 for ten midwestern cities. The 1950 and 1960 *Census of Housing* data on which this excellent descriptive study was founded could be exploited even more intensively to estimate the elasticity of supply of nonwhite housing by bringing together in some form of econometric model: population densities, the median incomes, average values and monthly rents, persons per room, and condition of housing of nonwhites relative to whites.

A projection of the Negro residential area boundaries, say, ten years hence is more than a piece of research curiosa. The long-range implications of the contemporary policy of carefully maintaining residential segregation by race may not be fully appreciated by many who ally themselves with this policy. Individual homeowners, neighborhood associations, and even whole political subdivisions may be grossly misinterpreting wherein their self-interest lies by not taking explicit note of the cumulative effect of their actions over an extended period of time. For example, individual white homeowners and their neighborhood associations located near the edge of the current boundary line separating Negro and white usually ally themselves with the more remote white homeowners in opposing mixed neighborhoods, that is, they also fight "open-occupancy" housing statutes which would help Negroes purchase houses in white neighborhoods anywhere throughout the urban area. By contributing to the white owner's power of resistance in the farther out and less vulnerable areas, opposition to open-occupancy housing concentrates the full force of an inexorable Negro population pressure on the more vulnerable nearby white neighborhoods. Prevented from spreading out thinly throughout urban areas, Negroes and other nonwhite groups are forced to exploit each new breakthrough to the fullest and consequently they inundate each new area into which they gain access. Neighborhoods pass from lily white to jet black with only a fleeting period of unstable racial mix.

By forcing on these nearby homeowners explicit recognition of the prospective growth of the Negro population over the coming decade, the current irrational community of interest between the various white neighborhoods may well be recast as a quite clear and healthy conflict of interest. The interests of the nearby white homeowners probably lie with those of the advancing Negroes, rather than with the far-out whites. That is, the nearby white homeowner stands to become a member of a dwindling white minority and will ultimately have to move primarily because he has helped create a situation in which his neighborhood must become nearly 100 per cent colored so that the neighborhoods a little farther out can remain 100 per cent white a little longer. The nearby homeowner is being sacrificed—is sacrificing himself unwittingly—to the interest of the farther out homeowner, so that the latter may enjoy the luxury of postponing his acclimation to a lesser amount of social and cultural change. We do not even have to argue the case for mixed neighborhoods as a rich experience for both parents and children to make a strong case for open-occupancy housing in the self-interest of the nearby residents. To do so, however, would be to argue open-occupancy as in the interest of all residents of the area—Negro and white, nearby and remote.

With a ten-year projection of the expansion of the Negro residential area, as it would occur under contiguous expansion and racial segregation, forced to the attention of the whole community, the balance of political power on the open-occupancy housing question might well shift dramatically. With the residents of white subdivisions now fully aware of and annoyed or even angered by their imminent sacrifice to the convenience of the more protected neighborhoods in the next ring outward, open-occupancy legislation and *practice* may not be so unattainable—so idealistic—as the "hard facts of political reality" supposedly ordain. Certainly, in a politically fragmented metropolitan area, where those about to be engulfed by a concentrated Negro housing invasion live in one jurisdiction (the central city) and those temporarily protected by distance live in another one (the suburbs), political recourse probably lies at the state level. Or, if the rural-suburban-dominated state legislature remains indifferent or hostile to the plight of the central city residents (both Negro and white), ultimate recourse lies at the federal level, in the executive division (through the HHFA and other housing offices) as well as in Congress and through the courts. But, in any event, the electoral power of the nearby white residents has been misdirected by lack of understanding and inadequate information.

The first step to be taken in creating a better balance of self-interest in the political bargaining process would be to clarify the implications of the present course of action if extended another decade into the future and the consequences of alternative positions. The relative ease with which the requisite calculations could be made and the high priority of the socioeconomic problem posed promises an exceptionally high rate of return on a very modest investment in research.

An Open-Occupancy Housing Model

An alternative projection of the prospective racial-residential spatial pattern could be built on an "open-occupancy" housing assumption. We might project the level and distribution of income among Negro families and assume that they behave and are treated like any other population group in the housing market. The implication is that Negroes will break out of their ghettos, at least to the extent that their prospective incomes permit them to compete successfully for the newer and better housing, and that they will express the same housing preferences as similarly circumstanced whites.[13] To assume that this minority group will scatter throughout the urban area is, of course, not to assume that they will be diffused so finely over the land or become so thoroughly blended into the social fabric of the community as to become just another "ethnic" group. A decade, even two, is probably much too short a time for accomplishing so radical a social change. But the urban socioeconomist can find much of interest in the implications of the "mere" scattering of the upper-income Negroes across the whole metropolitan area as it affects such diverse facets of urban living as housing, education, public finance, employment opportunities, and cultural assimilation.

An open-occupancy housing market might seem too remote at this time for serious consideration as a complement to the strict segregation/contiguous expansion model. But first reactions notwithstanding, one might argue open-occupancy almost as convincingly as contiguous segregation, as a first approximation of the residential pattern of 1970. The sixties give every evidence of being the Decade of the Negro, and we need not labor here the interesting question whether this great social change is more due to the acceptance of moral responsibility on the part of the white community (the pull) or to the wresting of these gains away from the white community by a new generation of Negroes with greater power and sense of that power (the push). With the courts on his side and with the once monolithic will to resist of the white community deeply divided and weakened by a complex mixture of guilt, compassion, and foreign policy, all that remains to validate the Negro's passport to suburbia is the economic power necessary to compete in the market for the newer and higher priced suburban housing.

For some time now the Negro has found greater opportunity in education and employment open to him, and the weakening of discrimination in these two realms may well provide the final ingredient

---

[13] According to the evidence marshaled by Eunice and George Grier, and the studies of others they have reviewed, the "new Negro middle class" looks for play space, good schools, personal safety, property maintenance, and neighbors with similar income and education—a fair description of middle-class white family residential values. And in the case of a "typical" suburban location near Philadelphia, 90 per cent of the Negro prospects moved 10 airline miles or more from their former neighborhoods (whereas only two-thirds of the white buyers moved this far) and nearly one-half of the Negro household heads had to commute 15 airline miles or more each way to work (only one-quarter of the whites did). We can, it seems, waive differences in taste patterns. Eunice and George Grier, "Market Characteristics in Interracial Housing," *The Journal of Social Issues*, Vol. XIII, No. 4, 1957, pp. 52–53.

needed to desegregate housing—rapidly rising economic productivity and income. Today, there is probably at least as much job discrimination in favor of the *well-educated* Negro as there is against him. Almost every business and government agency is looking for a skilled Negro to use as a public relations showpiece, as a sop to guilty consciences, or to satisfy some employment practices directive from above, or to nullify some local militant action group threatening a buyer's strike unless the enterprise employs Negroes at higher grades.[14] All in all, a strong case can be made for the assumption that Negroes with the highest skills will earn wages commensurate with their education and skill. (Needless to say, equality of opportunity in employment is a much rarer phenomenon among the unskilled and semiskilled.)

The specter of structural unemployment does cast a chill over the otherwise bright prospects of the Negro, as he is typically the marginal worker at all job levels, the first to be laid off and the last to be rehired, therefore the one most likely to be chronically unemployed. But this grave social problem is not especially relevant to the racial-residential spatial pattern of the future. Far more germane is the prospect of a rapidly increasing number of middle-income and even moderately high-income Negro households that promises to change residential patterns. The handmaiden of employment opportunity is income inequality, and the coming decade threatens to be one of great income inequality among Negroes, both because of their greater employment opportunities in skilled work and because of the disappearance of semiskilled work and the downgrading of semiskilled workers through the automation of these simpler tasks.

Our open-occupancy residential land use model began with the assumption that Negroes are free to compete in the housing market and that their ability to scatter throughout the urban area is constrained only by income. We now assume that the employment market is nondiscriminatory, in the upper strata, and that income is commensurate with personal productivity (education and skill). If we can project the educational level of the Negro labor force, especially the number of Negroes with an education necessary to qualify for employment which will pay a wage high enough to support payments on

---

[14] See Hannah Lees, "The Not-Buying Power of Philadelphia's Negroes," *The Reporter*, May 11, 1961, pp. 33–35, for an early account of the use of consumer strikes by Negroes against the products of employers who discriminate against Negro workers in hiring. For a detailed description of the strike tactics as they developed in the first few years, see *The New York Times*, November 25, 1962, p. 1. (Special report by John D. Pomfret.)

the higher priced suburban housing, we can project the number of Negroes who are financially able to leapfrog over the immediately bordering older housing to the next ring of newer housing—the "suburbs." In estimating the educational level of the Negro labor force of a decade hence, we would be for the most part working with a known stock. Within so short a time period, the educational background of most of the workers is already an accomplished fact. Only the fifth or so of the total labor force who are still in school when the projections are made constitute an unknown to any appreciable degree; here, we would have to estimate how long they will remain in school under rapidly changing social conditions.

The prospects seem quite good for moving from good educational information, via the assumptions of equal opportunity in the better-job market and open occupancy in housing, to racial-residential patterns that reflect expected income (current education). To illustrate, we might estimate the number of Negroes who will have a college education in 1970 and allocate them to the $20,000-and-up-house neighborhoods, and estimate the number who will have a high school education and two years of technical training or apprenticeship and move them into the $15,000- to $20,000-house neighborhoods and so forth. Thus residential segregation by race assumed in the first model is contrasted with residential segregation by income in this latter model. Whatever racial disproportions remain between neighborhoods will begin to reflect more unequal educational opportunities and cultural experiences that have cumulated over time and from roots deep in the past. The racial-residential pattern will, that is, reflect not current discrimination in the labor market but rather the legacy of past discrimination in education.

Racial Segregation in Housing and Neighborhood Conservation

The alternative racial-residential models discussed above were developed in an almost abstract analytical context with the single exception that a loose link to public policy was made in the course of pointing out that the near-in white residents may not be acting in their own self-interest by supporting racial segregation in housing. But another facet of the comparative analysis of these two models has considerable relevance to urban public policy. The continuation of a policy of strict racial segregation in housing generates both a residential environment and a housing market process which is most inimical to the neighborhood conservation programs being pursued in almost every urban area as a complement to the urban renewal effort. It is, in fact, difficult to see how more than a scattered handful of neighborhood conservation projects can succeed if strict segregation persists.

The process by which strict racial segregation in housing disrupts neighborhood conservation programs and contributes to urban blight runs something like this: First, white household resistance to the spread of nonwhite residences obstructs the orderly transfer of housing to a growing population group, packing the nonwhites into higher densities than parity in the housing market would dictate, even considering the lower income and housing buying power of nonwhites. This accelerates structural deterioration in the Negro neighborhood. Second, to the extent that the inevitable invasion is foreseen, it is probably planned for by reducing property maintenance and home improvement expenditures in the adjoining white neighborhoods to a minimum, assuming that a homeowner usually can recover only a small fraction of his renovation investments, especially in a forced sale. (It is the forced move from his home, not the color of the buyer, that is directly relevant, but color is precipitating the move.) Third, organized neighborhood conservation efforts to slow the rate of blight formation by renovation are encumbered, if not completely stymied, by massive population relocations. Our carefully planned and highly structured community development programs call for a neighborhood population that will sit still long enough to recapture the investment they must make in property improvements. Racial invasion followed by mass flight can deal a heavy blow to the most carefully planned neighborhood conservation program, and accelerate the need for another costly slum clearance project.[15]

[15] A number of observers, however, have pointed out that the very high rate of migration of rural Negroes to large cities, beginning with the labor scarcity during World War II, is due to slow down with the emptying out of the rural areas. Fiser, for example, points out that there "are now probably less than 3 million Negroes left on farms . . . [and with] . . . the increase in the white birth rate—our urban areas are approaching proportions of racial stability," Webb S. Fiser, *Mastery of the Metropolis* (Englewood Cliffs, N.J.: Prentice-Hall, Inc., Spectrum Books, 1962), pp. 54–55. Fiser emphasizes the connection between the rural Negro in-migrant and the extent of slums; we highlight above the *process* of slum formation.

Accordingly, the core area impacts and centrifugal shock waves emanating from nonwhite in-migration that have so destabilized neighborhood conservation efforts should become milder from now on. In addition, the new in-migrants will presumably come increasingly from small towns and other large urban areas, complete with urban values and social habits.

We in the United States are a long way from putting together a comprehensive neighborhood conservation strategy. None is offered here. It might be noted in passing, however, that one slender reed on which we might lean is the relative stability of central city neighborhoods that make appreciable use of private and parochial schools. Urban sociologists have long appreciated the high degree of solidarity of white Catholic neighborhoods in the face of nonwhite invasions and attributed this phenomenon to the fact that "by sending their children to Catholic schools, the parents avoided one of the major factors forcing otherwise unprejudiced families out of changing or mixed neighborhoods."[16] (The fact that many parochial schools have recently become integrated does not materially lessen their neighborhood stabilizing force in most cases because they are truly *mixed* schools, not *changing* schools.)

But there is room for an important public policy role here, too. Private schools are hard pressed for funds and we might be more co-operative in allowing joint use of certain expensive public school facilities, such as gymnasiums, auditoriums, and laboratories. In many cases these facilities could be used at off-peak times when the marginal cost of such use was near zero. By lowering the cost and improving the quality of core area private schools, we increase the solidarity and stability of near-in white populations. An important by-product here is that such sharing of public school plant would soften the resistance of an important element of the electorate who often resist tax increases for public school expenditures. Better schools for all may be the most critical factor of all in holding middle-income white families—Catholic and non-Catholic—in the central city.

Property Taxes and Housing Conservation

Good urban public management would use relative prices of various kinds to reward behavior which favors property conservation and to penalize that which accelerates depreciation. Especially at issue is the local property tax. A long line of thought, dating back to Henry George's *Progress and Poverty*, has pressed for taxing land values ("rent") very heavily because land is a gift of nature and yields its

---

[16] Mel J. Ravitz, "Effects of Urban Renewal on Community Racial Patterns," *The Journal of Social Issues*, Vol. XII, No. 4, 1957. For the empirically minded, the 1960 *Census of Population* has, for the first time, gathered tract data on public and private school attendance.

owners an "unearned income." Since, moreover, the supply of land is fixed, no level of taxation up to its full earnings would reduce the supply of land available to society. Heavy land taxes have, therefore, been championed on the grounds of ability to pay.

On the other hand, handsome buildings in good repair are not at all fixed in supply and depend on the profitability of investment in such capital. The local property tax, the "land-taxers" (intellectual heirs of Henry George) argue, acts in a most perverse fashion, by rewarding those who permit their property to depreciate into slums and penalizing with higher tax assessments those who improve their property. The "land-taxers" would eliminate or at least greatly reduce taxes on property improvements, and some have gone to the extreme to argue that our present heavy property taxes have almost single-handedly created our slums.

Without trying to assess the relative share that the local property tax has had in creating our slums, we can approach this subject constructively and programmatically by asking what our tax strategy should be. We quickly recognize that the local property tax cannot be rationalized on a benefit theory basis; it is clearly not a *quid pro quo* for public service benefits received. An old, dilapidated firetrap should pay more, not less, in benefit-type taxes than should a modern, fireproof building of higher value. Similarly, when a property owner puts in a new safer furnace or a garbage-disposal unit or paints the exterior of his building, he is causing the city less cost and creating social benefits—in return for which, perversely, his property is assessed at a higher value and his tax liability increased.

With respect to *rental* properties, one might make a strong case for a true benefit theory local property tax on buildings, distinct from but consistent with and even complementary to a heavy ability-to-pay land tax, to conserve and enhance urban capital. Such a tax package would not, moreover, impose any difficult income distribution problems or serious ability-to-pay questions; old, run-down *rental* properties do *not* imply poor owners. But when we turn to owner-occupied property, we need a fresh approach.

Deteriorating owner-occupied property poses a problem not unlike that of devising a way to make public assistance payments in a constructive way. One cannot realistically contemplate raising property taxes on rundown, owner-occupied dwellings—taxing the poor—no matter how much they may cost society in police and fire protection and public health services. But in discussing public assistance we argued there that rewards for socially beneficial behavior could be paid even if penalties for recalcitrant behavior could not be levied. A similar case can be made here for rewarding renovations on deteriorating residences by taxing them less heavily. Municipalities in New York State may now, in fact, grant property tax exemptions of up to twelve years on increased residential valuation created by installing hot water and central heating systems.

To sum up this section, the scope of public policy that bears on efficiency in urban blight and renewal clearly includes housing policies which provide for the orderly filtering down of aging housing in the great gray area. Considerable consensus exists that only by greatly retarding the rate of structural deterioration and slum formation can we even begin to solve the urban blight problem. Thus neighborhood conservation programs are central to urban renewal efforts and racial problems in housing and property tax policy are central to neighborhood conservation.

THE PRICE OF URBAN SPRAWL

Probably no recent phenomenon of urbanization has been more pointed to with alarm than urban "sprawl." Sprawl is used somewhat loosely to include both a haphazard intermingling of developed and vacant land on the urban-rural fringe and the siting of houses on lots of ever larger size.[17] Although there are some critics of big cities to whom size itself is an offense, the principal target of attack is not so much the growing total population and sheer land size of the urban area as it is the steadily falling density of residential development on the periphery where new building is occurring. Urban core areas tend, of course, to be solidly built up with very little vacant land available for new building and therefore they must grow by expanding centrifugally. But if the new residential subdivisions are too extravagant in their use of land—house lots too large—or if much usable land is skipped over in the march of urbanization outward, the urban area grows "unnecessarily large" and transportation, communication, utility

[17] While the antisprawl literature has stressed the leapfrogging of open land more than the trend toward large lots, the latter is probably more quantitatively significant and obviously has the greater long-run significance—the skipped-over places do usually fill in. For some feeling for the relative importance of various kinds of open space on the total size of an urban area, see Stanley B. Tankel, "The Importance of Open Space in the Urban Pattern," *Cities and Space, op. cit.*

services and local public services all become "unnecessarily" inefficient and uneconomical. A clear distinction between physical growth due to population growth and that due to low residential density should be made because it is density which is at issue in this country at this time, although in England aggregate size has been the subject of considerable thought and public policy for a couple of decades. How has this purported too extravagant use of land for urban dwellings come to be, if indeed such a problem really does exist?

Urban sprawl could be nothing more than a color word dramatizing an adverse value judgment on one particular urban living arrangement—a distinctive combination of land and structures. A group of confirmed urbanites, impassioned and articulate, may simply disapprove of suburbanites' taste patterns—the substitution of open space and privacy for frequency and ease of interpersonal contact—and seek to apprise the city deserters of the errors of their ways.

Perhaps the most impassioned protest against urban sprawl is the most questionable: the fear that the physical growth of cities is "devouring" prime farm land, with ominous long-run implications to our supply of agricultural products. Cities were founded and flourished, for the most part, in two contexts: as transportation centers and as market places for agricultural areas. In the former case, the city site was most often a good natural harbor and on land of mediocre quality at best. But in the latter case, the better the soil in the area, the more prosperous the local farmers, the faster their market town grew, the greater the conversion of prime quality agricultural land to sites for homes, streets, stores, and factories.

Even so, the considered opinion of most land economists is that the loss of agricultural land is a small matter and the major economic impact of sprawl is to be found elsewhere. Technological advances in fertilizers, hybrid seeds, and farm machinery have greatly increased output per acre, while advances in contour plowing, terracing, and irrigation continually replenish our supplies of land. Mason Gaffney[18] argues:

> We run no danger of running out of cropland. Consider the most extreme case, the destruction of southern California's Valencia citrus industry by the insatiable subdividers of Los Angeles. It is tragic, it is largely unnecessary, yet there remain in California, in the southern San Joaquin Valley alone, something like one million

[18] Mason Gaffney, "Containment Policies for Urban Sprawl," *Approaches to the Study of Urbanization* (Lawrence: University of Kansas Press, 1964).

acres with thermal conditions suitable for citrus, according to a recent report from the Riverside Citrus Experiment Station. The Central Valley Project, the Feather River Project, the San Luis Project, and a rash of Engineer Corps dams on San Joaquin Valley streams are bringing water to this land. Meantime Florida has run off with the lion's share of the U.S. citrus industry, easily filling the shortage left by Los Angeles. Italy and Israel are beginning to wonder where they will ever market the surpluses from all their new acreage soon to bear. The problem is going to be to find markets for the produce of all the new groves now coming into bearing—groves planted closer, with better stock, and managed more knowledgeably than the declining old Los Angeles groves they are replacing.

Homes, factories, stores, and theaters make very intensive use of land and these uses must be clustered because of the frequent movement back and forth and other heavy interaction. Farming, on the other hand, is an extensive land use, which suffers little from being isolated; the farmer makes relatively few trips to the various urban "buildings." It is not surprising then that farms will continually be displaced when they come in contact with expanding cities. The free market is, more often than not, doing its job very efficiently when it effects the orderly transfer of fringe land from rural to urban uses. This in no way denies that society may choose to subsidize the continuation of farming at the edge of a rapidly growing urban area to preserve "open space." But the farm becomes, in effect, an urban land use—its value lies in its spillover benefits as an urban amenity.

Urban Sprawl as a Problem in Consumer Economics

Perhaps the urban-fringe home builder is not simply reflecting a different taste pattern as he elects the distinctive mix of house and lot that so distresses his critic, but is indeed in danger of erring in a consumption decision; buying a new home in a new residential sub-division is a most complicated purchase. It is more than possible that the typical fringe area home buyer is not in possession of enough information to make a rational choice, even on the very narrow grounds of self-interest. Households may buy new homes built on sites considerably larger than they would have chosen had they been sophisticated enough to foresee the full and unending implications of their initial act. A home buyer may entrap himself in an inferior budgetary position by not anticipating the future context in which his present housing decision will place him, and a housing decision casts a die like no other consumption decision.

A city-dweller in first flight to the suburbs may in his inexperience purchase a full acre lot and complacently plant his house right in the middle of the lot, in such a way as to preclude future subdivision. This may seem to be, at the time, a quite rational act, considering the present low price of raw land and the value placed on privacy. Our naïve consumer reasons that for a few hundred dollars he can triple the width of his side yards, that is, his feeling of privacy and luxury. But with the advent of surrounding residential development and general urbanization through the community, even this low density area passes from rural to urban density. It reaches the stage when it must convert from dirt roads to paved and lighted streets, from septic tanks and well water to centrally supplied sewers and water. Then, what was gracious living on ex-urban lots becomes sub-urban sprawl, too densely populated to be rural and too sparsely populated to be efficiently urban, and property taxes rise to "confisca-tory" levels. For example, an assessment of $2,000 per acre for a storm drain trunk line comes to a staggering 14 per cent of the value of a $15,000 home, with laterals and catch basins still to come and sanitary sewers to follow.

The urban land and housing market operates, for the most part, in the classical economic framework of *caveat emptor,* but even the most sophisticated buyers are only vaguely aware of the pecuniary pitfalls that dot the long and uncertain path of urban-rural fringe development. Even if the fringe area home buyer is not so unsophisti-cated as implied above, one could be more confident that lack of consumer knowledge is not at issue here if some private or public agency were encharged with the responsibility to inform the prospec-tive urban fringe home buyer, *before purchase,* of the prospective costs he assumes over the next decade.

In the case of a new home, this information could be tendered to the buyer by the building department of the relevant local government at the time of application for a building permit, and to all subsequent purchasers of that house by real estate agents at the time of signing of the purchase agreement. A booklet which contained estimates of current, imminent, and ultimate property tax rates and special assess-ments and utility service costs for various size lots at different stages of urban development could be made available—a little like the "prospectus" that a corporation must make available to investors prior to offering a stock issue for public sale.

Of course we cannot know, precisely, the ultimate cost of owning various size lots because we do not know what level of public services will be demanded by the residents, so we cannot know future tax bills with neat accuracy. Nor do we now know the costs of construction of public plant at future dates under uncertain price levels and physical circumstances (e.g., storm drains or sanitary sewers that might have to be tunneled under expressways that do not now exist). Careful study by competent research groups could provide some rough guidelines that would make the housing decision a more realistic and rational investment process than it now is. Some of the seemingly harder problems of cost estimation may well soften under the pressure of good empirical work. For example, to a considerable degree, taxes are a substitute for private housing expenditures—public water and sewage disposal bills are substitutes for depreciation and maintenance costs on private pumps and septic tanks—so that total homeownership costs may be much more predictable than the precise composition of these costs.

To the extent, however, that expenditures on public services (local taxes and assessments) are a substitute for other expenditures unrelated to housing (automobiles and travel), various probable levels of public services must be priced out for various lot sizes so that the prospective home builder in a fringe area can rationally site his home—can delicately trade-off lot size against other goods. We may well have in urban "sprawl" a very subtle and serious information and communication problem in consumer economics.

Urban Sprawl as a Price Problem

Perhaps the fringe area home builder is not unmindful of the cost entailed by his land size decision. It may be, rather, that he anticipates that he cannot or will not be held liable for them. A large lot homeowner may escape paying for the luxury of consuming space because these costs are difficult to identify and to allocate by residence. Even if some of the costs of local public services attributed to lot size can be roughly estimated, the large lot homeowner may be able to indefinitely postpone legal liability for them by various obstructionist tactics. Taxpayer lawsuits to enjoin the construction of sewers, drains, water mains, and the like may so delay the construction of these facilities that those who desperately need these facilities, and are willing to buy peace at any price, may agree to a cost formula that greatly favors the large-lot holdouts.

The new facilities, for example, may be financed out of the general fund by increasing the general property tax rate, a levy that falls on the value of land *and buildings*. If the public service cost is primarily a function of the spatial extent of the service (e.g., the laying of pipes), recourse to the general property tax instead of a special assessment on land area alone (or frontage) clearly and unfairly favors the owner of a small house on a large lot over the owner of a large house on a small lot. Here, legal delay and hard bargaining provide a basis for arguing the economic inefficiency and inequity of urban sprawl. This is not a case that is usually made, but some careful thought and rigorous quantification might well show it to be a greater support to the urban sprawl critics than some of the slender reeds on which they now lean.

Both financial irresponsibility and institutional obstacles, such as the cumbersomeness of the legal process, stand in the way of imposing on the homeowner the full cost of his decision on size of lot. But neither of these problems may be as intractable as the sheer ambiguity of the cost accounting problems involved in allocating the joint costs of producing a collectively consumed public service. To illustrate, if a new residential subdivision on the edge of a city were to be platted in very large lots, subsequent residential subdivisions would have to be located farther out from the core of the central city than they would have been had the lots of the preceding subdivisions been smaller. With residential lots typically accounting for 50 per cent of total urban land area, the residential lot size decision dwarfs the influence of other land use decisions (e.g., streets, parks, parking space) in determining the radius of the urban area, the distance from the core of the central city to open space. Consequently, through the ensuing years the residents of each new layer of residential subdivisions will have to commute through this sparsely settled area, traveling farther and at greater time and money cost than if the large lots had never been created.

The cost of extending and impairing the lines of contact for everyone may be considerably in excess of the benefits of spaciousness derived by the homeowners from oversize lots, so that the total net social benefit is lower. Only if each property owner were both subject to some special assessment based on the increased transportation expense he imposes on other members of the total community in traversing his property and also informed, prior to making his decision, of the likely schedule of these charges over a period stretching into the future for the full life of his improvements on the property, could the resident rationally choose the proper mix of house and land to reflect not only his tastes and income but the social costs of his act as well. But, in practice, we do not assess the property owner for the construction and maintenance cost of the arterial streets that cross his area, streets that are made longer or shorter because of his lot size decision. Nor, on the other hand, do we credit him with the costs he does incur in "sprawling" which permit his neighbors to enjoy more fresh air, light, and openness than they would have otherwise. A full accounting of the social costs and benefits of large residential lots—of the external economies rendered to and diseconomies imposed on the community—is a difficult, if not impossible, labor.

Another and perhaps even more interesting aspect of sprawl applies at a grosser level: the by-passing of large blocks of vacant land. The urban fringe residential developments presumably leapfrog over potential building sites *en masse*, "despoiling" the natural countryside at an unnecessarily rapid rate by leaving half-eaten, hard-to-use patches of land behind in the race to greener and cheaper pastures.

In contrast to large-lot sprawl, where the land buyer underestimates the future cost of owning land when it and the adjoining land are fully developed and buys too much, leapfrog sprawl is caused more by the land seller who overestimates the future price of land and holds out too long. Gaffney[19] argues that the holders of urban-rural fringe land tend both to underestimate the future supply of urban land and overestimate the future demand for it. Misjudging the land supply is not too unexpected in the almost complete absence of information on the number of lots recently subdivided or on the current trend in land prices or any other relevant statistics.

There are misinformed speculators in many markets; what special problem do they pose in the urban land market? The answer is, in part, that land is a heterogeneous product; each parcel of land is unique in its spatial position. Ordinarily, if some potential sellers of a given product hold out for a very high price, the market proceeds to clear exchanges between those who are prepared to sell at a much lower price and buyers who will not pay the very high prices demanded by

[19] Mason Gaffney, "Urban Expansion—Will It Ever Stop?," *1958 Yearbook of Agriculture* (U.S. Government Printing Office, 1959), p. 517f.

the most optimistic sellers. But if we think of each land parcel as being numbered in order from the center of the urban area outward, then contiguous expansion—the avoidance of leapfrog sprawl—can occur only if the holders of the lower numbered parcels sell first. This will occur only if those who hold the lower numbered parcels are the most conservative in their estimates of land price trend and/or the least able to hold out for a long period. Otherwise some of the more distant parcels will be developed before some of the nearer-in ones, not because the land buyers would not prefer to stay in closer but because distant parcels were held in weaker and/or less optimistic hands.

When we add to this a propensity to employ flat rate utility charges irrespective of distance from the utility system centers, we weaken the buyer's preference to stay in close to the urban center. When a water line is extended outward across an open space to tie in a noncontiguous new consumer, this remote household requires its three-quarters of an inch of cross-section piping back through the system all of the way to the pumping and filtration plants. Usually the most that we require from the customer, regardless of how far removed he is from the plant, is his pro rata share of the cost of constructing the extensions from the nearest trunk lines. Clearly, then, the near-in households are subsidizing the leapfrog sprawl of the distant ones.

The combination of land buyers who do not have to pay the full costs of being remote from the urban center and speculative holders of near-in land who are highly optimistic about the trend in land prices, sets the stage for leapfrog sprawl. Urban sprawl in each of its two major forms is, then, a problem in pricing, and not without liberal elements of poor market information.

Urban Sprawl and Land Use Flexibility

Thus we have two possible interpretations of the basis of urban sprawl, both of which assume that the problem is a real one. First, sprawl was pictured as a problem in consumer economics, with the decision on proper lot size seen as a highly technical product evaluation, complicated by the fact that the very great durability of the housing investment introduces the uncertainties of the distant future into the calculations. Second, sprawl was seen as a product of external diseconomies of scale in which the large lot or remote lot owner passes off part of the cost of enjoying spaciousness on to others.

A third interpretation comes to mind. Sprawl may be seen as a temporary inefficiency in land use which lasts only until the open spaces have been filled in. For example, if a lot is twice too large and if the house is wisely located on one-half of the plot, then when the urban area has grown to such a size that the savings in transportation cost (in time as well as money) to a new homeowner by locating on the vacant half of the large lot, closer to the core of the city, is greater than the value of that amount of open space as an amenity to its owner, the lot can and should be subdivided. Both seller and buyer would benefit by the subdivision of the large lot and economic efficiency would be raised. The owner of the large lot, moreover, would have enjoyed the extra open space for the full interim period during which the lot was worth more as a private amenity than as a private transportation saving.

If the lot had been only one and a half times too big no such easy conversion could have taken place and the waste of space would have persisted over the full lifetime of the house. Thus one might argue that a lot twice the standard zoning requirement for the type of house involved, and with the structures thereon placed so that subsequent subdivision is possible, is a much more rational use of land than any lot size in between the minimum and twice the minimum. That is, a land platting that is less efficient in the short run may be more efficient in the long run, as flexibility becomes the key to maximization under conditions of change and uncertainty. An interim period of greater urban sprawl could lead to a lesser ultimate sprawl, for a net gain over all (all values discounted to present values).

What of the land speculator's role in the context of change and uncertainty? As he holds out longer and longer, the urban fringe gets farther and farther away and the transportation cost savings that would accrue to the owner of a new home at his location over a new home at the distant fringe become greater and greater. At some point of time the aging of other houses nearby, built an even longer time in the past (on land held in less strong or more anxious hands), begins to threaten the desirability of his land as a building site for new houses, and—to oversimplify—he sells when the decline in this environmental value per unit of time is exactly equal to the growing increase in distance-cost saving over the receding peripheral land.

In social cost terms, the crime of the land speculator appears to be that the residents of the urban area have to pass by his vacant land on the way to their destinations and have to bring utility pipes and wires farther than otherwise to pass his withheld land, thereby incurring a greater transportation cost than if the land area had been built up solidly from the beginning. But the future is unknown and the optimum land use pattern shifts with changes in technology, social institutions and the economic base of the community. It is not impossible that an unforeseen need will arise for a new land use pattern in the very area where the speculatively held land is located, and that this "wasted" open space will save the cost of wrecking a valuable building. Certainly, the land speculator (monopolist) in a free market would be in a position to bargain with the new land user—the city perhaps—for a price nearly equal to the cost of the expensive demolition pictured. Even so, the private land speculator would be much better off, and society no worse off (and more likely the gain would be shared), so that the total social product and income is greater.

One need only recall the eagerness with which builders of urban freeways and civic centers seize open (usually park) lands to relieve pressures in their redevelopment schemes to appreciate the value of having a little elbow room in which to maneuver when and if the need arises. Those who would impress all of the land in a developing area into its final form are either implicitly predicting little or no change in the major determinants of land use over the life of the structures implanted, or they show great confidence in their ability to foresee a changeable future. What needs careful quantification is the margin at which the cost (private interest plus social losses in current efficiency) of holding another unit of land supply vacant is roughly equal to the probable benefits of having another unit of land use flexibility with which to adjust to changing optima in urban spatial patterns—efficiency through time. It would be nice if we didn't have to lose a green park every time we gained a gray freeway.[20]

Public Entrepreneurship at the Fringe

The vacant fields in the urban-rural fringe area are an inviting place for the exercise of public entrepreneurship. Ebenezer Howard (*Garden Cities of Tomorrow*), the originator of the "garden city" concept, advised in 1898 that it would be well to acquire the suburban sites for these new detached communities before migration into the fringe lands raised land prices. Henry George, in *Progress and Poverty* (1879), would have had society tax away the full capital gain reaped by urban-rural fringe land owners, arguing that society by the simple

[20] See Chapter 2, footnote 21.

act of growing created the higher land values. More limited in aim, but in the same spirit, many urban-regional economists and planners today advocate public purchase of outlying lands well ahead of need; they would have government join in the land speculation.[21]

Local government as a land speculator has its strengths and weaknesses. Because local and state governments provide or control practically all of the critical social overhead on which new suburban developments depend—roads, water, sewers, gas, and so forth—they would seem to be in a highly advantageous position to speculate. While the local government may have only loose control over the amount of total local growth—the fortunes of local industry selling in competition with other cities in a national market—it has much more control over the spatial pattern of that growth.

The weakness of local government as a speculator is that long horizons are important; local government may be immortal but the mayor and council are not. Political horizons may be very close. Raising taxes or increasing bonded municipal debt now to acquire lands at low prices to the benefit of the community in the future is not likely to excite the politician. Not only is a political group likely to be more conservative about long-run land price trends than is an individual but a group cannot move as quickly to take advantage of shorter period oscillations in land prices. Apparently, much of the bold open space speculation that has given us our finest city parks is attributable to the entrepreneurship of wealthy, community-oriented private individuals.[22]

---

[21] In a very specific context, for example, Milliman suggests that a metropolitan agency might "purchase all or most of the adjoining lands when reservoir sites are chosen and acquired. . . . The collection of user-fees for use of reservoirs [for water recreation] plus the capturing of surpluses capitalized in land values would often seem to provide sufficient funds to compensate for the incremental costs imposed by multi-purpose operations"—that is, pay the recreation costs. J. W. Milliman, "Policy Horizons for Future Urban Water Supply," *Land Economics*, May 1963, p. 115.

Fagin asks: "What if we were to apply the principle not just to the new values created by man-made lakes but more broadly to the new values created by other key developmental activities of government—for example, highway construction or the provision of utilities to serve an erstwhile undeveloped area?" Henry Fagin, "Social Foresight and the Use of Urban Space," *Cities and Space, op. cit.*

Henry George's ghost still walks abroad through the urban-rural fringe lands.

[22] See William H. Whyte, Jr., "Urban Sprawl," *The Exploding Metropolis*, The Editors of Fortune (Garden City, N.Y.: Doubleday Anchor Books, 1957), p. 128f., for an interesting account of the role of private citizens in enterpreneuring the public parks of New York, Cleveland, Westchester County, and Boston. He argues:

There seem to be four clear lessons. (1) Getting something done is primarily a matter of leadership, rather than research. (2) Bold vision, tied to some concrete benefit, can get popular support fairly quickly. (3) The most effective policy is to get the land first and rationalize the acquisition later. (4) Action itself is the best of all research tools to find what works and what doesn't. (p. 131)

Some observers of urban-rural fringe land development problems would have the public sector go beyond speculation into land management. Clawson[23] would rationalize urban land development by creating "suburban development districts" as quasi-governments in advance of settlement. He would give the central city government the power to tax property, borrow, buy and sell land in its immediate hinterland. The main business of the district would be to prepare raw land for sale to private developers, subject to a land use plan which both reflects social costs and benefits and embodies the design advantages of exercising control over large parcels of land. His districts would be roughly the size of the subsequent political subdivisions that would follow. Private builders would fix their own house prices, so a number would be necessary, but each builder would be big enough to internalize most of the externalities of an individual lot. (The district would internalize other externalities, such as industrial and commercial tax base, and the broad regional authority would internalize the largest scale externalities, such as in transportation and utilities.)

Harvey Perloff in an unpublished paper has extended the concept of a planned suburban development to embrace a number of socioeconomic considerations that tie in with urban renewal. (They also will help to integrate our thoughts here at the end of the chapter with the material at the beginning.) His ideal public suburban development authority would select a site, acquire the land, and prepare it for sale to private builders, terminating in a municipal corporation. He would take great care to balance commercial and industrial property with residential, to balance tax base and public service needs and lessen commuting requirements. More unusual is his advocacy of mixing upper- and lower-income homes. A key feature of the Perloff model is, in fact, "open occupancy." A major purpose of his "new town" would be to create new communities so attractive that families without hardened segregation feelings—income level as well as racial— could be lured out of bland, safe homogeneous suburbs into experimenting with the exciting variety of small satellite "cities." Finally, Perloff implicitly recognizes the Lessinger[24] arguments against "com-

[23] Marion Clawson, "Suburban Development Districts," *Journal of the American Institute of Planners*, May 1960.

[24] Another not so readily apparent basis of slum formation lies in the tendency to build new housing in solid masses. With whole neighborhoods of almost identical age structures, whole neighborhoods wear out together. Thus we have large concentrated slums rather than occasional old, deteriorated houses. See Jack Lessinger, "The Case for Scatteration," *Journal of the American Institute of Planners*, August 1962.

paction" (massing buildings of the same age by building compactly—
not leapfrogging) by advocating that the new communities be built in
stages so that they would not wear out *en masse*.

The advantages of building a community in stages and of assembling
a wide range in the age distribution of housing is not just to prevent
the community from becoming dilapidated all at once. But, even more
fundamental, if the principal source of housing for the lower-income
classes is older housing, through the filtering-down process, then we
need houses of various ages in a community to bring together families
of various income levels.

The complementarity of the core renewal strategy discussed in the
first section of this chapter and the suburban development strategy
discussed immediately above is clear. Even as we are trying to attract
the well-to-do into the core area redevelopments, we should be moving
toward providing housing for the lower-income groups in our "new
towns." Cheap (subsidized?) new housing in the suburban developments would allow us to begin with lower-middle-class families, with
the lower-income group moving in later, as these houses aged and
filtered down. In this way the social transitions could be planned
better and implemented more gracefully. Metropolitan area-wide
housing authorities would, obviously, be necessary to initiate such a
policy. If all of this seems too naïve, or too complicated or too inter-
ventionist, the critic must frankly face the alternative: the central city
will become a massive ghetto for the poor and would at best be an
oversize *human* renewal area into which the suburbanite dispatched
tax money and/or educational missionaries, to the extent their consciences dictated.

CHAPTER 9

Traffic Congestion: Price Rationing and Capital Planning

The urban traffic problem, like most problems, arises out of the frustration of trying to reconcile a number of partly incompatible goals. Urbanites would like to move about their area (1) quickly, (2) comfortably, (3) cheaply, (4) mostly at the same time, and (5) mostly to or from the same places. Since the typical journeys are to work and shop, time spent in transit is time lost from a productive activity. The fact that the route is boringly repetitive and usually ugly further burdens urban movement. Urban movement, then, is largely an experience to be done with as quickly as possible; speed becomes a prime objective and traffic congestion, which slows movement, the main problem. But congestion is too seldom seen as a direct, if harsh, form of economizing; we economize on urban transportation plant and equipment (social capital) by crowding many vehicles on a narrow street or by carrying standing passengers in packed buses. Through congestion, the commuter trades his time for lower fares, fees, or taxes; the lost time may be regained only at the cost of additional investment in transportation plant and equipment.

The private automobile offers unparalleled quality of movement—flexibility, comfort, privacy—except in the worst of traffic jams where irritation and tension may tip the balance the other way. The quality advantage of the automobile may be gained, of course, only at the expense of economy, as personalized automobile movement is both the most capital using and land using form of transportation. But the use of the automobile would not be nearly so expensive if it were not for the sharp peaking in the demand for street and parking space, caused by the congruence of working hours. The quick remedy of staggering working hours has its own costs, as the number of business hours in common are reduced—an eight-hour day becomes a seven-

333

hour day if you open and close an hour earlier than those with whom you deal. If a significant increase in the cost of doing business results from delay in the transmission of messages and in the transactions of exchanges, then commuting congestion has been relieved only by intensifying communication congestion. Would a net gain ensue and if so how would the gain be distributed? And would those who might initiate the move to staggered working hours stand to gain?

The private automobile might operate with greater comparative advantage, even without staggering working hours, if trip patterns did not focus so intensively. The worst congestion results from the use of personalized transportation which peaks both in time and place —in the central business district at 5:30 P.M., for example, or at the gates of a large factory at the moment when the afternoon shift relieves the day shift.[1] But the flattening out of spatial peaks in movement also has its costs: smaller factories would be denied the internal economies of scale effected by large continuous-process assembly lines, and the external economies of agglomeration by quick and easy access to nearby suppliers, buyers, consultants, and other participants in production and distribution would be lost.

But trying to satisfy peak hour demand may be very expensive and perhaps uneconomic. Many persons now traveling off-peak to avoid the worst congestion would in the event of a new expressway shift to peak hour driving. Thus the additional public investment in transportation facilities sharpens the peaks and lowers the "load factor" (the ratio of average to peak use) and increases the per trip cost of the urban transportation plant. With a shift from traffic movement in off-peak hours that cost little or nothing before, the cost of the additional capacity per additional trip—the marginal cost of peak hour movement—becomes extremely high. So high, in fact, that if we employed marginal cost user charges in some way, very few drivers could afford this additional capacity. Paradoxically, to the extent that we do employ user charges we usually do so in a perverse way, such as *lower* prices to peak users. Witness the practice of offering a quantity discount on bridge tickets to commuters, who travel at peak hours.

---

[1] If the "load factor" is defined as the ratio of the average to the peak volume of use of the transportation system, the Chicago data exhibit a load factor of about .484 over all but only .294 for work trips. That is, if work trips were the only kind made, the streets would be used to only about 29 per cent of capacity, or 71 per cent idle, instead of the current 48 per cent utilization rate. Chicago Area Transportation Study, Vol. 1, *Survey Findings* (Chicago, 1959), p. 35, Fig. 15, reported in Lowdon Wingo, Jr., *Transportation and Urban Land* (Washington: Resources for the Future, Inc., 1961), p. 31.

All in all, the rationalization of urban transportation involves a very complicated trade-off between the joint goals of speed, comfort and cost.

Alternatively, we might express the urban transportation problem in a managerial context as two problems interrelated in time: pricing for today and investing for tomorrow. The immediate need is to effect a more efficient flow of traffic, given the existing network of transportation facilities and the existing land use pattern. This is basically a rationing problem in which a fixed supply of street, bridge, and parking space is allocated as between the competing demands of automobiles, buses, pedestrians, and so forth, and also between short-haul and long-haul users. While more basic long-run solutions are being worked out, the daily problems of moving people and goods about must be performed within the limitations of the current, nearly fixed, stock of transportation facilities and the current demand for movement originating in the temporarily immutable spatial pattern of homes, factories and stores. The analysis here might profitably be handled largely as a problem in rational price making or the simulation of the price function with more direct controls.

The second need is the long-run one of devising some new pattern of transportation facilities and land use which is superior to the current set of parameters, within which the community is trying to make the best of a bad thing. Long-run transportation planning finds expression in the form of public investment in very expensive transportation plant and equipment and in zoning and other controls over the land use pattern of the urban area.

TRAFFIC CONGESTION AS A PRICE PROBLEM

Distorted Prices

Fortunately, one of the major causes of the urban traffic problem is becoming increasingly well recognized, and at the level of the informed layman where it really matters most. In an article in *Fortune*,[2] the major blame for urban traffic congestion was attributed to relative price distortion.

The trouble is that the American consumer, in deciding between private and mass transportation, has for years and years been pre-

[2] Gilbert Burck, "How to Unchoke Our Cities," *Fortune*, May 1961, p. 120.

sented with a market heavily rigged in favor of using his own car in city traffic. . . . Specifically, let the consumer himself choose the way he wants to ride, but let him pay for his rides. Let his roads be financed not out of general tax funds, but by definite user charges. Let these charges be large enough to pay back the full investment in the facilities he uses. And let them be levied so that, as nearly as possible, he is always confronted with the true cost of his choice when he makes it.

It is most important that the user charges paid by motorists (e.g., tolls, gas taxes, license fees) not only cover the cost of the facilities provided in some aggregate fashion but that these charges be tied as specifically and as precisely as possible to the act of using the facilities. The individual operator of a private vehicle on city streets should pay for the streets and traffic control and other associated costs, not in some lump sum of which he is dimly aware, but consciously and as near as possible in time and place to the act of making the decision to drive rather than ride mass transit.

Imposing charges on the use of the private automobile in the more heavily traveled parts of the urban area, at least during the peak hours of traffic movement, would be a powerful corrective in that it would operate to alleviate the problem regardless of the economic response of the driver to the charge. (The *political* response might well take us right back to where this game began.) If the driver responds by abandoning his car to ride the public mass transit system, this economizes on scarce urban street space and greatly eases, if not solves, the traffic problem. Alternatively, if the driver chooses to pay the impost, the revenue is generated with which additional facilities can be created, that is, more street and parking space can be constructed.[3] Since some drivers will respond one way and some the other, the solution becomes the dual one of both adding more transportation space and economizing on its use—the treatment is partly to feed the patient a little more and partly to curb an excessive appetite. Such a solution should not be lightly regarded in a high-tax economy where consider-

[3] The fear has often been expressed that if most of the core of the urban area becomes paved for streets and parking lots then little reason will remain for going downtown. The very fear itself suggests the equilibrating mechanism at work: the excess demand to drive downtown is removed by shifting land from use as destinations (store, office, and theater sites) to transportation facilities, an action which both increases the supply of and reduces the demand for access. If, however, one's goal is not some static equilibrium efficiency condition but rather some normative or dynamic goal, such as a greater taste for and interest in "downtown," then some more comprehensive strategy is required.

able resistance is being encountered to further tax increases and where user charges offers a new source of public revenue.

The next step would seem to be to give some serious thought to the complexities of cost accounting and revenue collection. This does not mean that the simpler message of the responsibility of the private motorist to assume the burden of his acts does not still have to be carried in clear and forceful language to new audiences. The readers of *Fortune* may offer only token resistance to the argument for higher automobile movement prices in core urban areas both because they are more familiar with cost-price concepts and comprehend the nature of the case almost intuitively, and because they are the ones who would be the last to be rationed off the streets by a rising price. These upper-income drivers would not only stick in the market in the face of new user charges but might even look forward to the opportunity to be able to bid for a larger share of the limited street space through the price mechanism. The real challenge comes when the marginal automobile driver—the one already at the breaking point with the current gas prices and parking fees—is asked to vote for higher automobile service prices in urban core areas at rush hours—is asked to price-ration himself off the core streets. In short, raising the price may well increase the welfare of the high-income motorist but is almost certain to lower the welfare of the low-income motorist—initially.

While it is true that congestion tends to favor the middle-income motorist with more time than money to waste relative to the busy, high-income motorist, and thereby tends to redistribute income downward, surely a move toward full-cost pricing of urban transportation would not become complicated by an adverse redistribution of income in any significant way. Besides, in general, the more remote the suburbanite (e.g., "exurbanites"), the more affluent he is and the more he uses the subsidized automobile movement facilities. In contrast, the indigent members of the urban area who ride buses are probably overpaying for their mass transportation in the form of reduced speed and comfort and in poor service schedules on transit systems forced to operate over congested streets with inadequate patronage. If the relative prices for private and mass public transportation are biased in favor of the former, as almost all observers believe they are, then righting the imbalance would probably improve the lot of the mass transit users and redistribute real income more in favor of the poorer classes in the central city.

Instead of raising the price of operating a private vehicle in the core area of the city, we could, of course, right the balance by lowering the price of mass transit. A number of students of urban transportation have, in fact, argued for free buses or their equivalent.[4] Since all the evidence seems to indicate that the demand for mass transit is very price-inelastic, at least downward, it would probably take a price cut to near zero to transform any appreciable number of drivers into riders. And even then a mass shift from automobiles to buses would almost certainly call for a substantial improvement in both the quality and the speed of bus travel.

Just how important speed is to the choice of travel mode can be demonstrated most convincingly with a simple numerical example. Francis Bello[5] estimated the cost of automobile movement at five cents per passenger-mile at an average occupancy of 1.8 riders per car. We can compare this figure with the flat twenty-five-cent bus fare common in big cities, which also comes to five cents a mile for a five-mile trip. But, drawing again on Bello's figures, if the average automobile speed on main arteries during rush hour is twenty miles per hour and for buses only about two-thirds of that figure, then a five-mile trip "costs" fifteen minutes by automobile and about twenty-two minutes by bus. If we value commuting time at $1.00 per hour, much too conservative a figure for most automobile users, we can impute a time cost of an additional five cents per mile for a five-mile automobile trip ($1.00 × 15/60 ÷ 5) and one and one-half times that amount, 7.5 cents per mile, for bus travel. In total, the trip costs less by car (10 cents per mile) than by bus (12.5 cents per mile) if time costs are included. Only by extending the length of the trip to ten miles can the cost of bus movement be brought down to the automobile level of ten cents per mile (25-cent fare spread over ten miles is reduced to 2.5 cents, added to the 7.5-cent time cost per mile).

Of course, the accounting is not complete. At one rider per car the automobile cost rises to nine cents per passenger mile and the parking fee has not been accounted for. On the other side, Bello's figures reflect total depreciation instead of just use depreciation, and time spent walking between home or office and parking places or bus stops has still to be accounted for, to say nothing of comfort and convenience. But the purpose here is to emphasize the need to include time costs,

[4] See, for example, L. Leslie Waters, "Free Transit: A Way Out of Traffic Jams," *Business Horizons*, Indiana University School of Business, Vol. II, No. 1 (Spring 1959).

[5] Francis Bello, "The City and the Car," *The Exploding Metropolis*, Editors of *Fortune* (Garden City, New York: Doubleday Anchor Books, 1958), pp. 38–40 and 56–57.

and their impact on the relative advantage of various modes of travel is striking, even when we reckon time at only $1.00 per hour.

Another course is open: do nothing. Let the traffic congestion mount in hope that technological or institutional change will come to the rescue and in the belief that necessity is the mother of invention. Will congestion provide the crisis that will spawn the invention of a new vehicle or land use pattern which will save the day?

Cost Accounting and Costs of Collection

While recognition of the "fact" that the urban transportation price structure is rigged in favor of the motorist is quite common, pursuit of that insight to the point of a suggested program which would undo most of the mischief attributed to the purported public subsidy of urban automobile movement is quite uncommon. The obvious next step is to estimate the private and social costs associated with various kinds of traffic flow and to assign user charges in amounts roughly equal to these costs. But many of the costs are joint costs arising from common use of a facility that accommodates a number of diverse traffic movements, some of which impose greater physical demands on the facilities (e.g., trucks versus cars), and some of which create the need for investment in greater capacity while others conveniently utilize existing capacity at off-peak times (e.g., the journey to work versus the evening trip to the theater). Accordingly, perplexing problems of cost accounting arise. Imposing user charges on the motorist which approximate the costs he imposes, and making it clear to him that the exaction is levied because he chooses to drive, is a program easier to accept than to make operational.

The private operating costs of traveling by car (e.g., gasoline, oil, repairs, depreciation, and so forth) are probably roughly comprehended as well as fully paid for by the motorist. The costs of traffic control are, however, not borne directly by the user but are instead paid for out of the general fund, that is, out of property tax revenue in large measure. Allocation of traffic control costs would seem to be a manageable piece of public cost accounting. A rough apportionment of expenditures on traffic patrolmen and traffic signals and the like could probably be made by gross areas—the CBD, the "inner ring district" and the "outer ring"—and levied as flat charges on drivers according to their origins and destinations. The discrimination which arises out of the discreteness of zone prices, where a few city blocks one way or another might arbitrarily and inequitably double or halve the user charge is no worse than the zone pricing we live with in taxicab fares and is superior to one-price bus fares. Alternatively, the number of miles separating home and work place and the frequency with which the trip is made, that is, miles traveled in commuting to work, might become the basis for a flat quarterly or annual charge for the urban transportation service rendered by local government. Different co-efficients (rates) could be multiplied against total trip miles to adjust for the time of day and direction of the trip, reflecting cost differentials in servicing an automobile at on-peak and off-peak times and places.

Fully as difficult as determining what the urban motorist should pay for the privilege of using city streets and traffic control facilities is the task of devising an efficient means of collecting the appropriate user charges. Road tolls have long been disparaged as a cumbersome device which creates bottlenecks in traffic flow, with the value of the time lost by the driver in queuing up to pay the toll and the cost of collection to the road authority posed as a dead loss. Of late, however, we have become much more efficient in collecting tolls, witness the baskets in which motorists toss coins which are automatically counted with a photograph taken of the license plates of chiselers. In this age of automation, toll collection can be expected to become ever more automated and economical. However impressionistic in its present state, Vickrey's artistic work on the techniques of implementing urban transportation user charges has opened up a new medium for expression of engineering and managerial economics.[6] Finally, simplest of all, self-reporting of mode, time, direction, and distance of trips could be relied on, supported by the customary discipline of sample auditing, as in the administration of the income tax. This is probably quite practicable for the easy-to-check journey to work trips, and these are the most expensive trips to accommodate.

One might just as well argue that a grocery supermarket would be more efficient if the check-out counter were eliminated, that bottleneck which forms as the customers stop to pay the appropriate food "tolls." Surely, we would have traffic jams in the aisles of food stores and "shortages" of food if we tried to administer free food stores supported by general taxation. The food shortages would be analogous

[6] William S. Vickrey, "Pricing in Urban and Suburban Transport," *The American Economic Review*, May 1963, especially pages 453–60, and "General and Specific Financing of Urban Services," in *Public Expenditure Decisions in the Urban Community*, Howard G. Schaller (editor), (Washington: Resources for the Future, Inc., 1963).

to the shortages of street space per automobile (traffic jams) and the shortages of parking places that characterize our underpriced and tax-supported urban transportation industry.[7]

The fact, therefore, that user charges are almost certain to impose some costs of collection and compliance is not in itself a damning indictment. Taxes, too, impose these burdens and it is only the excess that is relevant. Perhaps even more important than efficiency in the public sector is the comparative effect of user charges and taxes on the distribution of income and area development. One of the most promising moves that can be made to restrain further increases in the overworked and increasingly inequitable local property tax is to resort to user charges whenever feasible to save tax rate millage to finance those public services which involve collective consumption (e.g., justice) or income redistribution (e.g., welfare) for which user charges are unworkable and inappropriate.

But if traffic control costs are all that is at stake, perhaps the game isn't worth the candle. What other costs are at issue? A common complaint from the urban commuter railroads is that they must both build their own roadbed *and* pay taxes on the land occupied. Motorists do, of course, pay gasoline taxes which are used to construct streets and highways throughout the state and to this extent they do provide their own roadbed, in statewide aggregate. If one could show that urban motorists paid a smaller share of the federal and state gasoline taxes than that which they received back in the form of state aid for city street construction and maintenance, then the gasoline tax would stand as a relatively underpriced city street user charge and overpriced highway user charge. But it is precisely the reverse that is usually claimed, that the urban motorist heavily subsidizes his rural counterpart, especially with reference to rural secondary roads. This leaves us with only that part of the city street costs which are paid for out of the general fund of local government, reduced by the net transfer from urban to rural motorists through the gasoline tax, as the measure of the deficiency in meeting urban roadbed costs. (Urban motorists remain aggregated at this point.)

---

[7] Another interesting illustration of the way in which not charging a price for a good or service increases physical efficiency is brought out by Leslie Waters in connection with his argument for free buses:

> Service would be fast because . . . passengers need not even walk by single file to pay their fares as they entered the bus or streetcar. The side of the vehicle would be opened for quick entrance and exit.

L. Leslie Waters, *op. cit.*, p. 107.

The contention that local property taxes fall on privately owned railroad land and capital and not on publicly owned street space and thus bias relative prices of rail and automobile travel in favor of the latter seems clear and valid,[8] although the resolution of the problem is more subtle and uncertain. From the standpoint of resource allocation one might argue, following a benefit theory of taxation, that the discriminatory differential be eliminated simply by exempting railroad roadbed from local property taxation. Abstracting from the revenue needs of local government, the argument would be that urban streets and expressways (and rails) do not have need of the ordinary general government services, such as education, justice, police and fire protection, welfare, and the like, and need not help support them.

The users of the streets do, of course, need a very selective set of public services, ones which are rendered most specifically to them and usually to them alone, such as driver education, traffic courts, traffic control, and so forth. But if these costs could be approximately reckoned and covered by user charges, as suggested above, the general local public economy could be divorced from the urban transportation segment, a segment which would be performing what was once the fashion to refer to as a proprietary function of government and pricing its services accordingly. One can stand, moreover, quite easily on benefit taxation or user charges in this realm of local public services in that

[8] Commuter railroads serving suburban communities of New York City paid state and local taxes of $12 million in 1959 out of operating revenues of $136 million. Those carriers serving the suburbs in New York State had operating deficits ($5 million) less than their state and local tax bill ($8 million) so that tax relief in New York could cover current deficits, although it is recognized that this could only be "a stop-gap remedy, since without capital investment in renewed equipment suburban rail deficits can be expected to climb above the present level." But in New Jersey, taxes of $4 million on suburban rail service fall far short of the $24 million operating deficit so that tax relief can only be a small part of the answer. *Commuter Transportation, A Study of Passenger Transportation in the New Jersey-New York-Connecticut Metropolitan Region with Particular Reference to Railroad Commutation*, Report Prepared for the Committee on Interstate and Foreign Commerce, United States Senate, 86th Congress (Washington: U.S. Government Printing Office, January 31, 1963), pp. 26 and 34.

A CED report also sees the property tax on commuter railroad roadbed and terminal facilities as a competitive disadvantage relative to tax-free highways. A minority dissent questions this tax-free characterization because the highway user is burdened with gasoline taxes and various excises. But this dissent seems to miss the point that the gasoline tax revenues are returned to the highway user through expenditures for the construction and maintenance of his roadbed. But very little, if any, of the property tax revenue raised from the railroads provides direct benefits to them. True, both forms of transportation are taxed, but the highway user receives a *quid pro quo* and is the net gainer competitively. *Guiding Metropolitan Area Growth*, Committee for Economic Development, August 1960, p. 22.

no critical redistribution of income seems to be at issue—no reason for rail commuters to subsidize a general public which consists largely of automobile commuters.

The principal cost resulting from urban traffic congestion is delay and irritation, both of which the motorist does pay, albeit not rationally. It is the adverse reaction of drivers to these time and energy costs which creates the existence of a traffic problem. This seeming paradox—traffic congestion which imposes one set of costs on the motorists (loss of time) because they escaped paying for part of another set of motoring costs (traffic control)—might be variously interpreted. First, the costs of delay and irritation due to traffic congestion are regarded, implicitly, by most motorists to be less than the alternative amenity cost of shifting to public mass transit or the money cost of higher taxes or user charges to expand automobile service facilities. In which case no real traffic problem can be said to exist; congestion is a form of economizing on public capital by trading time for money.

A second interpretation might be that the mass of motorists do not appreciate their alternatives as consumers of urban transportation services and would authorize higher taxes or user charges if the alternatives were more explicitly quantified and clearly articulated. In this case, research and communication would create a more responsive market mechanism.

Third, increasing the supply of streets, expressways, and parking facilities might involve a substantial redistribution of income from mass transit users to automobile users. An efficient mechanism to effect the necessary compensatory payments to balance the income transfer is lacking. If the central city bus riders and residents who are subjected to the noise, dirt, confusion, and delay of dense automobile traffic must be bought off by the automobile commuting suburbanites, a difficult transfer across political boundaries must be arranged. If the necessary compensatory payment is more than the automobile users are willing to pay, then again there is no traffic problem because an increased supply of expressway and street capacity costs more than it is worth, everything and everyone considered.

Finally, the act of making driving easier and of accommodating more motorists (the former seems to lead inevitably to the latter) may set in motion some set of forces which destroys some important characteristic of the central city which, while difficult to quantify, is judged to be a greater "cost" than the current congestion imposes. For example, the fear might arise that expressway capacity could become so great that automobiles would choke the central business district to the point where retail sales would decline and property tax valuations and yields would follow suit, endangering the fiscal position of the central city. Or perhaps important amenities of downtown, such as promenading, good conversation, and civic spirit, would be destroyed by a congestion which blurs the community's focal point, and repels the tourists who provide an important source of regional exports and earning power. While some of this might be quantified in rough measure in a very systematic and sophisticated cost-benefit analysis, considerations of judgment, personal tastes, and social values are so heavily involved that a fully objective solution is unlikely.

Urban Community Planning and Demand-Based Prices

The dilemma encountered in trying to rationalize a set of user charges to reflect the cost of operating a motor vehicle in the urban area at various times and places is that the most important costs inflicted by the motorist are usually the most difficult to quantify and allocate. As we move upward in expensiveness from traffic control to dirt, noise, and odors, then to congestion and delay, and finally to the alternative use of the scarce urban space, we move also from such manageable expenditures as traffic signals and patrolmen's salaries, up through the value of such amenities as fresh air and serenity, to far-reaching judgments on the nature and purpose of downtown.

The growing elusiveness of the relevant opportunity costs as the cost analysis becomes more significant suggests experimenting with an alternative approach to the rationalization of urban transportation. Beginning with master land use plans, local public finance objectives, the economic development plan for downtown, and other (somewhat inconsistent) statements of community goals and objectives, the urban transportation planners might work backward toward an appropriate set of user charges to effectuate these grand designs. The basic developmental plans might be synchronized with a compatible strategy of mixing full-cost and subsidized transportation services right down to a spelling out of the specific combination of flat fees, variable tolls, transit fares, and tax schedules, which would make operational the grand strategy. In this last stage of urban transportation policy, the tactics of price making, the estimation of demand elasticities would largely supplant careful cost accounting, as cost-based prices and a simulation of the competitive model give way to demand-based prices manipulated by a public monopolist to shape the spatial and functional development of the urban area.

To estimate the price elasticity of demand for automobile transportation in the urban area would probably prove to be a feat nearly as difficult as the assignment of costs to the users of the various urban transportation facilities. How would the typical motorist react to a given user charge on the act of driving a private vehicle within the urban area? By how much would he cut back his driving in reaction to successively higher user charges? This is a question highly critical to transportation planning. If the demand is elastic (price sensitive), user charges would tend to alleviate traffic congestion by greatly reducing the number of automobiles for which the transportation system had to provide. If the demand is inelastic, user charges would tend instead to leave the number of automobiles largely unchanged, generating instead a rich flow of public revenue with which additional facilities could be provided to handle the automobiles more efficiently.

These may not be equally acceptable "solutions" and in any case the urban transportation planner must respond quite differently to these two distinct possibilities, or any particular mix of them. Since one cannot proceed directly to some existing stock of relevant data and determine the price elasticity of automobile movement, some deductive analysis and a few experimental formulations might suggest methods by which elasticity estimates might be made.

The price elasticity of demand for automobile movement in urban areas is, of course, largely a function of the alternatives that the motorist has open to him. Depending on the nature of the user charges levied, the urban motorist may be able to substitute between routes, trip destinations, and time of movement as well as between modes of travel. More specifically, he may be able to switch to city streets to avoid expressway tolls, or to begin work earlier or later to avoid peak-period surcharges, or to shop in outlying retail centers in place of downtown, or to abandon the automobile for a mass transit vehicle. As the illustrations suggest, the degree of substitution is closely related to the purpose of the trip. A useful preliminary exercise might be to develop a set of cross-classifications which relates the various kinds of adjustments which can be made to user charges (route, destination, time, and mode substitutions) to the various kinds of trip purposes (work, shopping, social, and others).

Some careful empirical work may open up these relationships to reasonably close approximation. In any event, some preliminary deductive work is a near prerequisite to insights into and a feeling for the general nature of the material, preparatory to formulating a set of testable hypotheses. For example, the journey to work is of such a nature that it allows relatively little substitution between destinations for most people, in the short run anyway, and relatively little choice of the timing of the trip, at least at the individual decision making level. Individuals *en masse* (e.g., the union) and/or the management of the workplace may, of course, have much more power in the choice of working hours. On the other hand, considerably more latitude is possible in the choice of routes and mode of travel, especially in the case of employment in the core of the urban area, where the transportation system is the most fully developed and variegated.

Shopping trips are much more flexible and more sensitive to user charges. The shopper usually can dodge user charges by altering his or her route, destination, time of travel, or mode of travel. This sensitivity of the shopper to any change in the urban transportation environment is the basis of the current anxieties of the downtown merchant. Unfortunately, while this group of transportation users is the most sensitive to user charges, it is also the least troublesome in the management of efficient traffic flow. On the whole its members use the limited urban transportation plant mostly during the off-peak hours, traveling largely after the morning rush hour and before the evening one. Thus we have less need to manipulate their consumption of urban street space than that of the commuters.

While we have less potential for handling congestion as such through the shopping group, the fact that this group forms a significant off-peak demand for urban movement has significant indirect possibilities. To the degree that shoppers are sensitive to relative prices on the time and mode of movement they may provide an important handle for the financial rationalization of mass transit facilities. To the extent that the mass transit problem is one of insufficient patronage, not so much over all as at off-peak hours, then luring the shoppers to this mode of travel is much more likely to strengthen the financial position of the buses and subway systems than attracting a similar number of commuters. Shifting commuters to mass transit may relieve street congestion but the immediate effect on the mass transit system is to demand more buses, each of which may be idle all but a few hours each day and subject to the same operating loss per rider that characterized the system before the new rush hour business was acquired. In contrast, the shopper who abandons her automobile for the bus adds revenue to the system while imposing little or no extra cost, as she takes her seat in a half-empty vehicle.

A better understanding of the nature of shopping trips could improve our mass transit policy and, by strengthening mass transit, aid in rationalizing movement during the peak periods by permitting a more solvent mass transit system to offer more attractive peak period services—newer buses with more comfortable appointments. Certainly, the motoring shopper also uses the streets during off-peak hours and, by improving the load factor (reducing idle capacity) in this direction, helps finance better streets. But strengthening mass transit would probably contribute much more to improving rush hour transportation facilities than would adding to street improvement funds. On net, after careful reflection and observation, the case for first shifting the off-peak shopper to mass transit may provide almost as powerful a point of entry into the traffic problem as a frontal attack on the rush hour mess. Besides, the parking of automobiles in the core of the city is just as vexing a problem as moving them into that area, and the motoring shopper cannot claim the virtue of using parking facilities at off-peak times.

Social and recreational trips are sufficiently varied to require disaggregation but reflection on their general character will probably provide some feeling for their sensitivity to price and suggest ways to estimate that sensitivity. To illustrate, the family moves by private automobile with such ease and economy that alternative modes are quite unlikely to compete at any set of automobile user charges that are not punitive. One would, therefore, impose such user charges (e.g., bridge and expressways tolls on Sundays) with a clear appreciation that recreation movement would probably continue almost unabated at modest fees and at very high charges would probably cease without shifting to alternative modes of travel to any significant degree. And the demand for the automobile as the mode of movement for dating and courting is, we would probably all quickly agree, highly price-inelastic. But the masses of people who assemble at stadia for various spectator sports could probably be moved in and out by mass transit with relative prices only a bit more favorable to that mode than at present.

Strategy and Tactics in Setting User Charges

Once we have gained some feeling for the nature of the demand for urban movement for various purposes and over various paths and at various times, our transportation analysis might be profitably turned toward the form of the user charges. Consideration of the likely responses to changes in the level of tolls on movement, fees for parking, licenses to own vehicles or use them in select areas, and other such devices leads us right to the very heart of transportation and land use planning—the field tactics that implement the grand strategy. The user charges may be scheduled to ration time: the time of use of a facility (e.g., rush hour or off-peak), the length of time the facility is used (e.g., parking fees) or the number of times the facility is used in a given period (e.g., quantity discounts on bridge tickets). The user charges may be scheduled to ration space: the place of movement (e.g., expressways or streets), the direction of movement (e.g., centripetal or lateral) or the distance traveled (e.g., flat or zone tolls).

Because some of these charges attract and some repel, they may be poorly arranged so that various forces of push and pull work at cross-purposes to little or no avail, or they may be well articulated so that they reinforce each other as powerful determinants of traffic flow and land use patterns. Let us explore a bit the tactical framework within which policy-based strategy may be implemented.

For example, expressway tolls that vary directly with distance traveled favor the near-in motorist over the distant one, while flat charges reverse the advantage. Again, an urban expressway "license" which permits unlimited use of a core-area-oriented urban expressway for a given period of time, say, a month or a year, favors the regular downtown commuter who can spread the fixed charge over many trips, as against the occasional downtown shopper. And, in combination, a flat charge license fee, good for any number of trips of any length for some given period, favors the distant commuter, while a toll charge levied by zones—as on interstate turnpikes—favors the near-in, occasional shopper.

Parking charges may also have significant effects on urban spatial patterns of land use and movement. If the urban transportation authority should elect to raise the price of driving into town more by increasing parking prices and less by levying expressway tolls, this would tend to favor the short-period user of downtown facilities over the commuter in town for an eight-hour day, and would especially work to the disadvantage of the salesman with many stops to make (assuming the parking price schedules at a given lot exhibit decreasing marginal hourly rates). The salesman's requirements could be met by issuing parking tickets which are good at any core area parking lot any number of times on a given day or week or month. Flat, transferable weekly or monthly parking licenses or rents would clearly favor the regular commuter as well as the salesman. Moreover, greater dependence on parking charges rather than expressway tolls favors the distant commuter over the near-in one, as distance traveled becomes irrelevant. In sum, a preference for parking charges over road-use tolls especially favors the distant commuter, discourages the near-in shopper, and burdens the driver on business.

The possibilities are endless but the point is obvious: a sophisticated manipulation of tolls, parking charges, licenses, and other user charges by the urban transportation authority would tend to promote or penalize a given activity or land use pattern. By altering the relative transportation price structure that bears on job commuters, shoppers, and others as they move short or long distances at on- or off-peak hours and stay short or long periods at various sites, the public transportation authority could exert a significant, if not major, force on the form and function of the community.

The strategy of employing demand-based prices to achieve community development goals can be most efficiently pursued by beginning with a single or a very small subset of especially desirable developmental patterns and then working backward (in time) to the structure of user charges or some small number of substitute relative price structures—which would be most likely to achieve the desired effect. By beginning with objectives in land use and movement patterns, the analysis would probably assume manageable proportions. Even if the gains in manageability are modest, the normative approach does have the virtue of framing the objectives of the analysis in a most specific form, assuming that a clear set of community land planning goals does exist.

Suppose a large majority of the community has explicitly elected to create an urban area in which the core is primarily a professional, civic, and cultural center, with retail trade confined to unusual items and the servicing of downtown employees, then a set of user charges could be formulated which encourage a weekday-daylight population of higher-income professional workers and a weekday-evening and week-end cross section of the population of the whole urban area. Relatively expensive first class transportation services would be favored during the daylight hours of weekdays and the price of these services could be lowered (subsidized) to stimulate evening and week-end (cultural-recreational) use of the core area.

Cost-Based or Demand-Based Prices?

If we knew all of the costs associated with movement in the urban region, by mode, path, and time, including all the social costs, we might get away with cost pricing in urban transportation and not worry about the nature of demand. But if we can account for and allocate only part of these costs, and perhaps for only the lesser ones at that, we cannot blithely rely on prices equal to costs to achieve a rational pattern of resource allocation in the tradition of the free market. We may prefer to attempt to determine the consequences of our pricing acts—especially the frequent practice of setting the price at zero—to various community plans and goals. In this latter case, we price to achieve certain responses and the response is determined by the nature of the demand for the relevant service, hence we speak of demand-based prices as the alternative to the more conventional cost-based prices which simulate the free market economy.

Of course, in neither concept nor reality, is the demarcation sharp and clear between basing user charges for urban movement on cost criteria and using these prices programmatically to achieve certain social goals. One might argue that the distinction between these two approaches is but a question in semantics—what is a "cost"? The social cost of allowing privately operated motor vehicles to enter the central business district might soon be judged to be so great—so destructive in terms of urban aesthetics, amenities, efficiency, or some other critical facet of the vitality or viability of the city region—that the act must not occur. Thus the price might be set so high that even the wealthiest and most avid motorist would not pay the toll. Whether the demand for automobile movement was choked off by a high-price strategy or whether the automobile was priced out of the core area by such a cost rationalization, the effect is the same.

That the costs of preventing the central business district from being disorganized by traffic congestion cannot be precisely quantified is not critical in the pricing process, if it is generally agreed that the cost is so great that no one would pay it. Thus an outright ban on automobile traffic becomes an approximation of and a rational substitute for a cost-based price. Obviously, any price set to achieve some desired response on the part of the user (commuter, shopper) could also have been fabricated under a cost rationale by adding to objective money costs an "appropriate amount" (derived expost!) to reflect subjective

social costs. The more arbitrary the cost accounting, the more rational
becomes the frank and open use of prices as regulatory and developmental devices.

INVESTING IN MASS TRANSIT UNDER
CONDITIONS OF UNCERTAINTY

Most of the talk about the need to redress the inequity in relative
prices between automobile and mass transit movement in urban areas
is directed at the problem of allocating resources more efficiently under
conditions of existing technology, income levels, taste patterns, and so
forth. Raising the price of driving and/or lowering the price of mass
transit movement would tend to substitute buses for automobiles and
economize on street space—perhaps the scarcest resource of all. The
proposed solution is not merely a short-run tack designed to allocate
existing urban transportation plant more efficiently, for a favorable
long-run effect is also expected.

Reduced patronage has, in the view of many students of urban transportation problems, led to the decline of mass transit by setting in
motion a sequence in which the drop in patronage brought operating
losses on certain runs and on most runs at certain times of day,
necessitating reduced schedules and curtailed service, leading in turn
to a further reduction in patronage and so on to decrepitude and even
to its demise in some smaller urban places. In analogous fashion, the
hope is that an increase in patronage following from the imposition
of user charges on automobile drivers will strengthen the financial
position of mass transit lines sufficiently to enable them to improve
their service and thereby attract more riders which will further improve their financial position and service.

Efficiency or Progress?

While a price policy in urban transportation which eliminates the
bias in favor of the automobile driver might provide the fillip which
would lift mass transit out of its decline, localities have been apathetic
or reluctant to move on this front. This has turned attention to an
alternative strategy designed to promote the bus to the status of a
full-fledged partner of the automobile in a pluralistic urban transpor-

tation system—a widely, although not universally, accepted objective. The Federal Housing and Home Finance Agency has inaugurated a program of demonstration grants designed to encourage experimentation with new forms of urban mass transit. Implicit in these grants is the hope that we may be able to break into the developmental sequence sketched above at the second stage. Rather than wait for increased patronage to develop out of a revised set of relative prices that favors mass transit more than at present, rather than force commuters from their cars into buses, an effort will be made to lure them into buses by offering a service much superior to the one now available and perhaps even superior to the service they now get from their own cars.

Ideally, we should proceed on both fronts at once, pushing and pulling together. But a good political case can be made for starting with the improvement of the mass transit system first, via demonstration grants, rather than beginning by making driving more expensive. Disturbing the long-standing transportation environment of the dominant and vocal motorist group just by offering greater choice is more than enough social change to attempt at one time, without inviting their rebuke by crowding them into decrepit buses on erratic time schedules during the difficult transition period. Moreover, as important as it may be to redress the market price distortion that has long favored the automobile driver, the negative approach of rationing the automobile driver out of the core area of the city is not enough. The shift from automobiles to buses may reduce congestion but our purpose should also be to move people about the city in a manner which is pleasant and economical.

Even if the cost accounting for various alternative modes of urban transportation is handled with great care and the user charges can be administered faithfully and efficiently, this would still be only a very circumscribed "solution" to the urban transportation dilemma. Economic progress generally takes precedence over economic efficiency and progress rests not on the most rational arrangement of resources within the confines of existing institutions and technology but rather on breaking these bonds and creating new choices. So, while we are making the best of the current stock of transportation facilities within the current bounds of land use patterns, we should be experimenting with new forms of transportation and new land use arrangements that go beyond the optimum allocation of existing traffic among existing devices.

*Heavy Fixed Investment under Rapid Technological
and Institutional Change*

More and more, attention is turning to the revival of mass transit as the hope for eliminating core area traffic congestion. Typically, the impetus for reconsidering the contribution that mass transit might make to urban transportation is prompted not so much by the current traffic jams of private automobiles as by the future jams envisioned when urban traffic is doubled over the next couple of decades. Fresh from their population projections for 1975 and 2000, the planners contemplate with near horror the physical implications of these traffic magnitudes if privately operated, personalized transportation retains its present share of the urban transportation market. When one adds to the projected congestion the very long gestation period required to plan and carry out a mass transit system—subways, monorails, commuter railroads, or whatever—the urgency of tackling the long-range problem immediately is heavily underscored. Given this state of affairs, then, why has virtually every urban area which has toyed with mass transit ideas over the past decade been so timid? Despite all the talk about the inevitable great flood of automobiles, only San Francisco is building an "Ark."

One reason cities are reluctant to cast the die on mass transit is that the sums of money involved are very large and the investments are very fixed, both functionally and spatially. To guess wrong will be very expensive. As one reads these long-range urban area projections, such as the Washington Year 2000 Plan[9] (one of the better efforts, and in many ways a good one), an impression develops that if population is not quite the only variable that has truly been projected into the future, it is the one most liberally extrapolated. The accommodation of that future population, one is almost left to assume, will be handled by present day institutional, organizational, and technological arrangements and devices. The 1975 population is implicitly projected as living in 1962 homes, working in 1962 factories on forty-hour work-weeks, traveling in today's vehicles and engaging in today's patterns of leisure activities, all of which is, of course, even more damning when the year is 2000 A.D. Perhaps in some intuitive way, those who are responsible for making the mass transit investment decision are aware of the tremendous uncertainties that have been glossed over in most

[9] *The Nation's Capital, A Policies Plan for the Year 2000,* Prepared by the National Capital Planning Commission and the National Capital Regional Planning Council, May 8, 1961.

of these projections. It might be useful to quickly list some possible developments that could come to bear adversely on the value of a mass transit system oriented toward the CBD, a system that would take a decade to complete if begun today.

One does not find in most of these long-range urban transportation-land use projections any really keen appreciation for the fabulous force of technological change which is almost certainly going to create far-reaching effects on the socioeconomic fabric of urban life. Only in the most implicit or casual way do these projections incorporate the likely nature and demands of the automated factory. For over a decade now factories have been leaving central city sites for the suburbs in response to needs for both new sites for brand new plants and larger sites for one-floor operations. These ranch-type plants are distinctive for the extent to which they substitute capital for labor, and capital does not commute to the plant each day. The advent of dispersed manufacturing operations with small labor forces in each establishment eliminates one kind of clustered employment that is the hallmark of the traffic problem and the *forte* of mass transit.

Further, automation in manufacturing often leads to continuous processes which are operated around the clock; the impact of moving from massed employment in one shift to token forces of dial-watchers and maintenance men spread over three shifts smooths out in time, as well as disperses in space, the flow of commuting traffic. Where the trend is not to two or three shifts, the prospective shortening of the workday should make it much easier for firms to stagger their working hours so that the traffic peaks are flattened out a bit. First a seven- then a six-hour day will allow a great deal more latitude for variation in the working hours between places of employment, and insure some variation from chance divergence in tastes and situations.

Another way in which technological change may affect the urban transportation problem is by shortening the workweek. Employees may feel much more willing to undertake a long journey to work (in terms of time) if they only work four days a week in 1970—and three days a week in the year 2000. A related possibility is that the frequently observed shift from manufacturing employment to service employment may substantially alter the locale of work for many persons, especially in the professional services which will almost certainly be the fastest growing sector in an automated and highly educated society. The professional worker, moreover, may do a significant part of his work at home in his study, or at a nearby suburban office if he wishes to escape the home.

Not only may the work move, in part, to or near the home, but the homes may move closer to the work places. With the core of the metropolitan area serving an ever larger region and performing, therefore, ever more demanding services in finance (e.g., investment banking), education (e.g., the graduate and professional schools of the local university), government (e.g., metropolitan area authorities), and specialized entertainment (e.g., opera), downtown employees may come predominantly from the most highly educated and affluent classes. And, a decade or two from now the downtown area may well have a relatively high proportion of the newer and more desirable housing, as the near-in suburbs have aged and the central core has passed through the early renewal phases of the building life-cycle. Thus it may be quite easy for the downtown worker to live near his work in a style which compares favorably with any in the whole metropolitan area.

The possibilities for juxtaposition of home and work increase under multinucleation, and one of the simplest solutions to core area congestion is to create additional core areas. Furthermore, no great sacrifice in economies of agglomeration may result if care is taken to preserve the unity of the most intimate transportation and communication complexes. But this has come about quite naturally and rather easily in many urban areas, where separate specialized centers form. The legal-financial-government complex probably need not embrace the major retailing center of the city, and the cultural-educational center with the city university and libraries and museums can surely live apart from the other two, and the night life and convention area might also be separable from any of the foregoing, assuming that good lines of transportation string these centers together.

We noted in Chapter 4 that mixing diverse land uses in a given small area has the virtue of mixing day and night (and weekday and week-end) traffic and parking. We have a difficult trade-off here: clusters of like land uses minimize the total demand for movement, even though they cause it to peak sharply; clusters of diverse land uses smooth out the demand for movement and parking space, though they generate more movement. The particular combination that would minimize fixed investment and operating expenses would vary with the circumstances. Other considerations would weigh heavily, such as the usually superior aesthetics of variety in land uses and buildings, or perhaps an aversion of one of the political entities in the fragmented metropolitan area to sustaining the financial sacrifice of having a heavy concentration of tax-exempt land uses (e.g., churches, museums, and various cultural activities).

Again, the possibilities of closed-circuit television, substituting communication for personal transportation, has been frequently cited as a possible substitute for comparative shopping and the conveyance of documents. Television of sports events and first-run movies are a force which is hard to appraise, but striking shifts in the demand for personal movement cannot be left out of long-range projections. Technological change in housing also seems to be ignored in the urban transportation projections, despite the fact that a house which is nearly self-sufficient in utilities, with its own recycling water, a self-contained waste disposal system and with access to electricity by "radio" waves, smacks no more of science fiction today than today's automobiles and television sets would have in 1900. Houses without attachment to the core of the city in pipes and wires would greatly reduce the cost of "sprawl," and this form of low residential density seriously threatens the efficacy of mass transit.

The very simple geometric fact that the area of a circle increases with the square of the radius reminds one that the doubling of population increases the distance from the periphery to the core by only about 40 per cent, and the population would have to quadruple before the commuting radius doubled (assuming population density remains the same, which it hasn't in the past). Still, it is not at all inconceivable that during the next forty years total population in our large urban areas will a little more than double, average density will fall less than one-half—to current suburban practice—roughly quadrupling the total urban area. If, then, the speed of movement about doubled as the radius of the urban area about doubled, the travel time from the periphery to the core would remain unchanged between 1960 and 2000. The trip downtown probably has not, in fact, lengthened in time over the past one hundred years or so. Finally, some observers have speculated that the sheer joy of driving may outweigh relative cost considerations. Again, cost-based user charges may pale in the light of garish affluence. Viewed differently, driving to work may now be and may increasingly become an end in itself, a consumer good.

Urban transportation patterns are so intimately related to such a host of socioeconomic and technological variables and these variables are undergoing such dramatic change at the present time that a long-range transportation projection is extremely hazardous. The risk that this poses for the huge fixed capital investments entailed in mass transit systems all but paralyzes communities with vacillation. The failure of a few timid experiments in pseudo-mass transit—recombining existing facilities into minor variations on old patterns to convert motorists into transit riders—has only strengthened the feeling of the mass transit proponents that nothing short of radical changes will have a material impact on mass transportation usage. The hopes and doubts can be resolved only by more courageous experimentation with bigger pilot projects in the field of mass transit.

Federal Mass Transportation Demonstration Grants: An Experimental Approach

All of this has been increasingly well recognized over the past few years. Congress has authorized the Federal Housing and Home Finance Agency to stimulate local experimentation in urban mass transportation through direct subsidy and has made an initial appropriation of $42.5 million for capital grants covering two-thirds of the cost of mass transportation demonstration projects. The rationale advanced for placing this function in the hands of the HHFA is that improvement in mass transportation is a prerequisite to that agency's major objective of renewal and rehabilitation of core area blight. A simple listing of a few proposed local demonstration projects will give a rough idea of the kinds of mass transportation experiments which local experts throughout the country foresee as being the most promising forms of mass transportation.

Selected Requests for Mass Transportation Demonstration Grants:

Locality: Philadelphia, Pennsylvania
Purpose: To build 2.3-mile, high-speed transit link between airport and railroad station

Locality: Detroit, Michigan
Purpose: 25-mile monorail test line between center of Pontiac and Detroit CBD

Locality: Newark, New Jersey
Purpose: To pave Newark, N.J., subway line so that it could be converted to bus use for more flexibility

Locality: Ithaca, New York
Purpose: Free city bus service

Locality: Cleveland, Ohio
Purpose: To construct a 4-mile extension of the present Cleveland Transit System to Cleveland's Hopkins Airport

Locality: Philadelphia, Pennsylvania
Purpose: To purchase new electric and diesel commuter railroad cars

What are the general criteria by which a mass transportation demonstration grant request should be judged? Clearly, the federal government should be less in the business of solving any particular locality's current traffic crises than in sponsoring controlled experiments which lead to broad generalizations that could exert nationwide leverage. Since money is always a scarce commodity, both the size of the investment required to implement the proposed project and the risk of failure to which it is subject cannot be lightly dismissed. Both factors considered, the experiments to be preferred are those that (a) make maximum use of existing capital, (b) are reversible so that failures can be salvaged by a return to the original position with only a small loss and (c) reflect current trends or foreshadow the future in techniques and technology.

An illustration of a project which displays all of these attributes is the following. An application might be made for a grant to cover the costs of planning and implementing the conversion of a two or more lane thoroughfare into an exclusive right of way for buses, at least during the morning and evening rush hours. One lane might be reserved for local buses and the other for express buses, approximating the conventional arrangement of subways, with traffic signals synchronized at speeds as near subway or monorail speeds as safety will permit—at least 35 to 40 miles an hour. If only one of the two or more parallel main arteries serving a given string of communities were so set aside, the inconvenience to the motorist would seem to be nominal, especially if the experiment worked, relieving traffic on the adjoining streets. To be quite specific, a choice from the (northbound) set: Thirteenth, Fourteenth, or Sixteenth streets in Washington, D.C., or from the (northbound) set: Woodward, Second, Third, or Hamilton in Detroit, might be made. Clearly, the investment would be most modest and the decision would be almost perfectly reversible if it failed *as a solution*. (No well constructed experiment fails to add to our knowledge.) The planning value of a "failure" of a project which simulates rapid mass transportation is almost as great as a "success" to the home community which might then be saved from making a costly error, and it is just as valuable to other communities observing from afar.

While increasing the speed (reducing the trip time) of the bus is perhaps the most critical facet of mass transit experimentation, product innovation in rider comfort runs a close second. Raising or lowering the fare for mass transit produces only a minor response in patronage; apparently automobile drivers will abandon their cars only for buses of greater speed *and* comfort than those now offered. For example,

Moses and Williamson,[10] exploiting data gathered by the Cook County Highway Department, estimated that a zero bus price would convert only about 13 per cent of the automobile users to bus riders and that it would take a negative bus fare of over 30 cents to convert half of the Chicago area home-to-work drivers to bus riders. If this is an even roughly accurate reflection of commuters' taste patterns, then mass transit must be sold through improved product quality and not economy. Besides, a simple appreciation of our ever-growing national affluence is enough to impress us with the fact that "economy" transportation must surely be a declining industry.

Therefore, if a slightly greater investment can be afforded in the experiments which simulate rapid mass transit, requests for converting main streets to bus speedways might be fluffed out a little with a supplemental request for additional funds to acquire some new luxury buses—not just air-conditioned but with seats arranged so that there is more space per person, for both comfort and privacy. We probably greatly underestimate the role that privacy plays in making the automobile the favored means of transportation of the middle and upper income groups. The bus is almost as fast at rush hour and, counting the walk from the parking lot, the bus (with fringe area parking) is almost as flexible; what the bus is *not*, however, is gracious or luxurious. The luxury bus should charge a higher (probably even a full cost) price because, again, the objective is not to relieve traffic congestion in any given locality at any cost but rather to extend our knowledge of urban transportation parameters—in this case whether a luxury class, rapid mass transit system can be self-supporting. And a lower fare, standardized bus service should continue to run in competition with the luxury service to give additional evidence of the price and product quality structure of demand.

We need to know much more accurately what it is that people want out of their urban transportation system: speed, flexibility, frequency of schedules, or comfort. More specifically, how important is permission to smoke, privacy, opportunity to exercise full control over the vehicle or, the reverse, freedom from the responsibility of control. These highly subjective factors may yield a bit here and there to deductive effort but a very large role will almost certainly fall to the empiricist. Because large-scale empirical and experimental work is very

[10] Leon N. Moses and Harold F. Williamson, Jr., "Value of Time, Choice of Mode, and the Subsidy Issue in Urban Transportation," *The Journal of Political Economy*, June 1963, especially p. 259f.

costly and because whatever is learned will be almost as useful to other communities as the one which carries on the actual work, federal demonstration grants seem especially well suited to this kind of urban economic research. Inferring taste patterns, whether deductively or inductively, is a subtle and difficult business; therefore urban transportation economists must foresake the economist's traditional preoccupation with the deductive method and dabble a little in an even older scientific method, experimentation. It is probably through product development, market testing, and sales promotion that the major advances will be made in the business of moving people efficiently and comfortably about ever larger urban areas. But the experimental technique and the usefulness of the demonstration grant is only as great as the imagination and care with which the test is drawn up. And it is not at all clear that the Federal Mass Transportation Grants are being used to finance controlled experiments leading to broad generalization.

CHAPTER 10

Interactions among Problems: The Problems of ''Solutions''

The city is a complex, highly interrelated organism which must be seen as a whole and not just as the sum of its parts. We see, time and time again, "solutions" to one set of urban problems that then create new problems of their own, seemingly an endless chain.[1] The central city's tax base sags with the decline in downtown retail sales; expressways and municipal parking areas are hurriedly constructed to lure distant residents back to downtown stores; but the expressways force some and induce many more central city residents to move to the suburbs and the additional land area allocated to the expressways and parking areas cuts into the space available for destinations, reducing the motivation to come downtown and the pleasure of being downtown. And, to add insult to injury, the land pre-empted by the expressways is removed from the central city's tax rolls; and on and on. Thus, we find that "problems" often pose a Hobson's choice and "solutions" become merely a matter of finding the best trade-off between problems —the least uncomfortable spot between the horns of the dilemma. Thus this chapter parallels Chapter 5: there the "terms of trade" among the goals of affluence, equity, stability, and progress were considered at some length; here we trade off gains and losses in land use, transportation, public services, and antipoverty programs.

Still, at times, we may find that our solutions can do double duty. If we could, for example, encourage high-income, highly educated families to disperse throughout the metropolitan area so as to ensure that each political subdivision had about its pro rata share, then we would not only ease current fiscal problems by linking tax base to public service needs but probably also make a major contribution to economic growth by diffusing leadership throughout the total local

[1] For an excellent and highly readable account of the way in which the "solution" to one problem creates another, see Edward C. Banfield, *The Case of the Blighted City*, American Foundation for Continuing Education, Chicago, Illinois, 1959.

361

economy. Income mixing would also achieve greater equality of opportunity and ultimately a more equal distribution of income as closer contact between culturally advanced and culturally deprived classes fosters human resource development, especially among the young as in the big, consolidated, cross-cultural high school. Thus the complex of urban problems may exhibit the same characteristic of complementarity which we sometimes found tying the various income goals together. Moreover, just as complementarity between income goals could lead to either a happy couplet (e.g., affluence *and* growth) or the reverse, so too the wedding of problems and solutions may be for better or worse.

The fact that both problems and solutions may be complementary is highlighted by the way in which that part of the material of this chapter is treated. Beginning with the twin misfortunes of complementary problems—when it rains it pours—we proceed to strategies which offer the chance to treat both problems simultaneously—kill two birds with one stone. In general, then, this chapter seeks to take a short step toward building a matrix of solutions to a few of the problems detailed in Chapters 6 to 9: both solutions which produce new problems, and solutions which have extra cutting power. While this chapter is quite normative and programmatic in construction, the use of simple declarative sentences is for ease in exposition, and should not be interpreted as reflecting assurance that answers have been found to the very difficult and complex problems considered.

LA RONDE

Urban Land Use and Transportation

We might start with the interrelationship between land use patterns and transportation systems because it is so intimate and commonplace. The state of urban transportation technology gives the city its over-all form. The streetcar produced star-shaped cities and the automobile is bringing back a new form of the old circular city of hoof and foot. Beyond the over-all form, it is the ability to move about within an urban area that permits us to separate out various urban functions and create specialized subdivisions of the city—shopping centers, heavy industrial areas, residential subdivisions, and so forth. Moreover, the easier and cheaper we make movement the more spatial differentiation we can afford, assuming that there are economic reasons for the various activities to cluster in the first place.

Too often, however, transportation is seen as having an independent life of its own and transportation planning becomes an "engineering exercise" in static efficiency. Wingo and Perloff[2] argue that

> the choice of a transportation system is the *core developmental decision* that the metropolitan region can make. . . . The design of the transportation system "package" should logically be a process of successively constrained choices, in which the critical one is the first and most general—the setting of the long-run developmental objectives for the region . . . a criterion not of transportation efficiency but of . . . the productivity of the region as a producer of goods and services for itself and for the rest of the world . . . the achievement of the form and organization of the region which is most consistent with the collective aspirations of the community. Finally, long-run consumer satisfactions—related to the living and working conditions—need to be taken into consideration. . . .

The authors then proceed to criticize the creators of the 1959 Washington Transportation Plan for ignoring the locational feed-backs of their model and failing, thereby, to apprise the public of the full consequences of their plan.

In a more programmatic vein, they illustrate their argument by pointing out that a city which aspires to be a great regional and cultural capital would probably have to nurture the vitality of its core area and that this would require an appropriate transportation strategy, such as the development of a high-quality, high-speed mass transit system into the core area, to encourage centralization and compaction, and a peripheral transportation system which would congest under high volume use, to discourage decentralization and sprawl. At the tactical level, user charges on private vehicles could be manipulated so as to encourage or discourage driving at various times and in various directions and for various purposes, as was detailed in Chapter 9. All in all, urban transportation becomes more a means than an end, and most often must take its cue from the master land use plan.

But the reverse is true too, the land use strategy should also help implement the transportation plan. If, for example, one broad ob-

---

[2] Lowdon Wingo, Jr., and Harvey S. Perloff, "The Washington Transportation Plan: Technics or Politics?," *Papers of the Regional Science Association*, Volume Seven, 1961, pp. 250 and 257.

jective of the community is to encourage a shift from the use of private
vehicles to mass transit, this policy could be given a powerful boost
by insuring that homeowners pay the full cost of sprawl, including
social costs to the extent possible. For it is unlikely that low- to
middle-income families will ever be induced to crowd into high density
residential arrangements as long as we underprice large-lot sprawl
by using the general fund or flat rate user charges to finance various
public service costs, such as water supplies, sewage disposal, streets,
police and fire protection, and any others which are a function of
spatial extent. And without high density residential areas, mass transit
is uneconomic and impracticable.[3] Unless the land use and transportation plans are made mutually supporting, explicitly, they tend to be
mutually self-defeating, implicitly.

There are some reasons to hope that time is on the side of the rationalization of urban land use patterns and transportation efficiency.
Because urban areas grow centrifugally, the typical residential pattern
is one of more or less concentric circles of housing, with the oldest
housing in the center and the newest on the periphery. (Modified by
a tendency for high upper-middle and lower-middle income "sectors"
to develop—Hoyt's sector thesis.[4]) Insofar as the more affluent families
tend to live in the newest housing at the edge of the urban area but
work in the core area, and to the extent that the very low-income
families of the core area work in the suburbs (e.g., janitors in factories,
domestics in suburban households), job commuting is near a maxi-

[3] The 1960 *Census of Population* included a question asking what mode of transportation was used in commuting to work. Leo F. Schnore has analyzed the responses of residents of the central cities for the full 213 "urbanized areas" of the
country, with especial reference to the size, density, and age of the city. All three
variables are statistically significant in explaining the proportion of employed persons who travel to work by mass transit—large, densely populated, and old cities
make more use of mass transit. All three are statistically significant at the .01 level
and together yield a coefficient of multiple correlation of .80 (explained variance of
64 per cent). While density is rather highly intercorrelated with the other two, it
still exhibits a statistically significant partial correlation coefficient. City density
does, in sum, appear to have a distinct and separable influence on the demand for
mass transit services. Leo F. Schnore, *The Use of Public Transportation in Urban
Areas*, University of Wisconsin Urban Program (mimeographed).

[4] Homer Hoyt, "The Pattern of Movement of Residential Rental Neighbor-
hoods," *The Structure and Growth of Residential Neighborhoods in American
Cities* (Washington: Federal Housing Administration, 1939), pp. 112–22, reprinted in
Readings in Urban Geography, Harold M. Mayer and Clyde F. Kohn (editors)
(Chicago: The University of Chicago Press, 1959), pp. 501ff.

mum.[5] But as the urban area matures, the oldest housing literally crumbles away and a significant amount of core renewal may take place, part of which takes the form of upper- and upper-middle-income class housing (e.g., high rent apartments). Simultaneously, cheap, *old* housing begins to appear in the older suburbs and cheap, *jerry-built* housing begins to appear in some not-so-old suburbs. So, in time, the executive *could* live near his downtown work and the maid near her suburban employer. If, in fact, the aging of an urban area does bring about a more spatially random age-distribution of housing, the increased range of choice in housing everywhere should reduce the demand for movement and transportation capacity. Perhaps, the long-run solution to the urban transportation problem lies more in bringing home and work place closer together than in either of the two current panaceas: more capacity and/or less sprawl.

The opportunities for devising strategy and tactics to join land use and transportation objectives are limitless; one more illustration will suffice. Stricter licensing of motorists would operate both to revitalize mass transit and to contain urban sprawl. In particular, if we were more demanding in driver requirements, many elderly persons now driving would be denied licenses. This is equivalent to forcing them to live nearer to where they work and shop and to ride mass transit.[6] Clearly, both reactions operate to ease the urban transportation problem. Granting that this may be a politically difficult move, some combination of higher expressway speeds, greater congestion, and growing longevity may combine to increase the weight of the public safety factor to the point where it tips the balance against licensing older drivers *en masse*.

There are, then, many avenues toward harmonizing transportation and land use plans, if only co-operation and co-ordination between

[5] The recent New York study pointed up the phenomenon of "reverse commuting": "Negro and Puerto Rican men, travelling by car pool from Harlem and the Bronx to the New Jersey industrial belt . . . Negro women travelling from upper Manhattan and the Bronx to Westchester communities." Raymond Vernon, *Metropolis 1985* (Cambridge, Mass.: Harvard University Press, 1960, reprinted as a Doubleday Anchor Book, 1963), pp, 190-91. For a more complete treatment of reverse commuting in New York see Edgar M. Hoover and Raymond Vernon, *Anatomy of a Metropolis* (Cambridge, Mass.: Harvard University Press, 1959, also reprinted as a Doubleday Anchor Book, 1963), see index under "commuting, reverse."

[6] The relationship between stricter licensing and the demand for mass transit, particularly on the part of the elderly, is briefly mentioned in Webb S. Fiser, *Mastery of the Metropolis* (Englewood Cliffs, N.J.: Prentice-Hall, Inc., Spectrum Books), p. 17. The more programmatic aspects of this subject may deserve developing.

independent decision making bodies can be achieved. At present, city planning commissions charge that transportation planners see in every public park a cheap future expressway easement, while the state highway commission accuses the city planners of trying to use expressway appropriations as cheap slum clearance money as they bend the roads back and forth through one slum after another. "City efficient" and "city beautiful" can only be suboptimizations within some broader framework, as Perloff and Wingo caution.

Urban Transportation and the Local Public Economy

Probably the most powerful and socially significant connection between urban transportation and the local public economy is an indirect one, but one widely recognized and well publicized. Increased ease of movement about the urban area—the near universal ownership of the automobile in particular—has led to urban sprawl and, with fixed municipal boundaries, to growing political fragmentation. Earlier in this study we have detailed the tendency of the higher-income classes to move outward leaving the lowest income class behind, with a dwindling tax base, growing welfare loads, and a thinning leadership class. Here, we simply ask this further question: On net, do the freeways that speed and ease urban travel deflate or inflate the central city tax rolls?

Certainly, transferring private property from taxable uses to tax-exempt transportation corridors depletes tax rolls, but indirect effects on other property values must also be considered. Adjacent commercial property declines in value as potential customers speed past unable or unwilling to stop, except perhaps at certain entrances and exits. Again, residential property values adjacent to freeways may decline as neighborhood amenities are impaired by noise and exhaust fumes, and as local traffic and pedestrian circulation are impeded. Still, all of this could be offset, in aggregate, if the decline in commercial property values in the central business district were arrested by improved access to downtown stores and offices for suburbanite shoppers and professional workers. What the net balance of all these diverse forces may have on the central city tax base is largely a mystery at this time.[7]

[7] The City of Detroit's Department of Public Works in reporting to the City Council admitted that freeways had taken $35.2 million of property valuation off Detroit tax rolls, but they argued that no conclusive relationship between new free-

A full cost-benefit analysis of freeways would have to integrate the tax effect with the relevant expenditure effects, as displaced families will tend to reduce central city public service demands and increased numbers of shoppers and commuters will increase public expenditures. Finally, not only have we no sure feeling for the net impact of freeways on the central city public budget, but even this information would not be base enough from which to make good social decisions. Even though our large metropolitan areas are politically fragmented, some sense of the over-all balance of the net impact on all local public budgets in the urban area is needed, at least by federal and state authorities who should have the larger picture in view and who pass out the freeway money. And improved intergovernmental co-operation at the local level could come into being on the basis of a comprehensive approach to the economics of freeways.

As we noted at the beginning of this chapter, the transportation plan of an urban area must be evaluated in a much broader context than a cost-benefit analysis ordinarily captures, specifically as an integral part of the comprehensive land use plan and socioeconomic goals of the full community. The same user charges that would help unsnarl traffic jams could also ease local public finance problems. Tolls and license taxes on private vehicles which use key streets at rush hours would tend to shift motorists from space-extravagant cars to space-economizing buses, lessening congestion directly. Insofar as people chose to stay in their cars and pay, this would automatically generate the public revenue needed to build and maintain the expensive facilities they require. And in the long run, user charges on urban movement would tend to induce people to live closer to their work, econ-

---

ways and changes in over-all property assessments could be shown. This interpretation was at variance with an earlier report, prepared by the City Board of Assessors, from which the DPW statement was adapted. The Assessors stated: "Commercial properties have been on a decline for the past several years through the entire city, but these properties intersected by or paralleled by expressways have shown a greater decline, which has been reflected in the assessed values." The DPW admits that "temporary changes in value occurred in areas immediately adjacent to expressway construction . . . [but it] expects a recovery after a period of adjustment." The DPW points out that property in the west side industrial project (near downtown) has doubled in value and the initiation of other new construction near downtown has been due in some measure to the "convenient circulation provided by the expressways."

It is not surprising that the DPW, with a stake in street construction activity, and the Board of Assessors, more concerned with immediate valuation and revenue impacts, should interpret the same evidence quite differently. A broader and deeper interpretation by a more dispassionate observer is needed. Reported in the *Detroit News*, Wednesday, May 8, 1963, p. 10B.

omizing on public investment in transportation facilities. Either re-action relieves local financial problems, by increasing public revenue or by reducing public service costs.

The act of making local public transportation services more self-supporting would permit reductions in central city property taxes. Central city property tax rates are usually considerably higher than suburban rates and are often accused of driving business and wealthy residents out of the central city to suburban tax havens. Thus to the degree that we finance transportation facilities with property taxes rather than user charges, we compound ill effects. Why not turn to user charges, for what could be more appealing than a device which promises to reduce both traffic congestion and taxes? Or if we do not reduce property taxes we can use the revenue from that source to increase various public services which redistribute income and for which benefit taxation and/or user charges would be inappropriate or absurd (e.g., justice, welfare).

The alleged social crime is, moreover, not only that by making automobile travel too cheap we have increased the amount demanded to the point of financial distress, but also that freeways have led, through sprawl, to increased political fragmentation and to the divorce of tax base and public service needs. Thus it is argued, our failure to extend the price mechanism to the demand for movement within cities has both strained local public budgets and fragmented rational taxing and spending districts to the point where responsible levels of edu-cational and welfare services are endangered all over and are in default in the poorer subdivisions. Every advance in transportation tends to create more specialization in land areas, which in this context means greater separation of high- and low-income residential areas, but by underpricing movement we subsidize even greater social and spatial segregation—segregation which leads not only to greater distributive inequality but to allocative inefficiency as well.

Urban Land Use and the
Local Public Economy

The principal interrelation between land use and local public finance, especially relevant in the large, politically fragmented metro-politan area heavily dependent on the real property tax, is a simple, direct one: the tax base of the full metropolitan area should be shared by the many political entities in a way roughly commensurate with some pattern of public service needs. The simplest way to accomplish this would be to have only a very few, very large, political subdivisions so that each would contain (1) a random mix of industrial, commercial, and residential properties and (2) a random mix of upper-, middle-, and lower-income families that would tend to equalize both the tax base and welfare, police, and traffic control needs. As political subdivisions become smaller and more numerous, the land planning problem becomes more difficult if fiscal balance is to be achieved. But even if we could succeed in stuffing a little bit of industrial and/or commercial property into each small subdivision and in packing a fair share of the low-income persons and big families into each area, we would have achieved, at most, fiscal equity but almost certainly have sacrificed land use efficiency on the way.

An efficient land use plan for the full metropolitan economy probably requires the grouping of like uses into rather sizable enclaves. A big industrial park is more economical in its use of special utilities and transportation services and more conveniently arranged for internal exchange of complementary products and skills. The agglomeration of homely and ugly plants, warehouses, and railroad facilities in one place preserves residential amenities throughout the remainder of the urban area. If we were to start with the single objective of rational land use planning for the local economy as a whole, we would probably separate the industrial and residential areas with the industrial along the railroad tracks and in the valleys, down river, and the residential on the high ground with a view, up-stream above the pollution. The nonretail part of commercial (e.g., banking, corporate, and public administration and entertainment) would be concentrated in the core —the central business district. The retail trade properties would, however, tend to be distributed quite evenly throughout the area, with some concentration in the central business district.

Is it always necessary to choose between equity and efficiency? We could have both if we would give up political fragmentation. Then land use patterns can be rearranged endlessly within a single taxing-spending jurisdiction. But we would be sacrificing whatever values appertain to small, more intimate local government for equity *and* efficiency.

Still another course of action is open. We might try to devise some combination of local taxes and tax sharing arrangements which would distribute tax revenue to the various local public service units on some basis other than the spatial pattern of income and wealth. A familiar illustration of this, in a relatively simple situation, is the sharing of a local income tax between the political jurisdiction in which the tax-payer lives and the one in which he works. More difficult would be the case of the low-income, dormitory suburb which has neither resident nor work place earnings of much consequence to tax. The solution here might be to distribute the tax proceeds quite independently of the spatial source of the tax. Each subdivision might receive funds according to the number of resident children or households with incomes of less than $2,000 or some other index of revenue need. But, as more and more tax revenue is raised by one political unit and spent by some other unit, one of the chief virtues of small local government is lost: the disciplining effect of explicitly linking taxes and services, so that the opportunity cost, in private goods foregone, of expanding public budgets is fully appreciated by the citizen-taxpayer.

In addition to these hazards there is the risk of inefficiency in the public sector, if substantial economies or qualities of scale are lost by having too small public service units. Certainly, those public services with significant economies of scale could be purchased from larger political entities or consolidated public service authorities, such as water supplies from the central city. But the more this is done, the less these small subdivisions are true political entities. To pile multijurisdictional public service "authorities" on top of each other and to create area-wide taxing jurisdictions to equalize tax bases is to sap the vitality of these small political jurisdictions. Municipalities could become nominal entities confined to hiring a few recreational play leaders and organizing the annual Civic Day picnic. Perhaps the range and importance of local public services is really of minor consequence to the local residents, and it is only the image of a distinct local community which they care to preserve. Perhaps we can and should trade minor inefficiencies in a few relatively unimportant local public functions—the last refuge of small government—for a vital, efficient and equitable metropolitan area authority in the things that really count.

While it is most appropriate to outline alternative long-range objectives in land use and public finance planning, by which we hope to achieve both efficiency and equity in our politically fragmented metropolitan areas, we should remember the continuing battle that must be waged against destructive competition between the many political subdivisions. For example, high-income suburbs have been accused repeatedly of excluding low-income families indirectly by setting minimum lot sizes of a full acre or so. By zoning out low-price housing and low-income families, they can exclude households who impose public service demands in excess of their property tax contributions, and may not be welcome on other grounds as well. Thus a selfish public finance strategy is doubly disadvantageous to the full urban community as it further contributes to sprawl and external diseconomies for neighboring subdivisions.

It is a long gantlet to be run. Political fragmentation may be worth it, but the full cost, direct and indirect, private and social, in efficiency and equity, has seldom if ever been fully specified, much less quantified with care and rigor.

Urban Land Use and Unemployment and Poverty

By accelerating the formation of slums, chronic unemployment and unemployability of a large proportion of our urban labor force have a devastating impact on urban land use patterns. This was treated at length in Chapter 6. Here, let us consider less obvious associations between labor markets and urban land use forms. And this time let us start with land use patterns and trace some of their effects on unemployment.

At first blush, the impact of land use patterns on unemployment and poverty may seem nominal. We have repeatedly pointed out in earlier chapters that the metropolitan area is a single, integrated labor market. But that was a broad generalization. A small number of specialized labor markets are highly localized in some small part of the urban area. Two examples are especially relevant to local public administration and urban planning: the few market places for casual employment and the many market places for juvenile employment.

The location of a specialized labor market place may significantly affect its efficiency. One of the most distinctive labor markets in the metropolitan area is the casual labor market in skid row. Sudden, sporadic demands for short-lived jobs—odd jobs such as peddling handbills and shoveling snow off city streets, or salt onto them—are characteristic. The casual labor employment office should be placed so as to minimize the job commuting and maximize the frequency of contact between employers and employees. Typically, the job seeker reports in the morning and comes back again a couple of times during the day as repeated "shape-ups" are formed and dispersed, as the erratic demands of the market dictate. The creation of a well functioning casual labor market in skid row fosters both human reclamation and social economy, as even sporadic earnings reduces relief payments and dampens any inclination to acquire income through antisocial behavior, and work itself absorbs idle time and provides some daily discipline.

Skid row is as much a cheap living area as it is the home of alcoholics. We should, in fact, explicitly recognize that (at least) two distinct populations inhabit skid row: the alcoholics, to be sure, but also impoverished nonalcoholics searching for very low rents, cheap eating places, free outdoor recreation places (e.g., city parks), and free entertainment (e.g., people-watching in lively downtown places). We should also recognize that the skid row derelict, desperate for drinking money, preys on this latter group—elderly pensioners and physically handicapped or mentally retarded persons make easy marks. Accordingly, we should really create and/or preserve two distinct areas of cheap living: skid row and pensioners' row, both near downtown but sharply separated.

Differentiated and specialized casual labor markets could be created by establishing distinctive public employment offices and/or licensing differentiated private employment agencies in the two places. While further detail here would require some careful study of the labor force characteristics of the two groups, we might illustrate by speculating that the city could reinforce the distinctiveness of these two areas by channeling its emergency demands for heavy labor (e.g., snow removal) through its skid row employment office and its lighter work (e.g., public building or park attendant) through the pensioner area office. Differentiated casual employment offices would, of course, contribute not only to spatial efficiency in a static sense by easing job commuting, but also to long-run efficiency by reinforcing the effort to create and maintain these two distinctive and separated areas.

Let us turn now to the spatial aspects of the juvenile labor market, a very socially significant labor market for which we have few statistics and even less policy.[8] The linkage running from large, isolated

---

[8] What was especially shocking to me in my visits to the large cities in the last school year was the discovery that the employment of youth is literally nobody's affair. To be sure, there are groups concerned with various aspects of the problem, but no single agency in any of the cities has the data as to the unemployment picture in that city. There is little up-to-date information about youth unemployment even city-wide and only the estimate of school people about the

slums to personal development to employability has been developed in Chapters 3, 5, and 6. In brief, children of large slums in large cities seldom have nonslum experiences and are ill equipped in either aspirations or skills to find a place in an increasingly complex economy that has little need for unskilled labor. One smaller, more specific facet of the tie between big slums and employment warrants attention here.

Large urban areas may be no more residentially segregated by income class than small ones but a big enough difference in size does produce a difference in kind. The teenage children of poor families desperately need after-school jobs; this work may, in fact, be a prerequisite to their remaining in school. But the demand for their services, for such things as baby-sitting, grass-cutting, and snow-shoveling, lies largely in the middle- and upper-income neighborhoods. The rich and poor live within walking and talking distance of each other in the smaller places, but in the large urban area the supply of young labor may be many miles removed from the demand for it. In short, we really do not have an effective market for juvenile labor, and we are paying for this deficiency. Slum children without part-time work may drop out of school, virtually ensuring a lifetime of low-grade employment at best and perhaps chronic unemployment. More immediately, with lots of idle time and no spending money, they are ripe for juvenile delinquency.

The day of income-mixed communities is so far in the future that we should begin to find other ways to arrange communication between sellers and buyers in this market. Some small part of the federal appropriation for demonstration grants in techniques of juvenile delinquency control might be used to finance experiments with various forms of juvenile labor markets. Labor market counselors might be trained to ferret out jobs and then the spatial aspect of the market might be recognized by arranging regularly scheduled free or very cheap transportation between selected slum area pickup points and

---

slum neighborhoods. Seldom are figures available to distinguish between the unemployed who are high school graduates and those who have dropped out of school before completing the twelfth grade. Most important, it is not possible to say with any accuracy how the unemployed youth are distributed among various neighborhoods. There is much to be done in the gathering of reliable statistics. James B. Conant, "Social Dynamite in Our Large Cities," Address, Conference on Unemployed, Out-of-School Youth in Urban Areas, sponsored by National Committee for Children and Youth, Washington, D.C., May 24, 1961, reprinted in *Current*, August 1961, p. 45.

selected employment centers in the higher-income neighborhoods. No attempt will be made here to press the appropriate strategy, much less the tactics of "making a market." But it should not be necessary to labor the point that employed juveniles have both less need and less time to steal—not only does work itself reduce the idle time that leads to undesirable street corner loafing and evil associations but the very act of spending the earnings takes time (e.g., attending a movie).

Another aspect of the tie between residential land use patterns and employment and poverty originates in the racial residential pattern. The relationship between racial segregation and income segregation was discussed in Chapter 8. If we do move to open-occupancy housing and from racial segregation to income segregation the core area could lose most of its better-educated nonwhite residents to the suburbs. A major part of the actual and potential leadership class, as well as the tax base, of the central city would be lost. And the nonwhite professionals and managers are probably the group most aware of and most suited to the treatment of the welfare and human development problems of nonwhites. The mere presence of nonwhite lawyers, doctors, merchants, and technicians serves to set up valuable "models" for nonwhite youth to emulate—indispensable contrasts to the "successful" dope peddlers, gamblers, and pimps they see too often. In short, things could get worse.

But the brighter side is that if the nonwhite elite do aspire to live in mixed neighborhoods and if a large number of upper-middle-class and upper-class whites are quite willing and even desirous of associating with educated nonwhites it may be quite feasible to fashion new central city neighborhoods (via urban renewal) which are racially mixed, but educationally homogeneous at a high level. If racially mixed *middle-class* (or higher) neighborhoods could be dispersed throughout our large metropolitan areas, even a little, we might gain important leverage at the "community" (supraneighborhood, but subcity) level, as these key neighborhoods assumed leadership roles in interneighborhood co-operative activities with lower-class ones.

Urban Poverty and Transportation

A fascinating intellectual game (intriguing at least to the economist) is to assume that poverty has been eliminated and then to try to deduce which of the standard urban problems would still be troublesome.

Without being too sanguine about economics as the base of society, one could argue that eliminating poverty would go a long way toward effecting slum clearance, and would, by definition, eliminate welfare expenditures which, together with the increase in the tax base, would greatly relieve strained local public budgets. So far, so good. But widespread affluence could easily increase the urban traffic problem. A combination of the shift from mass transit to private vehicles and ever larger house lots, both hallmarks of affluence, would greatly increase the amount of movement (passenger-miles) and the street space needed per passenger-mile. We have a potential dilemma, easing the poverty problem increases the traffic problem. (There could be a way out if we would use our wealth to finance experimental work on developing speedy and luxurious forms of mass transit.)

Not only does widespread affluence intensify the traffic problem by substituting automobiles for buses but this very reaction ricochets back and intensifies the poverty problem. With the majority of the urban area residents, and practically all of the suburbanites, commuting by car, too few mass transit users remain to support good service. Thus an increase in per capita income has improved the transportation position of the majority, except perhaps in the peaks of traffic congestion but has left the poor worse off. Elderly residents, physically unable to drive, are also left worse off. We might argue then that to the degree that good urban transportation is an important element in the level of living of urbanites, the real income of the poor and the nondriving elderly is significantly reduced by widespread affluence and automobile ownership. And the spread of two-car families will enhance this effect, as the availability of a car for the housewife's midday shopping reduces the profitable (off-peak) demand for bus travel and further weakens the financial position of the mass transit companies and the quality of their service.

Simultaneously with the decline of mass transit, manufacturing, retailing, and other activities have been suburbanizing. With suburban densities far too low to support the extension of the lines of even a healthy mass transit system, the elderly, those financially unable to own a car, those unable to drive and others find that dependence on the central city mass transit system has narrowed their employment opportunities very appreciably. Clearly, growing affluence has led to greater mobility for most, but less mobility for a significant group, both in their roles as consumers and producers. A wide range of choice, the great virtue of the large city is more the prerogative of some than others.

The Local Public Economy and Urban
Unemployment and Poverty

The interconnections between urban unemployment and poverty and the local public economy are so varied that the illustrations below are random rather than representative. Clearly, heavy unemployment, especially chronic unemployment, loads tremendous responsibilities on the local public economy—welfare, retraining, relocation, and so forth. And poverty which results from unemployability is just as great a challenge, especially to the degree that the unemployables could be made employable with the proper public policies and programs. (This is particularly true of the children of the unemployables who offer a great potential for personal development.) No attempt will be made here to go beyond what was said in Chapter 6. Let it suffice to reiterate a point made briefly above: to the extent that local public services can be and are made wholly or partially self-supporting through user charges and fees of various kinds (e.g., expressways and recreational facilities), percentage points in local tax rates can be "saved" to support welfare, adult education, and other income redistributive activities. Thus we may have to introduce the price mechanism into urban transportation and land use management as much to facilitate local welfare programs as to rationalize urban movement and spatial form. Fortunately, these diverse objectives are complementary and therefore technically feasible, even though the strategy may be politically difficult to implement.

Heavy chronic unemployment leads to increased public expenditures in another way. While short layoffs can sometimes produce property improvements, as the temporarily idled worker repairs or paints his house, prolonged idleness leads to the postponement of property maintenance by impoverished homeowners or by landlords forced to reduce rents. Peeling paint, unrepaired cement work, broken electrical circuits, and the like hasten the formation of blight and speed the out-migration of the already small number of affluent families of the central city. Accelerated blight formation also enlarges federal urban renewal budgets and increases local appropriations necessary to take advantage of the federal grants, assuming some kind of local matching arrangement. For all of its critical importance to local, state, and federal budgets, we do not have any clear idea of even the *direct public cost* of chronic unemployment. We cannot adequately judge whether our present policy of repairing the ravages of chronic unemployment—slum clearance, direct relief, free food distribution, and so forth—is more or less expensive than some alternative, such as make-work projects of the WPA type.

This conjuncture of enforced idleness and urban blight formation suggests a variation on our current urban renewal theme which would allow us to make progress on two fronts simultaneously. We might use part of the federal urban renewal money to provide some form of outright or very generous matching grants (e.g., two-thirds or three-quarters federal money) to unemployed heads of households to buy materials for home maintenance and improvements. One advantage of these individual grants over the current big-project approach is that custom repairs and renovations are much more labor-intensive than projects, and the labor need be only semi-professional in many cases (e.g., house painting, minor carpentry) and therefore within the typical householder's capabilities.[9] In this way we could tap a vast reservoir of idle labor at the nominal cost of materials and promote fuller employment and neighborhood conservation at the same time, all at minimum public cost and at little or no social cost. And the social benefits to be derived from the provision of useful creative work would be considerable.

Even if this program were to be financed by shifting public expenditures from some other activity, a net increase in employment would almost surely occur because individual home maintenance and alteration work is typically much more labor intensive than the construction of housing projects or highways where heavy equipment replaces hand work. Often, in fact, all or part of the labor input is supplied by an idle householder who puts a very small price (opportunity cost) on his own time. To all this we might add the debatable value judgment of the large housing project critics, such as Jane Jacobs, that custom renewal is aesthetically superior to the "barracks-like" large renewal projects, and also is more efficient by better reflecting the subtle social purposes and processes which underlay the physical form of urban neighborhoods and communities.

Again, we find important complementarities which could convert multifaceted urban problems into simultaneous solutions, if we could but master the difficult problem of political implementation.

[9] The author is indebted to a colleague, Professor Norman Wengert, for pointing out the significant employment potential inherent in a home maintenance and improvement subsidy. Wengert has detailed his proposed program in a hectographed paper circulated privately.

TWO RECURRING THEMES

The Price System as a Disciplinary Force

While no single theme runs through this maze of interactions, the reader can scarcely fail to notice the frequent reference to user charges and full cost prices as potential instruments with which to rationalize the urban economy. In the first section of this chapter we saw how user charges on movement and greater recognition of acreage in fixing charges for utility services, police and fire protection, and other land-extensive services would support each other by forcing economy in movement and penalizing residential sprawl. Not only would these charges for services rendered and costs imposed promote efficiency in land use and transportation, but by freeing taxes for public services which redistribute income and opportunity they permit expanded public services in the fields of welfare and human resource development with the same or lower tax rates. These latter programs could reduce future welfare programs by expanding current programs designed to reduce the number of school drop-outs, adult illiterates, mentally disturbed and socially irresponsible persons, and so forth. At this point one is tempted to jump to the conclusion that a substantial part of our urban ills are attributable to the fact that too large a part of our urban environment is formed outside of the market place and does not have the disciplining force of the price system to guide it. Such a conclusion would be premature at this stage of our understanding of the city, but this is clearly one of the most promising avenues for further inquiry.

The Social Significance of Residential Patterns

A second pervasive theme deals with the social consequences of residential segregation by income. (This phenomenon will almost certainly persist well after racial segregation in housing has passed away and may well be the more basic problem even now.) At various places we have argued that segregation by income divorces public service needs from tax base, denies leadership and equality of opportunity to slum children, generates excessive traffic by unnecessarily increasing commuting distances, and separates slum juveniles from their potential employers, the upper-income classes. To turn this around and present it programmatically, if we would mix income classes at the "community" (high school district) level we would move a long way toward easing problems in local public finance, traffic congestion, welfare and human development, and juvenile unemployment, among others.

We might begin to achieve this intermediate level income mixing with the appropriate checkered pattern of land use zoning at the urban fringe and the appropriate urban renewal strategy in the core area. The former technique seems readily apparent, interspersing residential subdivisions with larger and smaller minimum lot sizes and varying multidwelling requirements. The renewal strategy is not quite so clear. We might, however, cast back to Chapter 8 where it was suggested that renewal not proceed in solid phalanx but leave carefully planned, *small* interstices of unrenewed areas which would be uplifted by the surrounding new developments. The rationale there was to create leverage by activating private renewal and thereby stretch the scarce public renewal money. We might add here that the slum families so surrounded would also feel the uplifting effect of the in-migration of better educated households, especially children in the formative early school years. The school district will, in fact, become the molecule of urban residential land use planning, if human resource development is given ever higher priority.

Such an arresting mass of complementarity makes one wonder whether there is not also a few painful trade-offs to be made. From Chapter 7 we recall that political fragmentation was reputed to have the advantage of affording greater consumer choice in public services. Those who preferred more educational services (higher taxes) would presumably settle in different municipalities than those who would minimize the public economy. To the extent that education, income level, and taste patterns are correlated, residential segregation by income is the means by which product differentiation in public services is achieved. And mixing incomes in local public service entities forces compromises. On what grounds can we judge whether it would be better to promote clustering by taste and income to achieve static efficiency in consumption, or better to promote income mixing to activate dynamic processes in human resource development?

THE CONTINUING TASK

The ultimate objective of the study of urban economics still lies ahead: to identify the half-dozen or so key variables that control the city's form and functioning. Western nations long ago discovered the great merit of using natural forces, such as the market, to make most of the small production and consumption decisions, confining the intervention of the state to the few key points that set the broad framework of economic life. For example, in the marketplace, our antitrust legislation was designed to avoid endless interference in petty price decisions by setting up a few broad rules designed to promote competition—breaking up monopolies, making entry into industries easier, prohibiting "unfair practices." Again, we hope that by controlling the supply of money through monetary policy and the level of total spending through fiscal policy, we can stabilize income and employment nationwide, without becoming enmeshed in innumerable small output, employment, and price level interventions.

What are the strategic points of the urban growth and development complex that afford powerful leverage over the whole urban environment with only a modest amount of manipulation? It would be presumptuous to suppose that our understanding of the urban economy has attained either the breadth or the depth to enable us to give a full answer. But this is the objective toward which we should move. This preface to urban economics began with the presumption that the shortest route to significant knowledge about the city was to first survey the full reaches of that complex organism, and not to follow doggedly the first promising path; let us end on the same note.

Here, now, at the "end of the beginning," the reader might find useful a rough map of the main avenues he has traveled. In Figure 9, the complex, but still incomplete, web encircling growth, size, and welfare is sketched in broad outlines. In brief, the figure depicts how urban growth leads to (a) large urban populations, (b) high population densities, (c) very large urbanized areas, and (d) political fragmentation, each of which creates important economies and/or diseconomies of size. Large size has, in turn, significant impacts—some positive, some negative—on the community's primary economic goals: affluence, equity, and stability. Finally, these welfare implications of growth and great size feed back to stimulate or depress further growth. The continued growth and ever larger size of our urban areas is, in fact, probably more dependent on our progress in local public administration—learning how to stave off the diseconomies of size in giant city regions—than any other single factor.

But this schematic representation of the web of urban growth and development is intended to be more than a convenient review and summary for the weary reader. The diagram symbolizes the objective: to see the *main* strands of the web in reduced form. If we could only keep improving that analytical "picture" of the city without increasing its detail; if we could only keep taking out some less significant line and box for each superior one we inserted, we would make steady progress toward the ultimate urban public policy objective: of strong and wise guidance, but with a light touch.

Consequences of urban growth   Consequences of very large city s

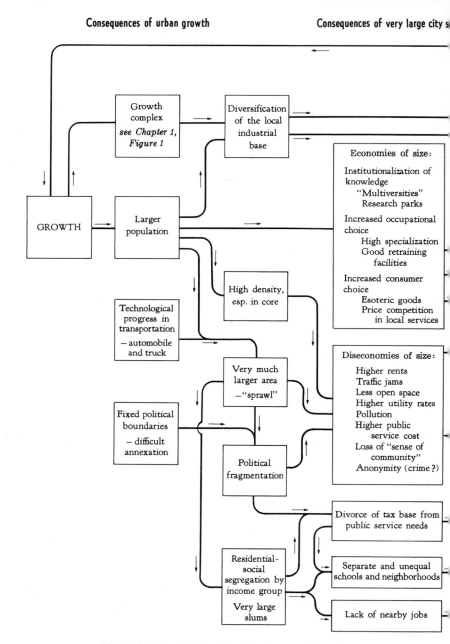

Figure 9. The consequences of urban growth and size.

Goals **Feedback on growth**

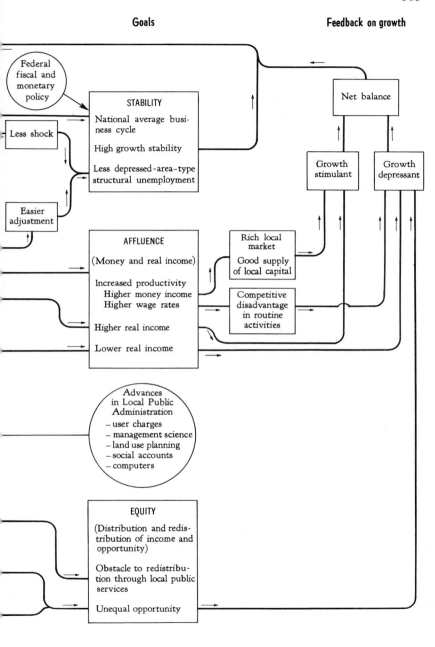

INDEX

A

Acculturation, 106, 117
Administrative skills, 279
Adult education, 138, 154, 222, 261
  financing, 376
  local government role, 215
  technical, 236
  user charges, 281
Advance Mortgage Corporation, 311
Advisory Commission on Intergovernmental Relations, 97
Affluence, 1, 4, 34, 113, 269, 356, 362, 364
  and city growth and size, 382–83 (f)
  destabilizing effect, 33
  and inventories, 151
  poverty amidst, 182
  transportation, and the poor, 375
  and unemployment, 224
Agglomeration, 12, 17, 92
Agricultural price support programs, 81
Agriculture
  labor force participation in and income analysis of, 66
  labor productivity, 11
  specialization, and income differentials, 66
  technology, 11
Aid to dependent children, 249
Airplane production, 21
Akron, O., 110, 111, 157
Alabama, 191, 193
Alaska, 101
Alexandersson, Gunnar, 17
Amenities, 6, 36, 98, 194, 284, 344
  of downtown, 344
  impairment by freeways, 366
  and interregional migration, 199
  and national growth, 197
  open space, 36, 87, 97, 382 (f)
  preserving income segregation as, 119
  residential, 57, 310, 369
  and urban growth, 57–58
"American Ruhr," 195
American Vocational Association, 235
Andrews, Richard B., 27, 304
Antipoverty programs, 361
Antitrust legislation, 380
API (see Average propensity to import)
Appalachian Mountain area, 36
Apparel manufacturing, 78
Apprenticeship
  fees and quotas, 134

Negroes in skilled trades, 113
Area development and public finance, 256
Area effect, wages, 74, 75, 77
Area Redevelopment Administration, 4, 189
Armour and Company, 233
Assessments, property, information for home buyer, 323–24
Atlantic City, N. J., 134
Automation, 33, 112, 115
  and displaced workers, 187
  and employment, 40, 187
  and industrial location, 58
  and labor skill and education, 203, 212
  and manufacturing, 111: and Negro employment, 113
  and Negro income inequality, 315
  in processing of raw materials, 195
  in transportation, 354
  and unemployment, 210, 222, 224
  unionization, and income distribution, 187
  vending machines, 240
  and wages, 86
Automobile industry
  and depression, 178
  and Detroit bankers, 55
  economies of scale and range of choice in, 266
  entrepreneurship in, 45–46
  management of, 26
  tapered vertical integration in, 152
  unemployment in, 20, 186
Automobiles
  affluence, and poverty problem, 375
  increased supply of street and expressway capacity, 343
  market for, compared with housing market, 303
  movement of: control by price strategy, 350; cost per mile and time cost, 338
  shift to mass transit, 351, 364, 367
  and sprawl, 366, 368
  subsidy of urban movement, 399
  and traffic congestion, 333–34
  transportation, estimating price elasticity of demand for, 345
  and trickle-down effect, 303
  user charges, 285, 336
Average propensity to import, 144, 145

R

A PREFACE TO URBAN ECONOMICS

WILBUR R. THOMPSON

designer:	Edward D. King
typesetter:	Monotype Composition Co., Inc.
typefaces:	Baskerville, Perpetua
printer:	Universal Lithographers, Inc.
paper:	Perkins & Squier, GM
binder:	Moore & Co., Inc.
cover material:	Columbia Riverside Linen